Rhythm,
the Poetic Idea:
Baudelaire, Rimbaud, Mallarmé

FAUX TITRE

254

Etudes de langue et littérature françaises
publiées sous la direction de

Keith Busby, M.J. Freeman,
Sjef Houppermans, Paul Pelckmans
et Co Vet

Rhythm, Illusion and the Poetic Idea
Baudelaire, Rimbaud, Mallarmé

David Evans

Rodopi

AMSTERDAM - NEW YORK, NY 2004

The paper on which this book is printed meets the requirements of
'ISO 9706: 1994, Information and documentation - Paper for documents -
Requirements for permanence'.

Le papier sur lequel le présent ouvrage est imprimé remplit les prescriptions
de 'ISO 9706: 1994, Information et documentation - Papier pour documents
- Prescriptions pour la permanence'.

ISBN: 90-420-1943-3
Editions Rodopi B.V., Amsterdam - New York, NY 2004
Printed in The Netherlands

CONTENTS

Acknowledgements

I would like to thank the A.H.R.B. for the three-year grant which enabled me to pursue this research and the *Ecole Normale Supérieure*, rue d'Ulm, for the opportunity to live and work in Paris for a year and for access to their excellent library facilities.

My grateful thanks to Dr. Peter Dayan and Dr. Mary Breatnach, whose time and patience, guidance and encouragement has been much appreciated throughout the project.

Pour leurs conseils et leur aide je tiens à remercier Bertrand Marchal, Steve Murphy, Michel Murat, Marie-Christine Bellosta, et tout particulièrement Julien Schuh, d'avoir discuté longuement et avec enthousiasme de mes recherches et de m'avoir indiqué bon nombre de lectures utiles.

Thanks to Graham Robb, Carrol Coates, Jean-Marc Hovasse, Angela Ryan, Richard Wakely, Maria Scott, Emma Wagstaff, Graham Chesters, Marion Schmid, Michael Brophy and Christa Stevens for bibliographical and practical assistance. I am indebted to Alan English for his technical guidance.

I would particularly like to thank John Oswald for his invaluable advice, and for his interest and support at every stage.

Til slutt vil jeg takke Anne-Signe Andreassen, for alt.

Cyflwynir y llyfr hwn i Eileen Mary ac Elwyn Owen Evans am eu cariad, eu cefnogaeth a'u hanogaeth drwy'r cyfan.

Introduction

Rhythm and Poetry

Rhythm is so often taken for granted as a fundamental characteristic of French poetry that we invariably assume that, in order to be 'poetic', a text must be 'rhythmic'. This is not just a critical assumption, since the notion of rhythm recurs obsessively in the discourse of both poets and critics alike, especially from the beginnings of modernity in the mid-nineteenth century. According to the Platonic world view which characterizes the first wave of romanticism, rhythms are to be observed in nature, the work of God. As Hugo argues in the 'Préface de Cromwell': 'Le christianisme amène la poésie à la vérité [...] car le point de départ de la religion est toujours le point de départ de la poésie. Tout se tient'.[1] Since creation appears to him cyclical, rhythmical and ordered, the Ideal, by analogy, is characterized by similar qualities. Thanks to this analogy, the obviously rhythmic vehicle of verse poetry, with its pre-existent structures of metre and rhyme, is the literary genre best suited to the projection of an aesthetic absolute.

In *Les Exilés*, Banville's gleefully stubborn, unfashionable lyrical collection of 1867, verse enjoys a privileged relationship with the absolute Rhythm of the Ideal:

> O Rythme, tu sais tout! Sur tes ailes de neige
> Sans cesse nous allons vers des routes nouvelles [2]

Crucially, this rhythm is only possible in verse, or 'poetry', and in his *Petit Traité de Poésie Française*, Banville sees fixed verse forms as 'tous les rhythmes qui existent', 'les rhythmes connus'. According to him, the poets who created these forms did so not randomly or

---

[1] *Préface du 'Cromwell' de Victor Hugo*, ed. by Edmond Wahl, Oxford: Clarendon Press, 1909, pp.11-12.
[2] *Les Exilés*, in *Œuvres poétiques complètes*, ed. by Peter J. Edwards *et al*, 8 vols, Paris: Champion, 1994-2001; IV, 1994, p.101.

arbitrarily, but in accordance with the regular laws of nature, validated by the Creator, 'obéissant aux mêmes lois qui régissent le cours des astres et modèrent toutes les forces de la nature'.[1] In 1852, only three years before his first prose poems, Baudelaire too argues that prose is devoid of rhythm: 'l'auteur qui poursuit dans une nouvelle un simple but de beauté ne travaille qu'à son grand désavantage, privé qu'il est de l'instrument le plus utile, le rythme'.[2] In this context, poetic rhythm is never in doubt, since it belongs to metrical verse, and despite the advent of so-called 'poetic prose' in Chateaubriand's more lyrical moments, the verse/prose opposition ensures that rhythm remains the privilege of poetry.

However, the well-documented *crise idéale* which creeps into poetry with Nerval's 'Le Christ aux Oliviers' – 'Dieu n'est pas! Dieu n'est plus!' (I, l.14) – means that the absolute which guarantees the significance of rhythm in nature can no longer be relied upon. The apparent order of nature might not, after all, correspond to a higher, transcendent Truth; indeed, nature might not be the perfectly ordered, regular system it had previously been thought to be. In the absence of this guarantee, the poeticity of regular rhythm cannot be taken for granted, and so the fixed forms which hitherto ensured the poeticity of a text also risk falling into obsolescence. Thus begins a fifty-year period, 1850-1898, when the idea of a poetic text is constantly pushed beyond the confines of predictable, fixed stanzaic and metrical forms to include prose poetry, *vers libre* and 'Un Coup de dés', which its author hoped would also set a generic precedent.[3] According to Banville's definition, none of these genres is rhythmic, since they lack the predictable formal mould which provides verse with its regular rhythmic pulse. We might expect, therefore, the rhythmic concept which had until now been the exclusive property of regular verse to disappear. In the event, it seems that at no time is it more vigorously

---

[1] Paris, 1872; Charpentier, 1883; Ressouvenances, 1998, pp.158-59 and 112 (hereafter *Petit Traité*).

[2] *Salon de 1846*, IV, 'Eugène Delacroix', in *Œuvres complètes*, ed. by Claude Pichois, 2 vols., Paris: Gallimard, coll. 'Bibliothèque de la Pléiade', 1975-76; II: 432 (hereafter O.C.).

[3] 'Le genre, que c'en devienne un comme la symphonie' (preface to 'Un Coup de dés', in *Igitur, Divagations, Un coup de dés*, Paris: Gallimard, coll. 'Poésies', 1976, p.407).

argued that rhythm defines poetry than during these years of revolution.

Dujardin, for example, refers to 'le rythme et les assonances d'un vers libre', insisting that the genre fulfil the same sort of restrictive formal requirements which were the downfall of its predecessors.[1] Repetitive devices and phonetic patterns are foregrounded in order to ensure the unity of the line, *enjambement* is strictly forbidden, as the genre symbolizing poetry's formal liberation, paradoxically, imports rhythmic techniques from the abandoned metrical model. Similar patterns, when foregrounded in prose poems, are invariably said by critics to fulfil a rhythmic function, as if the text's poeticity would disappear without them. In this way the poetry/prose dichotomy is replaced by an ever-diversifying verse/prose/*vers libre* corpus on the 'poetry' side of a hazier poetry/non-poetry divide. Poeticity is possible in prose, and 'prosaicness' is also possible in verse; it is precisely the 'prose rimée' of his predecessors that Rimbaud criticizes in 1871.[2] Although poetry and non-poetry can henceforth occupy the same formal media, the nature of poetic rhythm becomes infinitely problematic, from one model:

genre:	poetry	prose
form:	verse	prose
quality:	rhythm	non-rhythm

to another:

genre:	poetry	non-poetry
form:	verse / *vers libre* / prose	verse / *vers libre* / prose
quality	rhythm	non-rhythm?

The first model is clear: everyone can agree on where poetry and rhythm are thanks to a strict formal division. In the second, however, it becomes much more difficult to distinguish between the formal features of poetry and non-poetry. Stable notions of poeticity vanish, and it seems that not even the generic title 'poetry' can confirm whether the rhythms we discover in the text are poetic ones or lesser,

---

[1] *Mallarmé par un des siens*, Paris: Albert Messein, 1936, p.192.
[2] Letter of 15 May 1871 to Paul Demeny (*Poésies. Une saison en enfer. Illuminations*, ed. by Louis Forestier, Paris: Gallimard, coll. 'folio classique', 1999, p.87).

prosaic ones. Asking 'Peut-il y avoir des poèmes en prose?', Banville replies with an emphatic: 'Non, il ne peut pas y en avoir, malgré [...] les admirables *Poèmes en prose* de Charles Baudelaire'.[1] From the moment Baudelaire publishes his prose poems, both Poetry and Rhythm lose their absolute status and become dangerously flimsy categories which must be constantly re-motivated, challenged and justified by subsequent generations.

Yet such problematization has done nothing to puncture our faith in the necessary relationship between poetry and rhythm. Introducing his exploration of rhythm in all its formal manifestations, Henri Meschonnic maintains: 'la poésie, plus que le vers, est une pratique spécifique du rythme, et par là un terrain privilégié pour l'étude du rythme'.[2] How do we explain the obstinate critical, or indeed, authorial insistence on the importance of rhythm to the poetic text, in the face of the diverse structural qualities of all these poetic media? Surely different sorts of rhythm play such different roles in each that to claim that their poeticity results from 'rhythm' is infinitely more problematic than it is helpful. Yet numerous are the critics who, analyzing poetic texts, argue that certain foregrounded patterns of alliteration, assonance and repetition make the text 'rhythmic', as if the poetic nature of 'rhythm', these simple formal techniques, went without saying. It is surely highly dangerous to insist on the inherent poeticity of rhythm when as eminent a thinker as Valéry claims to be unable even to define 'rhythm' satisfactorily: 'J'ai lu ou j'ai forgé vingt "définitions" du *Rythme* dont je n'adopte aucune'.[3] In her exploration of rhythm in three twentieth-century French poets, Lucie Bourassa proposes ingenious solutions as to how rhythm is to be recognized in texts devoid of formal regularity, in which the rhythm does not strike the reader as metre does, but must rather be actively sought.[4] Rhythm is displaced, transposed from the purely temporal plane to the spatial, as if we were somehow obliged to interpret any poetic structural device as rhythmic. Yet were we able to imagine a

[1] *Petit Traité*, p.6.
[2] *Critique du rythme*, Lagrasse: Verdier, 1982, p.35.
[3] 'Questions de poésie', in *Œuvres*, ed. by Jean Hytier, 2 vols., Paris: Gallimard, coll. 'Bibliothèque de la Pléiade', 1957 and 1960; I: 1289.
[4] *Rythme et sens: Des processus rythmiques en poésie contemporaine*, Montreal: Les Editions Balzac, coll. 'L'Univers des discours', 1993.

poetic text independently of such rhythmic properties, such transpositions would be unnecessary.

This book explores the enduring relationship between notions of poetry and rhythm and its ultimate instability. I suggest that our refusal to accept a poetics without some sort of rhythmic quality results from a deliberate mystification of the poetic idea which begins in the mid-nineteenth century. Our obsession with the rhythms of poetry, or the poeticity of rhythm, is the result of careful aesthetic conditioning by the guardians of the temple of Poetry. Since this mystification of rhythm begins with Baudelaire, continuing notably in Rimbaud and Mallarmé, we will explore their rhythmic theory and practice, the relationship between the two, and the consequences for the poetic idea. All three authors are lauded by twentieth-century poets and critics alike as the founding fathers of poetic modernity. Yet the reasons for, and the mechanics of, their revolution of both poetic and rhythmic concepts still go largely unquestioned, since their synonymy so dominates the poetic idea that we cannot, or will not, scrutinize them too closely.

Studying *le vers*

Since 'rhythm' refers to both the intellectual concept and the very form itself, this study deals both with the poets' theoretical and epistemological writings on poetry and rhythm, and with their formal rhythmic practice. Each poet introduces a challenging new form into the poetic canon: Baudelaire the prose poem, Rimbaud the *vers libre* of certain 'Derniers vers', 'Marine' and 'Mouvement', Mallarmé 'Un Coup de dés'. The problematization of rhythm in these texts is discussed in terms of its importance to the poetics of a particular writer rather than to the genre of prose poetry or *vers libre* as a whole. Each poet is also known for revolutions within fixed forms, especially metrical innovation within the alexandrine, and my primary concern is to trace the unfolding drama of poetry within metrical verse, in the tension between regularity and irregularity.

Interest in metrical affairs has grown in France over the last twenty years, thanks largely to the work of metrician Benoît de Cornulier, researchers at his *Centre d'Etudes Métriques* at Nantes University, and a small but prolific group of critics including, notably, Jean-Pierre Bobillot, Jean-Michel Gouvard, Dominique Billy, Jean-Louis Aroui,

Jean-Luc Guilbaud and Jean-Louis Backès.[1] Cornulier's strictly
metrical stance has attracted criticism for its staunch insistence on
metrical regularity as a condition for the production of rhythm. It is
easy to see how this contradicts the modern approach to the
contingency of rhythm as explored by Meschonnic, or Bourassa, who
questions his 'définition restrictive du mètre'.[2] However, Cornulier's
work focuses on metre itself in the strictest classical terms according
to which the alexandrine, by definition, is not simply a dodecasyllable,
but rather, two hexasyllabic hemistichs clearly marked by a caesural
accent and pause. His system of *métricométrie* has provided
researchers with a useful common shorthand with which to classify
caesural infringement and to chart the decline of the alexandrine
throughout the nineteenth century and in its various manifestations
during the twentieth. Yet despite the clarity and the import of much of
his work, the object of his focus remains the *vers* itself: questions of
generic definition, and the rhythmical mechanics of problematic lines.
As a result, certain articles read as little more than statistical
catalogues of each poet's formal tendencies, with little or no attempt
to explore the significance of metrical minutiae beyond the historical
context of *le vers* itself. The opportunity is lost to examine the
importance of these details to the thematic development of each
artist's poetics.

   In this way the fertile yet dangerous ground between theory and
practice goes unexplored, and this provides one of the challenges
behind the present study. In the standard *explication de texte*, we are
used to interpreting formal features according to the sense which we
make of the individual poem. We assume, as sensitive readers of
poetry, that sound supports sense, and that both regularities and
irregularities convey this sense on a formal level. Nothing is arbitrary,
in the name of what Graham Chesters calls 'that cohesion in the use of
language which one inevitably associates with poetry'.[3] As he and
Peter Broome observe, 'there is no absolute key' to the interpretation
of formal techniques, which depend for their meaning on their

---

[1] General works on versification and works treating other poets are to be found in the
first bibliography to the present study; works pertaining in particular to Baudelaire,
Rimbaud or Mallarmé are classed in the other, author-specific bibliographies.
[2] *Rythme et sens*, p.53.
[3] *Some Functions of Sound-repetition in 'Les Fleurs du Mal'*, University of Hull
Publications, 'Occasional Papers in Modern Languages' 11, 1975, p.8.

contextual relationship to the content of the poem. *Enjambement* 'directs attention to itself as an irregularity', but this can carry many emotional resonances, such as enthusiasm, disobedience, humour, etc.[1]

However, in his article 'Baudelaire and the limits of poetry', Chesters interprets the technique in a more global context, since 'versification often serves as a sensitive gauge which can measure experiments taking place at other levels'. In terms of Baudelaire's forays into prose poetry, *enjambement* can be seen to create 'a type of verse which questions its classical symmetry and leans, however slightly, towards the rhythms, the unpredictability and the irregularity of prose'.[2] This wider interpretation of formal irregularities transcends the localized context of the individual line or poem, in favour of a global perspective of Baudelaire's whole career, an approach I apply to several areas of versification as catalogued in the appendices. I aim not for an 'absolute key' to these techniques, applicable to all poets, but for a tentative interpretative grid relating to close readings of each author's poetry and theory, in order to follow the drama of poetic rhythm as it unfolds in the form itself.

---

[1] *The Appreciation of Modern French Poetry 1850-1950*, Cambridge: C.U.P., 1976, pp.vii and 19 respectively.
[2] *French Studies* 32 (1978), 420-34; pp.421 and 426 respectively. I hope that the theoretical difficulties of deceptively simple expressions such as 'the rhythms of prose' will become clear during the course of this study.

PART ONE. BAUDELAIRE

1
Rhythm in Theory

The commonly accepted view of the Baudelairean revolution suggests a simple rejection of a supposedly restrictive verse form, with *Le Spleen de Paris* providing an escape from its shackles. Paradoxically, the poet who claims to enjoy the challenge of the sonnet form – 'Parce que la forme est contraignante, l'idée jaillit plus intense'[1] – is said to feel stifled by the verse mould, abandoning it in favour of the rhythmical freedom of prose. Albert Cassagne, in 1906, presents Baudelaire as a poet gripped by 'cette aspiration vers une facture plus libérée':

[...] un poète qui se soumet à des règles trop rigides pour lui, mais en gardant au cœur un désir persistant d'émancipation, désir le plus souvent refoulé et contenu, mais qui n'en perce pas moins en beaucoup d'endroits où le révèlent certains tâtonnements.[2]

Suzanne Bernard subscribes to a similar caricature: 'Baudelaire, en s'affranchissant du joug *du rythme* (comprenons du rythme *des vers*) et de la rime, entend varier le rituel de cette sorcellerie'.[3] Explaining the move to prose poetry, she too qualifies verse as a yoke. However, her use of the traditional synonym, 'rhythm', to designate verse, is problematic and requires a hasty parenthetical qualification. Having proclaimed rhythm to be restrictive, Bernard immediately specifies: verse rhythm, implying that prose rhythm is somehow acceptable, and, as she later claims, vital in defining these texts as poetic. Her analysis of the prose poems leads her into the self-contradiction of declaring their poeticity to spring from regularity, of the sort which the poet supposedly abandons along with verse. She identifies two opposing forces: 'tendance à la régularité, à la perfection formelle', which represents the 'poetic', and a 'tendance à la liberté, voire au désordre

---

[1] Letter of 18 February 1860 to Armand Fraisse (Baudelaire, *Correspondance*, ed. by Claude Pichois, 2 vols., Paris: Gallimard, coll. 'Bibliothèque de la Pléiade', 1973; vol.1 reprinted 1993, vol.2 reprinted 1999; I: 676) (hereafter *Corr.*).
[2] *Versification et métrique de Charles Baudelaire*, Paris: Hachette, 1906; Geneva: Slatkine, 1982, p.ii.
[3] *Le Poème en prose de Baudelaire jusqu'à nos jours*, Paris: Nizet, 1959, p.129; Bernard's italics.

anarchique', which in turn articulates the 'unpoetic' or the 'prosaic'. Thus the search for stable values of poeticity is complicated, rather than illuminated, by her search for poetic rhythm.[1]

This received idea, then, which has long gone unquestioned, is paradoxical. We are told that Baudelaire gradually tires of regular verse form, introducing irregularities into his verse before abandoning it for the rhythmical liberty of prose. However, critics simultaneously maintain that this rhythmical liberty cannot be poetic without elements of the former straitjacket being imported into prose. The prose poems repeatedly deemed most poetic are those which use techniques of alliteration, assonance and repetition usually associated with the abandoned verse rhythm. Yet verse form can and should be seen as more than simply a shackle to be thrown off, and it is only once we understand the thematic importance of verse rhythm to Baudelairean poetics that the rhythmical implications of his prose poems can be fully appreciated.

The meanings of *nombre*

Baudelaire's aesthetic reflections are never far from discussion of theological issues, a link supported by the concept of *nombre* and its various meanings. Meditating on the nature of the divine, Baudelaire wonders:

Comment le père *un* a-t-il pu engendrer la dualité et s'est-il métamorphosé en une population innombrable de nombres? Mystère! La totalité infinie des nombres doit-elle ou peut-elle se concentrer de nouveau dans l'unité originelle? Mystère! [...] tout ce qui est multiple deviendra-t-il un?[2]

The divine is One, whole, perfect, in comparison to *nombre*, the imperfect multiplicity of fallen human existence. Man is condemned to a multiple state, whereas in God all number is reconciled; God exists out of time, whereas man is forced every day to suffer its relentless ticking; whereas, before the fall, man spoke the perfect language of God, he is now trapped in the arbitrary linguistic apparatus of the word; whereas the absolute is *insensible*, like the women and sphinxes which haunt the poet, man is at the mercy of emotions, desires, aspirations and dreams.

---

[1] *Le Poème en prose de Baudelaire jusqu'à nos jours*, p.112.
[2] 'Victor Hugo' (O.C.II: 137-38).

Nombre, therefore, denotes the unpoetic disorder of human existence. Yet it also refers, very specifically, to verse rhythm and Baudelaire, referring to the defining formal features of verse, uses 'mètre', 'rythme' and 'nombre' interchangeably. Thus we find expressions such as 'l'aide de la rime et du nombre' and 'du mètre et de la rime' recurring alongside the terms 'du double élément du rythme et de la rime', or 'de rythmes et de rimes'.[1] It is metre which provides the rhythm, and in this sense, of course, only verse can be rhythmic. For Louis-Marie Quicherat, 'Le *nombre* est une succession de syllabes réunies dans un petit espace de temps distinct et limité. L'ensemble des nombres d'un vers en forme la *cadence*, le *rhythme*.'[2] Similarly, under 'nombre', Larousse gives first its mathematical meaning, then its Pythagorean interpretation, and finally the poetic definition:

Le *nombre* dans les vers résulte, chez les anciens, de la succession régulière des mesures; chez les modernes, en général, du *nombre* des syllabes et de la rime; chez tous, des césures, des repos et de la chute du vers ou de la phrase.[3]

Verse *nombre* thus refers to the metrico-syllabic mould which pre-exists the text; it denotes order and regularity, taking the disordered multiplicity of linguistic units and arranging them in a more beautiful structure. The voice of the poet's cat, 'subtil' and 'harmonieux', is compared to 'un vers nombreux' ('Le Chat', LI, 1.24 and 1.11). The same adjective is applied, in 'Tout entière', to the divine harmonies of the woman's body, described in terms of the recurrent musical metaphor:

Et l'harmonie est trop exquise,
Qui gouverne tout son beau corps,
Pour que l'impuissante analyse
En note les nombreux accords. (ll.17-20)

The *vers nombreux* is, therefore, synonymous with beauty and the rhythmical regularity of the metrical mould with its recurrent, fixed

---

[1] Respectively from: 'Auguste Barbier' (O.C.II: 145), 'Théophile Gautier' (O.C.II: 115 and 112) and both 'Théophile Gautier' (O.C.II: 105) and 'Auguste Barbier' (O.C.II: 145).
[2] *Traité de versification française*, Paris: Hachette, 1850, p.133.
[3] *Grand Dictionnaire Universel du XIXe Siècle*, Paris: 1875, 11: 1071.

accents. It creates the impression of harmony by which the elements of multiplicity are reconciled in a more perfect structure, elevating the poet and his poem out of unordered *nombre* and closer to the divine One. In *Du vin et du hachisch* (1851) the drug-taker enjoys a similar experience thanks to the multiplication of *nombre*:

> Les équivoques les plus singulières, les transpositions d'idées les plus inexplicables ont lieu. Les sons ont une couleur, les couleurs ont une musique. Les notes musicales sont des nombres, et vous résolvez avec une rapidité effrayante de prodigieux calculs d'arithmétique à mesure que la musique se déroule dans votre oreille.[1]

In *Les Paradis artificiels* (1860) the musical and mathematical analogies are once again linked in the same extravagant harmony:

> Les notes musicales deviennent des nombres, et si votre esprit est doué de quelque aptitude mathématique, la mélodie, l'harmonie écoutée, tout en gardant son caractère voluptueux et sensuel, se transforme en une vaste opération arithmétique, où les nombres engendrent les nombres.[2]

The result is a necessarily fleeting, highly intense illusion in which 'Toute contradiction est devenue unité. L'homme est *passé* dieu'.[3] The drug-taker overcomes the imperfect multiplicity of his fallen earthly state, achieving: 'sa propre nature corrigée et idéalisée'. The *nombre* of perfect harmony inspires 'la croyance de l'individu en sa propre divinité', as the dreamer cries: '*Je suis devenu Dieu!*' and 'Je suis un Dieu!'.[4]

Just as the multiplication of *nombre* brings the drug-taker closer to the divine, so too the impression of distance from the divine causes *nombre* to falter. In 'La Muse malade', the poet's muse appears to lose her faith in the absolute, overcome by 'la folie', 'l'horreur' (1.4) and 'la peur' (1.6). Significantly, she also loses faith in rhythm, and is unable to inspire the poet with verse, as he implores her:

> Et que ton sang chrétien coulât à flots rythmiques
> Comme les sons nombreux des syllabes antiques (ll.11-12)

---

[1] O.C.I: 392.
[2] 'Le Poème du hachisch', IV, 'L'Homme-Dieu' (O.C.I: 419).
[3] 'Du vin et du hachisch' (O.C.I: 394); Baudelaire's italics.
[4] 'Le Poème du hachisch', IV, 'L'Homme-Dieu' (O.C.I: 436, 430 and 437); Baudelaire's italics.

Similar vocabulary features in the opposite scenario in 'La Fontaine de sang', also from the mid-1840s. The rhythmic flow of blood recurs as the poet, in harmonious communion with nature, describes his vision of universal union:

> Il me semble parfois que mon sang coule à flots,
> Ainsi qu'une fontaine aux rythmiques sanglots. (ll.1-2)

There appears, therefore, to be a clear link between rhythm and faith in the absolute, be it religious or poetic, yet it also seems that, for Baudelaire, the time of such faith is past. Like the drug-taker, the poet of 'La Fontaine de sang' is simply enjoying a momentary illusion, which does not last beyond the quatrains, and in 'La Muse malade' only the regular metrical verse of antiquity, a bygone age of faith, might provide the rhythmic pulse necessary to restore the muse's poetic powers.

The universal analogy

For Victor Hugo, the embodiment of rhythmic and poetic faith, the significance of natural rhythm is absolute, guaranteed by the divine. The value of metrical rhythm lies in its correspondence to universal order, expressed in Pythagorean terms as *nombre*:

Celui pour qui le vers n'est pas la langue naturelle, celui-là peut être poëte; il n'est pas le poëte. Le rythme et le nombre, ces mystères de l'équilibre universel, ces lois de l'idéal comme du réel, n'ont pas pour lui le haut caractère de la nécessité. Il s'en passerait volontiers; la prose, c'est-à-dire l'ordre sans l'harmonie, lui suffit; et, créateur, il ferait autrement que Dieu. Car, lorsqu'on jette un regard sur la création, une sorte de musique mystérieuse apparaît sous cette géométrie splendide; la nature est une symphonie; tout y est cadence et mesure; et l'on pourrait presque croire que Dieu a fait le monde en vers.[1]

Yet whereas, for Hugo, these cycles and harmonies are proof of God's presence in the universe, Baudelaire sees this as mere conjecture. Indeed, this is part of his importance to poetic modernity: with Baudelaire, the theological certainties of old become unstable. The universal analogy is no longer certain; the natural order no longer

---

[1] *Œuvres complètes*, ed. by Jean Massin, Paris: Le Club français du livre, 18 vols., 1967-1970; VII: 700.

necessarily corresponds to any transcendent divine realm; and crucially, the value of poetic rhythm is no longer absolute.

In 1861 Baudelaire criticizes Hugo for using verse to present scientifically proven facts as if their divine meaning were guaranteed:

> Raconter en vers les lois *connues*, selon lesquelles se meut un monde moral ou sidéral, c'est décrire ce qui est découvert et ce qui tombe tout entier sous le téléscope ou le compas de la science, c'est se réduire aux devoirs de la science et empiéter sur ses fonctions, et c'est embarrasser son langage traditionnel de l'ornement superflu, et dangereux ici, de la rime.[1]

Science has proved that the universe functions according to certain laws, and that there is order in natural phenomena, just as there are certain correspondences within language which verse foregrounds in rhyme. Yet just as we have no proof of the divine meaning of natural order, the rhyming of *amour* with *jour* does not necessarily correspond to a higher, transcendent Truth. Thus we witness the poet of 'Le Soleil', from the early 1840s, 'Flairant dans tous les coins les hasards de la rime' (1.6), as if these phonetic echoes in language, like natural structures perhaps, were born not of a divine intention, but of chance. Baudelaire suggests that rhyme is 'dangerous' to Hugo's presentation of scientific fact as divine since rhyme, rather than confirming the significance of such correspondences, actually calls them into question. In a similar remark from 1861, he criticizes poets who describe only fact in their verse, railing against:

> [...] de pareilles dilapidations de rythmes et de rimes, [...] la plus insoutenable des erreurs, à savoir que le but de la poésie est de répandre les lumières parmi le peuple, et, à l'aide de la rime et du nombre, de fixer plus facilement les découvertes scientifiques dans la mémoire des hommes.[2]

Whereas science deals in demonstrable truths, the poetic beauty of rhythm and rhyme, no longer guaranteed by an absolute, belongs to the realm of conjecture. In 1852 Baudelaire insists on the incompatibility of rhythm and truth:

---

[1] 'Victor Hugo' (O.C.II: 139); Baudelaire's italics.
[2] 'Auguste Barbier' (O.C.II: 145); Baudelaire's italics.

Le rythme est nécessaire au développement de l'idée de la beauté, qui est le but le plus noble du poème. Or, les artifices du rythme sont un obstacle insurmontable à ce développement minutieux de pensées et d'expressions qui a pour objet la vérité.[1]

Rhythm no longer reflects divine universal significance, but rather, allows the poet to develop the idea of beauty, an eternal, unchanging absolute, whose existence is far from certain. Pierre Sauvanet confirms: 'Le rythme n'est pas de l'ordre de la vérité, tout juste de la beauté'.[2] As such the Hugolian notion of absolute rhythmical value might simply be an illusion to which the Baudelairean poet can only submit under the effects of intoxication. In 'Le Poème du hachisch', for example, universal rhythm only appears a Truth for the drug-taker who succumbs to harmony and regular rhythm:

L'harmonie, le balancement des lignes, l'eurythmie dans les mouvements, apparaissent au rêveur comme des nécessités, comme des devoirs, non-seulement pour tous les êtres de la création, mais pour lui-même, le rêveur, qui se trouve, à cette période de la crise, doué d'une merveilleuse aptitude pour comprendre le rythme immortel et universel.[3]

For Baudelaire, therefore, the poetic rhythm of metre and rhyme no longer corresponds to a stable universal analogy. Rather, rhythm is an artifice by which the poet might restore the notion of absolute significance which is lost as the universal analogy falters. The disappearance of absolute values, which rhythm is required to counter, is articulated through the recurrent Baudelairean image of the *gouffre*.

The *gouffre*

Les Fleurs du Mal charts the struggle between faith in theological and poetic absolutes and the bitter irony of doubt represented by notions of *ennui*, *spleen* and the *gouffre*, whose synonymy is suggested by the 'gouffre de l'Ennui' of 'Le Possédé' (l.4). Many critics, such as Morten Nøjgaard, agree that the *gouffre* represents the poet's loss of religious faith, a kind of existential terror.[4] Indeed, in 'De Profundis clamavi' (ll.2-4), 'Danse macabre' (ll.36-40) and 'Le Flacon' (ll.14-17) it is accompanied by recurrent references to vertigo,

---

[1] 'Edgar Allan Poe, sa vie et ses ouvrages' (O.C.II: 329-30).
[2] 'Ordre et chaos ou du rythme en philosophie', *Ritm* 1 (1991), 125-33; p.125.
[3] *Les Paradis artificiels* (O.C.I: 432).
[4] *Elévation et expansion*, Odense University Press, 1973, p.18.

horror, avant-Sartrean nausea and the *vide*. In a recent work on the subject, André Hirt develops this reading, declaring categorically that, for Baudelaire: 'Il n'y a pas de Ciel de vérités'. He insists: 'Il n'y a plus d'*ailleurs*. Et lorsqu'il arrivera à Baudelaire de célébrer dans l'élévation et la louange, ce sera sur le fond de cette noirceur'. According to this quasi-Mallarméan interpretation, poetry must now come to terms with the 'vide de l'idéal', 'cette stupeur devant le vide', and *Les Fleurs du Mal* is 'une œuvre exposée à la vérité de son vide'.[1] It is this godless reading that Laforgue, a fervent admirer and sensitive reader of Baudelaire, develops in his early poems.[2]

However, a reading which ignores Baudelaire's fundamental indecision obscures the constant tension between the desire to believe and the overwhelming waves of doubt. It is for his fixity, his refusal to acknowledge the impossibility of knowing, that Baudelaire criticizes Hugo's unquestioning belief in the divine and universal absolutes, and as such his own scepticism is anything but total. Thus in a letter of 1861, he tells his mother of the difficulty of maintaining the stable faith for which he yearns: 'Je désire de tout mon cœur [...] croire qu'un être extérieur et invisible s'intéresse à ma destinée; mais comment faire pour le croire?'.[3] Asking, 'Que reste-t-il, au XIXe siècle, de la foi religieuse, historique?', Benjamin Fondane acknowledges this fundamental uncertainty, observing: 'Dieu n'existe pas, peut-être'.[4] Indeed, it is in terms of the irresolvability of this 'peut-être' that the Baudelairean *gouffre* should be read if we are to preserve the poetic value of his constant hesitations.

A divine presence in the universe maintains the notion of absolute meaning upon which the stability of regular poetic rhythm depends. As Hirt asks: 'Qu'est-ce que Dieu, sinon l'universelle explication, le déploiement suprême?'.[5] Without God, the absolute value of rhythm, which guarantees the aesthetic superiority of metrical verse over

---

[1] *Baudelaire. L'Exposition de la Poésie*, Paris: Editions Kimé, 1998, pp.18, 13, 13, 33 and 57.
[2] In *Les Complaintes et les premiers poèmes*, Paris: Gallimard, coll. 'Poésies', 1979, pp.159-319.
[3] Letter of 6 May 1861 (*Corr.* II: 151).
[4] *Baudelaire et l'expérience du gouffre*, Paris: Seghers, 1947; Brussels: Editions Complexe, 1994, pp.338 and 245.
[5] *Baudelaire. L'Exposition de la Poésie*, p.11, quoting Leibniz's 'Discours du métaphysique'.

prose, simply disappears, and in his *carnets*, Baudelaire reflects on the gnawing suspicion of the instability of everything, the absolute value of which cannot be taken for granted:

> Au moral comme au physique, j'ai toujours eu la sensation du gouffre, non seulement du gouffre du sommeil, mais du gouffre de l'action, du rêve, du souvenir, du désir, du regret, du remords, du beau, du nombre, etc.[1]

The value of *nombre* is no longer stable, oscillating between absolute value and mere illusion, the possibility that it does not correspond to any higher Truth. Thus the *gouffre* threatens both the poet's faith in the divine and his art itself. All is not lost, however. The narrator of the prose poem 'Une Mort héroïque' considers an actor performing under the threat of execution:

> Fancioulle me prouvait, d'une manière péremptoire, irréfutable, que l'ivresse de l'Art est plus apte que toute autre à voiler les terreurs du gouffre; que le génie peut jouer la comédie au bord de la tombe avec une joie qui l'empêche de voir la tombe, perdu, comme il est, dans un paradis excluant toute idée de tombe et de destruction.[2]

Art provides a veil over the *gouffre*, inspiring an *ivresse* stronger than that of wine or hashisch, which stirs the poet's faith in the absolute value of his verse. Although neither the divine nor the *gouffre* can ever be proved true, the veiling power of art is irrefutable, the narrator insists. In verse, as we shall see, it is rhythm itself which provides the necessary veil, momentarily restoring faith in an unstable universal analogy.

The rhythmic veil

Les Fleurs du Mal is doubly written under the sign of the *voile*. Firstly, *la voile* acts as a naval metaphor for the poetic journey towards the hazy, distant Ideal:

> Vers ma pâle étoile,
> Sous un plafond de brume ou dans un vaste éther,
> Je mets à la voile   ('La Musique', ll.2-4)

---

[1] O.C.I: 668.
[2] O.C.I: 321.

Secondly, in an erotic context, *le voile* is the veil which both covers and affords tantalizing glimpses of the lover's body, and various lovers tempt the poet with the revelation of the naked truth. The vampire-woman, offering 'la science / De perdre au fond d'un lit l'antique conscience' ('Les Métamorphoses du vampire', ll.5-6) promises, in an alluringly balanced 3/3/3/3, 2/4/2/4 rhythm:

> Je remplace, pour qui me voit nue et sans voiles,
> La lune, le soleil, le ciel et les étoiles! (ll.9-10)

However, when the poet succumbs to the vampire's promise and lifts the veil, he finds nothing but skeletal remains, the crushing materiality of the afterlife, the *gouffre* itself. Similarly, in 'Delphine et Hippolyte', Delphine tempts her lover, promising to reveal the secret which lies behind the veil:

> Des plaisirs plus obscurs je lèverai les voiles
> Et je t'endormirai dans un rêve sans fin! (ll.39-40)

Yet there is only disappointment and *ennui*, as the unveiling reveals nothing but the *gouffre*, leaving Hippolyte consumed by an 'abîme béant' (l.76). Also, in 'Le Rêve d'un curieux', the curtain opens, yet the glorious revelation after death of a transcendent absolute never comes.

It is vital, therefore, to the perpetuation of faith in the poetic endeavour that the final veil must not be lifted. The tempting scenario offered in *La Fanfarlo* must always, necessarily, remain purely hypothetical:

Quel est l'homme qui ne voudrait, même au prix de la moitié de ses jours, voir son rêve, son vrai rêve poser sans voile devant lui, et le fantôme adoré de son imagination faire tomber un à un tous les vêtements destinés à protéger contre les yeux du vulgaire?[1]

Behind the veil there may be nothing more than a 'rêve' or 'fantôme', and so the veil itself is the key to a poetics of faith, allowing the projection of an unprovable absolute. Thus Baudelairean poetry can be read not simply as unproblematic faith in a stable Ideal, but rather as

---

[1] O.C.I: 576.

the creation of a veil which allows the poet to maintain the distance, between himself and this absolute, necessary to fuel his faith. In 'L'Irréparable', Satan who tempts the poet with the suspicion of God's absence is overcome by 'Un être, qui n'était que lumière, or et gaze' (1.46). The 'ailes de gaze' (1.50) provide the necessary filter by which the possible revelation of the existential *vide* is constantly deferred, and by which the notion of a glorious Ideal, a guarantee of absolute values, is maintained. Furthermore, the wing is a familiar metaphor for verse thanks to its suggestion of a regular *battement*, underlining the importance of rhythm to the poetic veil.

This veil of poetic illusion recurs throughout *Les Fleurs du Mal*. In 'Le Balcon' the poet reminisces on the bygone days of faith inspired by love: 'les soirs au balcon, voilés de vapeurs roses' (1.7). The same veiling vapour appears in 'Ciel brouillé', where the lover's gaze is 'd'une vapeur couvert' (1.1) recalling the deliciously *indicible* quality of 'ces jours blancs, tièdes et voilés' (1.5). In *Le Peintre de la vie moderne* (1863), Baudelaire highlights the importance of the veil to the necessarily vague impression of harmony and beauty:

La femme est sans doute une lumière, un regard, une invitation au bonheur, une parole quelquefois; mais elle est surtout une harmonie générale, non seulement dans son allure et le mouvement de ses membres, mais aussi dans les mousselines, les gazes, les vastes et chatoyantes nuées d'étoffes dont elle s'enveloppe, et qui sont comme les attributs et le piédestal de sa divinité; [...] une image inséparable de la beauté [...] de la femme et de la robe, une totalité indivisible.[1]

Vapeurs and *voiles*, then, provide the poet with the necessary distance from the object of his desire, stirring his faith that what lies beyond is more than just the *gouffre*.

In the poems of harmony, rhythm and faith in all manner of intoxicating correspondences, the plural *voiles* creates a convenient ambiguity between sail and veil, poetic journey and poetic illusion:

Je vois un port rempli de voiles et de mâts,
Encor tout fatigués par la vague marine   ('Parfum exotique', ll.11-12)

Tu contiens, mer d'ébène, un éblouissant rêve
De voiles, de rameurs, de flammes et de mâts ('La Chevelure', ll.14-15)

---

[1] Section X, 'La Femme' (O.C.II: 714).

In these poems, the image recurs of the rhythmic sea, whose tides and waves create an oscillation which inspires the poet with 'la plus haute idée de beauté qui soit offerte à l'homme'.[1] The woman of 'Le Beau navire' creates the mesmerising effect of a gently rocking ship, 'Suivant un rythme doux, et paresseux, et lent' (l.8), and in 'Le Port' a similar scene inspires the poet with a taste for rhythm:

Les formes élancées des navires, au gréement compliqué, auxquels la houle imprime des oscillations harmonieuses, servent à entretenir dans l'âme le goût du rythme et de la beauté.[2]

The beauty of the sea's oscillations provides a fleeting moment of reassuring Hugolian inspiration. It re-motivates faith in the incontrovertible aesthetic value of regular rhythm in nature, and thereby in poetic rhythm. In 'La Chevelure' the abundance of rhythm and harmony caresses the poet's mind with 'Infinis bercements' (l.25), and in 'La Musique' these 'bercements' cradle the poet over the *gouffre*, soothing his existential angst:

>   Le bon vent, la tempête et ses convulsions
>   Sur l'immense gouffre
>   Me bercent.   (ll.11-13)

Storms and convulsions hardly constitute regular rhythms, yet the poetic mind imagines their effect on a storm-tossed ship in terms of a regular vibration:

>   Je sens vibrer en moi toutes les passions
>   D'un vaisseau qui souffre (ll.9-10)

The pathetic fallacy, the sensation of a correspondence between human passions and natural phenomena, inspires the poet with faith in the possibility that there is, after all, absolute meaning in nature, providing a *bercement* which calms his existential fears.

The verb *bercer* and its cognates feature frequently in reflection on the sea's rhythmical qualities. The sobs of the natural world – again,

---

[1] 'Mon cœur mis à nu' XXX (O.C.I: 696).
[2] O.C.I: 344.

the reassuring pathetic fallacy of meaning in nature – have a cradling effect in 'Bien loin d'ici':

> La brise et l'eau chantent au loin
> Leur chanson de sanglots heurtée
> Pour bercer cette enfant gâtée. (ll.8-10)

'Mœsta et errabunda' features the same combination of musical and marine metaphors:

> Quel démon a doté la mer, rauque chanteuse
> Qu'accompagne l'immense orgue des vents
> De cette fonction sublime de berceuse? (ll.7-9)

The sea's rhythmical function is not guaranteed by God, but rather, granted by a demon, as if the temptation to believe in the universal analogy were but a fiendish illusion to which the poet succumbs. Thus, for the poet eager to escape the *gouffre*, the distinctly unsoothing winds and harsh roar of the waves create a quite illusory *bercement*. The word conveys the regular rhythmic motion by which fears are soothed away to sleep, an escape from the terror of the *néant*, and in 'La Fontaine de sang' the poet links sleep with the veiling effects of wine and love over existential terror:

> J'ai demandé souvent à des vins captieux
> D'endormir pour un jour la terreur qui me mine; [...]
> J'ai cherché dans l'amour un sommeil oublieux   (ll.9-12)

Similarly, in 'De profundis clamavi', he yearns for sleep as an escape from the *gouffre*:

> Je jalouse le sort des plus vils animaux
> Qui peuvent se plonger dans un sommeil stupide (ll.12-13)

The stupidity of a dozing beast recalls the 'stupidity' of blind faith to which Baudelaire sometimes wishes he could devote himself, and which he sometimes scorns. This can be applied to the rhythmical fabric of regular verse, as he declares: 'la grande poésie est essentiellement bête, elle croit, et c'est ce qui fait sa gloire et sa force'.[1] However, Baudelaire's lucid critical conscience forbids him from total submission to faith, and prevents him from writing 'la grande poésie'.

Happily, the illusory, fictional nature of these *bercements* is implied by the other sense of *bercer*, which can mean: 'chatouiller agréablement, nourrir de quelque illusion', as in the expression *se bercer d'illusions*, or: 'bercer quelqu'un d'un faux espoir, de vaines promesses'.[2] The regular rhythm of these marine poems, therefore, creates an illusion, veiling the *gouffre* temporarily and stirring poetico-religious faith in the meaningful link between a divine absolute and verse. This veil is synonymous with the *ivresse* which poetry inspires in the poet, and the verb *bercer* appears in 'La Pipe', where a veil of smoke soothes the poet's soul:

> J'enlace et je berce son âme
> Dans le réseau mobile et bleu (ll.9-10)

Rhythmical verse obscures the *gouffre* of doubt with an illusion of absolute meaning, by which faith in both the divine and aesthetic hierarchies might be sustained.

Verse multiplies structural correspondences which, through their harmony, take language closer to an imagined Ideal, thereby projecting the illusion of its existence. The more rhythmical and harmonic patterns, the more the impression of multiplicity is replaced by one of wholeness, the resolution of unpoetic, disordered *nombre* in a more meaningful, poetic *nombre*. Indeed, Banville describes the rhythms of speech as irregular, complicated and variable, in comparison to the apparent simplicity of poetic and musical rhythms:

Le son que produit la parole humaine est nécessairement rhythmé, puisqu'il exprime l'ordre de nos pensées ou de nos idées. Seulement, lorsque nous parlons, notre langage est réglé par un rhythme compliqué et variable, dont le dessin ne se présente pas immédiatement à l'esprit avec netteté, et qui, pour être perçu, veut une grande application; lorsque nous chantons, au contraire, notre langage est réglé par un rhythme d'un dessin net, régulier et facilement appréciable, afin de pouvoir s'unir à la Musique, dont le rhythme est également précis et simple.[3]

---

[1] 'Prométhée délivré par L. Ménard' (O.C.II: 11).
[2] Definition and example in Larousse, *Grand Dictionnaire Universel du XIXe Siècle*, 2: 569.
[3] *Petit Traité*, p.3.

These simple, regular poetic rhythms refer, yet again, to that rhythmical property which is theirs alone: the constant, periodic beat of metre which provides the poetic *bercement*. Banville implies that the simplicity and regularity of artistic rhythm is precisely what makes it artistic; speech rhythms are too irregular to be Art, and so the rhythmic veil of verse is poetic thanks to the simplicity of its regular rhythmic *évidence*.

It is the regular rhythms of poetry and music that function as a veil in a passage so crucial to Baudelaire's aesthetics that he uses it in essays on both Poe (1857) and Gautier (1858). In these texts of poetic propaganda, intended to glorify the poetic endeavour, Baudelaire insists on the existence of 'le rythme et la prosodie universels', maintaining the illusion of poetry's correspondence to an absolute:

C'est cet admirable, cet immortel instinct du Beau qui nous fait considérer la terre et ses spectacles comme un aperçu, comme une correspondance du Ciel. La soif insatiable de tout ce qui est au-delà, et que révèle la vie, est la preuve la plus vivante de notre immortalité. C'est à la fois par la poésie et *à travers* la poésie, par et *à travers* la musique que l'âme entrevoit les splendeurs situées derrière le tombeau.[1]

The prepositions italicized by Baudelaire himself indicate that the rhythmic structures of both poetry and music provide the veil through which the absolute might be glimpsed, and faith in the illusion of universal meaning restored.

Thus, in the absence of a universal Truth, the poetic veil acts as a vehicle of faith, with its rhythmic and harmonic correspondences which reassure the poet in a universe which constantly threatens to tumble into the *gouffre*. Baudelaire writes in his *carnets*:

Quand même Dieu n'existerait pas, la Religion serait encore Sainte et *Divine*.
Dieu est le seul être qui, pour régner, n'ait même pas besoin d'exister.[2]

By helping to fuel the poet's faith in a divine absolute, verse also helps to fuel his belief in Poetry, or absolute values of poeticity. Verse itself can perpetuate the illusion that its metre and rhyme correspond

---

[1] 'Notes nouvelles sur Edgar Poe' (O.C.II: 334) and 'Théophile Gautier' (O.C.II: 114); Baudelaire's italics.
[2] 'Fusées' I (O.C.I: 649); Baudelaire's italics.

to a cosmic order whose divine significance is guaranteed. Graham Martin asks:

> Is there, in French poetry, a connexion between the certainties of belief and the use of formal metre? [...] It looks as if a belief in certainty, even a certainty not yet found, expresses itself in formal rhythms [...]. Has rhythm something to do with belief, and with the nature of that belief?[1]

It certainly seems that, for Baudelaire, rhythm has everything to do not with the certainties of belief, but with the delicious illusion of belief which is the very aim of his verse poetry.

There is one problem, however: Baudelaire's verse is not simply a succession of constantly regular rhythms and harmonies. Indeed, as Verlaine admiringly observes, it is Baudelaire who writes the first metrically problematic lines in the history of French verse:

> Baudelaire est, je crois, le premier en France qui ait osé des vers comme ceux-ci:
>
> ... Pour entendre un de ces concerts riches de cuivre ...
> ... Exaspéré comme un ivrogne qui voit double ... [2]

Verlaine emphasizes Baudelaire's weakening of the caesural accent with two metrically unaccentuable words. Both lines can – just – be resolved as *alexandrins romantiques*, the 4/4/4 rhythm introduced into French verse by Hugo, which provides a substitute regularity when the caesura is threatened:

> Pour entendre un / de *ces* // concerts / riches de cuivre
> Exaspéré / comme *un* // ivro / gne qui voit double

However, Verlaine insists on these lines' problematic nature, indicating the extent to which the sixth-syllable accent forms the very essence of the alexandrine in the 1850s. Yet in the light of Baudelaire's critical writings on the poetic veil of rhythmical regularity, this begs the question: what exactly is the significance of this formal irregularity? Is the matter really as simple as critics have

---

[1] 'High Formal Poetry', in *Poetry in France: Metamorphoses of a Muse*, ed. by Keith Aspley and Peter France, Edinburgh University Press, 1992, pp.204-18; pp.217-18.
[2] 'Charles Baudelaire', in *Œuvres en prose complètes*, ed. by Jacques Borel, Paris: Gallimard, coll. 'Bibliothèque de la Pléiade', 1972, p.611.

always suggested: that Baudelaire rebels against the metrical straitjacket before plunging into the rhythmical liberties of prose? Let us examine the development of this formal irregularity throughout Baudelaire's career, in the hope that a comprehensive understanding of their appearance – and any trends which become apparent – might afford us a more subtle and sensitive understanding of the importance of irregularity to Baudelaire's poetic agenda.

2
Rhythm in Practice

The formal inscription of irony

In 'L'Héautontimorouménos' (1855) the poet revives his flagging faith with a rhythmical beating, as his victim's sobs provide the necessary regularity, 'Comme un tambour qui bat la charge!' (l.12). The poet's renewed hope is 'Comme un vaisseau qui prend le large' (l.9), recalling the hopeful departures of 'La Musique', 'Je mets à la voile' (l.4), and 'Le Beau navire', with its 'beau vaisseau qui prend le large [...] Suivant un rythme doux, et paresseux, et lent' (ll.6-8). The fourth stanza, however, heralds a sudden change of tone, and the poet is overcome by doubt as to the significance of this rhythm:

> Ne suis-je pas un faux accord
> Dans la divine symphonie,
> Grâce à la vorace Ironie
> Qui me secoue et qui me mord? (ll.13-16)

The poet's short-lived faith in the *divine symphonie*, the analogy by which universal and poetic order provide a reciprocal guarantee of meaning, is pierced by the ironic conscience from which he had tried to escape. Significantly, this irony is also expressed in terms of the musical metaphor, creating a *faux accord* in the harmony of verse and belief, such as in 'Le Poème du hachisch', where the artificial *ivresse* convinces the drug-taker that he is no longer 'une note discordante dans le monde d'harmonie et de beauté improvisé par son imagination'.[1] Could there be a connection between this *faux accord* and the versificatory irregularities in *Les Fleurs du Mal*?

In his 1861 essay on Banville, the poet of faith and illusion *par excellence*, Baudelaire makes the same connection between dissonance and Irony. Both of these, he writes, are absent from Banville's work, which is faithful, rhythmic and harmonious:

---

[1] *Les Paradis artificiels* (O.C.I: 432).

Comme l'art antique, il n'exprime que ce qui est beau, joyeux, noble, grand, rythmique. Aussi, dans ses œuvres, vous n'entendrez pas les dissonances, les discordances des musiques du sabbat, non plus que les glapissements de l'ironie, cette vengeance du vaincu.[1]

If regularity and harmony represent faith in both the divine absolute and verse, and if discord expresses the ironic conscience, what is the relationship between the two throughout Baudelaire's career? Do his first metrically problematic lines coincide with a more explicit presence of the ironic conscience in the content of the poems? Do the poems which articulate faith in rhythm conform to a more regular, harmonious model? Is there a significant development in the poet's versification after 1855, the date of both the first prose poems and 'L'Héautontimorouménos'?

In order to answer these questions, I propose to examine the chronological development of Baudelaire's versification according to the diachronic periods listed in the appendix (pp.339-47), studying the relationship between regularity and irregularity, faith and irony. We can identify six sites of verse tension, the critical points at which the clash between anticipated regularity and actual irregularity might create a *faux accord*:

1. Disruption of the caesural accent and pause.
2. Rhythmical hiatus caused by adjacent accents.
3. Tension in the syllable count and effects of asymmetry
   at the rhyme position.
4. Cases of *rejet* and *contre-rejet*
   (i.e. rhythmically problematic *enjambement*).
5. Rhyming and stanzaic irregularities in the sonnet form.
6. Questions of rhyme strength: reinforced or problematic
   rhymes.

These are the ways in which verse regularity, harmonic and rhythmic, might be reinforced or disturbed, the sites at which the ironic conscience might pierce the rhythmic veil with a *faux accord*.

---

[1] O.C.II: 168.

Tension at the caesura

The method of *métricométrie*, as proposed by Benoît de Cornulier and adopted by the current generation of French verse specialists, provides the starting point for our study of the Baudelairean caesura. In this system, different disruptive techniques are classified according to the hierarchical model FMEmCP6.[1] Expressed simply, the term F6 denotes a usually unpronounced, feminine 'e' at sixth position; Em6 a masculine 'e' such as 'de', 'le' or 'que'; M6 a caesura mid-word; C6 a monosyllabic article, pronoun, possessive or demonstrative adjective; and P6 a monosyllabic preposition:

F6	Forêts, soleils, rives, / savanes! – il s'aidait
Em6	Je me confesse de / l'aveu des jeunes crimes!...
M6	Eclatent, tricolo / rement enrubannés
C6	Ô feuillage, si **tu** / protèges ces mortelles
P6	Par ma lèvre: quand **sur** / l'or glauque de lointaines

According to prosodic tradition, each of these techniques represents a serious transgression of the alexandrine form.

Cornulier's approach is diametrically opposed to that of Banville and other critics who are happy to perpetuate the notion of poetic absolutes. Contrary to their mystification of poeticity, Cornulier insists that there is no absolute metrical mould which defines the line of verse as such:

Cette notion de schéma abstrait est ici superflue, puisque l'idée que les vers 'réalisent un *même schéma abstrait*' n'est qu'une conséquence automatique de l'idée qu'ils ont une *même propriété*, en l'occurrence le même nombre de syllabes. Un vers n'a pas à 'réaliser' un schéma préexistant dans un ciel des idées et des mètres: en général, la structure métrique est *immanente* au texte.[2]

As a modern metrician unconcerned with fuelling poetic illusions, Cornulier insists on the 'essentielle *relativité du nombre métrique*' in defining a line of verse.[3] Rejecting any sort of mythology as to the poetic significance of *nombre*, he concentrates on historical facts

---

[1] See *Théorie du vers: Rimbaud, Verlaine, Mallarmé*, Paris: Editions du Seuil, 1982, pp.134-43 for a more detailed discussion of these categories.

[2] *Théorie du vers*, p.39, Cornulier's italics; quotations are from Jean Mazaleyrat's *Eléments de métrique française*, Paris: Armand Colin, 1974, whose basic metrical model Cornulier rejects.

[3] *Théorie du vers*, p.37; Cornulier's italics.

rather than thematic interpretation in his analyses. His diachronic classification of the gradual decline of metrical regularity has given us a detailed history of the alexandrine's demise, yet in over twenty-five years of illuminating analysis of the metrically problematic, Cornulier has devoted only two rather unadventurous articles to Baudelaire.[1] Despite his pioneering role in the first caesural experiments, Baudelaire's form is generally considered rather regular, an opinion famously expressed by Rimbaud.[2] Furthermore, Cornulier's articles contain almost no discussion of what the data might mean in the context of Baudelairean poetics. By applying my own, augmented version of Cornulier's method to *Les Fleurs du Mal*, I hope to reveal the complexities of the Baudelairean verse fabric and to explore their possible significance in terms of his metaphysical and aesthetic considerations.

Cornulier's lack of interest in Baudelaire is understandable, since the categories with which he is most concerned – the metrically forbidden FMEm6 – do not appear in Baudelaire's verse. As for the P6 lines, if we include 'comme' and 'dont' where Cornulier does not, we still find only eight examples. However, these lines certainly encourage an accentual shift away from the hallowed sixth syllable, with 'comme', 'dont' and 'sous' unable to support the metrical accent:

> Les tables d'hôt / e, dont // le jeu / fait les délices
> > ('Le Crépuscule du soir', 1.23, 4-4+4)
> Hélas! et **j'a** / vais, comme // en **un** / suaire épais
> > ('Un voyage à Cythère', 1.55, M4, C8)
> Où l'Espéran / ce, comme // une / chauve-souris
> > ('Spleen' IV, 1.6, F8)
> Serré, four**mill** / ant, comme // un **mill** / ion d'helminthes
> > ('Au Lecteur', 1.21, M4, M8)
> Tes nobles jam / bes, sous // les **vo** / lants qu'elles chassent
> > ('Le Beau navire', 1.29, M8)
> Bien affilés, / et, comme // un **jon** / gleur insensible
> > ('A une Madone', 1.41, M8)

---

[1] 'Métrique des *Fleurs du Mal*', in *Les Fleurs du Mal: l'intériorité de la forme*, ed. by Martine Bercot, Paris: S.E.D.E.S., 1989, pp.55-76, and 'Pour une analyse du sonnet dans *Les Fleurs du Mal*', in *Lectures des Fleurs du Mal*, ed. by Steve Murphy, Presses Universitaires de Rennes, 2002, pp.197-236.
[2] 'Encore a-t-il vécu dans un milieu trop artiste; et la forme si vantée en lui est mesquine', in *Poésies. Une saison en enfer. Illuminations*, ed. by Louis Forestier, Paris: Gallimard, coll. 'folio. classique', 1999, p.93.

J'ai peur du **somm** / eil comme // on a / peur d'un grand trou
('Le Gouffre', 1.9, M4)
Les jambes **en** / l'air, comme // une / femme lubrique
('Une Charogne', 1.5, P4, F8)

Bernard highlights the 'effet de brusque rupture' produced by a pre-caesural 'comme', and Clive Scott also sees it as undermining the sixth syllable accent.[1] For Chesters, 'the sixth syllable loses almost all its privileges' with 'dont' before the caesura.[2] There is conflict, then, between metre and syntax, since these prepositional terms are syntactically subordinate to elements in the next hemistich. If the reader attempts to accentuate the sixth syllable, a *faux accord* is created in the verse harmony and the rhythm falters. Furthermore, only the first of the eight examples can be resolved as a compensatory *alexandrin romantique*; the other lines are left in a sort of rhythmical no man's land, conforming to no pre-existent metrical model. These lines are certainly at odds with Baudelaire's theoretical insistence on the veiling rhythmic *bercement* of metre, yet they are so few and so evenly distributed throughout his career as to provide little evidence of significant development.

The C6 lines prove more conclusive, since they are more disruptive at the caesura, and their distribution seems more significant. There are none before 1853, with four appearing between 1853 and 1857:

Vivre est un mal. / C'est un // secret / de tous connu ('Semper eadem', 1.4)
A la très belle, / à la // très bonne, / à la très chère ('Que diras-tu ce soir...', 1.3)
Et fait surgir / plus d'un // porti / que fabuleux ('Le Poison', 1.3)
Chacun plantant, / comme un // outil, / son bec impur ('Un voyage à Cythère', 1.31)

This increases to eight in 1858-59, both in a shorter period of time and in fewer poems:

Je te ferai / de mon // Respect / de beaux Souliers ('A une Madone', 1.19)
Volupté noire! des / sept Péchés capitaux ('A une Madone', 1.39)
O ma si blanche, / ô ma // si froid / e Marguerite ('Sonnet d'automne', 1.14)
Exaspéré / comme un // ivrogn / e qui voit double ('Les Sept vieillards', 1.45)
Pour entendre un / de ces // concerts, / riches de cuivre ('Les Petites vieilles', 1.49)
D'autres, l'horreur / de leurs // berceaux, / et quelques-uns ('Le Voyage', 1.10)

---

[1] *Le Poème en prose de Baudelaire jusqu'à nos jours*, p.111, and *A Question of syllables*, Cambridge: C.U.P., 1986, pp.77-82.
[2] 'Baudelaire and the Limits of Poetry', *French Studies* 32 (1978): 420-34; p.425.

Criant à Dieu, dans sa / furibonde agonie   ('Le Voyage', l.101)
O mon semblable, ô mon / maître, je te maudis   ('Le Voyage', l.102)

Finally, two more examples feature in poems from the 1860s:

Disait: 'la Terre / est un // gâteau / plein de douceur   ('La Voix', l.6)
Qu'il s'infiltre comme une / extase dans tous ceux'   ('L'Imprévu', l.51)

Furthermore, the first four examples all allow the substitute regularity of an *alexandrin romantique*, whereas four of the later C6 lines resist this alternative:

Volupté noi / re! des // sept **Pé** / chés capitaux   (M8)
Criant à Dieu, / dans sa // **furi** / bonde agonie   (M8)
O mon semblable, / ô mon // **maître**, / je te maudis   (F8)
Qu'il s'infiltre / comme une // extas / e dans tous ceux   (F4)

This development, from tentative beginnings to both increased frequency and increased disruptive force, suggests a move in the mid-1850s, confirmed in 1858-59, towards a more insistent inscription of the *faux accord* in Baudelaire's verse. Yet Cornulier's method can provide no further evidence either to support or to disprove this hypothesis.

However, caesural tension is not created by Cornulier's categories alone. He is at pains to emphasize his deliberate concentration on purely metrical disruption of the accent at the sixth syllable, but as Michèle Aquien observes, the caesura expresses both a metrical accent and a syntactic pause.[1] It is this pause, which can be disrupted by several other syntactic techniques, that Cornulier ignores in his concerted effort to eradicate the personal judgements of each reader's *pifomètre* from verse analysis. Yet Baudelaire exploits this very pause in the following line from the early poem 'A une Malabaraise', where it guides our interpretation of the second hemistich, whose two elements are in apposition, not with the 'flacons', as a compound noun, but rather with the verb:

De pourvoir les flacons / d'eaux fraîches et d'odeurs (l.7)

---

[1] *Dictionnaire de poétique*, Paris: Librairie Générale Française, coll. 'Livre de Poche', pp.75-78.

The caesura here, if respected, subtly yet firmly separates the 'flacons' from the 'd'eaux fraîches', providing a subtle syntactic nuance. In contrast, the following example from 'Le Reniement de saint Pierre' manipulates the reader's anticipation of metrical convention with a *trompe-l'œil* effect:

La crapule du corps / de garde et des cuisines (l.14)

The structure of this line, composed ten years later, is not: '/ de garde et des cuisines', but rather, 'du corps de garde / et des cuisines'. This subverts the caesural pause and confounds what appears at first sight to be a balanced second hemistich. Moreover, the line is syntactically tripartite, yet the F4 resists resolution in an *alexandrin romantique*. As it is, the alliteration 'c' and the 3-3 rhythm of the first hemistich lends a powerful accent to 'corps', and if the following 'de garde' is to close the syntactic unit successfully, its accent must be even stronger. This disrupts the anticipated second-hemistich balance which is so frequent elsewhere:

/ de viandes et de vins	('Bénédiction', l.42)
/ la terre et les enfers	('Bénédiction', l.66)
/ la Muse et la Madone	('Que diras-tu ce soir…', l.14)
/ de viande et de vins[1]	('Le Reniement de saint Pierre', l.3)
/ si brillants et si beaux	('Le Reniement de saint Pierre', l.21)
/ ni wagon ni vaisseau,	('Le Voyage', l.118)
/ sans vapeur et sans voile!	('Le Voyage', l.53)
/ d'un pontife ou d'un prince	('Le Masque', l.7) [2]

In this way the line ironically subverts the parallel construction with which Baudelaire often adds to the symmetrical balance of the second hemistich, and therefore, to the whole line. Tension is created between the reader's anticipation of the metrical accent, and the line's problematic syntactic structure.

Cornulier's CPFM6 categories, therefore, cannot cater for all methods of caesural disruption. Recognizing this, Jean-Luc Guilbaud, a contributor to the *Cahiers du Centre d'Etudes Métriques*, proposes the term D6, charting not what is strictly prohibited but rather,

---

[1] With diaeresis on 'vi-ande'.
[2] Examples taken from Chesters, *Some Functions of Sound-Repetition in 'Les Fleurs du Mal'*, p.56.

syntactic links which are sufficiently tightly bound to counteract both caesural accent and pause, 'ce qu'on appelle traditionnellement rejet et contre-rejet internes'.[1] He leaves this undeveloped, but an analysis of *Les Fleurs du Mal* according to my own *pifomètre* uncovers a number of caesuras which seem to resist simultaneous metrical and syntactic closure. These may be divided into ten categories:

adjective / noun
    Ils marchent, ces divins / frères qui sont mes frères ('Le Flambeau vivant', l.3)
noun / adjective
    Et qui sait si les fleurs / nouvelles que je rêve ('L'Ennemi', l.9)
complex verbal unit
    Et dont l'aspect aurait / fait pleuvoir les aumônes ('Les Sept vieillards', l.15)
bisyllabic preposition
    Viens-tu troubler, avec / ta puissante grimace ('Danse macabre', l.21)
other complex units
    Il était tard; ainsi / qu'une médaille neuve ('Confession', l.5)
subject / verb
    Et d'autres, dont la gorge / aime les scapulaires ('Femmes damnées', l.17)
verb / object
    Saint Pierre a renié / Jésus... il a bien fait! ('Le Reniement de saint Pierre', l.32)
compound nouns
    Vous êtes un beau ciel / d'automne, clair et rose ('Causerie', l.1)
plus, *moins*, *assez* or *aussi* / adjective
    Puisqu'il me trouve assez / belle pour m'adorer ('Bénédiction', l.38)
word pairs linked by *et*
    Une niche, d'azur / et d'or tout émaillée ('A une Madone', l.5)

This system certainly provides a more sensitive method of measuring caesural disruption, and the authors of poetic treatises from 1850 to 1950, such as Quicherat and Grammont, consistently dismiss such lines as discordant. Moreover, the numerous rhythmically irregular alexandrines in the work of Rimbaud and Mallarmé all fall into one of these ten categories.

In our Baudelairean corpus, the frequency of the D6 lines increases dramatically during the 1850s. During the 1843-46 period, out of thirty poems (754 alexandrines) there are thirty-seven D6 lines (in fifteen poems). There is a much higher concentration in the sixteen poems (359 alexandrines) of 1853-57: forty-two D6 lines (in fourteen poems). The eleven poems of 1858-59 (432 alexandrines) continue the

---

[1] 'L'Alexandrin dans l'œuvre de Guillaume Apollinaire', *Cahiers du Centre d'Etudes Métriques* 3 (1996): 25-54; p.31.

trend, with forty-seven D6 lines (in only eight poems). This increase in syntactically problematic lines coincides with both a similar increase in the number of metrically problematic C6 lines and also, more or less, with the appearance, in 'L'Héautontimorouménos' (1855), of a *faux accord* in the *divine symphonie*. The irony which causes the poet to doubt the absolute significance of both universal and metrical rhythms provokes a sustained questioning of the formal mould of verse, piercing the veil of regularity which the poet attempts to construct over the *gouffre*.

Adjacent accents

Although the D6 categories allow us more precision in our reaction to certain lines, they are somewhat subjective, and what might appear disruptive to one reader might be permissible for the next. However, a number of examples seem indubitably problematic, and the reason for this is purely accentual. Some possible examples of D6 lines are not counted since they are resolved in a regular 3/3//3/3 structure. This counteracts any disruptive force which the D6 syntactic link over the caesura may have, such as in the lines:

Dans le fiel: / son regard // aiguisait / les frimas	('Les Sept Vieillards', 1.18)
A travers / le treillis // recourbé / de tes côtes	('Danse macabre', 1.31)

Similarly, when the D6 syntactic link is resolved on the eighth syllable, although the line does not conclude with the complete regularity of 3/3, the resultant caesural disruption is not as forceful as that resolved on the seventh syllable. Compare, for example:

(2/4//2/4)   Pour fuir ce rétiaire / infâme; il en est d'autres
                                            ('Le Voyage', 1.119)

(3/3//1/5)   J'ai connu sous un dais / d'arbres tout empourprés
                                            ('A une dame créole', 1.2)

It seems that the D6 lines which are pulled up just after the caesura disrupt the rhythm of the line more significantly. They disturb the caesural accent and pause with a clash, at the sixth and seventh syllables, between the metrical and syntactic accents.

Investigating adjacent accents at the rhyme, Margaret Hudson observes: 'One of the fundamental rules of French versification is that between two stressed syllables there should be at least one unstressed syllable'.[1] Like other poetic rules, upon which critics, like Banville, insist in order to perpetuate a fallacious hierarchical aesthetic system, it is supposed to prevent discordance, as if 'good poetry' were synonymous with harmony and regularity, and 'bad poetry' with disturbance: 'Not only at the cesura and at the rime but even within a line of any length the immediate encounter of two stresses produces cacophony'.[2] Auguste Dorchain also declares in characteristically extravagant terms: 'l'oreille repousse, avec une gêne qui va jusqu'à la souffrance, la succession immédiate de deux syllabes accentuées', pronouncing such a horror to be 'interdite'.[3] Roger Pensom, more calmly, highlights 'the principle of alternating accent', 'the tendency in French to "space" semantically-loaded monosyllables by alternating them with polysyllables and clitics i.e. monosyllables whose frequency of occurrence is high and which are often semantically weak grammatical markers'.[4] In a well balanced, rhythmically soothing alexandrine, a line will have its four accents, two fixed: one at the sixth syllable and one at the twelfth, and two mobile: one in each hemistich. The position of the mobile accents is also regulated, as Quicherat asserts:

Dans le premier hémistiche, sur l'une des quatre premières syllabes;
Dans le second, sur la septième, la huitième, la neuvième ou la dixième.[5]

Cassagne also rules out syntactic accentuation of the syllable immediately preceding the two fixed metrical accents:

On sait qu'il est admis que deux toniques ne peuvent se suivre sans choquer l'oreille, et que le heurt de deux accents, sorte d'hiatus rythmique, doit être évité autant que le heurt de deux sons. Par conséquent, ni la 5e, ni la 11e syllabe ne doivent recevoir d'accent.[6]

---

[1] *The Juxtaposition of Accents at the Rhyme in French Versification*, University of Philadelphia, coll. 'Publications of the Series in Romanic Languages and Literatures' 19, 1927, p.7.
[2] *The Juxtaposition of Accents at the Rhyme in French Versification*, p.24.
[3] *L'Art des Vers*, Paris, 1905; 'Librairie des Annales', n.d., p.184.
[4] *Accent and Metre in French*, Berne: Peter Lang, 1998, pp.30 and 31.
[5] *Traité de versification française*, p.133.
[6] *Versification et métrique de Charles Baudelaire*, p.31.

Maurice Grammont asserts categorically that lines with hemistichs accentuated 1/5 or 5/1 lack sufficient balance: 'Comme ils n'ont pas de point de repère à l'intérieur de la mesure à 5 syllabes, leur harmonie n'est pleinement satisfaisante que s'ils sont divisibles de deux manières'.[1] And Dorchain, finding fault with certain Hugolian lines, asserts:

Quand nous rencontrons des vers, de coupe classique ou non, dont la prononciation nous inquiète, nous pouvons être sûrs que c'est parce que le poète a placé des accents rythmiques à la cinquième ou à la onzième syllabe:

L'être est un hi**deux tronc** / qui porte un di**vin buste**
Dont un bout est **nuit froide** / et l'autre bout clarté [2]

Although Dorchain and other critics find exceptions to these rules when the mood takes them, it appears that in the strictest possible terms, the more balanced and stable the line, the more pleasing the poetic *bercement*. Grammont insists: 'Les plus harmonieux sont ceux dans lesquels le rythme est du type 3-3-4-2, 3-3-2-4 ou 2-4-3-3, 4-2-3-3 et dans lesquels l'harmonie peut se diviser à la fois en dyades et en triades'.[3] Thus the accentual possibilities for the entirely partial concept of poetically rhythmic stability are limited to the following:

*	I	I	I	*	II	*	I	I	I	*	III
1	2	3	4	5	6	7	8	9	10	11	12

where * denotes an unaccentuable syllable, II the caesural accent, III the line-final accent, and I the possible positions of mobile accents, the respective strengths of the accents increasing from I to III.

Whenever Henk Nuiten observes a 3/3//3/3 line, the 'tétramètre régulier', he is enchanted by 'sa belle régularité'.[4] This 'symétrie rythmique' results from 'un rythme martelé de façon régulière, l'alexandrin étant parfaitement équilibré'.[5] An early version of 'Le

---

[1] *Le Vers Français. Ses Moyens d'expression. Son harmonie*, Paris: Librairie Ancienne Honoré Champion, 1923, p.418.
[2] *L'Art des Vers*, p.227.
[3] Grammont, *Le Vers Français. Ses Moyens d'expression. Son harmonie*, p.420.
[4] *Les Variantes des 'Fleurs du Mal' et des 'Epaves' de Charles Baudelaire*, Amsterdam: Academic Publishers Associated / Holland University Press, 1979, pp.143 and 139. (Hereafter *Les Variantes…*).
[5] *Les Variantes …*, p.206.

Vin des chiffonniers' contains a syntactic accent on the seventh syllable:

C'est ainsi que le vin // rè / gne par ses bienfaits (1.26)[1]

According to Nuiten's *pifomètre*, 'Le manque absolu de cadence rythmique rend ce vers aussi inexpressif qu'une ligne de prose banale'.[2] In another example, Baudelaire removes the first, rhythmically jarring, comma from line 4 of 'Les Chats', restoring balance to the line, from 1/5//3/3 to a regular 3/3//3/3 reinforced by internal rhyme:

Qui (,) comme **eux** / sont frileux / et comme **eux** / sédentair (es).

Observing 'la belle régularité à quatre temps forts' of the new line, Nuiten describes the alteration in similar, aesthetically biased, terms, resorting to that traditional staple of poetic criticism, the musical analogy: 'On voit, ou plutôt on entend que l'harmonie musicale, obtenue par la cadence équilibrée et la triple assonance intérieure, rachète largement la cacophonie initiale'.[3] This explicit value judgement must be seen for the bias it is – one of the aims of this study is to argue that, after Baudelaire, any claims to define poeticity in terms of an absolute hierarchical scale of values are fallacious.[4] Yet a 1/5 or 5/1 structure certainly creates imbalance in the hemistich; not, as Nuiten suggests, by accelerating one sense group,[5] but rather, by

---

[1] O.C.I: 1050. The line is later changed to: 'C'est ainsi qu'à travers / l'Humanité frivole' (1.25).
[2] *Les Variantes* ..., p.121.
[3] ibid., p.164.
[4] Although, as we shall see, this shared fiction among poetry enthusiasts, whether conscious or not, can be seen, after Baudelaire, as an illusion necessary to the perpetuation of the poetic idea.
[5] Quoting Jean Suberville, *Histoire et théorie de la versification française*, Paris: Editions de 'l'Ecole', 1965, Nuiten writes: 'Or, le rythme étant "le retour périodique des mêmes combinaisons de durée", la mesure de cinq syllabes sera sensiblement accéléré dans la diction' (*Les Variantes* ..., p.138). On line 11 of 'Que diras-tu ce soir...', 'Son fantôme dans l'air / dan / se comme un flambeau', Nuiten comments: 'La syllabe 'dans' occupe à elle seule une mesure entière. Le débit en sera considérablement ralenti.' (ibid., p.139). This theory of delivery speed is invalid. Since metrical accents do not obey the same relentless pulse as music, the idea that

pulling the rhythmic balance of the line up short with a 'thud', which Clive Scott calls 'accentual hiatus'.[1]

While studying the diachronic appearance of first- and seventh-syllable accents in Baudelaire's alexandrines, we must make the distinction between 'ordinary' accents and other, perhaps more significant, accents. It is quite common in French verse for an alexandrine to begin with a pause such as 'Et,...' or 'Qui,...', announcing a sort of syntactical parenthesis, and we should be wary of attaching too much disruptive value to a structural commonplace of which Baudelaire makes frequent use. It is immediately obvious that these pauses are far more common at first- than at seventh-syllable position. This suggests that a 1-5 *coupe* is much more acceptable in the first hemistich than in the second, thanks perhaps to the emphatic pause at the *entrevers* which dulls the hiatus between the previous rhyme accent and the following syllable. We should instead focus our attention on those semantically loaded monosyllables – nouns, adjectives or verbs – which seem to create a more emphatic pause. Rather than introduce parenthesis with a relatively weak syntactic accent, they demand attention with an emphatic rhythmical jolt.

This accentual notion is extremely pertinent to the investigation of the caesural *faux accord*, since almost fifty of the seventy seventh-syllable accents are not covered by the aforementioned D6 categories. Indeed, the sixth syllable is often syntactically and metrically accentuated, while the seventh syllable is also accentuated by the use of punctuation:

Et t'aime d'autant plus, // be / lle, que tu me fuis   ('Je t'adore à l'égal...', 1.3)
Mais de toi je n'implore, // an / ge, que tes prières   ('Réversibilité', 1.24)
– Mais pourquoi pleure-t-elle? // E / lle, beauté parfaite   ('Le Masque', 1.29)

In the previous D6 examples, the seventh-syllable accent weakens that of the sixth syllable and causes an emphatic accentual displacement. However, in the above examples, the metrical accent is reinforced at the sixth syllable, and the accentuation of the seventh syllable creates accentual hiatus between two semantically loaded syllables. This

---

five syllables have to be rushed out in order to keep up with an imaginary metronome is one which any reader of Cornulier would reject.
[1] *A Question of Syllables*, Cambridge: C.U.P., 1986; ch. 4, 'A privileged syllable: the articulated 'e' in *Les Fleurs du Mal*', pp.86-117; p.110.

juxtaposition of accentuated units causes a considerable jolt to the balanced, cradling effect of the rhythmic illusion. In 'Je te donne ces vers...' this technique particularly matches the content of the line it disturbs. The poem's first eight lines are all perfectly balanced alexandrines, as the poet describes the regular rhythmic effect he wishes them to have on the reader, 'ainsi qu'un tympanon' (l.6). Yet as soon as the woman appears, abandoned by God and facing doubt and existential terror alone, a *faux accord* in the *divine symphonie* is created:

> Être maudit à qui, / de l'abîme profond
> Jusqu'au plus haut du ciel, / rien, hors moi, ne répond! (ll.9-10)

This *faux accord* is the very monosyllable, 'rien', which represents the horrifying *vide* of the universe. The metre is disturbed and the *faux accord* is represented by the accentual clash between the predictable sixth-syllable accent, articulating the universal analogy, and the unpredictable seventh-syllable accent.

The concentration of accents at first- and seventh-syllable position increases from six and five in 1850-52, and three and nine in 1853-56, to eighteen and thirteen in 1858-59, supporting the theory of a significant increase in disruptive trends in this period. The increase is most dramatic among those adjacent accents placed at other points in the line, which progress from three (1850-52) and five (1853-56) to fourteen (1858-59) and thirteen (1860s). An examination of these other adjacent accents provides further evidence of a shift in Baudelaire's rhythmical practice around this time. Firstly, accent can be placed at the fifth syllable, causing hiatus when the caesural accent is pre-empted. The only two examples from pre-1846 poems come from 'La Muse vénale':

> Ranimeras-tu donc / tes épaules marbrées   (l.5)
> Récolteras-tu l'or / des voûtes azurées   (l.8)

According to the basic premise that syntactic accent falls on the last unit of a sense group, the juxtaposition of syntactic accent on the fifth syllable and metrical accent on the sixth causes a rhythmic 'bump', as the reader imagines a pause between the accents, just before the caesural pause. Even if the rhythmically aware reader compensates by accentuating the second syllable in the above lines, this compensation is a result of the poet's rhythmical problematization of the line, engaging the reader in an active search for, rather than passive reception of, a presumably 'poetic' regular rhythm.

Similarly problematic examples occur throughout the 1840s and 1850s. In the following examples, even if the first *accent mobile* were placed on the bracketed syllable, the fifth syllable would nevertheless require an even stronger accent. This would create a sort of tri-partite accentual crescendo towards the caesura, breaking the four-accent rule and problematizing rhythm still further:

> Qui (vers) son miroir penche / un lourd amas d'années
> > ('La Lune offensée', l.13)
> Un (vieux) Souvenir sonne / à plein souffle du cor!
> > ('Le Cygne', l.50)
> Ces (yeux) sont des puits faits / d'un million de larmes
> > ('Les Petites vieilles', l.33)
> Le trou (peau) mortel saute / et se pâme, sans voir
> > ('Danse macabre', l.54)

The same effect occurs when an accent is placed at the eleventh syllable, appearing first in 'J'aime le souvenir...' (1843-46):

> Que ronge et que nourrit / la débauche, et vous, vierges (l.26)

This frequency of this technique also increases, with two examples pre-1853:

> A travers la cité, / comme dans un champ clos ('La Fontaine de sang', l.5)
> C'est la clarté vibrante / à notre horizon noir ('La Mort des pauvres', l.6)

During the 1858-59 period, this increases to four:

> Tout se fera Benjoin, / Encens, Oliban, Myrrhe ('A une Madone', l.34)
> Faut-il partir? rester? / Si tu peux rester, reste ('Le Voyage', l.111)
> Divinement robuste, / adorablement mince ('Le Masque', l.5)
> Vers le ciel ironique / et cruellement bleu ('Le Cygne', l.26)

In this way the pre-existent metrical structure is undermined by the suggestion of other, unpredictable structures which act in counterpoint. Tension is created between the essential order of metre and the contingent syntactic patterns which are supposed to be subordinated to it. Of course, the scansion given above is not definitive; in the last two examples, the reader might shift the accent to the 'abl' and the 'ell' of the adverbs. However, this is a conscious choice on the reader's part to compensate for a rhythmically problematic hemistich with a sort of substitute regularity, and as Dorchain argues, such rhythmical problematization is to be avoided at all costs:

Toute suite de syllabes qui présente, ne fût-ce qu'une seconde, une énigme rythmique, c'est-a-dire qui laisse l'esprit et la voix hésiter un instant sur la place des toniques, *n'est pas un vers*, encore que le compte des syllabes y soit.[1]

Baudelaire also juxtaposes accents within the line itself, where the accentuation of both elements comes not from the clash of metrical and syntactic accent, but from two non-prescribed syntactic accents. The first two examples of this come before 1846:

Et vous, femmes, hélas! / pâles comme des cierges ('J'aime le souvenir…', l.25)
Ne me regarde pas / ainsi, toi, ma pensée! ('Delphine et Hippolyte', l.53)

As Dorchain stipulates, with an interesting qualification: 'on doit éviter de mettre, *sans raison*, plus d'un accent rythmique à chaque hémistiche'.[2] However, Baudelaire's use of this emphatic rhetorical accent becomes more frequent throughout the 1850s:

Vaincu, pleure, et l'Angoisse / atroce, despotique ('Spleen' IV, l.19)
Rubens, fleuve d'oubli, / jardin de paresse ('Les Phares', l.1)
Un être qui n'était / que lumière, or et gaze ('L'Irréparable', l.46)

Suggesting that this technique becomes part of a concerted effort to interrogate poetic rhythm, examples of adjacent accents within the line multiply around the critical 1858-59 period:

Bien affilés, et, comme / un jongleur insensible ('A une Madone', l.41)
Mais moi, moi qui de loin / tendrement vous surveille ('Les Petites vieilles', l.73)
'Amour… gloire… bonheur!' / Enfer! c'est un écueil! ('Le Voyage', l.36)
Et, folle maintenant / comme elle était jadis ('Le Voyage', l.100)

---

[1] *L'Art des Vers*, p.253; Dorchain's italics.
[2] ibid., p.230; my italics.

This increases the line's accentual total to five, adding a third *accent mobile* and swelling the line's essential tetra-accentual structure. Sure enough, the total number of lines featuring five accents also increases significantly, from one (1850-52) and six (1853-57) to eleven (1858-59) and six (1860s). If two adjacent *accents mobiles* are placed by a metrical accent, then the rhythmic fluidity of the line is disrupted even further, by the contiguity of three accents. This first appears in the mid-1850s, in 'L'Irréparable', where the sixth, seventh and eighth syllables are accentated by emphatic punctuation:

> Dis-le, belle sorcière, / oh! dis, si tu le sais (1.11, 1.15)

Indeed, from the mid-1850s Baudelaire includes lines whose accentual total is pushed to bursting point with six accents:

> Décrépit, poudreux, sale, / abject, visqueux, fêlé
> ('Le Flacon', 1.24)
> Je me souviens!... J'ai vu / tout, fleur, source, sillon
> ('Coucher du soleil romantique', 1.5)
> Et l'autre: 'Viens! oh! viens / voyager dans les rêves
> ('La Voix', 1.9)
> Guerre, science, amour, / rien ne veut plus de nous
> ('Bribes', 1.5)

In this way the anticipated regularity of the line is completely altered by a staccato effect which creates an unbearable cacophony for those for whom Poetry equals rhythmical equilibrium. The crowning glory of this technique is the following line from 'Les Sept vieillards', the only one of *Les Fleurs du Mal* to feature seven accents, where the realization of the meaninglessness of verse *nombre* and metrical obliteration coincide:

> Son pareil le suivait; / barbe, œil, dos, bâton, loques (1.29)

This line articulates the fundamental shift in Baudelaire's post-1857 poetics. In the poem, the poet faces the horrifying vision of a succession of seven identical figures, reflected formally in the seven accents. Suddenly, exact regularity provokes existential terror rather than rhythmical ecstasy, as the poet, terrified, realizes the ultimate meaninglessness of *nombre*. The mystery of *nombre*, explored in the essay on Hugo, no longer inspires his faith, but rather, he is 'Blessé par le mystère et par l'absurdité!' (1.48), and his soul is thrown into the infinite, 'sur une mer monstrueuse et sans bords!' (1.52). The line represents rhythmically a crisis in the poet's faith in regularity and order. As we have seen, the challenge made to the rhythmical veil of regularity by the disruptive *faux accord* has been growing increasingly more emphatic, and regular rhythm has now become, in 1858-59, simply monotonous and meaningless. Like the constant, eternal ticking of the clock which provides a backdrop to the poems of *spleen* and doubt, regularity no longer reflects absolute rhythmical value, but rather, 'le divin Hasard' ('L'Horloge', 1.21). This shift is similar to that whereby, for Baudelaire, Hugolian faith in meaningful linguistic correspondences is replaced by an acknowledgement of 'les hasards de la rime' ('Le Soleil', 1.6). This plummet, in the 1858-59 poems, from the divine significance to the absurdity of *nombre* is supported by a similar progression in the cases of *rejet* and *contre-rejet*.

Effects of *rejet* and *contre-rejet*

The generally accepted definition of *enjambement* is rather vague. According to Quicherat, it occurs 'lorsque le sens commence dans un vers et finit dans une partie du vers suivant'.[1] Over a century later, for Clive Scott, it is still simply 'the run-on of sense over certain prosodic divisions', or 'the run-on of a syntactical unit from one line to the next'.[2] Brandin and Hartog are slightly more helpful, suggesting that *enjambement* occurs when 'the first word of the second line completes the sense of the first', although numerous examples are given which hardly seem to transgress the boundary at all.[3] Becq de Fouquières dismisses this hazy definition as 'illogique', since in a long sentence sense can cross line boundaries without disrupting rhythmical regularity. He proposes instead a useful definition by which true *enjambement* is 'une extension de la période rythmique normale', not just a run-on in sense alone: 'Il y aura enjambement d'un vers sur un autre lorsque le rythme et le sens auront ensemble enjambé, c'est-à-dire franchi l'intervalle qui sépare ce vers du suivant [...] lorsqu'il y a suppression du temps respiratoire'.[4] This underlines the role of

---

[1] *Traité de versification française*, p.66.
[2] *French Verse-Art; A Study*, Cambridge: C.U.P., 1980, p.76, and *Vers libre: The Emergence of Free Verse in France 1886-1914*, Cambridge: C.U.P., 1990, p.307.
[3] *A Book of French Prosody*, London: Blackie & Son, 1904, pp.27-28.
[4] *Traité général de versification française*, Paris: Charpentier, 1879, pp.268 and 270.

enjambement in disturbing the rhythmical balance of adjacent lines: 'l'enjambement apporte une perturbation dans le temps et dans le nombre'.[1] It is only, therefore, the disruption of metrical rhythm by the postponed resolution of syntactic elements which interests us.

Here, Jean Mazaleyrat's distinction between *enjambement* and *rejet* is helpful. The former applies to the run-on of sense which does not necessarily disturb the rhythm of the following line. The latter is '*un élément verbal bref*'[2] which both drags the rhythm over the *entrevers* and immediately pulls it up short, creating syntactic tension over the pause and also, perhaps, accentual hiatus with the rhyme accent. Recalling the nuance which I apply to certain D6 lines, Becq de Fouquières argues that *enjambement* must not disturb the rhythm of the following line:

Ce à quoi les poètes doivent s'attacher non moins scrupuleusement, c'est à ne suspendre ni le sens ni le rythme avant la fin du second vers, sans quoi leur enjambement ne serait plus qu'un allongement irrégulier de l'alexandrin.[3]

Grammont explains this disturbance in musical terms similar to the Baudelairean *faux accord*: 'Le rejet est un effet de contraste produit par le fait que la phrase syntaxique ne cadre pas avec le mètre. Il y a discordance entre les deux'.[4] It is this transgressive quality which prompts Quicherat to label it a 'faute', 'une barbarie de fraîche date', declaring: 'L'enjambement est interdit au vers alexandrin, surtout dans les genres soutenus'.[5] Finally, Grammont insists that the metre must always be given precedence in cases of discordance: 'Quand il y a conflit entre le mètre et la syntaxe, c'est toujours le mètre qui l'emporte, et la phrase doit se plier à ses exigences'.[6] The notion of metre's absolute value is fiercely guarded by critical proscription, yet Baudelaire's practice displays a concerted effort to challenge it.

Only those examples of *rejet* and *contre-rejet* which either disturb the metrical rhythm of the following line, or leave the *contre-rejet* clearly unresolved, undermining the rhyme accent and pause, need

---

[1] *Traité général de versification française*, p.287.
[2] *Eléments de métrique française*, p.119.
[3] *Traité général de versification française*, p.271.
[4] *Le Vers Français. Ses Moyens d'expression. Son Harmonie*, p.35.
[5] *Traité de versification française*, pp.436 and 66.
[6] *Le Vers Français. Ses Moyens d'expression. Son Harmonie*, p.35.

concern us here. As we might expect, there is a significant increase in the concentration of rhythmically disruptive *rejet*, from two cases in 1843-46 to six in 1850-52, seven in 1853-57 and fifteen in 1858-59. The following lines provide several emphatic examples of this technique, such as preposition / noun, or subject / verb:

> Si ses balances d'or / n'ont pesé le déluge
> De larmes qu'à la mer / ont versé tes ruisseaux?
>> ('Lesbos', ll.10-11)

> Et, quand il s'en allait / sans rien voir, à travers
> Les champs, dans distinguer / les étés des hivers
>> ('Châtiment de l'orgueil', ll.23-24)

> Qu'ont les cierges brûlant / en plein jour; le soleil
> Rougit, mais n'éteint pas / leur flamme fantastique
>> ('Le Flambeau vivant', ll.10-11)

> Ainsi quand je serai / perdu dans la mémoire
> Des hommes, dans le coin / d'une sinistre armoire
>> ('Le Flacon', ll.21-22)

There is also a sharp fall in the number of poems to feature no *rejets*, from twenty-seven (1843-46) to twelve (1853-56) and five (1858-59). The 1858-59 examples feature a wide variety of disruptive techniques, such as *enjambement* between noun and adjectival unit, absent from Baudelaire's poetry until now: 'façon / Barbare', ('A une Madone', ll.11-12), 'cieux / Froids' ('Le Cygne', ll.14-5), 'gabarre / Sans mâts' ('Les Sept vieillards', ll.51-52); compound nouns: 'Souliers / De satin' ('A une Madone', ll.19-20); emphatic, monosyllabic *rejets*: 'une ville / Change' ('Le Cygne', ll.7-8) and 'la voirie / Pousse' ('Le Voyage', ll.15-16); two consecutive *rejets* ('Le Cygne', ll.14-16) and a *rejet* over a stanzaic barrier in 'Les Petites vieilles' (ll.16-17). Moreover, there is an increase in the number of *rejets* followed by emphatic mid-hemistich punctuation. There is only one example in 1850-52, 'Me bercent. D'autres fois' ('La Musique', l.13), and only one in 1853-57: 'Est poreuse. On dirait' ('Le Flacon', l.2). This increases to two in 1858-59: 'Et des flots; nous avons' and 'Que le cyprès? – Pourtant' ('Le Voyage', l.58 and l.74) and three in the 1860s: 'M'enveloppait. – Eh quoi!' ('Le Rêve d'un curieux', l.13), 'Se mêlaient. J'étais haut' ('La Voix', l.14) and 'Loin d'eux. Vois se pencher' ('Recueillement', l.9), which begins a new stanza. This certainly seems to confirm a progression, around the late 1850s, towards a more emphatic, sustained questioning of the apparently absolute verse mould.

These techniques undermine not only verse rhythm but also verse harmony. The *rejet* creates real tension between rebellious syntax and the totemic symbol of the rhyme, the most emphatic accentual marker, and definitive guarantee of poetic status. Banville insists that the rhyme is not just 'l'unique harmonie du vers', but rather, 'elle est tout le vers', providing 'la musique variée et triomphale'. In no uncertain terms he declares: 'Ceci est une LOI absolue'.[1] On the subject of *enjambement*, he is less forthcoming, stating simply: 'Dans la versification française, quand la Rime est ce qu'elle doit être, tout fleurit et prospère; tout décroît et s'atrophie, quand la rime faiblit. Ceci est la clef de tout'.[2] The rhyme, then, symbolizes the unassailable superiority of verse and its supposedly inherently meaningful rhythms. Since, for Banville, '*on n'entend dans un vers que le mot qui est à la rime*', any problematic *rejet* would undermine the sacred harmony of verse.[3] Furthermore, this would challenge the illusion of inherently meaningful rapports in language which, for Hugo, rhyme confirms and foregrounds.

According to Becq de Fouquières, 'l'accent rythmique de la rime, ne s'appuyant plus sur le repos de la voix et sur le temps aspiratoire, devient instable, de stable qu'il était, et subit le sort des accents mobiles qui peuvent s'éteindre sous l'influence d'un accent plus fort'. For staunch defenders of poetic absolutes such as himself, accentual displacement must be avoided, limiting any disruption of rhyme harmony. If *rejet* means that 'le rythme numérique du vers est sensiblement altéré', it is imperative to maintain 'une satisfaction suffisante dans l'intégralité du rythme musical'. To this end, 'le poète doit s'appliquer par l'exactitude des rimes à faire saisir à l'oreille la mesure dont une complexité momentanée du rythme a affaibli la sensation'.[4] Thus, for Becq de Fouquières, *enjambement* at a lowly *rime pauvre* is strictly forbidden.[5] If, as Cassagne, Bernard *et al*

---

[1] *Petit Traité*, pp.47, 47, 239 and 59; Banville's capitals.
[2] ibid., p.88.
[3] ibid., p.48; Banville's italics.
[4] *Traité général de versification française*, pp.271, 284 and 278.
[5] Useful further research could be carried out on the nature of the rhymes at which rhythmically problematic *enjambement* occurs. Three variables seem particularly

suggest, Baudelaire's poetic agenda were limited to a simple rejection of the verse straitjacket, we might expect his growing predilection for problematic *rejet* to be accompanied by neglect of the rhyme strength. However, as we shall now see, his later verse also features a concerted effort to strengthen rhyme harmony, which belies the simplistic critical reduction of his poetic enterprise. Since tension between harmony and discord is the very condition of the Baudelairean poetic journey, the counterpoint between disruptive effects of *rejet* and *contre-rejet* and a solid harmonic framework is an indispensable tool in the drama between illusory veil and piercing irony.

The reinforcement of harmony
     One of the rhymes which Baudelaire's ironic conscience destabilizes with *rejets* in 1858-59 is the strongest site of metrical harmony in all his poems:

> / 'Nous avons **vu des astres**
> Et des flots; nous avons vu des sables aussi;
> Et, malgré bien des chocs et d'impré**vus désastres** ('Le Voyage', ll.57-60)

The rhyme, counting nine identical elements, [v-y-d-e-z-a-s-t-r], is disturbed by the liaison to 'Et des flots', since the *'e' surnuméraire* is pronounced and the usually silent plural feminine ending [əz] creates phonetic asymmetry. Like the hepta-accentual line of 'Les Sept vieillards', the form reflects the content, since the tension between the veil of harmony and the irony of discord reflects precisely the interpretative instability of the universe for Baudelaire. For Hugo, the stars and their constellations are part of the divine cosmic order whose absolute value is fixed. However, as Baudelaire's travellers observe natural phenomena such as the 'flots' and the 'sables', they are confronted with 'imprévus désastres', which challenge the *cadre prévu* of the universal analogy. Just as Hugo's rhyming absolutes are for Baudelaire 'les hasards de la rime' ('Le Soleil', l.6), the travellers find that even 'les plus grands paysages' (l.65) cannot match up to

---

important: firstly, whether the *contre-rejet* is the first or second of a rhyme pair; secondly, the strength of the rhyme; and thirdly, the gender of the rhyme. In this third category the reader might be encouraged to pronounce the metrically uncounted 'e' of the feminine rhyme, if the *rejet* begins with a consonant, thereby creating a phantom thirteenth syllable and perhaps destabilizing the metrical *nombre*.

'l'attrait mystérieux / De ceux que le hasard fait avec les nuages' (ll.66-67). Thus the reader is drawn into this interpretative dilemma, torn between honouring Baudelaire's strongest rhyme, with its temptation to interpret phonetic correspondences as meaningful, and the *imprévu désastre* of an unforeseen syntactic irregularity.

Similar tension is at work in 'L'Héautontimorouménos', the very poem which introduces the notion of a *faux accord*. A subsequent stanza features numerous precious rhyming parallels, highlighting the conflict within the poet between both a merciless ironic conscience and the illusion of poetically meaningful harmonies:

*Je suis l*a plaie **et le couteau!**	*a*	[e lə u o]
*Je suis l*e soufflet *et la j*oue!	*b*	[e la u]
*Je suis l*es membres *et la r*oue!	*b*	[e la u]
Et la victime **et le b**ourreau! (ll.21-24)	*a*	[e lə u o]

While there is little drastic statistical progression in the strength of rhymes throughout Baudelaire's career, the percentage of *rimes léonines* does not fall during the 1858-59 period; indeed, it even increases slightly, and continues to rise in the poetic production of the 1860s. Furthermore, the poems of 1858-59 feature three trisyllabic rhymes, similar to the perennial critics' favourite of the 1840s, 'ta**mariniers** / **mariniers**' ('Parfum exotique', ll.12-14), which is so often cited as exemplary of Baudelaire's desire for harmony. As well as the aforementioned 'vu des astres / imprévus désastres', we find:

myst**érieuse** / s**érieuse**	('Chanson d'après-midi', ll.26-28)
Hum**anité** / ins**anité**	('Danse macabre', ll.58-60)

This attention to harmonic reinforcement provides a rich counterpoint to the weakening of metrical accents at the caesura and the *entrevers* during the same period. Rather than just expressing a straightforward rejection of the universal analogy, it seems that Baudelaire's later verse obliges the reader to tackle its fundamental instability.

Rhyme harmony is not the exclusive property of the canonical categories *pauvre*, *suffisante*, *riche* or *léonine*, and it is characteristic of Baudelaire's poetry that rhyme harmony is reinforced in other,

62   *Rhythm, Illusion and the Poetic Idea*

subtler ways which escape traditional modes of classification.[1] For example, as Clive Scott suggests, rhyme similarity is often increased by identical consonants before the eleventh syllable, frequently aided by isosyllabism.[2] Thanks to rhythmic as well as harmonic symmetry, the force of rhymes such as 'mystique / musique' ('La Vie antérieure', ll.6-7) or 'vestige / vertige' ('Tout là-haut', ll.13-15) is greater than just *suffisante* [ik]or *riche* [tiʒ]. Similarly, a divocalic rhyme is created by identical vowels at the eleventh syllable ('des cygnes / les lignes', 'La Beauté', ll.6-7), and this sort of echo is also found occasionally at the tenth syllable ('méchancetés / empestés', 'Bénédiction', ll.14-16). Reinforced rhymes over two syllables are strikingly common throughout Baudelaire's career, and their frequency does not drop, with thirty from 1853-57, twenty-nine in the 1858-59 period, and thirty-three in the 1860s. 'Chanson d'après-midi' (1860) includes several of these techniques, made even more noticeable thanks to the heptasyllabic lines which are unique in Baudelaire. The poem features six *rimes léonines*: 'méchants / alléchants' (ll.1-4), 'passi-on / dévoti-on' (ll.6-7), 'paresse / caresse' (ll.18-19), 'amoureuses / langoureuses' (ll.21-24), 'apaiser / baiser' (ll.25-28) 'guérie / Sibérie' (ll.37-40); and three divocalic rhymes: 'frivole / idole' (ll.5-8), 'ma brune / la lune' (ll.29-32) and 'de soie / grande joie' (ll.34-35). As for the other eleven rhymes, six are isosyllabic, which itself creates rhythmic if not harmonic symmetry thanks to the short metre: 'forêt / secret' (ll.9-12), 'rôde / chaude' (ll.13-16), 'forts / morts' (ll.17-20), 'satin / destin' (ll.33-36), 'couleur / chaleur' (ll.38-39) and 'moqueur / mon cœur' (ll.30-31).

The number of rhymes reinforced over three syllables increases noticeably, from one (1850-52) and two (1853-57) to eleven (1858-59) and nine (1860s), such as:

ma maîtresse / ma détresse	('A une Madone', ll.1-2)
comme les Cierges / Reine des Vierges	('A une Madone', ll.29-30)
s'abreuvent de pleurs / comme des fleurs	('Le Cygne', ll.46-48)
inquiétude / décrépitude	('Les Sept vieillards', ll.37-39)
le huitième / de lui-même	('Les Sept vieillards', ll.41-43)
se déplace / l'espérance n'est lasse	('Le Voyage', ll.29-31)

[1] See Graham Chesters, *Some Functions of Sound-Repetition in Baudelaire*, ch. 1 (i) 'Rhyme', pp.9-29.
[2] *The Riches of Rhyme*, p.30.

lumineux / ruineux	('Le Voyage', ll.76-78)
et stupide / et cupide	('Le Voyage', ll.89-91)
sans dégoût / dans l'égout	('Le Voyage', ll.90-92)
ta paresse / la caresse	('Chanson d'après-midi', ll.18-19)
sa guérite / marguerite	('Sonnet d'automne', ll.9-12)

The same technique is also extended to four syllables, twice in 1853-57, once in 1858-59 and four times in the 1860s:

et le couteau / et le bourreau	('L'Héautontimoroumémos', ll.21-24)
de vos désirs / de vos plaisirs	('Delphine et Hippolyte', ll.90-92)
m'humiliait / multipliait	('Les Sept vieillards', ll.34-36)
treize, nous avons / que nous savons	('L'Examen de minuit', ll.6-7)
elle croyait / elle noyait	('Un Fantôme' III, ll.9-10)
vraiment, est la sœur / en épaisseur	('Promesses d'un visage', ll.17-19)
de votre cendre / de pierre tendre	('L'Imprévu', ll.38-40)

Finally, this technique is pushed to five or six syllables, twice in 1853-57, and twice in 1858-59:

l'abîme de ta couche / habite sur ta bouche	('Le Léthé', ll.14-15)
Imbécile! – de son empire / cadavre de ton vampire	('Le Vampire', ll.21-24)
dans ton Cœur pantelant / dans ton Cœur ruisselant	('A une Madone', ll.43-44)
de cartes et d'estampes / à la clarté des lampes	('Le Voyage', ll.1-3)

It is hopefully now clear that, far from a one-sided rebellion against a versificatory straitjacket, Baudelaire's poetry comes more and more to demonstrate a simultaneous drive towards both harmony and rhythmic irregularity, veil and *faux accord*.

This is especially evident in 'Un Fantôme' (1860), one of only three poems written exclusively in decasyllables. On a rhythmical level, the poem features perhaps Baudelaire's most iconoclastic metrical irregularity. In 'Le Léthé' (mid-1840s) every line allows a standard 4/6 *coupe*, whereas 'La Mort des amants' (1851) presents a similarly acceptable, albeit less common, succession of 5+5 lines. As Cornulier observes, 4/6 and 5/5 are 'des mètres composés radicalement différents', presenting 'des combinaisons de longueurs qui n'ont rien de commun'; in traditional verse, it is forbidden to mix the two.[1] However, although the dominant metre of 'Un Fantôme' is 4+6, the first sonnet presents a rhythmical enigma:

> Je suis comme **un** / pein // tre / qu'un Dieu moqueur (l.5)

Firstly, the scansion 4+6 is prohibited by the metrically implausible C4; secondly, the recuperative 6/4 scansion possible in around twenty other lines of the poem is prevented by an even more implausible F6. The only possible scansion, therefore, is 5-5 which, with its *coupe italienne*, is rather untidy compared to the neat 5+5s of 'La Mort des amants' and the fifty-five remaining 4+6 lines of 'Un Fantôme'. Significantly, the *faux accord* comes just as the poet articulates his creative frustration, symbolizing the same sort of loss of faith in verse *nombre* as the hepta-accentual line of 'Les Sept vieillards'. However, the poem describes the memory of an absolutized 'Elle' (I, l.14) who returns to haunt the poet. Disillusioned with the present time of artistic difficulty, he finds comfort in the memory of the past:

> Charme profond, magique, dont nous grise
> Dans le présent le passé restauré!   (II, ll.5-6)

Just as the poet of 'La Muse malade' yearns for a bygone age of religious faith in rhythm and *nombre*, 'les sons nombreux des syllabes antiques' (l.12), the poet cherishes the fleeting vision of the 'spectre' (I, l.10) which graces him with a visit. This visit reaches its climax in the third sonnet, which features the tetra-syllabic rhyme quoted above and which marks a return to the most traditionally iconic model, the *abba abba ccd ede* sonnet form not used since 'Sed non satiata', 'Parfum exotique' and 'La Lune offensée' of the mid-1840s.

In 1872 Banville proclaims that only this sonnet form has eternal, absolute poetic value: 'Il faut toujours préférer le Sonnet régulier au Sonnet irrégulier'.[2] As Jacques Roubaud has shown, two principal sonnet forms are used in French after the sixteenth century, one by Marot (*abba abba ccd eed*) and the other by Peletier (*abba abba ccd*

---

[1] 'L'invention du "décasyllabe" chez Verlaine décadent: le 4-6, le 5-5, le mixte et le n'importe quoi', in *Verlaine à la loupe*, ed. by Jean-Michel Gouvard and Steve Murphy, Paris: Champion, 2000, pp.243-89; p.245.
[2] *Petit Traité*, p.197.

ede), with the latter constantly in the minority.[1] Banville's stipulation, therefore, is a pure fiction which stubbornly maintains, in his usual playful manner, a fallacious hierarchy of absolute values of poeticity. Cornulier, in contrast, has no such interest in maintaining poetic fictions, asserting: 'il n'existe pas un modèle unique, indépendant des époques et des cultures, absolument rigide, "du" sonnet seul "régulier" comme par droit divin'.[2] Therefore, the appearance of this form in 'Un Fantôme' reflects the poet's momentarily renewed faith in poetic absolutes, which might well be purely fictional. While new heights of ironic irregularity are scaled with the 5-5 line, this iconic sonnet form simultaneously appears to the poet in the night of his despair, a shimmering reminder of a bygone age of faith, further supported by the *rime léonine* '**vanté** / enchanté' (ll.2-3), and the reinforced '**dorure** / **bordure**' (ll.5-8) and '**du linge** / **du singe**' (ll.12-14).[3]

All this evidence of Baudelaire's later attention to verse harmony confirms that the evolution of his verse is not simply a move towards irregularity, but rather, an increasingly careful, intricate construction of tension between the rhythmic-harmonic veil and the *faux accord*. Indeed, although the variants reveal a number of corrections which disrupt verse harmony, Baudelaire often alters his text in the opposite direction, harmonizing discordant elements even in the numerous corrections made in 1860 for the 1861 edition. In 'Le Goût du néant', for example, a poem contemporaneous with the loss of faith in the absolute significance of *nombre* ('Les Sept vieillards'), and with the 1858-59 increase in disruptive techniques, a P6 line is removed from the version published in the *Revue Française* in January 1859:

(1859) Comme la neige <u>sur</u> / un corps pris de roideur
(1861) Comme la neige immense / un corps pris de roideur (l.12)

---

[1] *La forme du sonnet français de Marot à Malherbe*, Paris: Publications Langues' O, 'Cahiers de poétique comparée' 17-19, 2 vols., 1990; I: 146-55. For André Gendre: 'Banville, plus restrictif, n'admettait que le sonnet *Rg cr.* C'est mal comprendre la production du XVIe siècle, dont les sonnets sont aux deux tiers *Rg emb*' (*Evolution du sonnet français*, Paris: P.U.F., 1996, p.18, note 2).
[2] 'Métrique des *Fleurs du Mal*', p.62.
[3] In *Le Peintre de la vie moderne* the spectre also appears in an artistic context: 'Le passé, tout en gardant le piquant du fantôme, reprendra la lumière et le mouvement de la vie, et se fera présent' (O.C.II: 684).

Nuiten suggests that: 'Cette prédilection marquée de Baudelaire pour les constructions parallèles et symétriques se manifeste clairement dans les remaniements qu'il a apportés à un grand nombre de textes'.[1] This indicates, contrary to popular belief, that harmony is just as important as discord throughout Baudelaire's career. The tension might increase, certainly, with the addition of more and more disruptive elements, but this tension is dependent on a simultaneous reinforcing of the structural framework. The theory of Baudelaire's 'loosening' of the alexandrine at all costs is not, therefore, an accurate portrayal of his agenda, and this is far from being an isolated example.

When Baudelaire publishes 'Sur *Le Tasse en prison*' in the *Revue nouvelle* in 1864, the one D6 line has become a regular 6+6, as the metrical monotony mirrors the eternal regularity which provokes *ennui* in the doubting poet:

> (1844) Qui se penche à la voix / des songes, dont l'essaim[2]
> (1864) Ces grimaces, ces cris, / ces spectres dont l'essaim (l.10)

Similarly, as Alison Fairlie observes, the correction brought to line 28 of 'Les Litanies de Satan' restores balance to the line.[3] The D6 of 1857 becomes 6+6 in 1861:

> (1857) Toi qui frottes de baume / et d'huile les vieux os
> (1861) Toi qui, magiquement, / assouplis les vieux os

In the 1858-59 manuscript version of 'Sisina' the following D6 is crossed out, replaced with the formula published in the *Revue française* of 10 April 1859 and the 1861 edition:

> (ms.)   Et son cœur, délicat / et fier, garde toujours[4]
> (1861) Et son cœur, ravagé / par la flamme, a toujours (l.13)

---

[1] *Les Variantes* ..., p.110.
[2] O.C.I: 1151.
[3] '"Mène-t-on la foule dans les ateliers?"': Some remarks on Baudelaire's variants', in *Order and Adventure in Post-Romantic French Poetry: essays presented to C. A. Hackett*, ed. by E. M. Beaumont, J. M. Cocking and J. Cruickshank, Oxford: Blackwell, 1973, pp.17-37; p.30.
[4] O.C.I: 939.

Adjacent accents are also subject to removal, especially from the seventh syllable position. The first of the seven versions of 'Les Sept vieillards' features the following line, D6 with adjacent accents on the sixth and seventh syllables:

> Tous ces monstres avaient / l'air moins vieux qu'éternel! (l.40)

This has already been altered, by the second draft, to the regular 3/3//3/3 rhythm:

> Tous ces mon / stres hideux // avaient l'air / éternel. (l.40)[1]

The poem itself is by no means free from irregularity, but disruptive techniques are not employed indiscriminately. Between the second, third and fourth drafts of the same poem, line 52 fluctuates from regular to irregular and back again:

> (ii)   Sans mats [sic], sur une mer / indomptable et sans bords.
> (iii) Sans mats [sic], sur une mer / noire, énorme et sans bords.[2]
> (iv)   Sans mâts, sur une mer / monstrueuse et sans bords!

In the third draft, the adjective is changed to produce another D6 line, with an accent at the seventh syllable and five accents in total. By the fourth version, however, the poet reverts to his original idea, two trisyllabic adjectival units which restore regularity.

By the 1857 version of 'Don Juan aux Enfers', a seventh-syllable accent has been removed from that published in 1846 by the simple omission of two commas:

> (1846) Sganarelle en riant, / lui, réclamait ses gages [3]
> (1857) Sganarelle en riant / lui réclamait ses gages (l.9)

A similar correction is made between the 1857 proof and printed versions of 'Le Jeu':

[1] See F. W. Leakey and Claude Pichois, 'Les Sept versions des "Sept vieillards"', *Études baudelairiennes* 3, Neuchâtel: À la Baconnière, 1973, pp.262-89; pp.265 and 268.
[2] 'Les Sept versions des "Sept vieillards"', pp.268 and 273.
[3] O.C.I: 868.

> (épr.)   A de sales plafonds / <u>pen</u>dent de pâles lustres [1]
> (édn.)   Sous de sales plafonds / un rang de pâles lustres (1.9)

'Le Vin des chiffonniers', 'le poème dont les versions sont les plus nombreuses',[2] features several such corrections. Between the first manuscript, perhaps a copy of an 1843 version, and the 1857 edition, Baudelaire corrects:

> (ms.)   C'est ainsi que le vin / <u>rè</u>gne par ses bienfaits   (1.26)[3]
> (1857)   C'est ainsi qu'à travers / l'Humanité frivole   (1.25)

The same sort of correction is made between the 1854 version, published in the *Journal d'Alençon* in June 1857, and 1857's *Les Fleurs du Mal*:

> (1854)   Au fond de ces quartiers / <u>mor</u>nes et tortueux [4]
> (1857)   Au cœur d'un vieux faubourg, / labyrinthe fangeux (1.3)

Similarly, the following line progresses from balance to imbalance and back again:

> (1854)   Et des fumiers / infects // que rejett / e Paris (1.12)   (4/2//3/3)
> (1857)   Trou / ble vomissement // du fastueux / Paris (1.16)[5]   (1/5//4/2)
> (1861)   Vomissement / confus // de l'énorm / e Paris (1.16)   (4/2//3/3)

Finally, between the 1854 and 1857 versions, adjacent accents at the fifth and sixth syllables are displaced to create a regular 2/4//2/4 rhythm:

> (1854) Et par ses bien<u>faits</u> <u>rè</u>gne / ainsi que les vrais rois   (1.20)[6]
> (1857) Et <u>rè</u>gne par ses dons / ainsi que les vrais rois   (1.28)

Adjacent accents in other positions are also corrected. In a version of 'Danse macabre', published in the *Revue contemporaine* of 15 March 1859, line 16 features an initial accent, corrected in 1861:

---

[1] O.C.I: 1028.
[2] Pichois, O.C.I: 1047.
[3] O.C.I: 1047.
[4] O.C.I: 1050.
[5] Both variants: O.C.I: 1051.
[6] O.C.I: 1051.

(1859) C̲h̲arme de ce néant / follement attifé! [1]
(1861) Ô charme d'un néant / follement attifé!

A similar accent is removed from 'Au Lecteur' between the 1857 and 1861 editions, producing a rhythmically regular line which is simultaneously 6+6 and 4+4-4:

(1857) G̲r̲o̲uille, chante et ripaille / un peuple de démons [2]
(1861) Dans nos cerveaux / ribote // un peu / ple de démons (l.22)

And in 'Le Crépuscule du soir', the one line-initial accent from the 1852 *Douze poèmes* version is removed from the proofs in 1857:

(épr.) O̲u̲i̲, voilà bien le soir, […][3]
(édn.) O soir, aimable soir, […]   (l.5)

The run of adjacent accents in the proof version of 'Le Vin des amants' is smoothed out by the 1857 edition:

(épr.) Sans ép̲e̲r̲o̲ns̲, m̲o̲r̲s̲, s̲e̲l̲l̲e̲ ou bride [4]
(édn.) Sans mors, sans éperons, sans bride (l.2)

In the 1857 version of 'La Béatrice', Baudelaire retains the D6 quality of line 6, while removing the adjacent accents from the proofs:

(épr.) Un nuage l̲o̲u̲r̲d̲, n̲o̲i̲r̲ / et gros d'une tempête [5]
(édn.) Un nuage funèbre / et gros d'une tempête (l.6)

The adjacent accents in the 1857 version of 'La servante au grand cœur…', which create a 5/1 hemistich, have been replaced in the correction of 1861 by a 3/3//3/3 rhythm:

(1857) Et l'éternité f̲u̲i̲r̲, / sans qu'amis ni famille [6]
(1861) Et le siècle couler, / sans qu'amis ni famille (l.13)

---

[1] O.C.I: 1031.
[2] O.C.I: 831.
[3] O.C.I: 1026.
[4] O.C.I: 1056.
[5] O.C.I: 1068.
[6] O.C.I: 1039.

The copy of 'L'Amour du mensonge' sent to Poulet-Malassis in mid-March 1860 includes a line with accents on both the first and fifth syllables, both of which disappear by the poem's publication in the *Revue contemporaine* of 15 May:

> (Mar.) Est, comme son corps, mûr / pour le savant amour [1]
> (May)   Est mûr, comme son corps, / pour le savant amour (1.12)

Nor is *enjambement* exempt from regularization; in the 1861 edition, a monosyllabic *rejet* is removed from the 1857 version of 'La Musique':

> (1857) Je monte et je descends / sur le dos des grands monts
>   D'eau retentissante
> (1861) J'escalade le dos / des flots amoncelés
>   Que la nuit me voile   (ll.7-8)[2]

In 'Une Martyre', also, the correction of adjacent accents at eleventh and twelfth position erases the *contre-rejet*, as 'œil' replaces 'jarretière' as the subject of 'flambe':

> (1857) La jarretière, ainsi / qu'un œil vigilant, flambe
>   Et darde un regard diamanté.[3]
> (1861) La jarretière, ainsi / qu'un œil secret qui flambe,
>   Darde un regard diamanté. (ll.27-28)

Finally, the changes made to rhyme words invariably increase the richness. Those made to 'La Mort des artistes' between review publication in 1851 and the 1857 edition highlight the care with which Baudelaire reinforces the rhyme scheme:

(1851)			(1857)		
	vaux	[vo]		grelots	[e-lo]
	monture	[tyr]		caricature	[a-tyr]
	nature	[tyr]		nature	[a-tyr]
	repos	[o]		javelots	[e-lo]

---

[1] O.C.I: 1035.
[2] See Fairlie, '"Mène-t-on la foule dans les ateliers?": Some remarks on Baudelaire's variants', p.23.
[3] O.C.I: 1059.

travaux	[vo]		complots	[lo]
impure	[yr]		armature	[a-tyr]
figure	[yr]		Créature	[a-tyr]
sanglots	[o]		sanglots	[lo]
idole	[ol]		Idole	[dol]
affront	[frõ]		affront	[frõ]
front	[frõ]		affront	[frõ]
console	[ol]		Capitole	[tol]
nouveau	[vo]		nouveau	[vo]
cerveau	[vo]		cerveau	[vo] [1]

The first version is already meticulously structured; as in many of
Baudelaire's sonnets, the 'b' rhymes of one quatrain are bound
together tightly by a *consonne d'appui*, and there is similar
equivalence between the first 'a' rhyme of each quatrain. In the
second version, however, each 'a' rhyme receives the *consonne
d'appui* 'l'. In addition, those of the first quatrain become *léonine*, as
do all 'b' rhymes, and the equivalence between the 'c' rhymes which
begin each tercet is underlined by the addition of a pre-vocalic 'd' and
't', respectively voiced and voiceless dental plosives. The poem closes
the first edition with the hope that, through death, the poet might
encounter the 'Idole' (l.9), 'l'idéal figure' (1851, l.7) which has
constantly eluded him, an illusion which the precious rhyme harmony
helps to maintain.

Yet alterations of this sort are not confined to the pre-1857 poems.
The following examples show the poet increasing the richness of his
rhymes throughout his career:

(1851)	légères	[ɛr]		légères	[ʒ ɛr]
	jardinières	(*suff.*)	→	étagères	(*riche*)
					('La Mort des amants', ll.1-3)

(1857)	rangés	[ʒe]		rangés	[rãʒe]
	jais	(*suff.*)	→	étrangers	(*léonine*)
					('Les Hiboux', ll.2-3)

	patriarchal	[al]		patriarchal	[kal]
	final	(*suff.*)	→	chacal	(*riche*)
					('Abel et Caïn', ll.14-16)

[1] All variants: O.C.I: 1091-92.

élégante	[ãt]		élégante	[gãt]
pliante	(*suff.*)	→	fringante	(*riche*)
				('Une Martyre', ll.37-39)

(1861)	voluptueux [ø]		voluptueux	[ty-ø]
	paresseux (*pauvre*)	→	somptueux	(*léonine*)
				('Une Martyre', ll.2-4)

	bocagères [ʒ ɛr]		bocagères	[aʒ ɛr]
	légères (*riche*)	→	passagères	(*léonine*)
				('Un Voyage à Cythère', ll.21-24)

(1865)	épanouie [i]		épanouie	[u-i]
	pâlie (*pauvre*)	→	réjouie	(*léonine*)
				('Le Jet d'eau', ll.9-11)[1]

In all, it appears that Baudelaire's corrections are made, not according to a simply linear development, the supposed 'loosening' of the metrical straitjacket, but rather, in order to maintain the tension between regularity and irregularity, faith and irony. Corrections are made in both directions to the following lines from 'Spleen' IV:

(1857) Défilent lentement / dans mon âme; et, l'Espoir
         Pleurant comme un vaincu, / l'Angoisse despotique[2]

(1861) Défilent lentement / dans mon âme; l'Espoir,
         Vaincu, pleure, et l'Angoisse / atroce, despotique (ll.18-19)

The omission of 'et' from l.18 removes the adjacent accentuation whilst the re-working of the following line breaks the previous 2/4//2/4 regularity with accents on the second and third syllables. The same double process is applied to 'Le Flacon', between the *Revue française* version of April 1857 and the 1857 edition. Firstly, the balanced line below becomes D6:

(*Rf*)   Sentant l'odeur d'un siècle, / arachnéenne et noire
(édn.)   Pleine de l'âcre odeur / des temps, poudreuse et noire (l.6)

---

[1] Examples given by Chesters, *Some Functions of Sound-Repetition in Les Fleurs du Mal*, pp.72-73.
[2] O.C.I: 979.

Similarly, the following noun/adjective D6 line shifts to an altogether more problematic adjective/noun structure:

> (*Rf*)   On trouve un vieux flacon / jauni qui se souvient
> (édn.)   Parfois on trouve un vieux / flacon qui se souvient (l.7)

In line sixteen, however, the D6 line, with an accentuated seventh syllable, is altered to a decidely more regular 3/3//3/3 rhythm:

> (*Rf*)   Vers un gouffre où l'air est / <u>plein</u> de parfums humains[1]
> (édn.)   Vers un gouffre obscurci / de miasmes humains

Finally, in 'L'Ame du vin', two grammatically identical monosyllabic verbs, placed at the seventh syllable in various pre-1853 journal and manuscript versions are omitted in the 1857 edition:

> (1853)   Le soir, l'âme du vin / <u>chan</u>te dans les bouteilles
>   Un soir, l'âme du vin / chantait dans les bouteilles (l.1)
>
> (1853)   Comme le grain fécond / <u>tom</u>be dans le sillon
>   Grain précieux jeté / par l'éternel Semeur (l.22)

In the very next line, however, the correction process is reversed, as Baudelaire adds the same monosyllabic verb form to the seventh-syllable of a previously regular line:

> (1853)   Et de notre union / naîtra la poésie[2]
> (1857)   Pour que de notre amour / <u>nai</u>sse la poésie (l.23)

It is clear that the progression towards the irregularities of the 1858-59 poems is by no means one-sided. Baudelaire accompanies his discordant elements with an equally important reinforcement of the metrical and harmonic framework without which they would lose all their effect. Regularity and irregularity are required to articulate on a formal level the necessarily irresolvable question of the absolute significance of both the cosmos and verse itself. The 1858-59 poems display a higher proportion of disruptive elements, but this is not just a rebellion against a repressive verse framework. Rather, it suggests a

---

[1] All variants: O.C.I: 921.
[2] All variants: O.C.I: 1045-46.

more thorough, determined interrogation of the unstable poetic and theological absolutes. Verse irregularities articulate the *faux accord*, challenging received notions of aesthetic values and the *divine symphonie*, and puncturing the rhythmic and harmonic veil. Baudelaire's verse fabric, therefore, allows the exploration of the irresolvable tension between his conflicting drives towards faith in absolutes and the *gouffre*, a tension subtly articulated by the final object of this analysis: syllabic uncertainty at the rhyme.

Poetry as irresolvable tension

For Baudelaire, one of Gautier's many achievements is 'la pourpre régulière et symétrique d'une rime plus qu'exacte'.[1] Poe, however, is said to augment the pleasure of the rhyme by adding 'cet élément inattendu, l'étrangeté, qui est comme le condiment indispensable de toute beauté'.[2] Similarly, in the first 'Projet de préface' of 1860, the function of verse is not simply to reflect unproblematic universal regularity. Rather, Baudelaire argues: 'le rythme et la rime répondent dans l'homme aux immortels besoins de monotonie, de symétrie et de surprise'.[3] As the poet of 'Les Sept vieillards' discovers, exact regularity with no surprises soon appears meaningless. Some formal 'imprévus désastres' ('Le Voyage', l.59) are required in order to acknowledge the fundamental instability of regularity, the tension between faith and irony, and the constant questioning of the universal analogy into which the poet draws us.

It is the rhymes of Leconte de Lisle in particular which, for Baudelaire, provide the necessary symmetry and surprise: 'Ses rimes, exactes sans trop de coquetterie, remplissent la condition de beauté voulue et répondent régulièrement à cet amour contradictoire et mystérieux de l'esprit humain pour la surprise et la symétrie'.[4] The rhyme, therefore, has the power both to resolve and to disturb, and therein lies its importance to the indissociable elements of the poetic practice, harmony and discord, faith and irony. It provides a pleasing harmonious balance which satisfies the ear eager for poetic 'beauty', yet one of Baudelaire's most noted achievements is to disturb this

---

[1] 'Théophile Gautier' (O.C.II: 126).
[2] 'Notes nouvelles sur Edgar Poe' (O.C.II: 336).
[3] O.C.I: 182.
[4] 'Leconte de Lisle' (O.C.II: 179).

traditionally poetic harmony with incongruous correspondences which shock the reader, such as in 'Une Charogne': 'âme / infâme' (ll.1-3), 'pourriture / Nature' (ll.9-11), 'ordure / Nature' (ll.37-39), 'infection / passion' (ll.38-40) and 'vermine / divine' (ll.45-47), or 'L'Examen de minuit': 'dévotion / putréfaction' (ll.22-23). However, verse tension also manifests itself at the rhyme on a more subtly irresolvable formal level.

Two of the above examples feature diaeresis 'i-on' on both rhyme words, which, by artificially 'stretching' the pronunciation of the final vowel sound, creates a strong, resonant *rime léonine* over two syllables: [si-ɔ̃]. If the poetic mind requires symmetry, then the matching of diaeresis at the rhyme is one method of reinforcing harmony, while simultaneously underlining the poetic artifice of the technique. As Mazaleyrat remarks, underlining the verse/prose opposition, the artificial pronunciation of a vowel sequence[1] as two contiguous vowels is one of the formal laws by which verse poetry is defined: 'La diérèse étale, déroule plus largement le mot sur le vers; la synérèse le fait passer plus vite, à la manière de la prose'.[2] Anxious to guard against formal inconsistency which might undermine verse, Grammont highlights the artificiality of diaeresis, horrified to observe contradictions in the work of many poets:

C'est la marque la plus évidente d'une langue artificielle, et bien que ce ne soit en apparence qu'une chose sans importance elle peut avoir les conséquences les plus graves et devenir un germe de mort pour la poésie qui l'admet.[3]

Michel Deguy proposes a useful thematic reading of diaeresis as 'la figure de l'infini dans la diction', 'la marque formelle de l'infinité dans le langage de "vraie poésie"' with the alexandrine itself representing the 'diminutif de l'infini'.[4] Yet while Deguy offers only one example ('expansi-on', 'Correspondances', l.12), a more thorough

---

[1] Since the term 'diphthong' used by Banville, Dorchain *et al* is no longer used in relation to French, I use the term 'vowel sequence' to refer to any contiguous vowels irrespective of how they are pronounced.

[2] *Eléments de métrique française*, p.54.

[3] *Le Vers Français. Ses Moyens d'expression. Son Harmonie*, p.470. The vowels in *ouest, truie, hier, rouet, fouet, chouette, suicide, miasme*, and *opium* can all be pronounced with either synaeresis or diaeresis (ibid., pp.468-70).

[4] 'L'infini et sa diction ou de la diérèse (Etude baudelairienne)', *Poétique* 40 (1979), 432-44; pp.434, 438 and 435.

study of synaeresis and diaeresis throughout Baudelaire's verse reveals the importance of this technique to the necessarily irresolvable tension between faith and irony.

Although Baudelaire's practice is entirely traditional, convention serves Deguy's argument well. The infinite can certainly be apprehended in the artificial pronunciation of words central to Baudelairean poetics: *expansi-on*, *dévoti-on*, *passi-on*, *visi-on*, *ondulati-on*, *imaginati-on*, *tri-omphe*; *pri-ère*; *harmoni-eux*, *radi-eux*, *mystéri-eux*, *religi-eux*, and *préci-eux*, which itself underlines the precious artifice of the technique. By extension, the vowel sequences which cannot be contracted to one syllable also seem to express a similar expansion: *spiritu-el*, *monstru-eux*, *voluptu-eux*, as well as *po-ète* and *po-ésie* themselves. When such artificially expansive words appear at the rhyme they reinforce both the rhythmic and harmonic symmetry, creating a veil which simultaneously draws attention to its own artifice.[1] There are fifty-one such examples from Baudelaire's verse, such as:

passi-ons / convulsi-ons	('La Musique', ll.9-11)
mystéri-eux / harmoni-eux	('Le Chat', LI, ll.21-24)
inou-ïes / éblou-ies	('Rêve parisien', ll.29-31)

The rhyme 'déli-er / réconcili-er' ('Le Vin de l'assassin', ll.18-19) articulates the dual function of these rhymes, which first undo prosaic pronunciation by the versificatory artifice of diaeresis, before re-uniting the elements in a different configuration.

Baudelaire himself highlights his sensitivity to these rhymes. On the proofs of 'La Fontaine de sang', his editor corrects 'capti-eux' to 'capiteux', to which the typically cantankerous poet replies: 'Mais non! s'il y avait *captieux*, c'était fort bien; *des vins captieux*, et non pas capiteux qui d'ailleurs ne rime pas'.[2] Yet the more common expression, *vins capiteux* or 'heady wines', would rhyme, albeit poorly, and it certainly seems to make sense. However, the tercets in

---

[1] This is perhaps why Dorchain argues: 'Il est certain que l'oreille n'aime pas à rencontrer deux fois de suite la diérèse [...]. On fera bien d'accoupler, le plus souvent possible, un mot où se produit la diérèse avec un mot où la même terminaison forme diphtongue' (*L'Art des Vers*, p.130).
[2] O.C.I: 1064; Baudelaire's italics.

question show the poet attempting to escape from existential terror via the artificial illusion of harmony provided by wine and love-making:

> J'ai demandé souvent à des vins capti-eux
> D'endormir pour un jour la terreur qui me mine;
> Le vin rend l'œil plus clair et l'oreille plus fine!
>
> J'ai cherché dans l'amour un sommeil oubli-eux (ll.9-12)

As Larousse explains, the word on which Baudelaire insists means 'propre à tromper ou à séduire, par une apparence de raison, [...] par des raisons spécieuses'; 'ce qui est *captieux* séduit par de fausses apparences'.[1] The wine is not simply 'heady', but rather, it is an instrument of illusion by which the poet tries to trick himself into belief in the universal analogy, such as the 'rythmiques sanglots' of his blood (l.2). Although the wine cannot provide an effective veil, only making him see more clearly, the rhyme itself remains firmly, perhaps ironically, harmonious, and this in a text from the 1840s.

If poetry, for Baudelaire, articulates the search for meaning in an unstable universe, the verse fabric itself can represent the object of this scrutiny. Often, the reader is tricked in the search for harmony, since some rhyme elements are graphically identical, giving *la symétrie pour l'œil*, but with diaeresis on one element and synaeresis on the other. At first sight, the rhyme appears harmoniously *léonine* – 'ce qui est *captieux* séduit par de fausses apparences' – but the anticipated phonetic harmony is confounded. In 'pi-eux / Dieux' ('Le Vin du solitaire', ll.11-14), for example, the artificial pronunciation of the first diaeresis attracts our attention, and we anticipate resolution on an equally artificial rhyme element. This anticipation is confounded, however, by the synaeresis on 'Dieux' and so, from the possible *rime léonine* [i-ø], reinforced by the similarity between the pre-vocalic voiceless and voiced plosives 'p' and 'd', comes just a *rime pauvre*: [ø]. Roy Lewis remarks: 'the second element of the rime can always bear more stress than the first, since it completes an aesthetic pattern; the mind waits for it, and is satisfied when it arrives'.[2] Yet the anticipated correspondence never comes, disappointing our ear's

---

[1] *Grand Dictionnaire Universel du XIXe Siècle*, 3: 337.
[2] 'The Rhythmical Creation of Beauty', *Forum for Modern Language Studies* 6 (1970), 103-26; p.120.

desire for the unproblematic, symmetrical satisfaction of harmony. The surprise of this *imprévu désastre* is compounded by the visual similarity between the two rhymes, which, like natural phenomena perhaps, are not exactly what they seem. The phonetic difference is only slight between [i-ø] and [jø], so that the richer rhyme is not completely lost, and a subtle echo of what we were expecting remains in the *harmonie manquée*. The rhyme thus remains unresolved, wavering between *léonine* and *pauvre* without settling definitively on either, like the poet contemplating the thorny problem of the meaning of these linguistic correspondences.

Thanks to this irresolvability, the anticipated harmony remains unfulfilled. It destabilizes the poetic illusion yet quivers on the edge of resolution in the discrepancy between the visual and the aural. 'Femmes damnées' features the highly significant example: 'païens / anci-ens' (ll.14-16). The adjective 'ancien', like 'antique', is often used to refer to those bygone days when faith in absolute Truth was never in doubt, when Art and Religion were entirely compatible:

> Les cloîtres anciens sur leurs grandes murailles
> Étalaient en tableaux la sainte Vérité   ('Le Mauvais moine', ll.1-2)

'Ancien' refers to 'le souvenir de ces époques nues', where the artifice of illusion and veil was unnecessary, since *jouissance* was attainable 'sans mensonge'.[1] 'Païen', on the other hand, refers both to polytheistic cults and the 'mécréant, personne qui manque aux devoirs religieux les plus essentiels'.[2] It is symptomatic of the poet's uncertainty as to the absolute value of the cosmos that the rhyme 'païens / anci-ens' puts into conflict two different faiths and ways of interpreting the world. The irresolvable tension between the metre and the rhyme, which are usually meant to combine in verse, highlights the *mise en scène* of our interpretative uncertainty in the verse form itself.

Of course, perfectly unloaded examples of such rhymes occur frequently in all French poetry. Chateaubriand's *Premières Poésies*, full of youthful, romantic exuberance for natural beauty and harmony, contain the unstable rhymes 'préci-eux / cieux', 'silenci-eux / cieux',

---

[1] 'J'aime le souvenir...', l.1 and l.4 respectively.
[2] Larousse, *Grand Dictionnaire Universel du XIXe Siècle*, 12: 29.

'solaci-eux / cieux', 'peupli-ers / sentiers', with no suggestion of doubt or discord.[1] However, in the context of Baudelaire's merciless ironic conscience, and his sensitivity to the intricacies of the versificatory exploration of meaning, the instability of these rhymes, which confound potential harmonies only partly realised, dramatizes precisely the instability of absolute meaning in language and the world. In two early versions of 'Un voyage à Cythère', line 48 is variously:

> (1852) Le long fleuve de fiel / de mes douleurs anciennes
> (1855) Le long fleuve de fiel / de mes amours anciennes [2]

In the 1857 version, however, the possessive adjective is removed, creating the rhyme:

> Ridicule pendu, / tes douleurs sont les miennes! [...]
> Le long fleuve de fiel / des amours anci-ennes   (ll.45-48)

The first versions, with synaeresis on the 'ie' phoneme, feature a *rime riche* between 'miennes' and 'anciennes': [jɛn]. With the correction, prosodically permissible,[3] Baudelaire simultaneously regularizes the metre to 3/3//3/3, with rhyme at the seventh syllable clitics followed by two disyllabic nouns, and disrupts the rhyme harmony. The line presents irresolvable tension, therefore, between the rhythmic regularity of faith and the subtle harmonic asymmetry of doubt. This inspires the reader to play an active role in an interpretative dilemma, to which neither solution is wholly satisfactory. We may either lean towards harmony by matching the rhymes, to the detriment of metre, or towards regular rhythm by respecting the metre to the detriment of rhyme harmony. By putting the two constants of poetic form, to which he frequently alludes as the defining characteristics of verse, into conflict – metre versus rhyme, rhythm versus harmony – Baudelaire defines the nature of Poetry and the poetic condition as a tension which is, necessarily, irresolvable on both a philosophical and a

---

[1] See 'Tableaux de la Nature' in *Pensées et Premières Poésies*, ed. by Alain Coelho, Nantes: Le Temps Singulier, 1980; pp.95-136.

[2] O.C.I: 1073.

[3] As Banville observes: 'dans *ancien* on peut à volonté le prononcer en une ou deux syllabes' (*Petit Traité*, p.34).

formal level. In doing so he also seems to question the validity of a pre-existent poetic form whose regular rhythm and harmony are challenged by 'la vorace Ironie', the doubt as to whether they correspond to any absolute values.

As we have ascertained, for Baudelaire, unlike Hugo, the existence of universal, eternal absolutes cannot be proved. Pierre Campion highlights the fundamental need for tension, or drama, in the investigation of such irresolvable questions as those of theology and poeticity:

> Nous soutenons que certaines propositions philosophiques, concernant la liberté de l'homme, par exemple, ou la mort, ou la nature de l'immortalité poétique, ou le statut du poète [...] ne peuvent se poser et se développer que sur le mode du dramatique. Pourquoi?
>
> Parce que ces questions, qui relèvent pleinement de la réflexion philosophique, sont des questions problématiques, qui devraient rester problématiques. Ou plutôt, leur nature demanderait que le problème y soit pensé de manière à ce que son caractère problématique soit respecté jusqu'au bout, entendons: qu'il ne soit pas résolu, au sens de liquidé, par le travail de la pensée; que, précisément, son caractère de problème ne soit pas perdu en chemin.[1]

Prose cannot articulate this essentially problematic property since it lacks the inherently regular metre which represents, in verse, one side of the dilemma. Only verse can create discord, since verse alone can represent a dynamic relationship between essential (metrical) and contingent (syntactic) rhythms, as Mazaleyrat observes:

> Fondée sur un processus d'écart entre des structures syntaxiques naturelles et des structures métriques données par la tradition, l'habitude ou le mouvement d'un contexte, la discordance est un phénomène logiquement lié au vers régulier.[2]

Verse provides a pre-existent metrical and rhyming structure which, when interpreted as a microcosm for meaningful universal order, can be interrogated by the 'imprévus désastres' of syntactic and phonetic devices which work in counterpoint. Encapsulating the necessary oxymoron by which this poetry functions, Hirt states: 'La poésie tend à promouvoir une harmonie nécessairement discordante'.[3] The essence of verse poetry, then, for Baudelaire, is not the rhythmic

---

[1] *La littérature à la recherche de la vérité*, Paris: Editions du Seuil, 1996, p.217.

[2] *Eléments de métrique française*, p.130.

[3] *Baudelaire. L'Exposition de la Poésie*, p.276.

illusion alone, nor the expression of an ironic conscience, but rather, the creation of a rhythmic, harmonic veil over the *gouffre* and its simultaneous piercing by the discordant voice of *la vorace Ironie*. As Campion suggests, it is vital to a philosophically valid investigation that no conclusion be reached. However, in the 1858-59 poems the poet appears to do just that, preparing as he does so a move towards perhaps the most radical and influential revolution in French poetry.

The meaninglessness of rhythm

This is the breaking point in the evolution of Baudelaire's versificatory agenda, the moment when the struggle between regularity and irregularity is at its most insistent and irony appears to emerge victorious. At this point Baudelaire has already composed and published two prose poems and the first edition of *Les Fleurs du Mal*. The verse poems composed during 1858-59, added to the 1861 edition, mark in both their content and their form a radical departure from the 1857 edition, and hold the key to our understanding of the move to prose poems, which come with unprecedented frequency after 1861. Whereas it was once hoped that rhythmic regularity might create the illusion of its correspondence to the universal analogy, the 1858-59 poems appear to accept the *gouffre* as the truth. The poet has seen through the veil of regularity, and now uses it to symbolize precisely its own meaninglessness.

In 'Le Possédé', for example, probably composed in 1858, the poet bids his companion: 'plonge tout entière au gouffre de l'Ennui' (1.4).[1] 'Ennui', capitalized, is now made as absolute as the former divine, since, in the absence of this divine guarantee, the *gouffre* and *ennui* are the only Truth. Significantly, with 'Un Fantôme', 'Le Possédé' is Baudelaire's only other iconic 'Banvillian' sonnet written since the mid-1840s, and in 1861 it is placed immediately before the former poem, as if to announce the return of the poetically obsolete 'spectre'. In 'Le Possédé', as the rhythmic veil and absolute hierarchies of poeticity disappear, the poet finds, in their absence, that canonical forms of poetic regularity – and beauty – are meaningless and provoke not *extase* but *ennui*.

---

[1] Pichois notes: 'Environ 5 novembre 1858: manuscrit adressé à Poulet-Malassis', a text which Baudelaire describes as 'un morceau inédit' (O.C.I: 899-900).

Revising 'Sur *Le Tasse en prison*' for *Les Epaves*, in 1864, Baudelaire both reinforces the sense of existential angst which grips the poet-hero and also removes the one D6 line, creating the sort of monotonous rhythmic regularity which, in 'Les Sept vieillards', accompanies the terrifying realization of the *gouffre*.[1] Already, in the 1840s version, Tasso is tormented by doubt (1.7), and his reason may give way to the absurd (1.6). He feels existential vertigo before the abyss: 'L'escalier de vertige où s'abîme son âme' (1.4), and Baudelaire even considers changing the line to: 'Le gouffre de vertige'.[2] Elsewhere, the new text echoes more explicitly the 1858-59 thematics: 'la terreur' (1.3) and 'l'horreur' (1.12) recall 'Horreur sympathique' or 'Danse macabre'. 'Le Doute' (1.7) is now capitalized, becoming absolute, invincible, acquiring an almost divine status like the 'divin Hasard' of 'L'Horloge' (1.21). Moreover, the fear which grips the poet is 'Hideuse et multiforme' (1.8). Realising the lack of inherent meaning or aesthetic superiority of certain sacred poetic forms hitherto guaranteed by the absolute, he recoils from the dizzying infinite possibilities of form. With the collapse of the universal analogy comes the collapse of the formal hierarchy by which verse is more poetically significant than prose. As if to demonstrate the monotonous meaninglessnes of regularity, 'Sur *Le Tasse en prison*' features seven consecutive *rimes plates*, as dull and inevitable as the wheezily ticking clocks of the 'Spleen' poems, as insignificant as the rhythm of eternal return in 'Les Sept vieillards'.

'A une Madone' also dramatizes the inherent meaninglessness of regularity. The poem displays a wealth of disruptive techniques: two P6 lines, one C6 line, four D6 lines, four cases of adjacent accent, two five-accent lines and three cases of *rejet*. The poet will build an altar for his mistress:

> Avec mes Vers polis, treillis d'un pur métal
> Savamment constellé de rimes de cristal   (ll.7-8)

Verse is elevated to absolute status, as the cristal-clear rhymes create a *constellation savante*, a veil of vapours reminiscent of the rhythmic illusion: 'En Vapeurs montera mon esprit orageux' (1.36). Yet the poet

---

[1] For this variant, see page 66 of the present work.
[2] All variants: O.C.I: 1151. Pichois observes: 'C'est l'angoisse, la certitude de la mort et du néant'.

is now fully aware of the vanity of verse, using it *en connaissance de cause*. As if to ironize the universal number significance which he has seen through, he stabs his madonna with seven knives, recalling the symbolic figure at which the meaninglessness of *nombre* is apprehended in 'Les Sept vieillards':

> Je les plan / terai tous // dans ton Cœur / pantelant,
> Dans ton Cœur / sanglotant, // dans ton Cœur / ruisselant! (ll.43-44)

The regularity of these lines is highlighted by their 3/3//3/3 rhythm, with the nasal /ã/ marking the first accent of five tri-syllabic groups and the last accent of four of them. Indeed, the final three hemistichs are identical but for the changing adjective, always a trisyllabic present participle. In this way the surfeit of rhyming richness is only achieved by the use of identical words, which transgresses a basic law of verse harmony. Baudelaire ends this metrically problematic poem by ironizing the regularity which had once fuelled his poetico-theological illusion and which now only symbolizes the ultimate meaninglessness of *nombre*.

As the title suggests, the poet of 'Le Goût du néant' (1858) also intends to plunge into the *gouffre* of *ennui*. He too confronts meaningless regularity which is symbolized by a relentless, eternal ticking: 'Et le Temps m'engloutit minute par minute' (l.11). And so, the poem features only regularly balanced alexandrines, and the P6 line in the first draft is removed in order to create total rhythmic monotony.[1] In this context, a P6 line would alleviate precisely the intensely repetitive rhythm by which the poet provokes an *ennui* compounded by the use of only two rhyme sounds throughout the poem: [yt] and [dœR].

The only other poem with just two rhyme elements throughout is the contemporaneous 'Sonnet d'automne' (1859), rhyming on either [al] or [it]. This sonnet is notable for its full-stop at the end of the seventh line, another *imprévu désastre* which disturbs the form's traditional syntactico-prosodic coherence. As Roubaud remarks, if a full-stop is placed anywhere but the end of lines 4, 8 or 14, 'il met en cause la hiérarchie des positions de fin de strophe'.[2] In this way

---

[1] For this variant, see page 65 of the present work.
[2] *La forme du sonnet français de Marot à Malherbe*, I: 215.

Tasso's 'Peur ridicule, / Hideuse et multiforme' (ll.7-8) is realised as the iconic formal hierarchy of poeticity begins to crumble. Only two other sonnets feature this striking irregularity, 'L'Aube spirituelle' (1853?) and 'Causerie' (1854?), the former emphasizing the irregularity by also removing the full-stop at the end of line 8. Indeed, its second quatrain deals with 'l'inaccessible azur' (l.5), and the possibility that man's 'rêve' (l.6) of the absolute is mere illusion. It is precisely when the infinite blue sky 'S'ouvre et s'enfonce avec l'attirance du gouffre' (l.7) that the full-stop appears, and the poet's dizzying tumble into the *gouffre* is also expressed on a formal level, reminiscent of 'Les Sept vieillards'. For André Gendre, 'Faire du vers 7 un vers final représente une transgression, certes, mais aussi un hommage au nombre sacré que tout sonnet comprend deux fois'.[1] In the context of the *gouffre*, however, this is not a hommage but an ironic reference to the once-hallowed icons of a now obsolete poetics.

It is now clear that an analysis of Baudelaire's verse irregularities can only do him justice by acknowledging that his agenda is not simply a rebellion against a restrictive yoke, but rather, a matter of matching the suitable verse structure to the process of spiritual and philosophical inquiry particular to each individual poem. Such a reading allows us to differentiate between the thematic importance of regularity in the fourteen 6+6 alexandrines of 'Parfum exotique' (1840s) and those of 'Le Goût du néant', where the optic through which verse form is to be interpreted is so different. Just as *nombre* is interpreted differently, so too is the verb *bercer*, of the former rhythmic illusion. As the poet of 'Chant d'automne' (1859) listens to the sound of falling wood, which conjures up images of death, he feels not repulsed by the sound, but soothed: 'bercé par ce choc monotone' (l.13). The meaningless regularity of eternally identical thuds, 'les coups du bélier infatigable et lourd' (l.12), causes him an ironic pleasure similar to the 'plaisir mystérieux et aristocratique' felt by the narrator of 'Le Port', who recognizes the ultimate vanity of 'le goût du rythme et de la beauté'.[2] The function of regular rhythm, then, changes as the poet loses faith in its inherent correspondence to the order of universal phenomena. The taste for and rejection of the rhythmic illusion are henceforth two sides of the same coin; neither is

---

[1] *Evolution du sonnet français*, Paris: P.U.F., 1996, p.192.
[2] O.C.I: 344.

more 'true' than the other, and the poet uses verse regularity after 1858 to articulate both.

In this way two more poems added to the 1861 edition, although rhythmically similar to 'Le Goût du néant', present an entirely different attitude towards *nombre*. 'Le Masque' (1859) and 'L'Amour du mensonge' (1860) maintain perfect 6+6 alexandrines over 36 and 24 lines respectively.[1] In the latter, the woman appears to have heeded the poet's plea in 'Le Possédé', and displays 'ennui' in her 'regard profond' (1.4). Her eyes are 'Plus vides, plus profonds que vous-mêmes, ô Cieux!' (1.20), as the fundamental emptiness of the *azur* is acknowledged, situating the poem firmly in the *gouffre*. Yet whereas, in 'Le Goût du néant', all is despair – 'L'amour n'a plus de goût' (1.6) – 'L'Amour du mensonge' heralds 'le savant amour' (1.12), recalling the *prise de conscience* of the meaninglessness of rhyme's *constellation savante* in 'A une Madone' (1.8). Praising the woman's beauty in regular lines of canonical poetic beauty, the poet sighs:

> Mais ne suffit-il pas que tu sois l'apparence
> Pour réjouir un cœur qui fuit la vérité? (ll.21-22)

Having come to terms with the hollowness of poetic regularity, the poet expresses a detached pleasure at the rhythmic veil which he recognizes as nothing more than a pleasant illusion, as he tells the statue of 'Le Masque', 'tout encadré de gaze' (1.11): 'Ton mensonge m'enivre' (1.27). There can no longer be any doubt: the rhythmic illusion is a pure lie, and it seems that the tension articulated the length of *Les Fleurs du Mal* has come to an end, the poet having reached a decision. At this critical point, the vanity of the verse-rhythmic illusion appears the only reality, and in 1859 Baudelaire acknowledges the truth of the *gouffre*, writing of artifice: 'Ces choses, parce qu'elles sont fausses, sont infiniment plus près du vrai'.[2] Poetry, for Baudelaire, can no longer ignore the *gouffre*, and after 1860 the rhythmic illusion is employed less and less.

Whereas the *gouffre* once terrified the poet, he resolves in 'Danse macabre' (1858), in a moment of bravado, to confront his existential vertigo:

---

[1] With the exception of a minor D6 line: 'Où la Fatuité / promène son regard' ('Le Masque', 1.9).
[2] *Salon de 1859*, VII, 'Le Paysage' (O.C.II: 668).

Les charmes de l'horreur n'enivrent que les forts! (1.36)

This is the challenge which prose poetry will present us. *Le Spleen de Paris* is a far cry from the unproblematic, joyous release which certain critics' reductive reading of verse rhythm would have us believe. Indeed, in the absence of the universal analogy, the prose poet lifts the veil on the world in order to investigate the consequences of the loss of an illusion which makes of verse poetry a sham. However, the result is an infinitely problematic interpretative instability which challenges our perception of both the world and poetry. It is to this instability that the poet and his readers will be obliged to respond, necessitating an irrevocable re-definition of both the role and the mechanics of poetic rhythm.

3
Rhythm and Prose Poetry

Into the *gouffre*

The second edition of *Les Fleurs du Mal* ends with a departure for a new voyage, and the shift to prose poetry can be read as an attempt to write a poetics not of illusion, but of the *gouffre*. The poet of 'Le Voyage' loses interest in the veil of verse and the rhythmic illusion, declaring new enthusiasm for a different poetics:

> Nous voulons voyager sans vapeur et sans voiles! (l.53)

The poetic journey is not at an end; the poet vows to continue onwards, but without the traditional methods of propulsion, steam or sails. The double meaning of *vapeurs* and *voiles*, as hazy vapours and veils, also suggests a rejection of the regular rhythmic and harmonic structure of the versificatory veil. Indeed, the poet expresses the desire to confront exactly what has hitherto been veiled:

> Plonger au fond du gouffre, Enfer ou Ciel, qu'importe?
> Au fond de l'Inconnu pour trouver du *nouveau*! (ll.143-44)

The *gouffre*, symbolizing the loss of absolutes and inherent meaning in nature and verse, is no longer to be feared, but rather, it is positively to be sought. 'Chant d'automne' (1859) announces the same departure with its 'chocs funèbres' (l.3), 'ce choc monotone' (l.13): 'Ce bruit mystérieux sonne comme un départ' (l.16). Here the verb *plonger* also recurs: 'Bientôt nous plongerons dans les froides ténèbres (l.1).

The poem's images of scaffold (l.10) and coffins (l.12) create an atmosphere of death and mourning, and in 'Le Voyage', humanity, 'ivre de son génie' (l.101), curses God: 'Criant à Dieu, dans sa furibonde agonie' (l.103). Although the antecedent of the possessive is ambiguous, this certainly suggests the rejection of the divine absolute and, by extension, the universal analogy it maintains. Indeed, in two poems of 1860 placed side by side in the 1861 edition, the link between the scrutiny of natural phenomena and the mourning of the divine is made clear. 'Alchimie de la douleur' suggests that it is indeed God, the guarantee of meaning, who has died:

> Dans le suaire des nuages
> Je découvre un cadavre cher (ll.11-12)

Similarly, 'Horreur sympathique' depicts the skies torn asunder, confirming the absence of the divine. The poet is proud to have seen through the illusion of meaning in natural phenomena, whilst the clouds mourn perhaps their lost significatory stability:

> Cieux déchirés comme des grèves,
> En vous se mire mon orgueil;
> Vos vastes nuages en deuil […]. (ll.9-11)

The absence of God, or man's rejection of a meaningful link between the divine and the world, is also reflected in the prose poems. In 'Le Joueur généreux', for example, the devil explains 'l'absurdité des différentes philosophies' to a faithless poet who ends the day 'faisant encore ma prière par un reste d'habitude imbécile'.[1] Similarly, the fourth little boy of 'Les Vocations' declares: 'Dieu ne s'occupe pas de moi et de mon ennui'.[2]

In a passage from his 1860s *carnets*, Baudelaire wonders whether the fall of unity into multiplicity might indicate a flaw in the divine:

> La Théologie.
> Qu'est-ce que la chute?
> Si c'est l'unité devenue dualité, c'est Dieu qui a chuté.
> En d'autres termes, la création ne serait-elle pas la chute de Dieu?[3]

If the absolute is no longer perfect, then the universal analogy and aesthetic hierarchy upon which Art rests collapses. If there is no absolute *Beau*, no stable formal values, then the qualitative verse/prose distinction carefully perpetuated by poets is untenable. Thus 'les principes de la nature d'après lesquels nous sommes déterminés à regarder certaines formes comme belles et gracieuses, et d'autres comme laides et désagréables', seen as an absolute truth by

---

[1] O.C.I: 326 and 327.
[2] O.C.I: 334.
[3] O.C.I: 688.

William Hogarth in his *Analysis of Beauty*, become unstable, since the notion of perfection depends on the concept of the absolute.[1] In this context, Banville's argument against prose poetry, which rests upon the same fiction, is also obsolete:

Peut-il y avoir des poëmes en prose? Non, il ne peut pas y en avoir, malgré [...] les admirables *Poëmes en prose* de Charles Baudelaire et le *Gaspard de la Nuit* de Louis Bertrand; car il est impossible d'imaginer une prose, si parfaite qu'elle soit, à laquelle on ne puisse, avec un effort surhumain, rien ajouter ou rien retrancher.[2]

Once the rhythmic veil and illusion are abandoned, the apparent superiority of verse over other forms, for Baudelaire, falters. Without metre and rhyme, which were inextricably bound up in this fiction of inherent meaning, prose poetry rejects the supposedly absolute hierarchy of old, and acknowledges the challenge of the *gouffre*.

In such a paradigm, anything might have the potential to be poetic, and this is the importance of the notion of chance to the Baudelairean prose poem. Whereas the staunch young aesthete of 1846 proclaims: 'Il n'y a pas de hasard dans l'art',[3] Baudelaire informs Sainte-Beuve in 1866 of his intention to create 'un nouveau Joseph Delorme accrochant sa pensée rhapsodique à chaque accident de la flânerie'.[4] In 'Le Poème du hachisch' (1860) he twice defines *rhapsodique* in terms of *le hasard*, first quoting an acquaintance's experience of hachisch:

'J'étais, disait-il, comme un cheval emporté et courant vers un abîme, voulant s'arrêter, mais ne le pouvant pas. En effet, c'était un galop effroyable et ma pensée, esclave de la circonstance, du milieu, de l'accident et de tout ce qui peut être impliqué dans le mot *hasard*, avait pris un tour purement et absolument rhapsodique'.[5]

The experience of chance and circumstance draws the mind directly into the abyss, or the *gouffre*. In 'L'Homme-Dieu', Baudelaire defines the word in terms of a world liberated from the tyrannical grip of a Hugolian world view: 'le mot *rhapsodique*, qui définit si bien un train

---

[1] *Analysis of Beauty*, 1753; *Analyse de la Beauté, destinée à fixer les idées vagues qu'on a du goût*, 1805, trans. by Jansen; revised by S. Chauvin, Paris: Ecole nationale supérieure des Beaux-Arts, 1991, p.45. On Baudelaire's knowledge of Hogarth's work, see: *Charles Baudelaire. Nouvelles Lettres*, Paris: Fayard, 2000, pp.75-77.

[2] *Petit Traité*, pp.6-7.

[3] *Salon de 1846*, IV, 'Eugène Delacroix' (O.C.II: 432).

[4] Letter of 15 January and 5 February 1866 (*Corr.* II: 583).

[5] *Les Paradis artificiels* (O.C.I: 414); Baudelaire's italics.

de pensées suggéré et commandé par le monde extérieur et le hasard des circonstances'.[1] The prose poet, therefore, will not attempt to force meaning upon objects. Rather, he hopes to allow the *imprévu désastre* to provide a new source of meaning when examined without the interpretative optic of the universal analogy. It is as a recognition of the difficulties of such a project that the prose poems will now be read.

The instability of the sign

Although *Les Fleurs du Mal* is the site of a self-consciously illusory poetics, the word *illusion* does not appear in any poem. *Le Spleen de Paris*, however, features three occurrences of the word, all in 'La Corde', where the poet's friend suggests that the loss of an illusion can have a positive force:

Les illusions, – me disait mon ami, – sont aussi innombrables peut-être que les rapports des hommes entre eux, ou des hommes avec les choses. Et quand l'illusion disparaît, c'est-à-dire que nous voyons l'être ou le fait tel qu'il existe en dehors de nous, nous éprouvons un bizarre sentiment, compliqué moitié de regret pour le fantôme disparu, moitié de surprise agréable devant la nouveauté, devant le fait réel.[2]

The former rhythmic poetics imposed a religious bias on the interpretation of natural phenomena. Hugo could only see nature as proof of the divine absolute and a guarantee of the significance of order. For the poet of the *gouffre*, however, there can be no such bias, since in the absence of a guarantee, divine meaning in the universe is a fallacy. The prose poet's friend tempts him to lift the veil in order to examine 'l'être ou le fait tel qu'il existe en dehors de nous'. This corresponds to the doctrine of the realist, or *positiviste*, as explained in the 1859 *Salon*: 'les choses telles qu'elles sont, ou bien qu'elles seraient, en supposant que je n'existe pas', a study of 'l'univers sans l'homme'.[3]

The problem of knowing what 'reality' is once absolutes disappear preoccupies Baudelaire for much of the 1859 *Salon*. He scorns the bourgeois faith in the stability of external meaning, those who declare: 'Je crois à la nature et je ne crois qu'à la nature', or who pose for a

---

[1] O.C.I: 428.
[2] O.C.I: 328.
[3] IV, 'Le Gouvernement de l'imagination' (O.C.II: 627).

portrait misguidedly believing there is only one way of interpreting an object: 'Je pose, et en réalité c'est moi'.[1] In 'La Corde', Baudelaire is careful to put such a deceptive simplification into the mouth not of the poet, but of a friend who claims that maternal love is 'un phénomène évident, trivial, toujours semblable, et d'une nature à laquelle il [est] impossible de se tromper'.[2] He proves himself wrong, however, in his own anecdote which details exactly why we should be wary of the notion of universal, absolute interpretation. The prose poems explore the poet's interpretative uncertainties once the veil of inherent meaning is lifted.

Without a guarantee, natural phenomena are no longer the dependable signs of a constant underlying meaning. In 'Le Chien et le flacon' the poet describes the wagging of a dog's tail, but he is willing to offer only a hypothesis for what is a universally accepted sign: 'ce qui est, je crois, chez ces pauvres êtres, le signe correspondant du rire et du sourire'.[3] In 'Une Mort héroïque', the prince's intentions go unexplained, provoking speculation on the meaning of his act: 'signe évident, ajouteraient les esprits superficiels, des tendances généreuses du Prince offensé'.[4] Yet the poet offers only cautious interpretation, admitting that his theory is 'infiniment plus probable', but nevertheless not entirely certain. In 'Le Joueur généreux' the poet hesitates to describe what he sees, unsure whether his version is 'correct', offering only a tentative: 'Si je voulais essayer de définir d'une manière quelconque l'expression singulière de leurs regards, je dirais que [...]'.[5] In 'Portraits de maîtresses' the men's air is beyond the poet's descriptive faculties: 'cet indescriptible je ne sais quoi'.[6] In this way the universal semiotic system becomes unstable. 'What does this really mean?', the poet of 'La Fausse monnaie' wonders, lost in an infinity of possibilities, 'tirant toutes les déductions possibles de toutes les hypothèses possibles'.[7] This hesitation, or inability, to interpret signs is so frequent in the texts that Steve Murphy resumes

---

[1] II, 'Le Public moderne et la photographie' (O.C.II: 617) and VI, 'Le Portrait' (O.C.II: 654).
[2] O.C.I: 328.
[3] O.C.I: 284.
[4] O.C.I: 320.
[5] O.C.I: 325.
[6] O.C.I: 345.
[7] O.C.I: 324.

the prose poet's agenda thus: 'ne jamais livrer au lecteur un simple jugement de valeur en tant qu'auteur-autorité'.[1]

The narrator realizes that, without the imposition of significance on phenomena, they mean nothing. The sign freed from the tyrannical universal analogy is not a source of meaning, but simply a blank page onto which meaning might be projected. Yet the prose poet is unable to commit to one interpretation. Observing a beautiful widow he comments: 'cette pauvreté-là, si pauvreté il y a', unsure of what he sees.[2] 'Le Gâteau' reveals a lack of interpretative stability as the poet discovers 'un pays superbe où le pain s'appelle du *gâteau*'.[3] This instability is reflected in *Le Spleen de Paris*, where we observe *un pays où la prose s'appelle de la poésie*. In 'Les Yeux des pauvres' the poet is surprised to find that his pity for the poor is not shared by his intolerant companion: 'Je tournais mes regards vers les vôtres, cher amour, pour y lire *ma* pensée', only to find his interpretation of events is not the only one possible.[4] In 'Le Miroir', therefore, the poet acknowledges the importance of context, or an interpretative grid, to deciding a meaning which is no longer absolute: 'Au nom du bon sens, j'avais sans doute raison; mais, au point de vue de la loi, il n'avait pas tort'.[5]

In the prose version of 'Le Crépuscule du soir', the poet admits that it is common 'de voir la même cause engendrer deux effets contraires'. The additions to this poem, often rejected as 'unpoetic' by critics inadvisably sure of their aesthetic criteria, can now be seen as central to Baudelaire's prose poetics. The first madman is horrified by a chicken 'dans lequel il croyait voir je ne sais quel insultant hiéroglyphe'. This entirely idiosyncratic interpretation isolates him from conventional modes of sign recognition – he dies 'incapable de reconnaître sa femme et son enfant' – but that does not necessarily mean that his vision of the world is invalid, since there is no such thing as absolute truth.[6] It does, however, indicate that once agreed modes of phenomenal interpretation are abandoned, only madness can

---

[1] 'Le Complexe de supériorité et la contagion du rire: "Un Plaisant" de Baudelaire', *Travaux de littérature* 7 (1994), 257-85, p.273.
[2] O.C.I: 294.
[3] O.C.I: 299.
[4] O.C.I: 319.
[5] O.C.I: 344.
[6] All quotations: O.C.I: 311-12.

follow. Such is the tragic case of Mademoiselle Bistouri, who mistakes the poet for a doctor and cannot be dissuaded.

Sure enough, the poet is soon exasperated by this constant uncertainty, the liberating effects of which he had anticipated with relish in the verse texts of 1858-59. Once he buries his Ideal in 'Laquelle est la vraie?', reality taunts him: 'tu m'aimeras telle que je suis'.[1] Yet he cannot see 'le fait tel qu'il existe en dehors de nous', precisely because *le fait n'existe pas en dehors de nous*. It seems that the 'objective' poetics of the *gouffre* should only be imagined from within the reassuring safety of the meaningful verse structure, as an attractive but illusory possibility. The poet ought to have heeded the advice of the narrator of 'Les Projets': 'à quoi bon exécuter des projets, quand le projet est en lui-même une jouissance suffisante?'.[2] As soon as the poet steps outside the guarantee of meaning, the promise of glory vanishes, and he is overcome with vertigo, madness and creative frustration. The scenarios of 'Les Métamorphoses du vampire' and 'Le Rêve d'un curieux' prove prophetic: as soon as the veil is lifted, the anticipated magnificent revelation turns to dust and the poet is left with nothing.

Rejection of an objective poetics

The former rhythmic illusion was a window through which a tyrannical system of significance was projected onto exterior objects. The prose poet opens that window, just as in the 1859 *Salon*, misguided painters attempting to reproduce 'le fait tel qu'il existe en dehors de nous' do the same:

Or un poème ne se copie jamais: il veut être composé. Ainsi ils ouvrent une fenêtre, et tout l'espace compris dans le carré de la fenêtre, arbres, ciel et maison, prend pour eux la valeur d'un poème tout fait.[3]

Poetic meaning and value, therefore, does not simply leap out at the artist from objects released from the universal analogy. The introduction to Aloysius Bertrand's prose texts is often ignored by critics in their haste to see Bertrand's influence on Baudelaire in the

---

[1] O.C.I: 342.
[2] O.C.I: 315.
[3] VII, 'Le Paysage' (O.C.II: 661).

form alone.[1] Since a study of the form of *Le Spleen de Paris* is best approached in the context of interpretative stability, this introduction is as important as Bertrand's prose texts themselves. The narrator, a disillusioned poet, meets the devil in disguise who explains that, in his search for 'l'art absolu', he too opened a window: 'J'enjambai la fenêtre, et je regardai en bas. O surprise!'.[2] Similarly, the Baudelairean prose poet eagerly opens the window, lifting the veil to see what surprises await him.

The poet of 'Le Mauvais vitrier' does just this, gripped by both 'un courage de luxe pour exécuter les actes les plus absurdes et souvent même les plus dangereux' and, in keeping with the 1858-59 verse, 'une espèce d'énergie qui jaillit de l'ennui'. He succumbs to temptation and it is, of course, the cause of his misery: 'j'ouvris la fenêtre, hélas!'. The poet soon despairs of the lack of stable meaning which he finds in place of the 'reality' he had anticipated. When the exasperated poet invites the glazier up to his garret, he is enraged to find only plain windows, with no tinted or stained glass:

Comment? vous n'avez pas de verres de couleur? des verres roses, rouges, bleus, des vitres magiques, des vitres de paradis? [...] vous n'avez pas même de vitres qui fassent voir la vie en beau![3]

The rhythmic veil of verse obscured the emptiness of 'le fait tel qu'il existe en dehors de nous', projecting an illusion of meaning onto it. The prose poet, however, wondering what the poetic charge of the exterior object might be, can find absolutely nothing, and Poetry itself cannot function. Therefore, the poet, in his anger, destroys all the glazier's panes with a symbolic weapon, 'un petit pot de fleurs'. Disillusioned with objectivity, he reaches automatically for the verse poems of *Les Fleurs du Mal*, the rhythmical windows *qui font voir la vie en beau*.

As a consequence of this terror, the poet of 'Les Fenêtres' emphatically closes the window again, returning to the safety of

---

[1] For example, D. H. T. Scott, who highlights Bertrand's consistent brevity, his visual use of the page, juxtaposition of images and sense of organization (Barbara Wright and D.H.T. Scott, *La Fanfarlo and Le Spleen de Paris*, London: Grant & Cutler, 1984, pp.41-42).
[2] *Gaspard de la nuit*, Paris: Gallimard, coll. 'Poésie', 1980, pp.75 and 62.
[3] All quotations: O.C.I: 285-87.

poetically projected meaning: 'Celui qui regarde du dehors à travers une fenêtre ouverte, ne voit jamais autant de choses que celui qui regarde une fenêtre fermée'.[1] In this context, what J. A. Hiddleston calls 'a paradox [...] which blatantly goes counter to common sense and experience' is anything but.[2] By shutting the window the poet rejects external reality with its infinity of possible meanings and significatory instability. The acknowledgement of the object's lack of inherent poeticity, however, means that meaning must once again be somehow projected onto the object. The poet cannot return to the abandoned universal analogy, since this is inextricably linked to the verse vehicle whose artifice is all too apparent in its metre and rhyme. Yet he must nonetheless impose some sort of poetic meaning on the world. Hiddleston suggests that the window now functions as 'a kind of mirror in which there is some reflection of the poet himself'.[3] Indeed, following the loss of the universal analogy the poet now projects his own personal interpretation on an unstable world.

As he shuts the window, rejecting an 'objective' poetics, the poet himself, looking out, becomes the unique source of meaning, projecting significance on the outside world. He is unconcerned with the question of whether his version of events corresponds to 'reality', since there is no reality beyond his gaze:

Peut-être me direz-vous: 'Es-tu sûr que cette légende soit la vraie?' Qu'importe ce que peut être la réalité placée hors de moi, si elle m'a aidé à vivre, à sentir que je suis et ce que je suis?[4]

Indeed, *le moi* occurs with significant frequency in the post-illusory texts. In 'Le Cygne' (1859), the poet declares: 'tout pour moi devient allégorie' (1.31), elevating himself to the centre of the significance of all that he observes. In 'La Mort héroïque', it is only the poet who can see Fancioulle's halo, 'auréole invisible pour tous, mais visible pour moi'.[5] As we have seen, Baudelaire tells Sainte-Beuve of his intention to create 'un nouveau Joseph Delorme'.[6] In his flagship work, Sainte-

---

[1] O.C.I: 339.
[2] *Baudelaire and Le Spleen de Paris*, Oxford: Clarendon Press, 1987, p.28.
[3] ibid., p.29.
[4] O.C.I: 339.
[5] O.C.I: 321.
[6] Letter of 15 January and 5 February 1866 (*Corr.* II: 583).

Beuve's lyrical hero claims that the poet is born with the key to universal significance: 'il a reçu en naissant la clef des symboles et l'intelligence des figures'.[1] However, it is only the key to universal meaning as guaranteed by the divine Creator that the lyric poet receives; he is in tune with the *divine symphonie*. Baudelaire's version of the hero, in 'Les Fenêtres', holds his own key to universal significance, rather than that imposed on him by a fallacious universal analogy. This method is ascribed, in the 1859 *Salon*, to 'l'imaginatif', who declares: 'Je veux illuminer les choses avec mon esprit et en projeter le reflet sur les autres esprits'.[2]

'La Femme sauvage...' dramatizes the opposition between the former universal analogy and the poet's new interpretative freedom. Having asserted his right to replace the divine as a possible source of meaning, the poet rejects that which his mistress tries to impose on him. The poem begins with his version of the motives behind her actions: 'Si au moins vos soupirs exprimaient le remords, ils vous feraient quelque honneur; mais ils ne traduisent que la satiété du bien-être et l'accablement du repos'. Refusing to play his mistress's game, the poet imposes his own interpretation on her sighs which no longer have the desired effect of winning his attention. Whereas the sigh or the sob once signified a beautifully unspoken 'poetic' yearning for the *au-delà*, the poet chastises his companion for the sighs by which she tries to convey to him her melancholy: 'Et que peuvent signifier pour moi tous ces petits soupirs?'. Recalling the *voiles* and *vapeurs* of the rhythmic illusion, she sighs at the skies through a veil of tears, 'les yeux tournés vaporeusement vers le ciel'. Indeed, the poet compares her to 'une jeune grenouille qui évoquerait l'idéal' as if she still had faith in absolutes. Her naïve yearning towards a fictional Ideal now simply annoys a poet who has left the previous window of poetic illusion, and he angrily threatens the woman with the same defenestration: 'je vous jetterai par la fenêtre, comme une bouteille vide', where the empty bottle suggests that the *ivresse* of illusion has run out.[3] Her punishment will be the same terrifying plunge into the *gouffre* as that experienced by the poet of 'Le Mauvais vitrier'.

---

[1] *Vie, Poésies et Pensées de Joseph Delorme*, 1829; Paris: Editions d'Aujourd'hui, coll. 'Les Introuvables', 1985, p.237.

[2] IV, 'Le Gouvernement de l'imagination' (O.C.II: 627).

[3] All quotations: O.C.I: 290.

The problem of authority

Although this re-motivation of *le moi* as guarantee might seem to solve the problem of meaning, it is, in fact, highly problematic. If the poet articulates his own interpretation of signs, there is no guarantee that his version is any more authoritative than any other. This is highly dangerous for Poetry in that, if the poet sees beauty and poeticity where his reader does not, both the author and his work lose all credibility. The prose poet risks inviting question and contradiction, and many are the critics who argue that certain Baudelairean prose poems do not fulfil their own personal criteria for what makes a poetic text.[1] Without the universal aesthetic stability symbolized by the formal poetic constants of metre and rhyme, the prose poet struggles constantly to convince himself and his reader that his text is poetic.

Before the statue of Venus, 'l'immortelle Déesse', the poor *fou*, 'le dernier et le plus solitaire des humains', feels he has lost his poetic superiority. Yet he nevertheless retains an irrepressible sense of his acute sensitivity to an aesthetic absolute: 'Cependant je suis fait, moi aussi, pour comprendre et sentir l'immortelle Beauté!'.[2] Likewise, in 'A une heure du matin' the poet tires of his unstable poetics of the *gouffre*, and turns in desperation to the security of the previous poetics, to both God and verse, the complementary cornerstones of aesthetic stability:

---

[1] For example: Hiddleston's rejection of 'Un Plaisant', which Murphy soundly counters in 'Le Complexe de supériorité et la contagion du rire: "Un Plaisant" de Baudelaire'. Or D. H. T. Scott, who argues: '*Petits Poèmes en prose* seems to define a *genre* as much as suggest a title and the definition it proposes is somewhat problematic since the question of whether all the texts grouped under this heading are in fact prose poems is an open one' (*La Fanfarlo and Le Spleen de Paris*, pp.47-48). Scott defines 'poetic' as 'elaboration in terms of images and through sensuous and imaginative assocation [...] rather than through logical or narrative links' (ibid., p.53). This definition is at odds with the narrative verse poems 'Don Juan aux enfers' and 'Châtiment de l'orgueil', to name but two, but Scott proposes his own system of generic classification for the fifty texts, intended 'as much as a basis for argument and discussion as a fixed and immutable system'. Refusing purely poetic status to many of them, he suggests instead: 'Poème' (17), 'Poétique' (3), 'Poème-boutade' (7), 'Moralité' (9), 'Essai' (4), 'Conte' (10) (ibid., pp.73-80).
[2] O.C.I: 284.

Seigneur mon Dieu! accordez-moi la grâce de produire quelques beaux vers qui me prouvent à moi-même que je ne suis pas le dernier des hommes, que je ne suis pas inférieur à ceux que je méprise![1]

Indeed, this prayer is preceded by a fleeting echo of the verse rhythms which the poet now regrets giving up in his plunge into the *gouffre*:

Âmes de ceux / que j'ai aimés,	(8)
âmes de ceux / que j'ai chantés,	(8)
fortifiez-moi, / soutenez-moi,	(8)
éloignez de moi / le mensonge	(8)
et les vapeurs / corruptrices du monde [2]	(10)

Here the world itself, not poetry, is seen as 'mensonge' and 'vapeurs'. The struggle to return to the previous safety of regular rhythm is shown by the rhythmical imperfection necessary in order to make verse of these 'lines', which demand irregular synaeresis on 'iez', as if the poet cannot quite submit to the rhythmic illusion for which he now yearns.

In 'Mademoiselle Bistouri' the prose poet doubts of his new poetics, wondering whether God inspired him with his difficult rebellion simply in order to restore his faith in divinely guaranteed absolutes. Without God the world has lost all its stable meaning, and the poet, exhausted by his search for the poetic, returns to the Father to pray for salvation, for the restoration of guaranteed poetic significance:

Seigneur, mon Dieu! vous, le Créateur, vous, le Maître; vous qui avez fait la Loi et la Liberté; [...] vous qui êtes plein de motifs et de causes, et qui avez peut-être mis dans mon esprit le goût de l'horreur pour convertir mon cœur, comme la guérison au bout d'une lame.[3]

The prose poet's despair convinces him that Poetry cannot exist without the divine absolute and structural constants. In 'Le Gouffre' (1862) he retreats into a recognizable sonnet form and the safety of meaning as guaranteed by recognizable verse structure. Fleeing the 'abîme' (l.2) and the 'vertige' (l.12) of his 'cauchemar multiforme'

---

[1] O.C.I: 288.
[2] Adapted from the original (O.C.I: 288).
[3] O.C.I: 355-56.

(1.8), he recoils from the window, through which he sees a dizzying infinity of formal and poetic possibilities: 'Je ne vois qu'infini par toutes les fenêtres' (1.11). Whereas the prose poet sought to explore 'les innombrables formes de roman et de nouvelle',[1] the verse poet restores *nombre* as an absolute: 'Ah! ne jamais sortir des Nombres et des Êtres!' (1.14).

'Enivrez-vous' constitutes a similar flight from the *gouffre* and back to the veil of *ivresse*, as the poet asserts: 'Il faut être toujours ivre'. One of the most structurally repetitive prose poems, its numerous parallels and structural correspondences herald a moment of respite from the *gouffre*. The poet recommends intoxication, 'De vin, de poésie, de vertu', in the kind of lyrical ternary rhythm so common in *Madame Bovary*, where Emma's faith in absolute values of love and beauty is treated with similar irony.[2] The notion of virtue restores the abandoned moral hierarchy where *le Mal* is an absolute, and of which God is the guarantee. Yet Baudelaire acknowledges in 1863 that virtue is '*artificielle*, surnaturelle'.[3] It does not correspond to transcendent, absolute values, but rather, requires an imaginative effort, and in 1859 Baudelaire asks: 'qu'est-ce que la vertu sans imagination? Autant dire la vertu sans la pitié, la vertu sans le ciel'.[4]

In 'Le *Confiteor* de l'artiste', the poet finds momentary relief from the worrying instability of poetry as seen by *le moi*.[5] He succumbs to

---

[1] 'Théophile Gautier' (1858-59) (O.C.II: 119).

[2] O.C.I: 337. Baudelaire uses this ternary rhythm frequently in the prose poems, especially in 'Le Vieux saltimbanque', where we find, among others: 'Partout s'étalait, / se répandait, / s'ébaudissait', 'elles piaillaient, / beuglaient, / hurlaient', 'un mélange de cris, / de détonations de cuivre / et d'explosions de fusées', 'le vent, / la pluie / et le soleil', 'la joie, / le gain, / la débauche', 'sans amis, / sans famille, / sans enfants' (O.C.I: 295-97).

[3] *Le Peintre de la vie moderne*, XI, 'Eloge du maquillage' (O.C.II: 715); Baudelaire's italics.

[4] *Salon de 1859*, III, 'La Reine des facultés', (O.C.II: 621).

[5] The poem begins: 'Que les fins de journées d'automne sont pénétrantes!', announcing the same autumnal, vespertine setting as 'L'Ennemi' (1855), with its 'automne des idées' (1.5), contemporary with the appearance of the *faux accord* in 'L'Héautontimorouménos'. The same context abounds in the post-illusory texts 'Sonnet d'automne' (1859), 'Chant d'automne' (1859), 'Chanson d'après-midi' (1860) and 'La Fin de la journée' (1861). The setting autumn sun announces, with the death of the previous poetics, the advent of the new; as the poet writes in 'Un Cheval de race': 'Elle aime comme on aime en automne; on dirait que les approches de l'hiver allument dans son cœur un feu nouveau' (O.C.I: 343).

the illusion that the meaning he projects corresponds to a real meaning inherent in objects. Again the sea is the object of his scrutiny, with its typically post-illusory 'mélodie monotone de la houle'. The 'real' nature of the sea is a fallacy which the poet recognizes in the cold light of day, but the monotonous melody – a sort of rhythmic illusion – lures him into confusing his own poetic interpretation of the melody with its illusory 'inherent' nature: 'toutes ces choses pensent par moi, ou je pense par elles (car dans la grandeur de la rêverie, le moi se perd vite!)'. This loss of *le moi* is central to the illusion of 'true' universal aesthetic constants and provides the prose poet with welcome relief from his task of searching for values of poeticity, and presenting them to a sceptical reader.

The illusion bypasses logic and presents itself not as the result of a long process of deduction, 'mais musicalement et pittoresquement, sans arguties, sans syllogismes, sans déductions'. In *Le Peintre de la vie moderne* (1863) Baudelaire highlights the poet's struggle, following the collapse of aesthetic absolutes, to prove what is poetic: 'Tout ce qui est beau et noble est le résultat de la raison et du calcul'.[1] In 'Le *Confiteor* de l'artiste', however, there is no need for calculation, since the truth of Beauty is seen as an incontrovertible *évidence*. Strikingly, this illusion is expressed in another echo of verse rhythm, the bygone guarantee of the stable aesthetic hierarchy, which falters only when the illusion bursts:

mais musicalement / et pittoresquement,	(6+6)
sans arguties, / sans syllogism(es), / sans déductions.	(4/4/4)
Toutefois, ces pensées,	(6)
qu'elles sortent de moi / ou s'élancent des choses,	(6+6)
deviennent bientôt trop intenses.[2]	(8)

Of course, this requires effort on our part as well as the poet's, a similar need to search for reassuring, stable guarantees of poeticity, since in order to release these rhythms reminiscent of verse, inconsistency is required in our treatment of the 'e' *caduc* and certain vowel sequences. But just as the poet is unsure of where Poetry disappears in a prose poetic paradigm, so too the reader is equally lost,

---

[1] O.C.II: 715.
[2] Adapted from the original (O.C.I: 278).

and equally grateful for the fleeting illusion of the former poetics to which both poet and reader succumb together.

Yet like any Baudelairean illusion, such as the vision of 'La Chambre double', it cannot last long. When the illusion vanishes, the intensity of the infinite – 'il n'est pas de pointe plus acérée que celle de l'Infini' – overpowers the poet. This plunges him back into his 'cauchemar multiforme' ('Le Gouffre', 1.8), his inability to recognize the poetic from an infinity of possibilities. Hugo's faith allows him to see the infinite as a delicious religious mystery, and in 1861 Baudelaire explains: 'Ainsi est-il emporté irrésistiblement vers tout symbole de l'infini, la mer, le ciel [...] il se meut dans l'immense, sans vertige'.[1] By contrast, the prose poet is overwhelmed by vertigo before an infinite in which any one of countless choices is possible, like the fourth little boy of 'Les Vocations' who remarks: 'il est toujours très difficile de se décider à n'importe quoi'.[2] The poet of 'Le Confiteor de l'artiste' now wishes to escape the contemplation of nature, and the temptation of elevating the visions of *le moi* to the status of truth: 'Nature! [...] laisse-moi! Cesse de tenter mes désirs et mon orgueil!'. The prose poetic search for aesthetic values appears, in a moment of doubt, to be doomed to failure in the face of a silent nature which remains *limpide* and *insensible*: 'L'étude du beau est un duel où l'artiste crie de frayeur avant d'être vaincu'.[3] Once the notion of universal absolutes – *le Beau* – disappears, the study of beauty with a small 'b' is an irresolvable problem, since neither the poet nor his readers can be sure of relative values of poeticity.

In 'Obsession' (1860), the intrusion of *le moi* again frustrates the poet. He longs to embrace the *gouffre*: 'je cherche le vide, et le noir, et le nu' (1.11), but the wind screams like a cathedral organ, calling him back to the religious interpretation of nature, and he is dismayed to find that the rhythms of the sea correspond to something within him:

> Je te hais, Océan! tes bonds et tes tumultes,
> Mon esprit les retrouve en lui   (ll.5-6)

However much he might long to see the night sky with no stars at all, devoid of all temptation towards the former poetic ordering

---

[1] 'Victor Hugo' (O.C.II: 136).
[2] O.C.I: 335.
[3] All quotations: O.C.I: 278-79.

interpretation, he simply cannot, since patterns spring from his own eye:

> Mais les ténèbres sont elle-mêmes des toiles
> Où vivent, jaillissant de mon œil par milliers,
> Des êtres disparus aux regards familiers.   (ll.12-14)

The temptation to see constellations in the stars is too great, but whereas they were once imposed on the poet by the universal analogy, here they seem, on the contrary, to be a product of *le moi*. In the end, it is the poet's own leaning towards order which foils his attempts at objectivity, since the very source of these patterns is his own mind.

This suggests a fundamental shift in the poet's understanding of the value of apparent order in natural phenomena. Perhaps order is not simply bound to the universal analogy; perhaps, rather, it is a product of the poet's own gaze. In the 1862 additions to the prose poem 'Le Crépuscule du soir', twilight creates a veil as if providing a glimpse of the spectre of the old poetics, much as in 'Un Fantôme':

On dirait encore une de ces robes étranges de danseuses, où une gaze transparente et sombre laisse entrevoir les splendeurs amorties d'une jupe éclatante, comme sous le noir présent transperce le délicieux passé; et les étoiles vacillantes d'or et d'argent, dont elle est semée, représentent ces feux de la fantaisie qui ne s'allument bien que sous le deuil profond de la Nuit.[1]

Here the stars no longer represent meaningful constellations. They are simply 'ces feux de la fantaisie', like the 'fantasmagories' which the poet imagines in the clouds in 'La Soupe et les nuages'.[2]

This might suggest a sort of success, as if order had been recuperated by the poet from a distorting theological framework and re-situated in the artistic gaze. Indeed, in the 1859 *Salon* the artist, 'un homme imaginatif', declares: 'La nature est laide, et je préfère les monstres de ma fantaisie à la trivialité positive'.[3] Yet later in the same text Baudelaire qualifies fantasy as personal, idiosyncratic – a product of *hasard* and *le moi*, and therefore poetically risky:

---

[1] O.C.I: 312.
[2] O.C.I: 350.
[3] III, 'La Reine des facultés' (O.C.II: 620).

Mais la fantaisie est vaste comme l'univers multiplié par tous les êtres pensants qui l'habitent. Elle est la première chose venue interprétée par le premier venu; et, si celui-là n'a pas l'âme qui jette une lumière magique et surnaturelle sur l'obscurité naturelle des choses, elle est une inutilité horrible, elle est la première venue souillée par le premier venu. Ici donc, plus d'analogie, sinon de hasard; mais au contraire trouble et contraste, un champ bariolé par l'absence d'une culture régulière.[1]

Fantasy and *le moi*, therefore, endanger Art since they replace absolute values with a possibly infinite number of different personal interpretations. Significantly, this danger is compared to that of the prose poem: 'la fantaisie est d'autant plus dangereuse qu'elle est plus facile et plus ouverte; dangereuse comme la poésie en prose, comme le roman', 'comme toute liberté absolue'.[2] In the absence of the structural guarantee of verse which maintains the universal analogy, prose poetry risks presenting its poet's interpretative authority as mere fantasy. Indeed, in 'La Fausse monnaie', the narrator, 'tirant toutes les déductions possibles de toutes les hypothèses possibles', admits: 'ainsi ma fantaisie allait son train'.[3]

In 1846 Baudelaire explains the dangers of *le moi* which introduces doubt and instability into the aesthetic hierarchy:

Cette glorification de l'individu a nécessité la division infinie du territoire de l'art. La liberté absolue et divergente de chacun, la division des efforts et le fractionnement de la volonté humaine ont amené cette faiblesse, ce doute.[4]

However, in 1859 he offers one alternative to the equally untenable poetic positions of the *positiviste*, with his faith in absolutes, and the *imaginatif*, with his equally unsatisfactory acceptance of the relative. This solution is the *poncif*, the commonly agreed interpretation which is so universal that it becomes a mere cliché.[5] He asks: 'existe-t-il [...] quelque chose de plus charmant, de plus fertile et d'une nature plus positivement *excitante* que le lieu commun?'.[6] The notion also features in his *carnets*, as Baudelaire tells himself: 'Créer un poncif, c'est le génie. Je dois créer un poncif'.[7] In the *Salon* Baudelaire

---

[1] O.C.II: 644-45.
[2] O.C.II: 644.
[3] O.C.I: 324.
[4] *Salon de 1846*, XVII, 'Des Ecoles et des ouvriers' (O.C.II: 492).
[5] *Salon de 1859*, IV, 'Le Gouvernement de l'imagination' (O.C.II: 628).
[6] *Salon de 1859*, I, 'L'Artiste moderne' (O.C.II: 609); Baudelaire's italics.
[7] 'Fusées' XIII, O.C.I: 662.

stresses the need for an impression of universality in poetry, as the notion of 'une impression poétique, religieuse, universelle', suggests a highly significant synonymy between the three adjectives.[1]

Having realized the possibility of recuperating the notion of order by displacing its value from an external divine absolute to an internal source, Baudelaire also recognizes the need for this source to be common to all mankind if an absolute notion of Poetry is to survive. If this is shared by all mankind, then the poet who presents as poetic his insights into meaningful order will not be contradicted, since what seems to be the personal opinion of *le moi* will in fact strike the same chord with every other *moi*, tapping into a common well of poeticity. This idea pre-occupies Baudelaire in his *carnets*, as he writes: 'Moi, c'est tous; Tous, c'est moi', or more obliquely: 'De la vaporisation et de la centralisation du *Moi*. Tout est là'.[2] Once *le moi* as source of mere fantasy has been vaporized, an absolute *Moi* can become the source of poetic meaning. Of 'Le Crépuscule du soir', Chesters observes: 'the stars are made to represent the workings of the human imagination'.[3] Thus the poet's obsession with order, which so frustrates him in 'Obsession', actually leads him towards a possible solution to the problem of interpretative instability in prose poetry.

Let us look again at Baudelaire's remark in the first 'Projet de préface', written around 1860: 'le rythme et la rime répondent dans l'homme aux immortels besoins de monotonie, de symétrie et de surprise'.[4] There is no unstable authorial *moi* here, only man with his 'immortels besoins', and so it is likely that the order to which the poet is drawn will satisfy all his fellows. If the poetry of the universal analogy was defined by formal ordering elements, it is not because God created an ordered universe. Rather, this passage implies, it is because of a fundamental leaning in mankind towards order, which the surprise of certain 'imprévus désastres' protects from the *ennui* of predictability. By extension, man cannot conceive of an absolute, be it divine or aesthetic, without the notion of perfect order, devoid of the imperfections which its ideal status overcomes. Thus Baudelaire insists in the Poe criticism of the late 1850s: 'le principe de la poésie

---

[1] V, 'Religion, histoire, fantaisie' (O.C.II: 634).
[2] O.C.I: 651 and 676.
[3] *The Poetics of Craft*, p.168.
[4] O.C.I: 182.

est, strictement et simplement, l'aspiration humaine vers une beauté supérieure'.[1]

This fundamental shift in Baudelaire's understanding of the significance of rhythm allows a new interpretation of the marine images of his earlier verse poems. The significance of the regular rhythms and *bercements* lies not in the divine guarantee, but rather, in the human mind itself, whose natural penchant towards order and regularity is satisfied by the observation of these structural patterns. 'Fusées', from the 1860s, shows a newly refined comprehension of the source of aesthetic beauty. The human mind, inclined to appreciate order over disorder, is charmed by the evidence of order in the object, but it is only within our imagination that this order assumes poetic significance:

> Je crois que le charme infini et mystérieux qui gît dans la contemplation d'un navire, et surtout d'un navire en mouvement, tient, dans le premier cas, à la régularité et à la symétrie qui sont un des besoins primordiaux de l'esprit humain, au même degré que la complication et l'harmonie, – et, dans le second cas, à la multiplication successive et à la génération de toutes les courbes et figures imaginaires opérées dans l'espace par les éléments réels de l'objet.[2]

The poet, therefore, does not simply observe the object itself, the rocking ship, but he uses its periodic motion as the inspiration for seeing imaginary figures traced in the air. Elsewhere the same process is applied to a carriage as observed by the artist:

> Dans quelque attitude qu'elle soit jetée, avec quelque allure qu'elle soit lancée, une voiture, comme un vaisseau, emprunte au mouvement une grâce mystérieuse et complexe très difficile à sténographier. Le plaisir que l'œil de l'artiste en reçoit est tiré, ce semble, de la série de figures géométriques que cet objet, déjà si compliqué, navire ou carrosse, engendre successivement et rapidement dans l'espace.[3]

Thus the apparent order of the exterior object alone does not constitute Poetry. Poetry lies only in the significance which order assumes in the imagination of the observer.

These two passages contain a slight inconsistency which is vital to Baudelaire's prose poetics. In the first, regularity is said to fulfil

---

[1] 'Notes nouvelles sur Edgar Poe' (O.C.II: 334).
[2] O.C.I: 663.
[3] *Le Peintre de la vie moderne*, XIII, 'Les Voitures' (O.C.II: 724).

'l'esprit humain', whereas in the second it is 'l'œil de l'artiste' which is satisfied. Do all humans, we wonder, possess an artistic eye? This question, as we shall see, is fundamental to the recuperation of Poetry from the universal analogy by Baudelaire, Rimbaud and Mallarmé. In the 1859 *Salon*, Baudelaire considers the common features that unite 'une foule d'individus différents'. The familiar notion of order returns, satisfying a fundamental need in yet a third figure:

Il est évident que les rhétoriques et les prosodies ne sont pas des tyrannies inventées arbitrairement, mais une collection de règles réclamées par l'organisation même de l'être spirituel.[1]

'L'homme' is now replaced by a mysterious 'être spirituel'. Who is this spiritual being whom order is meant to satisfy? Are we all spiritual beings, sensitive to a higher realm of meaning? Certainly, the cast of motley characters in the prose poems would suggest not. In 1858 we are told: 'Comme les différents métiers réclament différents outils, les différents objets de recherche spirituelle exigent leurs facultés correspondantes', but not all mankind is predisposed towards such spiritual investigation.[2] Is this 'être spirituel' perhaps to be seen as the poet himself, or his readers who possess more refined taste than their fellows? The need for a universal poetic sentiment, for a certain agreement between the artistic *moi* and all mankind, suggests that this too is unsatisfactory.

In the prose poems the adjective *spirituel* certainly seems to designate a poetic sensibility, from 'Le Vieux saltimbanque' with its 'homme occupé de travaux spirituels', to the wondrous 'Chambre double', 'une chambre véritablement *spirituelle*', italicized as if to highlight its importance. With its 'Idole' veiled in muslin, the room allows another return to the former rhythmic illusion. Here 'l'esprit sommeillant est bercé' and eternal monotony inspires not *ennui*, but delight, in a fleeting echo of metrical rhythm, an *alexandrin à coupe épique*: 'minute par minut [e], seconde par seconde'.[3] In *Le Peintre de la vie moderne* Baudelaire highlights the spirituality of the artifice celebrated in the post-illusory verse poems: 'la haute spiritualité de la toilette', 'la majesté superlative des formes artificielles' and 'leur

---

[1] O.C.II: 626-27.
[2] 'Théophile Gautier' (O.C.II: 112).
[3] O.C.I: 295 and 280-81.

dégoût pour le réel'.[1] Thus Poetry is a spiritual endeavour, now synonymous with a poetic yearning in man. Yet this poetic sentiment must be both universal and somehow exclusive, and the relationship between the artist and mankind is henceforth a problematic one over which Baudelaire maintains an air of mystery. This replaces the obsolete religious mystery of infinity and unity explored in the Hugo essay[2] with an equally irresolvable question: the necessary mystery of Poetry itself.

Authorial insight and poetic mystery

We have discerned a clear development in Baudelaire's aesthetics from an externally meaningful order to an untenable experiment with the poetic potential of chance, followed by a re-definition of order as internally meaningful for all mankind. Yet although we all have the potential to sense poeticity in phenomena or indeed, in a text, it appears that only some of us, the *êtres spirituels*, are inclined to search. And so begins the greatest achievement of the prose poet: a mischievous re-mystification of the poetic idea which provokes his readers into a search for what we hope to be absolute, universal values of poeticity. Surely, we assume, the poet knows what Poetry is, despite occasional critical rejection of certain poems as unpoetic. If Poetry is to survive its plunge into the *gouffre*, the poet must restore his authorial superiority which the interpretative instability has challenged. He must maintain the paradoxical notion that poeticity is both a fundamental human quality, yet one to which only a privileged few have access, as if the artist enjoyed a keener insight into our collective soul. Indeed, this leads us back to perhaps the most traditional poetic notion of all, which many poetry enthusiasts happily accept. Previously, the poet's authority came from a superior insight into the universal analogy, a fiction maintained the length of Banville's *Les Exilés*. Now it comes from privileged authorial sensitivity to the equally mysterious notion of Poetry itself. After 1859 Baudelaire repeatedly insists that the meaning of natural phenomena can only be decided by the artist, as he declares: 'un site naturel n'a de valeur que le sentiment actuel que l'artiste y sait mettre'.[3] Nature is

---

[1] XI, 'Eloge du maquillage' (O.C.II: 716).
[2] 'Victor Hugo' (O.C.II: 137-38). See also page 22 of the present study.
[3] *Salon de 1859*, VII, 'Le Paysage' (O.C.II: 660).

but 'un amas incohérent de matériaux que l'artiste est invité à associer et à mettre en ordre'.[1] There is no underlying significance to natural phenomena which present only a disordered mass with which poetic order might be created. The poetic imagination is the source of all significance, and the word *imagination* recurs obsessively in Baudelaire's post-illusory theory, sixty-nine times in the *Salon de 1859*.[2]

The prose poems themselves maintain this hierarchy. In 'La Fausse monnaie', the 'éloquence muette de ces yeux suppliants' can only be interpreted correctly by 'l'homme sensible qui sait y lire'.[3] In 'Les Veuves', as the poet studies 'ces rides profondes et nombreuses', he concludes that only 'un œil expérimenté [...] déchiffre tout de suite les innombrables légendes d'amour trompé'.[4] In 'Le Joujou du pauvre', we learn that 'l'œil du connaisseur devine une peinture idéale sous un vernis de carrossier'.[5] And finally, in 'Les Foules', since the poet alone, 'le poète actif et fécond', knows the inherent meaninglessness of all things, he is the sole judge of their worth: 'Pour lui seul, tout est vacant; et si de certaines places paraissent lui être fermées, c'est qu'à ses yeux elles ne valent pas la peine d'être visitées'.[6]

Until this point, it was the poet of 'A une heure du matin', 'Le Confiteor de l'artiste' or 'Le Fou et la Vénus' who had been forced to search for aesthetic stability, like the disillusioned narrator of *Gaspard de la nuit* who tells the mysterious stranger his occupation: 'Poète, si c'est poète que d'avoir cherché l'art!'.[7] In 'Fusées', however, Baudelaire declares his search at an end: 'J'ai trouvé la définition du Beau, – de mon Beau'.[8] The capital 'B' elevates the personal aesthetic ideal to the same status as the former divine Ideal. By restoring the necessary notion of authorial superiority, Baudelaire solves the

---

[1] Cut from 'Peintures murales d'Eugène Delacroix' (1861) since re-used in *L'Œuvre et la vie d'Eugène Delacroix* (1863) (O.C.II: 752).
[2] I am grateful to Graham Robb for a copy of his unpublished article 'Baudelaire: Révolutions et contre-révolution', which includes this statistic.
[3] O.C.I: 323.
[4] O.C.I: 292.
[5] O.C.I: 304-5.
[6] O.C.I: 291.
[7] *Gaspard de la nuit*, p.60.
[8] O.C.I: 657.

problem of his own worrying search for poeticity by inciting his reader to do it instead. In the first 'Projet de préface', for example, he disingenuously asks 'quelques questions très simples' such as: 'qu'est-ce que la Poésie? quel est son but?'.[1] By mischievously refusing to give the answer, claiming that it is too obvious to mention, Baudelaire challenges us to identify constant, absolute values of poeticity.

The prose poet himself operates a similar mystification, as explanations for the myriad questions posed continually elude the reader. When the hapless father of 'Les Dons des fées', 'sans doute un de ces raisonneurs si communs, incapable de s'élever jusqu'à la logique de l'Absurde', asks the fairies: 'pourquoi?', he is met only with the eternally elusive: 'Parce que! parce que!'.[2] Prose poetry itself now obeys this 'logique de l'Absurde', or the 'singulière logique' of 'Mademoiselle Bistouri', eluding our attempts to reason our way towards poeticity.[3] In 'A une heure du matin', the poet reflects on a day in which he completely subverts the notion of meaningful action, refusing, or unable, to explain his motives: 'm'être vanté (pourquoi?) de plusieurs vilaines actions que je n'ai jamais commises, et avoir lâchement nié quelques autres méfaits que j'accomplis avec joie'.[4] The poet of 'Le Mauvais vitrier' claims to be unable to explain the motives for his actions: 'Il me serait d'ailleurs impossible de dire pourquoi'.[5] And although the poet of 'Les Yeux des pauvres' might attempt an explanation, he infuriatingly claims that his companion would not understand: 'Ah! Vous voulez savoir pourquoi je vous hais aujourd'hui. Il vous sera sans doute moins facile de le comprendre qu'à moi de vous l'expliquer'.[6]

In 'Les Veuves', confronted with the widows' sorrow, the poet asks the strange question, 'Quelle est la veuve la plus triste et la plus attristante?', only to reply 'Je ne sais'.[7] The question suggests there is a hierarchy between the widows, in the same way as aesthetic considerations rest upon a hierarchy of beauty. However, the poet refuses to conclude. This highlights the difficulty of deciding on the

---

[1] O.C.I: 182.
[2] O.C.I: 307.
[3] O.C.I: 307 and 355.
[4] O.C.I: 288.
[5] O.C.I: 286.
[6] O.C.I: 317.
[7] O.C.I: 293.

criteria by which one defines a hierarchical system, yet it simultaneously hints that one exists. Similarly, observing 'La Belle Dorothée', the poet asks, for no obvious reason, 'Pourquoi a-t-elle quitté sa case?'.[1] Yet the poetic reason for such a question is clear: by asking these questions, the poet creates his own mysteries, and the asking pre-supposes an answer for which the reader must search. In the same way, a prose poem asks a disturbed reader: *pourquoi la poésie a-t-elle quitté sa forme?*, inspiring a search for new values of poeticity which, as we shall see later in this chapter, is to be carried out in the form itself. Rather than searching a mute universe for meaning, the poet is now free to posit his own mysteries to which only he, perhaps, has the key. In prose poetry, absurdity and inexplicability act as a new poetic veil by instigating a search for problematized meaning. The poet himself replaces the divine absolute as the privileged guardian of poetic essence, and in order to guard the necessary mystery of poeticity, he remains mysterious. 'L'Etranger' transposes the notion of mystery from an inscrutable divine to the 'homme énigmatique' who refuses to give his interlocutor a straight answer.[2] This cloud-lover is later identified, in 'Perte d'auréole', as the poet himself.

The narrator of 'Mademoiselle Bistouri' emphasizes the pleasure of mystery, delighting in the tension it creates, the anticipation of a resolution, the hunt for an explanation: 'J'aime passionnément le mystère, parce que j'ai toujours l'espoir de le débrouiller'.[3] This is precisely the attitude which the reader of the prose poems must adopt. We are invited to participate in a similarly delicious search, to scrutinize the poems for clues as to the nature of Poetry, pursuing a particularly elusive, non-committal narrator. This narrator constantly confronts us with 'les actes les plus absurdes et souvent même les plus dangereux', which echoes the expression of 1859, 'dangereuse comme la poésie en prose'.[4] His only explanation, however, is: 'l'esprit de mystification qui, chez quelques personnes, n'est pas le résultat d'un travail ou d'une combinaison, mais d'une inspiration fortuite'.[5] It is

---

[1] O.C.I: 327.
[2] O.C.I: 277.
[3] O.C.I: 353.
[4] 'Le Mauvais vitrier' (O.C.I: 285) and Salon de 1859, V, 'Religion, Histoire, Fantaisie' (O.C.II: 644).
[5] 'Le Mauvais vitrier' (O.C.I: 286).

this 'esprit de mystification' which defines the poet's role in re-motivating the necessary mystery of poeticity once the formal veil is removed, and the divine guarantee banished.

Jacques Derrida discusses at length the narrator's 'misérable cerveau, toujours occupé à chercher midi à quatorze heures'.[1] As he explains, this expression means: 'se torturer l'esprit pour trouver ce qui, par définition, ne peut pas se trouver là ou on le cherche, et surtout pas au moment où on le cherche', 'travailler de façon fatigante à chercher ce qui ne se trouve pas au lieu où cela devrait naturellement se trouver'.[2] We might usefully apply this concept to the question of the prose poems' poeticity. The reader searches for clues to solve the mystery of what makes them poetic, signposts to what we assume lies just beyond us, but never so far that we abandon our search. It is crucial that the poet encourage, exploit and maintain the reader's curiosity. Although their poeticity might not be obvious, we must continue to believe it is in there somewhere, if only we knew where and how to look. To cite Derrida out of context: 'la possibilité de ce secret est lisible sans que le secret puisse jamais être accessible'.[3] Poetry can henceforth be defined as the pleasure of the search for meaning which must not be allowed to come to an end. The task of the prose poet is to prolong indefinitely the journey by which we travel towards poeticity, the hope inspired by the *départ éternel* of 'Le Voyage', 'L'Invitation au voyage' or 'Les Vocations', whose musicians are constantly on the move, fixed 'nulle part'.[4]

'Déjà!' warns of the dangers of allowing such a journey to reach a conclusion. Like the reader of prose poetry, the poet enjoys his journey in unknown waters, which allows him the pleasure of a search for significance in the unfamiliar: 'contempler l'autre côté du firmament et déchiffrer l'alphabet céleste'. Arrival, however, brings disappointment, and the poet sighs: 'Moi seul j'étais triste,

---

[1] 'La Fausse monnaie' (O.C.I: 324). Significantly, the same expression is used in the *Salon de 1859*, where Baudelaire speculates on the possible meanings of Frémiet's 'Cheval de saltimbanque' before being told off by a bourgeois, with his faith in 'objective' reality: 'Un voisin que j'irrite veut bien m'avertir que je cherche midi à quatorze heures, et que cela représente simplement le cheval d'un saltimbanque' (VIII, 'Sculpture', O.C.II: 676).
[2] *Donner le temps I: La fausse monnaie*, Paris: Galilée, 1991, pp.51 and 161.
[3] ibid., p.193.
[4] O.C.I: 334.

inconcevablement triste'.[1] Whereas the poet of 'Le Voyage' announced the plunge into the *gouffre* with hope and enthusiasm for poetic novelty, the prose poet realizes that the search for this novelty must not be allowed to come to an end. In order to preserve the mystery of Poetry, to allow Poetry to remain an untouchable absolute, our curiosity must be maintained yet never entirely satisfied. It is imperative that, whilst we suspect that the poet knows what Poetry is, we allow the exact poeticity of form to elude us, and it is in this light, as we shall see, that the form of Baudelaire's prose poems can most fruitfully be read.

The problematization of poetic form

According to the former verse illusion, Poetry was defined on a purely formal level. It was to be recognized by the formal signposts of metre and rhyme, or rhythm and harmony, whose significance was guaranteed by the universal analogy. However, in 1861 Baudelaire imagines the mistake of another poetically misguided friend whose work, despite these formal signposts, does not fulfil the mysterious poetic requirement:

Un de mes amis a travaillé à un poème anonyme sur l'invention d'un dentiste; aussi bien les vers auraient pu être bons et l'auteur plein de conviction. Cependant qui oserait dire que, même en ce cas c'eût été de la poésie?[2]

According to the formal definition, anyone with a minimum of training could create Poetry simply by writing in metre and rhyme, yet for Baudelaire *de bons vers* are no longer necessarily synonymous with Poetry. In the 'Projets de préface' he teasingly declares that:

Appuyé sur mes principes et disposant de la science que je me charge de lui enseigner en vingt leçons, tout homme devient capable de composer une tragédie qui ne sera pas plus sifflée qu'une autre, ou d'aligner un poème de longueur nécessaire pour être aussi ennuyeux que tout poème épique connu.[3]

The implication is that true values of poeticity are not found in the outward formal signs by which we are used to recognizing them.

---

[1] Both quotations: O.C.I: 337 and 338 respectively.
[2] 'Auguste Barbier' (O.C.II: 145).
[3] O.C.I: 183.

Familiar form is no longer a stable guarantee of Poetry. Indeed, it is vital to Poetry's survival that the poet destroys this notion.

Once again, the preface to Baudelaire's beloved *Gaspard de la nuit* contains a similar idea, as the devil, incognito, tells the narrator: 'Le diable existe'. However, he does not assume the form by which we traditionally recognize him: 'Nulle part le diable en cornes et en queue'.[1] Poetry is not to be found in familiar forms, but it does exist, and this is the mystery that prose poetry inaugurates. *Nulle part la poésie en rythmes et en rimes*, it cries, *mais la poésie existe*! Poetry also plays hide-and-seek with the reader, occasionally disappearing like Bertrand's devil who slyly confides: '[le diable] n'existe pas'.[2] It is within this dilemma of the (non-) existence of Poetry that the formal characteristics of the prose poems assume all their value, and that the faith and resolve of the reader are tested to the full.

Just as pure regularity is to be avoided in verse, so too prose poetic form must not be allowed to settle or become predictable. Baudelaire realises in the 1860s that *nombre* is no longer the privilege of verse; since rhetorical structures spring from the same human source as prosody, *nombre* can also be found in prose texts: '*Tout* est nombre. Le nombre est dans *tout*. Le nombre est dans l'individu. L'ivresse est un nombre.'[3] Simply writing in prose, therefore, is not enough to safeguard Poetry, and the *nombre* of prose must be problematized in the same way as that of verse if Poetry is to avoid another crisis of formal fixity and predictability. Just as Baudelaire's later verse problematizes metrical rhythm, *Le Spleen de Paris* presents a revolutionary notion of form as a process rather than a product. This is articulated through two recurrent symbols of the prose poetic endeavour: the urban model and the clouds.

Baudelaire's remark in the *dédicace* indicates that the structural complexity of the urban landscape was the inspiration behind his prose poems: 'C'est surtout de la fréquentation des villes énormes, c'est du croisement de leurs innombrables rapports que naît cet idéal obsédant'.[4] Whereas nature was always assumed to be a divine creation, the city itself is purely man-made. It is obviously structured,

---

[1] *Gaspard de la nuit*, p.73.
[2] ibid., p.75.
[3] 'Fusées' I (O.C.I: 649); Baudelaire's italics.
[4] O.C.I: 276.

proof of a penchant in creative man, architect or poet, towards order. However, it is not simply in the static plan of a city that the inspiration for prose poetics is to be found, but specifically in the 'croisement' of 'innombrables rapports'. The 'rapports' are multiple in a city constantly in movement, and this constant evolution, this resistance to settling down in one realisable form means that they are literally 'innombrables', inexpressible in any fixed formal *nombre*. The verse poet of 'Le Cygne' sighs: 'la forme d'une ville / Change plus vite, hélas! que le cœur d'un mortel' (l.7-8). For the prose poet, however, this is a cause not for dismay, but rather, for poetic enthusiasm.

In the 1859 *Salon*, Baudelaire praises Méryon's Parisian etchings for their poetic quality, which is the result of multiple drives, always clashing, never fixed yet *sur le chantier*, in constant process towards a deferred state of completion:

J'ai rarement vu représentée avec plus de poésie la solennité naturelle d'une ville immense. Les majestés de la pierre accumulée, les clochers *montrant du doigt le ciel*, les obélisques de l'industrie vomissant contre le firmament leurs coalitions de fumée, les prodigieux échafaudages des monuments en réparation, appliquant sur le corps solide de l'architecture leur architecture à jour d'une beauté si paradoxale, le ciel tumultueux, chargé de colère et de rancune, la profondeur des perspectives augmentée par la pensée de tous les drames qui y sont contenus, aucun des éléments complexes dont se compose le douloureux et glorieux décor de la civilisation n'était oublié.[1]

Such is the importance of this passage to Baudelaire's new aesthetics that he also includes it in a letter to Hugo and repeats it word for word in his 1862 article 'Peintres et aquafortistes', preceded by the following description of Whistler's Thames etchings: 'merveilleux fouillis d'agrès, de vergues, de cordages; chaos de brumes, de fourneaux et de fumées tirebouchonnées: poésie profonde et compliquée d'une vaste capitale'.[2] Contrary to much critical opinion, the prose poems' poeticity springs not simply from the disorder of multiplicity, the 'chaos de boue et de neige', the 'mille carosses', 'ce tohu-bohu', 'ce vacarme',[3] or 'ce chaos mouvant' of the busy street,[4] but rather, from the countless 'rapports' to be observed therein. This disordered, unartistic swarm of multiplicity actually creates an

---

[1] 'Le Paysage', VII (O.C.II, 666-67); Baudelaire's italics.
[2] Letter of 13 December 1859 (Corr. I: 628), and O.C.II: 740.
[3] 'Un Plaisant' (O.C.I: 279).
[4] 'Perte d'auréole' (O.C.I: 352).

impression of poetic harmony in the observer: 'Il admire l'éternelle beauté et l'harmonie de la vie dans les capitales, harmonie si providentiellement maintenue dans le tumulte de la liberté humaine'.[1] Restored to his elevated position in 'Le Crépuscule du soir', the poet maintains the necessary distance which transforms this urban discord into harmony:

Cependant du haut de la montagne arrive à mon balcon, à travers les nues transparentes du soir, un grand hurlement, composé d'une foule de cris discordants, que l'espace transforme en une lugubre harmonie.[2]

Once again, it is distance which allows discord to create the mysterious impression of poetic harmony, the same distance which separates us from our goal on our search for poeticity. Just because the poet writes in prose, without the former source of harmony, rhyme, we should not be so quick to assume that Baudelaire's prose poetics is simply one of discord alone. This idea stems from a gross over-simplification of, and an anachronistic attachment to, the obsolete verse/prose dichotomy. Nor is harmony alone the goal, but rather, a constantly evolving series of fleeting poetic correspondences.

The clouds in the post-1858 texts present the same unsettled form. In 'Le Voyage', both natural landscapes and urban forms are surpassed by the clouds, products of chance:

Les plus riches cités, les plus grands paysages,
Jamais ne contenaient l'attrait mystérieux
De ceux que le hasard fait avec les nuages. (ll.65-67)

Since the poet initially wishes to embrace the poetic potential of chance, the apparently random constructions visible in the sky provide the perfect metaphor for a prose poetics which refuses the universal analogy. The mysterious figure of 'L'Etranger', therefore, has only one preoccupation: 'J'aime les nuages... les nuages qui passent... là-bas... là-bas... les merveilleux nuages!'.[3] In 'Le Port', 'l'architecture mobile des nuages' amuses the poet endlessly, since the clouds present a structure which is constantly in a process of becoming, and

---

[1] *Le Peintre de la vie moderne* (O.C.II: 692).
[2] O.C.I: 311.
[3] O.C.I: 277.

which never settles on one fixed form.[1] The verse poet of 'Les Plaintes d'un Icare' failed 'Pour avoir étreint des nuées' (1.4). In contrast, the prose poet does not try to embrace a form which refuses to be fixed, but rather, observes from a distance the clouds' perpetual formal evolution. In this way the poet can project various interpretations onto them – the simple game of finding shapes in the clouds – which constantly elude reductive finality.

In 1860's 'Un Mangeur d'opium', cloud formations in constant movement provide similar stimulation for the poetic imagination: 'D'étonnantes et monstrueuses architectures se dressaient dans son cerveau, semblables à ces constructions mouvantes que l'œil du poète aperçoit dans les nuages colorés par le soleil couchant'.[2] A similar sunset image from the 1859 *Salon* underlines its importance to Baudelaire's poetics: 'les bouffées de ma pipe qui sont nuancées par le soleil couchant'.[3] This sunset recalls 'Le Coucher du soleil romantique' where the universal analogy ('le Dieu qui se retire', 1.9) gives way to the 'ténèbres' (1.12) of poetic uncertainty. In this new poetics, the poet enjoys the interpretative freedom to see poeticity in exquisitely impalpable forms. Similarly, in 'Les Bienfaits de la lune' (1863) the poet recovers from the 'cauchemar multiforme' of 'Le Gouffre' (1862), and claims to love 'l'eau informe et multiforme'.[4] Whereas, under the universal analogy, the sea displayed clearly recognizable regular rhythms, it now presents a succession of forms constantly in motion. Never settling on one alone, it gives the impression of formlessness, or form as a continual process.

In 'La Soupe et les nuages' the poet observes similarly intangible, constantly shifting clouds through an open window: 'par la fenêtre ouverte de la salle à manger je contemplais les mouvantes architectures que Dieu fait avec les vapeurs, les merveilleuses constructions de l'impalpable'.[5] Interestingly, God reappears, replacing *le hasard* as creator of the clouds. However, just as the poet of 'Obsession' realizes that the significance of the stars comes from his own eye, the poetic gaze and God are no longer incompatible. The

[1] O.C.I: 344.
[2] *Les Paradis artificiels* (O.C.I: 482).
[3] I, 'L'Artiste moderne' (O.C.II: 613). For other occurrences of the sunset image, see page 99 of the present work, note 5.
[4] O.C.I: 341.
[5] O.C.I: 350.

Creator may well have made the clouds, but the responsibility for their interpretation lies in the poetic gaze. This usurps the obsolete universal analogy which confused creation of form with responsibility for meaning. Similarly, the prose poet creates a text devoid of the obvious markers of metre and rhyme which, like the sea, might appear 'informe et multiforme'. Responsibility for the poems' interpretation lies in the reader's response to a text, the meaning of which the author himself claims is beyond his control.

Poetry and the search for rhythm

Like God offering the clouds up for interpretation by the poetic gaze, the prose poet refuses the traditional link between his authorial authority and the reader's interpretation of the text. In the 1840s, Baudelaire had insisted on this very link, praising three artists in the 1845 *Salon* since: 'ils disent juste ce qu'ils veulent dire'.[1] Similarly, lauding Delacroix in the 1846 *Salon*, he declares: 'Une chose heureusement trouvée est la simple conséquence d'un bon raisonnement [...] tout a sa raison d'être, si le tableau est bon'.[2] For the Baudelaire of the 1840s there is only one correct way to see a work of art, hence the disadvantage of sculpture:

C'est en vain que le sculpteur s'efforce de se mettre à un point de vue unique; le spectateur, qui tourne autour de la figure, peut choisir cent points de vue différents, excepté le bon, et il arrive souvent, ce qui est humiliant pour l'artiste, qu'un hasard de lumière, un effet de lampe, découvrent une beauté qui n'est pas celle à laquelle il avait songé. Un tableau n'est que ce qu'il veut.[3]

Poe, the major poetic influence on Baudelaire's later aesthetic theories, claims in 'The Poetic Principle': 'it is an obvious rule of Art that effects should be made to spring as directly as possible from their causes'.[4] However, when Poe dissects this theory in 'The Philosophy of Composition', his mischievously ironic tone suggests that his insistence on the absolute link between cause and effect is a playful mystification. Yet this mystification reinforces the fiction which we

---

[1] O.C.II: 356.
[2] O.C.II: 432.
[3] O.C.II: 487.
[4] *Complete Poems and Selected Essays*, ed. by Richard Gray, London: Everyman, 1993, p.160.

are keen to believe: that the significance we attach to the carefully scrutinized form is a desired poetic effect of the author, the guarantee of poeticity, and not simply a fantasy of our own confection.

The prose poet, however, abandons his text to the reader's gaze, since there is not one absolute Beauty to impose on the reader, but rather, a plethora of possibilities to be sought and relished. Appearing now to accept the sculptor's humiliation of 1846, Baudelaire declares in 1859: 'l'esprit du vrai poète doit être ouvert à toutes les beautés'.[1] He claims in the *dédicace* to be unsure of what exactly he has achieved: 'quelque chose (si cela peut s'appeler *quelque chose*)', an 'accident dont tout autre que moi s'enorgueillirait sans doute, mais qui ne peut qu'humilier profondément un esprit qui regarde comme le plus grand honneur du poète d'accomplir *juste* ce qu'il a projeté de faire'.[2] Baudelaire re-motivates the mystery of poeticity in the most effective way possible, pleading his own ignorance, denying his reader any explanation of either the poetic intentions or features of his prose poems whilst proclaiming, nevertheless, that these are *Petits Poèmes en prose*. Similarly, in the 1861 essay on Wagner, he asserts: 'La poésie a existé, s'est affirmée la première, et elle a engendré l'étude des règles'.[3] Poetry, therefore, is posited as a mysterious given and any investigation of what defines Poetry can only come, necessarily, *après coup*. We sense that it exists, the poet insists, before we know how it is to be recognized, and our task as readers of the prose poems is to search for the signs which maintain our faith in the texts' poeticity.

Much analysis of the prose poems has concentrated, therefore, on a search for values of poeticity: how do we know that these texts are poetic? Which common features guarantee their status? How can we be sure what makes a prose poem poetic? Answers are most often assumed to lie in the form alone, and for this reason I have preferred to leave the form until last, since formal studies ignoring the vital theme of interpretative instability are dangerously simplistic and reductive. Bernard, for example, proposes 'cette règle du *court poème*' as 'une des lois essentielles du poème en prose'.[4] Contributors

[1] *Salon de 1859*, V, 'Religion, histoire, fantaisie' (O.C.II: 630).
[2] O.C.I: 276; Baudelaire's italics.
[3] O.C.II: 793.
[4] *Le Poème en prose de Baudelaire jusqu'à nos jours*, p.145.

to *The Prose Poem in France: Theory and Practice* offer a variety of suggestions. Tzvetan Todorov, searching for 'a transcultural, transhistorical "poeticity"', agrees that brevity must surely be a 'requirement' of the poet's.[1] Michael Riffaterre, supposing that there must be something 'that makes up for the lack of meter in a prose poem', 'the features that substitute for verse', decrees that a prose poem must necessarily contain constant features which define the text as a formal and semiotic unit.[2] Robert Greer Cohn, defining the essence of prose poetry as the intersection of horizontal and vertical elements, even goes so far as to decree that certain *Petits Poèmes en prose* are 'marginal to the genre' which they themselves instigate, a pronouncement which confirms the worst fears of the prose poet.[3] It is striking that every critic, like Hermine Riffaterre, is equally sure that it must be possible to define 'the poetic feature of the text, or what makes this prose a poem'.[4] However, as I hope to have shown, the texts must both maintain our faith and guard their secret. The hope of revealing the key to their poeticity, therefore, must be tempered by an acceptance of the necessary irresolvability of the enterprise, a willingness to be confounded at every turn for the common good: the preservation of the mystery of Poetry. Poetic form remains perpetually one step ahead of the seeker, and manages thereby to maintain our interest, an active search for poeticity to which the vast critical litterature devoted to the prose poems attests.

The most common misconception about rhythm in Baudelaire's prose poems is that, in order to be poetically meaningful, it must imitate the rhythms of verse. This is in no small part due to the infamous description of the new aesthetic Ideal made in the *dédicace*, a dream of 'le miracle d'une prose poétique, musicale sans rythme et sans rime'.[5] Baudelaire suggests that the creation of poetry in a prose text, without the former guarantees of metre and rhyme, would be a miracle. The implication, therefore, is that it is impossible, as if, in the absence of a miracle, prose really did require rhythm and rhyme in order to be poetic. This notion of prose rhythm and rhyme has

---

[1] Ed. by Mary Ann Caws and Hermine Riffaterre, New York: Columbia University Press, 1983; 'Poetry Without Verse', pp.60-78; p.60 and p.69.
[2] 'On The Prose Poem's Formal Features', pp.117-32; pp.117-18.
[3] 'A Prose-Poetry Cross', pp.135-62; p.149.
[4] 'Reading Constants: The Practice of the Prose Poem', pp.98-116; p.108.
[5] O.C.I: 275.

invariably been interpreted as an invitation to search for the phonetic and structural strategies which make this poetic prose 'musical'. Indeed, as we have seen, the prose poetic journey has so far comprised: the realization of the instability of meaning; a consequent search for meaning; and the suggestion, in 'Obsession', that this search will naturally be for recognizable, familiar patterns of order. However, prose poetry also demonstrates that, in the absence of absolute values, the poeticity of any rhythms and harmonies we might find is far from guaranteed.

Of course, the prose poems certainly foreground certain rhythmic and harmonic patterns, in 'Le *Confiteor* de l'artiste' and 'A une heure du matin' to name but two. Yet here the most obviously verse-rhythmic segments articulate not the poeticity of regularity, but precisely the prose poet's despair at the loss of this certainty, and a longing for the rhythmic security he has abandoned. Furthermore, each echo lasts only an instant, and the reader has to work hard for a problematic rhythm by searching for regularity in an uncertain haze of 'e's and vowel sequences.[1] These segments are certainly not the source of the prose poems' poeticity, since, as I hope to have demonstrated, the post-rhythmic poet of the 1860s suspects that the formal guarantee of regularity is a pure fiction, albeit an occasionally desirable one. Naïve critical insistence that the texts' poeticity lies in regular form ignores the poet's own post-rhythmic theory, and his re-definition of rhythm, in the 1860s, as independent of the primitive verse/prose dichotomy. Indeed, in 'Les Veuves', the poet reads 'les innombrables légendes d'amour trompé' in 'ces rides profondes et nombreuses'.[2] This co-existence suggests that at a certain post-illusory point, the distinction between *nombre* and the *innombrable*, which the previous poetics kept carefully separated, is now blurred, preserving a healthy air of mystery around the relationship between rhythm and the poetic idea.

Nevertheless, many critics insist that the poeticity of Baudelaire's prose lies in its verse-rhythmic qualities. Antoine Fongaro confidently informs us: 'Baudelaire, lui, savait qu'il avait farci sa prose avec des rythmes de la versification', wondering in a startlingly simplistic aside: 'Est-ce pour cela qu'il a mis "Poème" dans le titre?'. In support

---

[1] See pages 98 and 100 of the present work.
[2] O.C.I: 292.

of his hunch, Fongaro teases the following, variably pertinent, metrical segments from 'Le Poème du hachisch' (1860):

Ne possèdes-tu pas (6) // ce mépris souverain / qui rend l'âme si bonne? (12: 3/3//3/3)
De nouveaux éléments / de plaisir et d'orgueil (12: 3/3//3/3)
À mon implacable appétit (8) //
    d'émotion, / de **co** // nnaissance / et de beauté (12: M6, 4+4+4)
Ce cri culbuterait les anges // disséminés / dans les chemins du ciel (8+10)[1]

Whereas the poet knows that these rhythms no longer define the poetic text, critical thinking shows itself to be stuck in a pre-Baudelairean rut where Poetry really is reducible to a predictable formal definition. Confronted with a prose poem, the reader's natural reaction is to cling to the very definition of poeticity which the prose poet challenges us to relinquish.

In a recent article, Roger Pensom sets out to 'comprendre un peu mieux ce qu'est un "poème en prose"', and formal elements occupy most of his analysis. He interprets numerous rhythmic structures of 'Un hémisphère dans une chevelure' as metrical, such as 'la réalisation toute métrique' of the ternary rhythm: 'tout ce que je vois! tout ce que je sens! tout ce que j'entends'. Yet 5/5/5 is a rare metrical rhythm indeed, and a 4/4/4 reading would be ametrical thanks to the Em6 on 'que'. Similarly, the unit 'parfumée par les fruits, par les feuilles et par la peau humaine' is said to be 'surdéterminée sur le palier métrique'. For Pensom, the phrase 'de chants mélancoliques, d'hommes vigoureux' presents 'une équivalence métrique', while 'dans la nuit de ta chevelure je vois resplendir l'infini de l'azur tropical' contains 'l'interruption d'une série de "pieds anapestiques"', defined as 'une unité métrique de deux ou trois syllabes qui comporte un seul accent de mot'.[2] Cornulier *et al* would insist, however, that metrical rhythm is the privilege of verse alone. Units conforming to these rhythms can exist in prose, of course, and eager critics search for them and identify them, but cannot conceive of poetically meaningful rhythm without resorting to the verse analogy which remains, so long after Baudelaire, an outdated symbol of poeticity.

---

[1] All quotations from 'Segments métriques dans la prose d'*Illuminations*', Presses Universitaires du Mirail-Toulouse, 1993, p.4.
[2] 'Le poème en prose: de Baudelaire à Rimbaud', *French Studies* 56:1 (2002): 15-28; pp.15, 18, 19, 19 and 21 respectively.

This thirst for rhythm can even drive the critic to impose the most tenuous of metrical grids on the texts. Bernard suggests that the reader should apply a metrical *coupe enjambante* after each feminine 'e' in the prose poems, claiming: 'Plus les terminaisons féminines seront nombreuses, plus le rythme, en général, sera balancé', before setting out the first two sentences of 'La Chambre double' in verse format in order to demonstrate: 'Le règne de l'impair est ici évident'.[1] Jean Pellegrin's faith in the poetic significance of rhythm is such that he arranges 'Enivrez-vous' in *vers libres*, claiming that the metrical 'scansion' is clearly marked by punctuation:

Dans *Enivrez-vous*, les virgules marquent bien la scansion: trois ou quatre segments longs (de 12 à 25 'pieds' ou syllabes) sont consacrés au *Temps*, l'ennemi juré de l'ivresse; ils sont enveloppées, assaillis, harcelés par la foule des segments brefs (de 2 à 7 ou 8 syllabes).[2]

Clive Scott feels similarly free to re-arrange the penultimate paragraph of 'Un hémisphère dans une chevelure' as verse, explaining:

I choose a free-verse disposition not only because it gives added definition to the rhythmic segments, but because I believe that this is, in many ways, the new hidden verse that the prose poem proposes. [...] Does not this 'stanza' have a rhythmic concertedness just as great as that to be found in its metrical 'twin'?[3]

Declaring perhaps too categorically that 'any attempts to scan this prose into alexandrines or octosyllables will yield no results', Anne Jamison suggests that, in 'La Chambre double', 'other forms of scansion produce other, less regular, patterns, patterns suggestive of the metrical feet central to English prosody'. Thanks to Baudelaire's knowledge of Poe, 'the "metre" is of course far from regular, but much of it scans into approximations of English metrical feet'.[4] This improbable rhythmic enthusiasm is also applied to texts which do not even claim to be poetic. Barbara Wright, in a discussion of *La Fanfarlo*, asserts: 'The Poet/Dancer sequence of La Fanfarlo is written in metrical prose. It aims at combining the unexpected and the

---

[1] *Le Poème en prose de Baudelaire jusqu'à nos jours*, pp.133 and 138 respectively.
[2] 'Rythmes baudelairiens', *Cahiers de Sémiotique Textuelle* 14 (1988), 51-63; p.57.
[3] *Vers Libre: The Emergence of Free Verse in France 1886-1914*, pp.113-14.
[4] 'Any Where Out of this Verse: Baudelaire's Prose Poetics and the Aesthetics of Transgression', *Nineteenth Century French Studies* 29 (2001): 256-86, pp.273-74.

predictable in a metrical prose best typified by the description of the Dancer's movements, "pleins d'une cadence précise"'.[1] Under careful scrutiny, however, the passage yields little which justifies such a claim. Graham Robb, albeit cautiously, finds similar examples of 'metrical' prose:

> L'on devine, dans *La Fanfarlo*, d'autres souvenirs de l'idylle en vers – des hémistiches et des rythmes de l'alexandrin: 'mais le souvenir n'est qu'une [douleur] nouvelle'; 'la fatigue des songes'; 'où nos yeux clairs riaient à toute la nature'; 'vivait et jouissait'; 'sans bruit et sans orgueil'.[2]

Yet Robb's replacement of 'souffrance' with 'douleur' in the first example, in order to avoid a thirteen-syllable 'line', suggests that the critical eye is perhaps so eager to search for regular rhythm, that it is blind to the necessarily problematic, irresolvable rhythms with which the text preserves its poetic mystery.

Taken out of context, the verse segments inserted at critical points of prose poetic crisis can easily distort Baudelaire's problematization of the relationship between rhythm and Poetry. Having located the following 'hemistich', 'alexandrine' and 'decasyllable' in the prose poems, should we take them as 'metrical prose', proof of the poet's intention to make prose poetic by importing verse rhythms?

(6)   sans dents et sans cheveux /
(6+6)   Consolez-moi par-ci, / caressez-moi par là
(5-5)   Les Chinois voient l'heur / e dans l'œil des chats [3]

Which segments, we might wonder, are meaningful, and which are not? Which ones did the poet 'intend'? How do we know we have found them all? How do we know where to draw the line in our search for meaningful poetic rhythm? To which the prose poet, carefully avoiding any stable declaration of intention, might reply: the search for meaningful rhythm must never come to an end, for the sake of Poetry itself. It is when verse rhythm became predictable that the poetic idea found itself under serious threat, and prose poetry restores the veil over poeticity by problematizing this rhythm.

---

[1] *La Fanfarlo and Le Spleen de Paris*, p.32.
[2] *La poésie de Baudelaire et la poésie française 1838-1852*, Paris: Aubier, 1993, p.34.
[3] O.C.I: 277, 278, 279 and 299 respectively.

Although this critical search for a verse-rhythmic definition of poeticity does an injustice to the complexity and subtlety of the prose poet's formal agenda, it remains, Baudelaire assures us, perfectly natural. As lovers of poetry, as *êtres spirituels*, are critics not naturally pre-disposed, like the poet himself, to see meaningful constellations in the stars? If critics are eager to find rhythmic, structural devices in the prose poems, and interpret them as meaningful sources of poeticity, it is perfectly understandable since they believe in Poetry and retain, consciously or unconsciously, a need for faith in aesthetic absolutes. The vital nuance, then, which Baudelaire suggests we make to our understanding of these rhythms is that we interpret them as evidence, not of an external guarantee of poeticity, but rather, of our own dedication to the poetic and aesthetic Ideal which defines us as lovers of Poetry. In this way study of the prose poems might be allowed to progress from a backward-looking study of 'what makes them poetic' to a more productive study of the mechanisms by which the prose poet encourages us to see them as poetic.

In this context, the commonly abused expression 'prose rhythms' is redundant since the prose poem can present as many rhythmic interpretations as it has readers. Like the sculpture criticized in the 1846 *Salon*, or like nature before the artist's gaze, God and the artist offer up their creations without an absolute guarantee to their meaning. In this light, F. W. Leakey's admiration for 'the unerring sureness of Baudelaire's ear for prose rhythms' is rather a recognition of his own rhythmical observations.[1] The prose poet cannot 'create' a prose rhythm; he can only write prose in which he knows his readers will search for rhythm. He may then exploit this anticipation, sometimes to satisfy, sometimes to disappoint our rhythmic expectations, by foregrounding, complicating and problematizing rhythm to varying degrees. In the 1861 essay on Wagner, Baudelaire insists that, were the verse text removed from Wagner's opera, its poetic quality would survive thanks to a certain formal technique:

En effet, sans poésie, la musique de Wagner serait encore une œuvre poétique, étant douée de toutes les qualités qui constituent une poésie bien faite; explicative par elle-même, tant toutes choses y sont bien unies, conjointes, réciproquement adaptées, et,

---

[1] *Baudelaire and Nature*, Manchester University Press, 1969, p.259.

s'il est permis de faire un barbarisme pour exprimer le superlatif d'une qualité, prudemment *concaténées.*[1]

According to Larousse, concatenation is a 'figure qui consiste à lier plusieurs membres d'une période, au moyen d'un ou de plusieurs mots que l'on emprunte au membre précédent'.[2] This complicates the rhythm by erasing the boundaries between one segment and the next, creating the impression of a structural *flou* which resists being fixed in one form by the analytical eye. Wagner's complex structural concatenation is 'prudent' since it problematizes the search for rhythm, hindering our arrival at a concrete, analyzable formula for poeticity. The prudent prose poet, therefore, operates a similar rhythmical problematization, from the obvious patterns of repetition in 'Les Bienfaits de la lune' and 'Enivrez-vous', to the subtler echoes which close 'Déjà!' and 'Les Bons chiens',[3] and to all rhythmical and lexical concatenations which inspire our curiosity and enthusiasm for Poetry.

Conclusion

The weakness of the inherited regular verse form, in thrall to the universal analogy, was that by defining Poetry as regular rhythm and harmony, it both ignored the unstable poetic value of these notions and de-mystified the essence of Poetry itself. By problematizing the formal signs by which we recognize Poetry, Baudelaire ensures that it escapes our clutches. The prose poem, in this context, stands not simply for 'freedom' and 'fluid rhythms', but rather as a defence of Poetry as an eternally mysterious essence, as Roubaud argues:

L'alexandrin vacillant, le vers *n'est* plus aussi évidemment *la poésie*; l'affaiblissement d'un canon absolu du vers menace. En *rompant* l'identification de la poésie au vers, la naissance du *poème en prose*, loin de préparer l'effacement de la distinction prose/poésie, vise à la préserver en lui donnant un statut absolu, en essence.[4]

Roubaud, as crafty as Baudelaire, makes no attempt to define this essence. This silence is the ultimate achievement of the prose poet: to

---

[1] O.C.II: 803; Baudelaire's italics.
[2] *Grand Dictionnaire Universel du XIXe Siècle*, 4: 825.
[3] In the former, the final paragraph takes up images from four paragraphs earlier; in the latter, it repeats elements from three paragraphs earlier.
[4] *La Vieillesse d'Alexandre*, Paris: Maspero, 1978; Ramsay, 1988, p.109; Roubaud's italics.

have inspired generations of poets, critics and readers to ask the unanswerable question to which we must constantly return: what is Poetry? Baudelaire's prose poems take us deeper into this mystery, lifting the protective formal veil of metre and rhyme only to leave another, altogether more problematic veil in its place: the notion of a poetic rhythm which will forever elude us. Roger Bodart concludes:

> A partir de Baudelaire nous ne savons plus où est la poésie: elle est partout, elle est dans la prose, elle est dans le vers, et c'est là la fécondité de Baudelaire; cette inquiétude qu'il a introduite.[1]

The title *Petits Poèmes en prose* confidently proclaims Poetry to be alive and well, sending us searching for the constants which, we assume, must be discernible, without knowing exactly where. As Jean-Michel Maulpoix observes, 'Se mettant ainsi elle-même en procès, la poésie devient poursuite, et d'abord de sa propre identité'.[2] By insisting that each prose text is poetic, Baudelaire posits poeticity as the sole link between them, and by problematizing this poeticity the prose poems act as a much more efficient veil around the absolute notion of Poetry than verse ever previously could.

From this point onwards, poetry becomes a matter of faith. Whilst many commentators read 'Le Thyrse' as describing the prose poem, with its rigid baton and its 'méandres capricieux' (still the verse/prose dichotomy dominates the analogy), fewer note that the 'thyrse' itself is: 'un emblême sacerdotal dans la main des prêtres ou des prêtresses célébrant la divinité dont ils sont les interprètes et les serviteurs'.[3] The poet wields the prose poem as a symbol of his authority, his superior sensitivity to Poetry, and as readers we must put our faith in his hands. He presents us with a poem, and only our faith allows the text to function as such. Indeed, in the *dédicace* does Baudelaire not tempt us to believe in 'le miracle d'une prose poétique, musicale sans rythme et sans rime'? A miracle is precisely that inexplicable yet undeniable *évidence* which must bypass our reason in order to fuel our faith. Since the poet of 'Déjà!', on arrival in the marvellous new world, is

---

[1] *Journées Baudelaire, Actes du colloque Namur-Bruxelles, 10-13 octobre 1967*, Brussels: Académie Royale de Langue et de Littérature Françaises, 1968; Robert Guiette, 'Vers et prose chez Baudelaire', pp.36-46; discussion, pp.44-45.
[2] *La poésie malgré tout*, Paris: Mercure de France, 1996, p.13.
[3] O.C.I: 335.

'semblable à un prêtre à qui on arracherait sa divinité', the journey of poetic faith must never be allowed to come to an end.[1] In the monetary terms which, as Mallarmé later observes, replace religious faith, Poetry is now a matter of credit, or to borrow an expression from Derrida: 'acte de foi, de crédit, de créance, voire de crédulité'. For certain critics, some texts seem more 'authentic' than others, yet 'tant que de la monnaie passe pour de la (bonne) monnaie, elle n'est tout simplement pas différente de la monnaie que, peut-être, elle contrefait'.[2] Since the poetic endeavour becomes a refusal to allow the satisfactory revelation of constant measures of poeticity, the irresolvable question of authenticity is vital to Baudelaire's defence of Poetry.

In conclusion, Baudelaire saves the poetic idea from obsolescence by a dangerous plunge into the *gouffre* from which he emerges aware of the fundamental instability of the poetic idea. Poetry requires a re-definition of its most basic elements: poet, poem, rhythm and reader, who henceforth undertakes a necessarily irresolvable search for a poetic value constantly deferred by a set of mystificatory mechanisms. The continuing critical interest in the rhythms of poetry in both verse and prose proves the success of the gesture by which Baudelaire saves the poetic idea from extinction, and yet also suggests a failure on the part of many critics to apprehend the full extent of Baudelaire's rhythmic revolution. If rhythm articulates the necessary aesthetic hierarchy by which the people who believe in Poetry, we *êtres spirituels*, find certain structures more beautiful than others, it is imperative that critical understanding of Baudelaire's poetry advance beyond the reductive verse/prose dichotomy. The 'defeat' of which some find evidence in Baudelaire is an inaccurate evaluation of the salutary gesture by which the prose poet makes of poetry an active

---

[1] O.C.I: 338.
[2] *Donner le temps I: La fausse monnaie*, pp.207 and 194.

search for rhythmical values.[1] The fact that even today, we cannot agree on what exactly makes the prose poems poetic, whilst refusing to believe that they might not be, attests to the success of his re-affirmation and rhythmical re-mystification of Poetry itself.

---

[1] For John E. Jackson, 'la poésie ne vit désormais que sur un mode crépusculaire', 'elle ne vit que d'avoir accepté sa défaite' ('Baudelaire', in *Dictionnaire de Poésie de Baudelaire à nos jours*, Paris: P.U.F., 2001, pp.47-53; p.48).

PART TWO. RIMBAUD

4
Challenging an Exclusive Poetics

The thematic development of Rimbaud's poetic career is strikingly similar to that observed in Baudelaire. Firstly, from the 'Cahiers de Douai' (1870) to the 1871 poems, the poet questions the reductive interpretative grid of the universal analogy – the fiction of inherent meaning in natural phenomena – and the restricted forms of metrical verse which it supports. 'Le Bateau ivre' (September 1871) narrates an experiment with an objective poetics which, like the Baudelairean prose poet's search for 'le fait tel qu'il existe en dehors de nous', proves impossible. Since there can be no return to the universal analogy, the poet explores in 1872 his own poetic visions via a new formal inclusivity, since, in the absence of absolute aesthetic values, any form has the potential to be poetic.[1] However, the infinity of poetic possibilities eventually leads to madness, and the endeavour is abandoned as the poet realizes that the poetic idea cannot survive without a certain aesthetic exclusivity. In *Illuminations*, therefore, he re-motivates this exclusivity whilst problematizing notions of form and rhythm, and re-mystifies poeticity by situating the source of poetic value in an evasive yet provocative poet figure.[2] Let us first examine the move away from interpretative conventions in the 'Poésies', as the poet challenges both the inherited view of nature as a meaningful system of rhythms and the value of verse form.

---

[1] In keeping with the most recent editions – *Rimbaud: Œuvres complètes I*, ed. by Steve Murphy, Paris: Champion, 1999, and *Rimbaud: Poésies. Une saison en enfer. Illuminations*, ed. by Louis Forestier, Paris: Gallimard, coll. '*Poésies* classique', 1999 – I refer not to the 'Derniers vers' or 'Vers nouveaux et chansons', but simply to the '1872 poems', the twenty poems written between May and September 1872.
[2] This suggests, perhaps, an excessively tidy development at odds with the often contradictory, non-linear appearance of Rimbaud's work. Also, the uncertainty as to the dates of many texts, as well as to the object of certain self-referential passages of *Une saison en enfer*, allows the critic a dangerous margin for imaginative but tenuous interpretations. The progression observed above does not claim to be definitive, but it nevertheless provides a useful thematic framework *dans les grandes lignes*.

The meaning of rhythm

Jean-Pierre Bobillot suggests, in one of several excellent articles on Rimbaldian form, that the inherited verse mould symbolizes the religious, social, political and aesthetic order against which the young poet instinctively rebels:

> Si Rimbaud part en guerre contre l'"hexamètre', c'est qu'il a reconnu, dans cette persistance d'une commune mesure abstraite, une implicite organisation de la société, une implicite conception du monde, strictement pré-déterminée, et réglée, – où le sujet n'a pas sa place, pas plus que le hasard, le désordre du vivant.[1]

The disruption of metrical order is seen as part of 'le projet anti-chrétien de Rimbaud', namely: 'en finir avec le jugement de Dieu'.[2] Rimbaud's first poems display a lyrical enthusiasm for a nature whose poetic significance comes not from God but from a harmonious communion with man. 'Sensation' depicts the poet at one with an absolutized 'Nature' (1.8) which inspires him with 'l'amour infini' (1.6); and as 'Soleil et Chair' suggests, nature's beauty is independent of the Christian God, 'l'autre Dieu' (1.47). It comes instead from a universal harmony, which has been lost in modern times and requires restoration through poetry: 'Je regrette les temps de l'antique jeunesse' (1.10). This bygone age is characterized by a universal *bercement*, 'les arbres muets berçant l'oiseau qui chante, / La terre berçant l'homme' (ll.22-23), as all unites in a regular rhythm. The poem faithfully follows the Banvillian theme of the redemptive power of universal harmony, as gods, man and nature finally reunite in a musical metaphor:

> L'Amour infini dans un infini sourire!
> Le Monde vibrera comme une immense lyre (ll.77-78)

However, the first line, above, is one of Rimbaud's first two P6 lines (along with 'Tout le dieu qui vit, sous / son argile charnelle', 1.70), as the faith in the rhythmic regularity implied by the verbs *bercer* and

---

[1] 'Le clinamen d'Arthur Rimbaud. Travail du rythme et matérialisme dans les vers de 1872', in *Rimbaud 1891-1991. Actes du colloque d'Aix en Provence et de Marseille*, ed. by André Guyaux, Paris: Champion, 1994, pp.89-102; p.99.
[2] ibid., p.100.

vibrer is punctured by actual rhythmic imbalance. The poem also features eight D6 lines, including:

– Car l'Homme a fini! l'Homme / a joué tous les rôles!	(l.65)
Au front de Zeus; ses yeux / sont fermés; elle meurt	(l.100)
S'avance, front terrible / et doux, à l'horizon!	(l.112)

There are also eight seventh-syllable accents which either undermine the pre-caesural accent (1-4) or clash with it (5-8):

L'eau du fleuve, le sang / <u>ro</u>se des arbres verts	(l.15)
Sur la rive, en voyant / <u>fuir</u> là-bas sur les flots	(l.88)
Zeus, Taureau, sur son cou / <u>ber</u>ce comme une enfant	(l.95)
– Et tandis que Cypris / <u>passe</u>, étrangement belle	(l.106)
Où le sol palpitait, / <u>vert</u>, sous ses pieds de chèvre	(l.17)
– Oui, l'Homme est triste et laid, / <u>triste</u> sous le ciel vaste	(l.49)
Il ressuscitera, / <u>libre</u> de tous ses Dieux	(l.67)
Contempleur des vieux jougs, / <u>libre</u> de toute crainte	(l.73)

In the version sent to Paul Demeny, line 48 gains six accents, dislocating the regular 3/3//3/3 rhythm, with internal rhyme, of the earlier version sent to Banville:

Mais c'est **toi** / la Vé<u>nus</u>! // c'est en **toi** / que je **crois**!	(Banville)
<u>Chair</u>, <u>Mar</u>bre, <u>Fleur</u>, Vé<u>nus</u>, / c'est en <u>toi</u> que je <u>crois</u>!	(Demeny)

Furthermore, when 'Credo in unam' is edited to become 'Soleil et Chair', the thirty-six consecutive lines omitted from the definitive text all present a perfect 6+6 rhythm with no metrical irregularities.[1] It is as if the poet, a product of a faithless age, cannot entirely submit to the regular rhythms which might restore universal harmony. The lines asking the crucial *Pourquoi?* of existence, which echo Nerval's 'Le Christ aux oliviers', a source text for much nineteenth-century poetic questioning of absolute values, are among those omitted. In these lines, the poet wonders:

Un Pasteur mène-t-il cet immense troupeau
De mondes cheminant dans l'horreur de l'espace? (ll.12-13)

---

[1] See *Poésies. Une saison en enfer. Illuminations*, ed. by Louis Forestier, Paris: Gallimard, coll. 'folio classique', 1999, pp.278-79 (hereafter 'folio').

In the face of doubt as to the origin of universal significance, 'Soleil et Chair' posits instead 'L'Idéal, la pensée invincible, éternelle' (1.69) as an internal truth, independent of an external divinity yet absolute nonetheless.

In 'Ophélie', it appears that the heroine's madness and death result from her horror of an absurd existence in which these universal rhythms and harmonies lose their inherent meaning. The wind reveals to her 'l'âpre liberté' (1.20), a pre-existential vertigo, and the infinite no longer inspires faith in universal love, but terrifies her: 'l'Infini terrible effara ton œil bleu' (1.32). The sea, which inspires so much Baudelairean reflection on the meaning of exterior phenomena, also plays its part:

> C'est que la voix des mers / <u>fol</u>les, immense râle,
> Brisait ton sein d'enfant, trop humain et trop doux (ll.25-26)

Fittingly, in the first line, the realization of universal emptiness is accompanied by a seventh-syllable accent on 'folles' and the collapse of rhythmic regularity. Soon rhythmical equilibrium is lost in an asymmetrical five accents:

> <u>Ciel</u>! A<u>mour</u>! Liber<u>té</u>! / Quel <u>rêve</u>, ô pauvre <u>Folle</u>! (1.29)

Regularity is also challenged by the poem's three seventh-syllable verbs, each monosyllabic bar the *e caduc* at the eighth. Suggesting a coherent disruptive strategy, the lines are strikingly similar, both grammatically (article + [noun-adjective] / verb + adverbial unit) and rhythmically (2/4//1/5):

> La blanche Ophélia / <u>flot</u>te comme un grand lys   (1.2)
> Les saules frissonnants / <u>pleur</u>ent sur son épaule   (1.11)
> Un chant mystérieux / <u>tom</u>be des astres d'or…   (1.16)

Reference is made to Ophélie's veils in three 6+6 lines, as if, after the lifting of the rhythmic veil, they were replaced in a hasty retreat to the blinkers of faith and the safety of regular *bercement*:

> Flotte très lentement, / couchée en ses longs voiles   (1.3)
> Ses grands voiles bercés / mollement par les eaux   (1.10)
> Et qu'il a vu sur l'eau, / couchée en ses longs voiles   (1.35)

Indeed, the girl's phantom floats in a lyrical atmosphere of universal harmony, where nature seems alive with meaningful correspondences which veil the *gouffre*:

> Les saules frissonnants / pleurent sur son épaule,
> Sur son grand front rêveur s'inclinent les roseaux.
>
> Les nénuphars froissés soupirent autour d'elle [...]
> – Un chant mystérieux / tombe des astres d'or... (ll.11-16)

The two seventh-syllable accents, however, pierce the rhythmic illusion with the suggestion of its ultimately fictional nature. Once the veil has been lifted on universal meaninglessness, no attempt to return to the former safety can be entirely successful.

As Yves Reboul demonstrates, by July 1871 and 'L'Homme juste' Rimbaud parodies Victor Hugo's poetry of cosmic harmony and meaningful rhythms.[1] Stanza nine describes how the notion of order is used to dominate universal chaos, and this victory of order over disorder is represented on a structural level:

Cependant que, silen / cieux sous les pilastres	[M6, 4/4/4?]	[e – astr]
→ D'azur, allongeant les / comètes et les nœuds	[C6, no 4/4/4]	
→ D'univers, remuement / énorme sans désastres,	[D6, no 4/4/4]	[dezastr]
L'ordre, éternel veilleur, / rame aux cieux lumineux	[1/5//3/3]	
Et de sa drague en feu / laisse filer des astres!	[4/2//4/2]	[dezastr]

The first three lines disrupt the formal order of the universal analogy: each caesura is undermined and the pauses at two *entrevers* are threatened by the *enjambement* of two tightly-knit compound nouns. However, the disruption is gradually weakened as the stanza progresses: the third caesura is metrically plausible, with only a relatively mild D6, and the second *rejet* ('D'univers') is trisyllabic. Order arrives with a monosyllabic thud, bringing to an end the flouted metrical accents with two 6+6 alexandrines. Steve Murphy suggests that the 'les astres' (l.45) given in Verlaine's copy and current editions

---

[1] 'A propos de l'*Homme juste*', *Parade Sauvage* 2 (1985), 44-54. Rimbaud directs the attack 'en parodiant très visiblement cette poésie cosmique [...] [et] la figure si hugolienne du contemplateur d'infini' (pp.47-48), since 'bolides ou astres monstrueux soudainement apparus, c'est bien la vision de l'univers que développe la poésie du temps de l'exil' (p.48).

is, in fact, 'des astres' in Rimbaud's version.[1] Thus the *a* rhyme, which at the end of the third line is only *riche*, ends the stanza with emphatic *léonine* resolution, further reinforced by the internal rhyme /ø/ which marks the return to a 3/3 rhythm and creates a *rime batelée*. This versificatory order reflects the universal order which, in Hugo's verse, gives meaning to the stars themselves.

For Cornulier, this return to order represents an 'ordre rassurant, donc, mais qu'on ne peut évoquer sans évoquer l'angoisse du chaos universel (désastres) dont il nous garde'. He suggests: 'Dans tous ces cas l'angoisse métrique de la rupture avec la mesure binaire exprime l'angoisse inhérente à l'atmosphère du sujet'.[2] However, this rupture is desired by the subject, who by questioning the metrical mould repeatedly challenges the poetic validity of the universal analogy in which Hugolian poetics is firmly anchored. Indeed, the poet leads a confident, impatient rebellion against this outdated world view via a series of progressively more disruptive formal techniques.

The Rimbaldian alexandrine

Much excellent material has been written on Rimbaud's use of metre, rhyme, syllable count and the sonnet form. Cornulier renews interest in versificatory techniques with his landmark article of 1980, in which *la métricométrie* is applied to 1,716 dodecasyllables.[3] The 1872 poems contain only sixty-five, in just two texts ('Qu'est-ce pour nous,…' and 'Mémoire'), yet these few lines count for seven of the eight F6, four of the five F7, and eight of the twelve M6 lines of the whole corpus.[4] Since these categories are more transgressive than C6 and P6, and given this remarkable concentration of iconoclastic lines, the majority of criticism focuses on the 1872 verse, with its high proportion of rhyming and syllabic irregularities. This is the case for

---

[1] Champion edition, p.458.

[2] 'Métrique du vers de 12 syllabes chez Rimbaud', *Le Français Moderne*, 48:2 (1980), 140-74; p.154.

[3] It is important to distinguish between alexandrines, whose defining characteristic is the recurrent accentual structure 6+6, and dodecasyllables such as they are found in 'Mémoire'. The latter feature twelve syllables, but without a common, pre-determined accentual structure. Cornulier and Bobillot repeatedly insist, therefore, that these lines are not alexandrines, lacking the necessary common metre.

[4] 'Métrique du vers de 12 syllabes chez Rimbaud', p.143. Cornulier does not count '*L'Enfant qui ramassa les balles…*' in his 1872 poems, whereas Steve Murphy does.

Cornulier's analysis in *Théorie du vers*.[1] Of the 'Poésies', he simply states that each alexandrine is metrically divisible as either 6/6, 4/4/4 or 8/4, 'ces deux dernières mesures ne servant que d'*accompagnement* à la mesure binaire 6-6'.[2] This shows the importance of the metrical mould to Rimbaud's project:

Ces observations permettent de conclure que jusqu'à l'époque même où Rimbaud traite l'alexandrin de manière relativement souple comme dans 'Le bateau ivre', il ne cesse pas d'être un poète métrique, et même *très métrique*, ce qui rend son évolution ultérieure d'autant plus significative.[3]

Until 1872, therefore, the canonical 6+6 structure provides the framework against which Rimbaud's various dislocatory techniques work in counterpoint.

A tripartite rhythmical evolution from the 'Cahiers' (1870) to the poems of 1871 and 1872 is immediately apparent.[4] The first F6 line in the history of French poetry, the revolutionary value of which, despite its 4/4/4 recuperation, has been amply demonstrated by Cornulier, appears in 'Les Poètes de sept ans' of 1871:

Forêts, soleils, / rives, // savan / es! – il s'aidait (l.33)

This is not repeated until the iconoclastic dodecasyllables of 1872, none of which allows 4/4/4 resolution:

'Mémoire':	sous les murs dont quelque / pucelle eut la défense'	(l.4)
'Qu'est-ce...':	Et de braise, et mille / meurtres, et les longs cris	(l.2)
	Et toute vengeance? / Rien!... – Mais si, toute encor	(l.5)
	Périssez! puissance, / justice, histoire, à bas!	(l.7)

---

[1] Ch. 6, 'Rimbaud faussaire'. Since Cornulier's list of Rimbaud's FMEm6 lines can be found in his 'Listes méthodiques' (*Théorie du vers*, pp.302-03), I do not reproduce all his examples here.

[2] 'Métrique du vers de 12 syllabes chez Rimbaud', p.156.

[3] ibid., p.156.

[4] Although, as Steve Murphy warns in his Champion edition, 'il est hasardeux de procéder comme si l'on connaissait intimement l'évolution stylistique de Rimbaud pendant l'été de l'année 1870, et rien ne permet de présupposer une évolution strictement linéaire' (p.279). Suggesting that 'Les Corbeaux' might have been composed in 1872, contrary to the generally accepted theory of late 1870, he argues: 'La datation la plus répandue suppose le caractère linéaire de l'évolution stylistique de Rimbaud et son incapacité de revenir, dans un cadre pragmatique ou littéraire particulier, à des techniques anciennes' (ibid., p.803).

A nous! Romanesques / amis: ça va nous plaire.   (1.15)
Notre marche venge / resse a tout occupé   (1.18)
Cités et campagnes! / – Nous serons écrasés!   (1.19)

The first ever M6 lines also appear in 1871, leaping from three to eight in 1872; the Em6 lines appear even earlier, including one in Rimbaud's first published poem, with three in the 'Cahiers', two in 1871 and eight in 1872. Although this is enough to confirm the importance of the Rimbaldian alexandrine to the revolution of the French canon, and the marked difference between Rimbaud's verse in 1870-71 and 1872, a study restricted to the categories FMEm6 is insensitive to significant early development from the 'Cahiers' to the 1871 poems.

Firstly, the P6 category, which Cornulier hardly mentions, features twelve times in the 'Cahiers' alone:

Tout le dieu qui vit, sous / son argile charnelle	('Soleil et Chair', 1.70)
L'Amour infini dans / un infini sourire!	('Soleil et Chair', 1.77)
Morts de Valmy, / Morts de // Fleurus, / Morts d'Italie	('Morts de 92', 1.10)
Qui palpite là, comme / une petite bête	('Roman', 1.16)
Le notaire pend à / ses breloques à chiffres	('A la musique', 1.8)
Le prit rudement par / son oreille benoîte	('… Tartufe', 1.6)
Sifflent tout le jour par / l'infini du ciel bleu	('Le Mal', 1.2)
L'hiver, nous irons dans / un petit wagon rose	('Rêvé pour l'hiver', 1.1)
Tu fermeras l'œil, pour / ne point voir, par la glace	('Rêvé pour l'hiver', 1.5)
Un petit baiser, comme / une folle araignée	('Rêvé pour l'hiver', 1.10)
Un schako surgit, comme / un soleil noir… - Au centre	('…Sarrebrück', 1.12)
Du jambon tièd / e, dans // un plat / colorié	('Au Cabaret-vert', 1.11)

In all but two examples, resolvable as 4/4/4, the syntactic accent is emphatically displaced from the sixth to the fifth syllable, as Rimbaud obstructs the anticipated 6+6 regularity. As we shall see, the resulting 5/7 rhythm, simple accentual displacement by one syllable, is the principal method of metrical subversion in Rimbaud's early poems. By 1871, the thirteen P6 lines demonstrate more varied rhythmical problematization, with only four examples of a 5/7 rhythm:

D'où le soleil, clair comme / un chaudron récuré	('Accroupissements', 1.3)
A se renfermer dans / la fraîcheur des latrines	('Les Poètes de sept ans', 1.15)
– Ils auront couché sur / ta Haine inviolée	('Les … Communions', 1.131)
Qui courais, taché de / lunules électriques	('Le Bateau ivre', 1.77)

Four lines feature a stronger syntactic accent at the fourth than at the fifth or sixth syllables:

Et vous su<u>ez</u> / pris dans // un a*troce* entonnoir	('Les Assis', 1.32)
Comme le <u>su</u> / cre sur // la den*ture* gâtée	('L'Homme juste', 1.48)
Il se dé<u>mèn</u> / e sous // sa couver*ture* grise	('Accroupissements', 1.6)
Un bateau <u>frê</u> / le comme // un papi*llon* de mai	('Le Bateau ivre', 1.96)

The reader is lured into anticipating a 4/4/4 rhythm, since syntactic and metrical accents coincide at the fourth syllable, but this expectation is disappointed; although the accent at the sixth syllable is undermined, the next *accent mobile* avoids the eighth syllable, deferring resolution of the syntactic unit until the ninth or tenth.

The C6 lines, of which Cornulier also makes disappointingly little, present a striking development. The 'Cahiers' feature only three, of which the first is easily recuperated in a 3/3//3/3 rhythm, and the third allows a 4/4/4 structure:

C'est très bien. / Foin de leur // tabatièr / e à sornettes!	('Le Forgeron', 1.96)
Au Cabaret-Vert: je / demandai des tartines	('Au Cabaret-Vert', 1.3)
Comme des lyr / es, je // tirais / les élastiques	('Ma bohème', 1.13)

In the 1871 poems, however, the number of C6 lines leaps up to twenty-nine, of which only nine are *alexandrins romantiques*:

Et noires, fier / de ses // premiers / entêtements	('Les Sœurs de charité', 1.6)
Le déchirer / de leur // auguste / obsession	('Les Sœurs de charité', 1.28)
Ils ont greffé / dans des // amours / épileptiques	('Les Assis', 1.5)
Dans la colère, / ou les // ivress / es pénitentes	('Voyelles', 1.8)
Sur sa poitrine, / en une // horribl / e pression	('L'Orgie parisienne', 1.36)
D'astres lactés, / et les // essaims / d'astéroïdes	('L'Homme juste', 1.5)
Vraiment, c'est bêt / e, ces // églis / es de village	('Les ... Communions', 1.1)
Elle verra, / sous les // tristess / es du bonheur	('Les ... Communions', 1.110)
Et les ressacs / et les // courants: / je sais le soir	('Le Bateau ivre', 1.30)

Ten demand a 5/7 scansion, emphatically pre-empting the metrical accent:

Ouvrant lente<u>ment</u> leurs / omoplates, ô rage!	('Les Assis', 1.23)
Les bercent, le <u>long</u> des / calices accroupis	('Les Assis', 1.42)
Aux contours du <u>cul</u> des / bavures de lumière	('Accroupissements', 1.32)

L'orage a sac<u>rée</u> ta / suprême poésie	('L'Orgie parisienne', 1.65)[1]
Alors, mettrais-<u>tu</u> tes / genouillères en vente	('L'Homme juste', 1.13)
D'azur, allon<u>geant</u> les / comètes et les nœuds	('L'Homme juste', 1.42)
Les vieilles cou<u>leurs</u> des / vitraux irréguliers	('Les ... Communions', 1.6)
Se gorgent de <u>cire</u> au / plancher ensoleillé	('Les ... Communions', 1.18)
J'ai vu fermen<u>ter</u> les / marais énormes, nasses	('Le Bateau ivre', 1.49)
Fileur éter<u>nel</u> des / immobilités bleues	('Le Bateau ivre', 1.83)

Three lines complicate the rhythm further with a monosyllabic preposition at the fifth syllable. As with the similar P6 lines, any 4/4/4 recuperation which the reader might anticipate is confounded by the second *accent mobile* falling on the ninth, tenth or seventh syllable:

Où, pomma**dé**, <u>sur</u> un / guérid*on* d'acajou	('Les Poètes de sept ans', 1.45)
Et rythmes **lents** <u>sous</u> les /rutile*ments* du jour	('Le Bateau ivre', 1.26)
Et les loin**tains** <u>vers</u> les / gou*ffres* cataractant	('Le Bateau ivre', 1.52)

Other C6 lines of 1871 postpone the syntactic resolution over a similar succession of unaccentuable syllables:

S'entre<u>lac</u> / ent pour les // ma*tins* et pour les soirs	('Les Assis', 1.8)
Quelque <u>cho</u> / se comme un // oi*seau* remue un peu	('Accroupissements', 1.19)
Conver<u>saient</u> / avec la // dou*ceur* des idiots!	('Poètes de sept ans', 1.25)
Noire et <u>froide</u> / où vers le // crépus*cule* embaumé	('Le Bateau ivre', 1.94)

Finally, three other lines confound our expectations of an *alexandrin romantique*, with the second *accent mobile* falling in each case on the ninth syllable:

– Huit ans, – la **fill**e des / ouvri*ers* d'à côté	('Les Poètes de sept ans', 1.37)
Adona**ï**!... / – Dans les // terminai*sons* latines	('Les ... Communions', 1.57)
Je vis **assis**, tel qu'un / ange aux *mains* d'un barbier	('Oraison du soir', 1.1)

In 1871, therefore, the rebellion against metre involves more varied strategies of rhythmical problematization, with accents pushed further and further apart.

---

[1] Most editors give the following version of the line: 'L'orage t'a sacrée / suprême poésie', which restores to the line a symmetrical 6 + 6 structure. However, as Murphy points out in his critical edition, this is not the version given in Vanier's edition of 1895 – it is a correction brought to the text by subsequent editors; see Murphy's Champion edition, pp. 426-46.

A study of the variants confirms the sustained inscription of a 5/7 or 7/5 *faux accord* in the 1870 poems.[1] The different versions of the 'Cahiers' poems – mostly an early version sent to Georges Izambard and a later one to Demeny – reveal from the outset a concerted effort to disrupt regular 6+6 lines with a 5/7 or 7/5 rhythm. Rimbaud's first P6 line replaces a previously regular line, as if the preposition were shifted only for its rhythmically disruptive force; line 69 of 'Credo in unam', sent to Banville in April 1870, becomes P6 in the May version, sent to Demeny in the Autumn:

> Tout ce qu'il a de Dieu / sous l'argile charnelle   (Banville)
> Tout le dieu qui vit, <u>sous</u> / son argile charnelle   (Demeny)

Line 65 becomes D6, with adjacent accents on the fifth and sixth syllables, and the new punctuation clearly highlights a 5/7 syntactic structure:

> Et l'Homme n'est pas fait / pour jouer tous ces rôles!   (Banville)
> Car l'Homme a fini! <u>l'Homme</u> / a joué tous les rôles!   (Demeny)

The seventh-syllable accent added to line 15 suggests a 7/5 rhythm:

> L'eau du fleuve jaseur, / le sang des arbres verts   (Banville)
> L'eau du fleuve, le sang / <u>rose</u> des arbres verts   (Demeny)

That added to line 17 creates accentual hiatus with the pre-caesural accent, and since it closes the syntactic unit of the previous hemistich, the line leans towards 7/5:

> Où tout naissait, vivait, / sous ses longs pieds de chèvre   (Banville)
> Où le sol palpitait, / <u>vert</u>, sous ses pieds de chèvre   (Demeny)

A D6 seventh-syllable accent is added to line 25 between the copies of 'Ophélie' sent to Banville in May 1870 and to Demeny that autumn:

---

[1] Indeed, both Cornulier and Bobillot apply this metaphor to Rimbaud, referring to 'la discordance à la coupe' ('Métrique du vers de 12 syllabes chez Rimbaud', p.151) and 'la dissonance' at 'les "positions sensibles" (c'est-à-dire: métriques) du vers' ('Vers, prose, langue', *Poétique* 89 (1992), 71-91; p.75).

C'est que la voix des mers, / comme un immense râle   (Banville)
C'est que la voix des mers / <u>foll</u>es, immense râle   (Demeny)

'A la musique' presents the most emphatic example of irresolvable tension between the metrical mould and syntactic structure. The symmetrical 3/3//3/3 rhythm of line 8 in the Izambard version is forcefully dislocated in the 5/7 imbalance of the new P6 line:

Les notair / es montrer // leurs brelo / ques à chiffres   (Izambard)
Le notaire / pend <u>à</u> // ses **bre** / loques à chiffres   (Demeny)

The new line is also F4 and M8, impeding 4/4/4 recuperation, and the syntactic pattern of the line suggests yet another 5/7 *coupe*. Line 18 becomes D6, with an accent on the seventh syllable, dislocating the same 3/3//3/3 symmetry, with the punctuation urging towards 7/5 in the new P4, Em8 line:

Un bourgeois / bienheureux // à bedain / e flamande   (Izambard)
Un bourgeois **à** / boutons // <u>clairs,</u> **be** / daine flamande (Demeny)

The shift from 6/6 to 7/5 is also visible in line 91 of 'Le Forgeron':

Pleins de menus décrets, / de méchants droguailles   (Izambard)
Pleins de jolis décrets / <u>ro</u>ses et de droguailles   (Demeny)

The juxtaposition of accents at sixth- and seventh-syllable position in lines 83 and 97 produces post-caesural hiatus:

Et je vais dans Paris, / le marteau sur l'épaule   (Izambard)
Et je vais dans Paris, / <u>noir,</u> marteau sur l'épaule   (Demeny)

Nous en avons assez, / de tous ces cerveaux plats!   (Izambard)
Nous en avons assez, / <u>là,</u> de ces cerveaux plats!   (Demeny)

As Murphy observes, the alteration to line 96 introduces one of the first C6 lines to Rimbaud's verse.[1] The simultaneous alteration to line 95 creates yet more accentual hiatus and a 7/5 rhythm:

Pour débiter là-bas / des milliers de sornettes
Et ne rien redouter / sinon les baïonnettes   (Izambard)

---

[1] Champion edition, pp.336-37.

> Pour ne rien redouter, / rien, que les baïonnettes...,
> C'est très bien! Foin de leur / tabatière à sornettes!   (Demeny)

Thus Rimbaud takes his first steps towards rejecting the metrical verse form, towards a liberty twice announced in seventh-syllable position in 'Soleil et Chair':

> Il ressuscitera, / libre de tous les Dieux   (l.67)
> Contempleur des vieux jougs, / libre de toute crainte   (l.73)

This early predilection for 5/7 or 7/5 displacement of the alexandrine's 6+6 equilibrium is further reinforced in 'Au Cabaret-Vert' by a typographical shift:

> – *Au Cabaret-Vert*: je / demandai des tartines (l.3)

Cornulier, a staunch defender of the strictest possible definition of the metrical mould, refuses this 5/7 *coupe* metrical status: 'je ne vois pas sur quelle base on pourrait considérer que la division 5e forme une coupe *métrique*'. For him, this undermines any isometric notion of an alexandrine:

Ces sortes de scansion 'à vue de nez' peuvent être classées comme absolument fantaisistes. Elles paraissent, certes, pouvoir s'autoriser du 'bon sens', mais ce n'est qu'une apparence; car si le 'bon sens' peut indiquer judicieusement les principales possibilités naturelles de division rythmique, il ne saurait garantir l'identité de ces divisions manifestes avec les divisions déterminées en poésie par un système contextuel de mesure; et c'est vraiment le contraire du bon sens, que de croire qu'une particularité individuelle, imprévisible et non réglée, puisse servir de mesure, car toute chose a forcément les dimensions qu'elle a (si toute articulation était rythmique, il n'existerait pas de prose).[1]

The introduction of this 'particularité individuelle, imprévisible et non réglée' is precisely Rimbaud's agenda, challenging the metrical structure traditionally seen as inherently meaningful, with insistent *faux accords*.

A study of adjacent accents reveals more varied techniques of rhythmic interrogation. The second 'Cahier' introduces a new method,

---

[1] 'Métrique du vers de 12 syllabes chez Rimbaud', p.150.

a dissonant accentual clash produced by reinforcing both fifth- and sixth-syllable accents:

> Et tu me di<u>ras</u>: "<u>Cherche</u>!", / en inclinant la tête   ('Rêvé pour l'hiver', 1.12)
> J'allais sous le <u>ciel</u>, <u>Muse</u>! / et j'étais ton féal   ('Ma bohème', 1.3)

Only two of the adjacent accents in 1871 occur at the caesura, both in 'Les Poètes de sept ans'. The first creates fifth/sixth-syllable hiatus, the second a 5/7 rhythm:

> Quand venait, l'œil <u>brun</u>, <u>folle</u>, / en robes d'indiennes   (1.36)
> Il n'aimait pas <u>Dieu</u>; <u>mais</u> / les hommes, qu'au soir fauve   (1.48)

Similar examples now multiply at different points throughout the line, disrupting the rhythm at any point:

> <u>I</u>, <u>pourpr</u>es, sang craché, / rire des lèvres belles   ('Voyelles', 1.7)
> <u>U</u>, <u>cycl</u>es, vibrements / divins des mers virides   ('Voyelles', 1.9)
> <u>Dis</u>: <u>Frère</u>, va plus loin, / je suis estropié!   ('L'Homme juste', 1.10)
> <u>Mais</u>, <u>vrai</u>, j'ai trop pleuré! / Les Aubes sont navrantes   ('Le Bateau ivre', 1.89)
> En <u>bas</u>, – <u>seul</u>, et couché / sur des pièces de toile   ('Poètes de sept ans', 1.63)
> Golfes <u>d'ombre</u>; <u>E</u>, candeurs / des vapeurs et des tentes   ('Voyelles', 1.5)
> De journaux illustrés / <u>où</u>, <u>rouge</u>, il regardait   ('Poètes de sept ans', 1.34)
> Dévorant les azurs / <u>verts</u>; <u>où</u>, flottaison blême   ('Le Bateau ivre', 1.23)
> Je suis maudit, tu sais! / Je suis <u>soûl</u>, <u>fou</u>, livide!   ('L'Homme juste', 1.23)
> De honte, ruminant / toujours mon en<u>nui</u>, <u>doux</u>   ('L'Homme juste', 1.47)
> Le bonhomme mijote / au feu, bras tor<u>dus</u>, <u>lippe</u>   ('Accroupissements', 1.16)

The number of accents per line also increases to five, with eleven examples in the first 'Cahier' and twenty-three in the 1871 poems. Indeed, 'Les Poètes de sept ans' features the most accentually irregular line to date, with six accents:

> <u>Qui</u>, ché<u>tifs</u>, fronts <u>nus</u>, <u>l'œil</u> / déte<u>ignant</u> sur la <u>joue</u> (1.23)

It is the D6 categories with which I supplement Cornulier's method that provide the clearest evidence of a dramatic increase in disruption between the 'Cahiers' and the 1871 poems. The first 'Cahier' features forty-five D6 lines out of 524 (8.6%), whereas the second, composed soon afterwards, displays a much higher concentration: twenty-two in only ninety-eight lines (22.4%). In 1871 the same high concentration is sustained over a larger corpus for a much longer period, with 152 D6 lines from 652 alexandrines (23%). Almost every D6 category increases between the 'Cahiers' and 1871, some dramatically: from four compound verbal constructions to thirteen; from one bisyllabic preposition to eleven; from four compound nouns to seventeen. Since the categories which emerged from my Baudelairean study feature so prominently in Rimbaud, increasing in frequency alongside the FMC6 lines, it certainly seems that the D6 system is a valuable tool for measuring a subtler level of metrical tension, lending support to the reader's *pifomètre*. For example, compared to only one example in the 'Cahiers', the 1871 poems feature eight examples of the adjective/ noun category, including only one *alexandrin romantique*:

Par lesquelles de fiers / bureaux seront bordés	('Les Assis', 1.40)
Il craignait les blafards / dimanches de décembre	('Les Poètes de sept ans', 1.44)
Où les crieurs, en trois / roulements de tambour	('Les Poètes de sept ans', 1.50)
Des soins naïfs, / des bons // travaux / abrutissants	('Les ... Communions', 1.20)
L'air s'emplit du lointain / nasillement des danses	('Les ... Communions', 1.39)
L'amant rêver au blanc / million des Maries	('Les ... Communions', 1.111)
Christ! ô Christ! éternel / voleur des énergies	('Les ... Communions', 1.133)
Illuminant de longs / figements violets	('Le Bateau ivre', 1.34)

Most clearly of all, the noun/adjective category jumps from twenty-six in the 'Cahiers' to fifty-six in 1871, fifteen of which present a 7/5 rhythm thanks to a monosyllabic adjective:

Tes haines, tes torpeurs / fixes, tes défaillances	('Sœurs de charité', 1.21)
Cachant de maigres doigts / jaunes et noirs de boue	('Poètes de sept ans', 1.24)
Lumineuses, parfums / sains, pubescences d'or	('Poètes de sept ans' (1.53)
Font baiser leurs longs doigts / jaunes aux bénitiers	('Pauvres à l'église', 1.36)
De mourir, idiots / doux aux chansons soudaines	('Pauvres à l'église', 1.54)
Par un badigeon d'eau / bleue et de lait caillé	('Communions', 1.14)
Le cœur, sous l'œil des cieux / doux, en les devinant	('Communions', 1.88)
Elle eut soif de la nuit / forte où le cœur qui saigne	('Communions', 1.91)
Elle passa sa nuit / sainte dans les latrines	('Communions', 1.97)
Dans la cour où les cieux / bas plaquaient d'ors vermeils	('Communions', 1.102)
Tels que les excréments / chauds d'un vieux colombier	('Oraison du soir', 1.5)
Puis par instants mon cœur / triste est comme un aubier	('Oraison du soir', 1.7)
Je pisse vers les cieux / bruns, très haut et très loin	('Oraison du soir', 1.13)
Et des taches de vins / bleus et des vomissures	('Le Bateau ivre', 1.19)
Dévorant les azurs / verts; où, flottaison blême	('Le Bateau ivre', 1.23)

The most frequent methods of caesural disruption in the 'Cahiers', noun/adjective (26) and subject/verb (19), also feature a high frequency of seventh-syllable accents: twelve and ten respectively. Most are from the first 'Cahier', in which twenty D6 lines feature a post-caesural monosyllable. Very few of these lines allow a 4/4/4 scansion, and even in 1871, as the variety of disruptive rhythms increases, the D6 lines featuring bisyllabic prepositions and subject/verb constructions include fifteen and ten seventh-syllable accents respectively. The constant presence of this mode of accentual displacement in all these categories confirms Rimbaud's early enthusiasm for the rhythmically awkward 7/5 structure.

Certain poems from 1870-71 seem almost to be *exercices de style* in disruptive techniques, as the young poet experiments with clash and discord, with one dominant trend per poem: three post-caesural monosyllabic verbs ('Ophélie', ll.2,11,16) or three monosyllabic post-caesural adjectives ('Oraison du soir', ll.5,7,13); three noun/adjective lines ('Le Dormeur du val', ll.5,10,14), and three subject/verb lines in 'Ma bohème', all in the second quatrain, where the first-person possessive + noun is followed in each case by a third-person imperfect verb (ll.5,7,8); three line-initial monosyllables in the space of five lines ('Le Dormeur du val' ll.4,7,8) and four cases of accentual hiatus in identical fifth- and sixth-syllable positions ('Rêvé pour l'hiver', ll.1,5,10,12). In all, Rimbaud's earlier poems rebel against the metrical mould with line-initial accents and 5/7 or 7/5 lines providing rhythmic jolts, whereas later poems vary the rhythmic disruption beyond simple displacement of the caesural accent. They begin to blur the metrical structure in preparation for its obliteration in 1872, as the rhythmical *points de repère* fade from view. Rebellion against a predictable metrical framework gradually gives way to the submersion of this framework in increasingly unpredictable structures.

The role of rhyme harmony

Whereas Rimbaud concentrates his early attention on the caesura, by 1871 the wider variety of disruptive techniques extends more frequently to the *entrevers*. Rhythmically problematic *enjambement* in all metres increases from eleven and seven examples in the 'Cahiers' to thirty-one in 1871, featuring several different constructions such as compound noun: 'une tête / De femme' ('Vénus anadyomène', ll.1-2), 'tartines / De beurre' ('Au Cabaret-Vert', ll.3-4), 'des haillons / D'argent' ('Le Dormeur du val', ll.2-3); noun / adjective: 'citoyens / honnêtes' ('Le Forgeron', ll.121-22), 'poitrine / Tranquille' ('Le Dormeur du val', ll.13-14), 'Promenades / Immenses' ('Les Sœurs de charité', ll.37-38), 'houles / Lumineuses' ('Les Poètes de sept ans', ll.52-53), 'l'épouvante / Bleuâtre' ('L'Homme juste', ll.11-12); verbal unit: 'tu sens / Sourdre' ('L'Orgie parisienne', ll.54-55); conjunction: 'quand / L'air s'emplit' ('Les Premières Communions', ll.38-39); and adverb: 'très / Intelligent' ('Les Poètes de sept ans', ll.5-6). Moreover, the first 'Cahier' features the first appearance of a Pv *contre-rejet* ('sous / Sa chaste robe noire', 'Le Châtiment de Tartufe', ll.1-2), while in 1871 three Cv *contre-rejets* are introduced, as the poet's disrespect for the hallowed rhyme position becomes gradually more pronounced: 'nos / Lèvres' ('Les Mains de Jeanne-Marie', ll.58-59), 'la / Strophe' and 'une / Cabane' ('Ce qu'on dit au poète...', ll.45-46 and 82-83).

There is also an increase in monosyllabic *rejets*, which create a sharp jolt in the metrical *nombre*:

'Cahier' (i)	'Ophélie / Passe'	('Ophélie, ll.5-6)
	'croupe / Belle'	('Vénus anadyomène', ll.13-14)
	'route / Blanche'	('Les Reparties de Nina', ll.57-58)
'Cahier' (ii)	'met / Belge'	('La Maline', ll.3-4)
	'table / Verte'	('Au Cabaret-Vert', ll.5-6)
	'gousse / D'ail'	('Au Cabaret-Vert', ll.12-13)
1871	'bagues / Vertes'	('Les Assis', ll.1-2)
	'nos / Lèvres'	('Les Mains de Jeanne-Marie', ll.58-59)
	'sens / Sourde'	('L'Orgie parisienne', ll.54-55)
	'plantes / Froides'	('L'Homme juste', ll.31-32)
	'amoureuse / Est'	('Les Premières communions', ll.121-22)
	'la / Strophe'	('Ce qu'on dit au poète...', ll.45-46)
	'volets / Clos'	('Ce qu'on dit au poète...', ll.83-84)
	'peaux / D'hommes'	('Le Bateau ivre', ll.46-47)

Alterations made to the first 'Cahier' provide clear evidence of Rimbaud's early fondness for disruptive line-initial monosyllables. In 'Le Forgeron' the imperfect form 'Poussaient' becomes present, as the 2/4 rhythm becomes 1/5:

Pou / ssent leurs régiments // en habits de gala (l.169)

A line-initial accent is also added to line 111:

| Couvrant son vaste corps / de la peau du lion | (Banville) |
| Fort, ceint son vaste corps / de la peau du lion | (Demeny) |

As line 144 assumes a D6 quality, with emphatic mid-hemistich punctuation disrupting the previously regular rhythm, line 143 gains a line-initial accent:

> – Tout ce qu'on ne sait pas, / c'est peut-être terrible
> Nous prendrons nos marteaux, / nous passerons au crible   (Izambard)
>
> Plus! – Ce qu'on ne sait pas, / c'est peut-être terrible
> Nous saurons! Nos marteaux / en main; passons au crible   (Demeny)

Indeed, 'Le Forgeron' alone features twenty-eight line-initial accents, including numerous exclamations: 'oh!', 'Non.', 'Sire,', 'Moi,', 'Folle!', 'Plus!'. Along with Rimbaud's first C6 line and fifteen D6 lines, this sustains a sense of rhythmic dislocation throughout the poem. Just as the blacksmith confronts his ruler, rebelling against the imposed social order, so too the poem constantly rejects rhythmic equilibrium. No poem from 1871 features such a wealth of line-initial staccato effects.

Yet as with Baudelaire, these challenges to the authority of the rhyme accent are accompanied by a simultaneous increase in rhyme strength. As the *rimes pauvres* fall from forty-nine in the first 'Cahier' to three in the second and twenty-nine in 1871, the *rimes riches* rise from ninety-three (first 'Cahier') and eighteen (second 'Cahier') to 155 in 1872, with *rimes léonines* rising from twenty-five (first 'Cahier') and six (second 'Cahier') to eighty-three in 1871. Representative of this development, the revision of 'Credo in unam' strengthens the *rime suffisante* 'plier / foyer' to *léonine* 'ployer / foyer' (ll.153-54). The number of rhymes reinforced over two syllables increases from seventeen (first 'Cahier') and three (second 'Cahier') to twenty-nine (1871), with the number of rhymes reinforced over three syllables increasing from three ('Cahiers') to seven (1871):

têtes fêlées / sombres mêlées	('Le Bal des pendus', ll.21-23)
cigare aux dents / regards ardents	('Rages de Césars', ll.2-4)
sa narine / sa poitrine	('Le Dormeur du val', ll.12-13)
ces éclanches / casser les hanches	('Mes Petites amoureuses', ll.37-39)
des latrines / des narines	('Les Poètes de sept ans', ll.15-16)
abrutissants / brunissants	('Les Premières Communions', ll.20-24)
Acajous / sapajous	('Ce qu'on dit au poète', ll.73-75)
des réclames / et des lames'	('Ce qu'on dit au poète', ll.98-100)
ces dorades / mes dérades	('Le Bateau ivre', ll.57-59)
et des îles / et t'exiles	('Le Bateau ivre', ll.85-87)

In 1871, two rhymes are even strengthened over four syllables:

mollet marquant / or débarquant   ('Les Premières Communions', ll.41-42)
des pommes sures / des vomissures   ('Le Bateau ivre', ll.17-19)

This reinforcement of the harmonic verse framework provides an effective counterpoint against which effects of *rejet* can be measured. Likewise, the shift highlighted by Michel Murat away from the eleven *sonnets libertins* of the 'Cahiers' to sonnets in 1871 with only *ab* elements in the quatrains ('Voyelles', 'Les Douaniers', 'Oraison du soir') creates: 'une tension plus forte entre l'affirmation brillante de la règle et l'infraction faite à la règle'.[1]

Following the collapse of faith in the inherent meaning of cosmic harmony, and therefore of rhyme, the increase in rhyming richness seems ironic, and is often used in a parodic context. Unlike in *Les Fleurs du Mal*, rhymes matching synaeresis and diaeresis are rather rare, whereas the number of rhymes matching diaeresis, or two contiguous pronounced vowels, leaps from two in the 'Cahiers' to fifteen in 1871. An early example comes in 'Ma bohème', where the possibly ironic tone and the imperfect tense throughout suggest a move, by October 1870, away from the poet's childish pre-occupation with lyrical matters. All is poetic *ivresse*, and the significance of cosmic harmony is not in doubt, but the poem reduces the scene, in the sub-title, to a mere 'fantaisie', recalling Baudelaire's dismissal of the artistic value of the same concept. The poet's exclamatory derision of his former beliefs features the rhyme 'idé-al / fé-al' (ll.2-3), where the adjective 'idéal' designates that which is physically non-existent. Since fidelity to the old Ideal and faith in harmony were misplaced, the *rime léonine* now rings hollow.

The ironic tone of these rhymes is maintained in their proliferation in the poems of 1871. Two appear in 'Les Sœurs de charité', a poem with such strong Baudelairean overtones it is almost in places another *exercice de style* bordering, as ever with Rimbaud, on the parodic.[2] Four are foregrounded by the octosyllables of 'Ce qu'on dit au poète à

---

[1] 'Rimbaud et la poétique du sonnet', *Parade Sauvage* 13 (1995), 5-23; p.17.

[2] 'Le Buffet' features similar overtones, particularly recalling 'Le Flacon'; indeed, 'Le Buffet' contains one of the rare examples in Rimbaud of the 'adjective / *et* adjective' construction, 'De linges odorants / et jaunes, de chiffons' (l.6), a particularly common feature of Baudelairean caesural transgression.

propos de fleurs', sent to Banville as either a parody or a defence of lyrical values in the face of bourgeois materialism, and three feature in the Hugolian parody 'L'Homme juste'. The use of two such rhymes seems similarly ironic in 'Les Premières communions', which rejects organized religion with forty-six D6 lines, ten post-caesural monosyllables and five cases of rhythmically problematic *rejet*. The presence of these rhymes in poems parodying three poets of the previous generation and their obsolete faith in absolutes, indicates the irony with which the verse framework is now treated. The inherent meaning of both natural phenomena and verse form can no longer be taken for granted, and 'Le Bateau ivre' narrates the rejection of this analogy, the opening of the interpretative window which forces the narrator, the boat itself, to confront 'le fait tel qu'il existe en dehors de nous'.

Into the Rimbaldian *gouffre*

'Le Bateau ivre' is traditionally read as the last of Rimbaud's metrical poems before the experiments of 1872, although Murphy warns: 'Il n'y a aucune certitude que *Le Bateau ivre* ait été le dernier des poèmes qu'il ait composés avant son départ pour Paris'.[1] The poem can be read as an exploration of the difficulties of interpreting external phenomena without the guidance of the universal analogy, and of the consequences for the writing of poetry. Indeed, it is striking that Rimbaud uses the same naval metaphor and marine images as Baudelaire does in 'Le Voyage' to announce a similar change of aesthetic. Although boats, of course, as inanimate objects, have no will to impose on phenomena, Rimbaud's boat enjoys an independent consciousness and a poetic will, yet without a crew it is at the mercy of the external elements, unable to impose its desires on the sea. The boat is thus obliged to observe external phenomena 'as they really are', and to confront the many problems this inevitably brings.

At the outset the boat is suddenly freed from the course imposed on it by man. The 'haleurs' (1.2) had previously confined it to 'des Fleuves impassibles' (1.1), the capital 'F' suggesting absolute status within a fixed universal value system where everything has its place and meaning. This restrictive interpretative grid is reflected in the regular form of the first seven lines, as the boat is confined to a 6+6

---

[1] Champion edition, p.547.

structure until the 'haleurs' are overcome by red indians. They represent a pre-Christian paradigm, developed in *Une saison en enfer* in terms of the pagan or the savage upon whom a new world view is unfairly imposed. Line 8, the critical point at which the boat is freed from its constraints, features the first D6 line, pulling us over the metrical barrier with the movement of the boat itself:

> Les Fleuves m'ont laissé / descendre où je voulais.

Immediately after liberation the boat abandons itself to the waves which are released from their traditional poetic role in the pathetic fallacy, with its rhythms and *bercements*.

In the next stanza a host of disruptive devices underlines the plunge out of rigid form and into interpretative and rhythmic freedom. Line 9 is D6, and line 10 begins with the emphatic monosyllable 'Moi', underlining a shift from imposed interpretative system to glorious celebration of the subject's opportunity to look at the world anew. This 'Moi' is repeated with line-initial, rhythmically disruptive emphasis in lines 71, 74 and 81. Lines 11 and 12 are both M6, the metrical disruption reflecting the initial impression of chaos as the received world view is undone. The first depicts the 'Pé / ninsules démarrées', as nature enjoys new freedom from its accepted configurations; as Cornulier remarks: 'la césure *Pén* + *insules* figurerait précisément cet arrachement, par le détachement métrique des "insules" libérées'.[1] Similarly, the second features 'tohu- / bohus', the image of the world before God's imposition of order, as Larousse explains: 'la terre, après avoir été créée, mais avant d'avoir été séparée des eaux, éclairée par les astres, couverte des végétaux et des animaux, offrait une espèce de chaos'.[2] Yet the stanza also features what is, with 'paladins / Saladins' ('Le Bal des pendus', ll.2-4), 'damassées / ramassées' ('Le Mal', ll.9-12) and 'bandoline / mandoline' ('Mes Petites amoureuses', ll.17-19), the joint-strongest rhyme of Rimbaud's career, 'des marées / démarrées' (ll.9-11), underlining the strength of both the belief in the inherent meaning of order, and the verse mould against which the boat-poet rebels.

---

[1] 'Métrique du vers de 12 syllabes chez Rimbaud', p.153.
[2] *Grand Dictionnaire Universel de XIX Siècle*, 15: 251.

Thus the initial impression, once the blinkers are removed, is one of chaos, in which the boat delights: 'Plus léger qu'un bouchon j'ai dansé sur les flots' (l.14). The image recalls 'Les Sept vieillards', where the Baudelairean poet realizes the absurdity of regular poetic *nombre* and tumbles into the *gouffre*:

> Et mon âme dansait, dansait, vieille gabarre
> Sans mâts, sur une mer monstrueuse et sans bords! (ll.51-52)

Similarly, as the water engulfs the boat in the fifth stanza, 'dispersant gouvernail et grappin' (l.20), it loses the tools by which to impose its course on the waves. It is now completely at the mercy of external forces, and the metrical *nombre* is overwhelmed by a D6 line with seventh-syllable accent, even more discordant since the sixth syllable is reinforced by a *rime batelée*:

> L'eau verte pénétra / ma coque de sap**in**
> Et des taches de v**ins** / <u>bleus</u> et des vomissures (ll.18-19)

In the next stanza the versification undergoes its most sustained dislocation yet:

> Et dès lors, je me suis / baigné dans le Poème   [D6]
> → De la Mer, infusé / <u>d'astres</u>, et lactescent,   [D6, 7/5]
> Dévorant les azurs / <u>verts</u>; <u>où</u>, flottaison blême   [D6, 7/5; 7-8 hiatus]
> → Et ravie, un noyé / pensif parfois descend   [D6]

Each line features a D6 technique, and there is a seventh-syllable accent in the second and third lines, the latter followed by another accent at the eighth syllable. The former, 'infusé / d'astres', shows the stars released from their constellations, dissolving in the sea at the point where metrical *nombre* falters. The search for poetic value in these liberated external phenomena is confirmed by the expression 'Poème de la mer'. Dislocated at the *entrevers*, it encourages the pronunciation of a subtle *'e' surnuméraire*, highlighting its incompatibility with verse form, like the Baudelairean *imprévu désastre*. As Murphy notes, Verlaine's copy of the poem gives the variant 'azurs / vers', underlining the antagonism between the sea-poem and traditional verse as the expression erases the caesura with a

7/5 scansion.[1] As the 'real' sea engulfs the boat, therefore, it washes it clean of 'des taches de vins bleus et des vomissures' (1.19), the *ivresses* of the former poetics.

The interpretative dilemma

As we know from the Baudelairean poet's lifting of the veil and plunge into the *gouffre*, the attempt at an objective poetics, the study of external objects to see what they might 'really mean', is doomed to fail. The boat repeatedly describes what it sees – 'j'ai vu' (ll.32,33,49, 85) – but without an interpretative grid, phenomena resist reduction to values of order or disorder, and the boat offers no meaningful poetic interpretation. The 'archipels sidéraux' (1.85) are compared to stars, site of the ultimate interpretative dilemma: are the constellations proof of meaningful external order, or not? We are shown 'les ressacs et les courants' (1.30), 'la houle à l'assaut des récifs' (1.42), 'les marais énormes' (1.49), 'Glaciers, soleils d'argent, flots nacreux, cieux de braise' (1.53) but nowhere are they structurally significant, nowhere do they represent recognizably poetic regularity. On the contrary, we witness 'Des écroulements d'eaux au milieu des bonaces' (1.51), a 'bonace' meaning: 'état de la mer pendant un calme plat, quand ses eaux n'éprouvent aucune agitation'.[2] For Baudelaire, this 'calme plat' provokes despair in 'La Musique' when unrhythmed by the waves; and there is no rhythm in Rimbaud's poem, only 'écroulements' signifying 'tomber en débris en s'affaissant', 'tomber ensemble confusément'.[3] This suggests a disorder incompatible with the traditional poetic view of marine rhythms. Yet the boat initially gains poetic pleasure from this new experience of the sea, expressed by two verbs usually associated with the former poetics of regular rhythm:

> – Des écumes de fleurs ont *bercé* mes dérades
> Et d'ineffables vents m'ont *ailé* par instants.   (ll.59-60; my italics)

Whereas Baudelaire was *bercé* by the sea's regular motion, and the poet of the highly regular 'Elévation' soars 'd'une aile vigoureuse' towards the Ideal (1.15), Rimbaud's boat takes poetic pleasure from the ineffable, which resists interpretation and expression.

---

[1] Champion edition, p.528.
[2] Larousse, *Grand Dictionnaire Universel du XIXe Siècle*, 2: 915.
[3] ibid., 7: 171.

The *ivresse* of the old poetics, the remnants of which are washed away in stanza five, is replaced in stanza seven by a different *ivresse*, a shift which also heralds a formal evolution. The sea-poem is the site of fermentation of 'les rousseurs amères de l'amour' (1.28), 'Plus fortes que l'alcool, plus vastes que nos lyres' (1.27). With both hemistichs grammatically and metrically (2-4/2-4) identical, the line echoes the preciously lyrical 6+6 structure which is to be overcome. This fermentation model can be applied to poetic form; as Larousse explains, fermentation is a dynamic process in which an existing structure is undone in order to create a new configuration: 'Travail qui s'opère dans un corps organisé, et par suite duquel les parties qui le composent se combinent entre elles dans des proportions différentes de celles qui existaient auparavant'.[1] The initial rejection of the imposed order does not, therefore, preclude all order *per se*, but rather, sets off an active search for new poetic formal values. The poem features a series of funnels and cones, from the 'trombes' (1.29) to the 'nasses' (1.49) and the 'entonnoirs' (1.80), suggesting the chemical apparatus of fermentation.[2] Thus re-examination of the natural world, and the collapse of the universal analogy, announce the promise of new poetic forms. The boat's keel is also a 'cône', a 'corps qui diminue d'épaisseur de la base au sommet', situating this process firmly in the observing subject.[3] Yet when the keel is mentioned – 'O que ma quille éclate! O que j'aille à la mer!' (1.92) – it expresses the self-destructive despair of the poem's conclusion. The problems caused by the boat's attempt at an objective poetics, freed from a restrictive universal analogy, create interpretative difficulties which soon prove too much to bear.

The boat overwhelmed

By stanza sixteen the boat's initial enthusiasm for the objective observation of natural phenomena turns to fatigue. It is a 'martyr

---

[1] ibid., 8: 254.
[2] According to Larousse, a 'trombe' is an 'amas de vapeurs épaisses' having 'la forme d'un cône dont la base est dirigée le plus souvent vers les nuages, le sommet vers la terre' (15: 543); an 'entonnoir' is an 'ustensile ayant le plus souvent la forme d'un cône évasé, ouvert par la base et le sommet, et servant à transvaser les liquides' (7: 643) and a 'nasse' is a 'panier d'osier, de forme conique, servant à prendre du poisson' (11: 850).
[3] *Grand Dictionnaire Universel du XIX Siècle*, 13: 543.

lassé' (1.61) tired of the interpretative instability which occurs when the subject cannot find stable meaning in objects. This is reflected in the problematic poetic *nombre* of line 65:

Presque île, ballottant / sur mes bords les querelles

Highlighting the importance of the semantic nuance, Murphy notes that 'Verlaine a commencé à écrire *Presqu' [île]*, rectifiant tout de suite en biffant l'[']'.[1] *Presqu'île* alters the sense from 'almost an island' to 'peninsula', but the resulting correction also has important metrical consequences. According to metrical rules, both would be pronounced [prɛskil], and so in order to emphasize the meaning upon which the spelling insists, the reader is obliged to pause and accentuate the masculine 'e' of 'Presque'. This undoes the liaison, both creating hiatus [prɛskə'il] and adding a *syllabe surnuméraire* to the line as the verse mould cracks. The reader can ignore this nuance, of course, but only at the expense of a semantic precision which defines the nature of the object, out there, in 'reality'. By putting into irresolvable conflict the sound and the sense, traditionally meant to coincide in verse, the poet draws his reader into the difficulties involved in making interpretative decisions when rhythmical certainty disappears.

The fermentation has produced an *ivresse* too strong to bear; the boat is now a 'carcasse ivre d'eau' (1.72), 'jeté par l'ouragan dans l'éther' (1.70), the chemical sense of 'éther' suggesting the subject's loss of consciousness. Indeed, the boat's initial urge was to escape the dominant poetic consciousness and examine nature afresh, but once the universal analogy is abandoned, no inherent meaning leaps out from external 'reality'. The loss of guiding aesthetic constants, 'gouvernail et grappin' (1.20), has set the poet adrift like Baudelaire's eclectic: 'il n'a donc pas d'idéal, il n'a pas de parti pris; – ni étoile ni boussole'.[2] Thus the poem reveals the instability of interpretation in an objective poetics, and just as we no longer know whether natural phenomena represent order or disorder, the poem features a formal mixture of both regularity and irregularity.

---

[1] Champion edition, p.529.
[2] *Salon de 1846*, XII, 'De l'éclectisme et du doute' (O.C.II: 473).

The former includes rhythmically balanced alexandrines such as
1.92, hemistichs with a Baudelairean sense of balance such as:
'gouvernail et grappin' (1.20), 'des pôles et des zones' (1.61), 'que tu
dors et t'exiles' (1.87) and 'des drapeaux et des flammes' (1.99), and
the rhymes **'des marées / démarrées'** (ll.9-11), **'ces dorades / mes
dérades'** (ll.57-59) and **'et des îles / et t'exiles'** (ll.85-87). Yet as
Bobillot notes, the poem's 'dissonance dans le mètre' constitutes
'l'éclatant adieu à cette phase [...] d'*obstination métrique*'.[1] Indeed,
the poem features two M6, six C6 (the most in one poem) and four P6
lines, with 25 D6 lines including eleven noun / adjective cases. There
are also seven line-initial monosyllables and six seventh-syllable
accents, four hepta-accentual lines (ll.10, 23, 73, 89) and two cases of
rhythmically problematic *rejet* (ll.21-22, 46-47). In this way the reader
is drawn into the same interpretative dilemma as the boat, scrutinizing
the text as the poet does the world, confronting the 'imprévus
désastres' which challenge our preconceived notions of what is poetic.
Yet without a guarantee of poeticity, we cannot be sure whether
regularity is more poetic than irregularity.

This interpretative difficulty is highlighted by the following lines,
in which the succession of compound nouns is actually obscured by
the metrical *points de repère*:

> Mêlant aux fleurs des yeux / de panthères à peaux
> D'hommes!   (ll.46-47)

If we respect the sixth- and twelfth-syllable accents and pauses, the
syntactic links across them are lost: the first 'des' seems prepositional,
and both 'yeux' and 'peaux' appear to close a sense-unit, whereas
each is the first element of an albeit unfamiliar compound noun. Even
if we pause after 'fleurs', anticipating an *alexandrin romantique*, this
possibility is confounded in the second hemistich. The reader, like the
boat, loses the guarantee of the relationship between metrical rhythm
and reliable meaning; if metre is discarded, syntactic units are saved,
whereas metrical stability can only be preserved at the expense of
sense. The incompatibility of interpretative liberty and the verse

---

[1] 'Quelque chose comme le rythme existe-t-il?', *Ritm* 1 (1991): 55-80; pp.70 and 59;
Bobillot's italics.

mould is underlined as the line-initial monosyllable disrupts the metrical equilibrium:

<u>Libre</u>, fumant, monté / de brumes violettes

Having initially revelled in this liberty, releasing the 'Péninsules démarrées' (1.11), the boat is now only 'Presque île'. Its 'liens frêles' (1.67) suggest that it is no longer completely free, but rather, has returned to the moorings triumphantly thrown off at the outset, closing the window like the poet of 'Les Fenêtres'.

Eventually, the boat goes mad with the interpretative uncertainty, becoming a 'Planche folle' (1.78). It finally admits: 'Je regrette l'Europe aux anciens parapets!' (1.84), yearning to return to the interpretative and structural safety of the previous poetics. Larousse gives a useful definition of 'parapets' which matches the relationship between the veil of verse and the former illusion of inherent meaning:

On nomme *parapets* ou garde-fous des barrières pour préserver d'une chute un observateur placé sur le bord d'une plate-forme, d'un balcon ou d'une corniche élevée, soit dans un monument, soit sur un pont, soit sur un quai, soit, enfin, sur un escarpement naturel. Un parapet doit avoir assez de hauteur pour préserver le corps de la chute, sans être pour autant assez élevé pour obstruer la vue.[1]

The parapets of poetically meaningful rhythm are indeed 'garde-fous', guaranteeing the meaning of nature and preserving us from the *gouffre*. Without them the confrontation with the natural world is fraught with danger, and in the penultimate stanza the boat yearns not for the sea, but rather, a puddle upon which a child releases a model boat. Having initially rejected the former poetic representation of nature, the boat would now happily leave the 'real' sea for a safer representation of it, in order to restore a degree of interpretative certainty. For the child, the puddle *is* the sea, just as for the poet who represents the sea in his poem, his literary interpretation *is* the sea, the rhythmical significance of which is created by the poetic veil. Yet the boat does not simply call for a return to the universal analogy, since the child's vision of the world, on the contrary, is fresh and personal. Indeed, it is to the child's gaze that Baudelaire compares the *artiste*

---

[1] *Grand Dictionnaire Universel du XIXe Siècle*, 12: 296.

moderne in 1863: 'L'enfant voit tout en *nouveauté*; il est toujours *ivre*'.[1]

The 'Poème de la Mer', therefore, does not exist in the sea itself. It must be imposed on the sea by a new poetic gaze which also requires formal novelty in order to distance it from the verse form associated with the universal analogy. Indeed, whereas the 'haleurs' imposed a metrical course on the boat, the child simply lets it go (ll.95-96). This allows new poetic representations to be expressed in similarly fresh forms, in contrast to metrical verse which only presents novelty as irregularities disrupting the canonical mould, imposing a reductive value judgement on them. Whereas the boat initially rejected both the poetic representation of nature and the metre which articulated it, the puddle restores the necessarily representative aspect of poetry yet without the verse mould which would confine it to only one absolute interpretation. This conclusion supports the ideas first expressed in the 'Lettre du voyant', where Rimbaud demands a fresh way of seeing the world and new forms in which to express these visions. A study of this agenda will lead us to the formally and thematically revolutionary poems of 1872.

'La Lettre du voyant'

For Rimbaud, traditional poetic forms have until now hidden from poets the possibility of looking at the world in new ways: 'Musset n'a rien su faire: il y avait des visions derrière la gaze des rideaux: il a fermé les yeux'.[2] The formal veil which Baudelaire used to stir his flagging faith in the universal analogy must now be lifted so that the poet might see the world differently, liberated from the fallacious romantic paradigm. However, as Baudelaire's prose poet and Rimbaud's boat discover, once we open the window or lift the veil, notions of interpretation and poeticity become unstable. It is the visions of the child-poet which henceforth assume poetic value, and Poetry is to be measured on a scale of *voyance*. The problems of authenticity and universality experienced by Baudelaire loom large, since the personal visions of *le moi* are open to contradiction by other subjects. Therefore, a new understanding of the nature of *le moi*, the

---

[1] *Le Peintre de la vie moderne*, III, 'L'Artiste, homme du monde, homme des foules et enfant' (O.C.II: 690).
[2] folio, p.93.

poetic subject, is required, which elevates the personal visions of the poet to a universal plane. The imaginings of *le moi* are no longer to be rejected by romantic poets peddling the universal analogy as if it were the only Truth, and Rimbaud asserts: 'Si les vieux imbéciles n'avaient pas trouvé du moi que la signification fausse, nous n'aurions pas à balayer ces millions de squelettes'.[1]

The infamous 'Je est un autre' suggests that *le moi* is no longer to be seen as a subject observing an external 'objective reality'.[2] Rather, *le moi* becomes a conscious observer of itself, scrutinizing its poetic insights and presenting them as more than just fictions, since any notion of an 'objective reality' is entirely fallacious. What the poet sees, then, must be believed to exist outside-yet-within this split subject. Rimbaud's revolution is to elevate the personal, traditionally labelled 'subjective', suggesting a certain unreality or invalidity, to the status of the objective. The problematic nature of this project is acknowledged by the ambiguity of the word 'vision'. As Larousse explains, 'vision' can designate either the 'action de voir', as if the object were unproblematic, or a 'perception surnaturelle, par les yeux du corps ou par l'intelligence, de choses que la nature a cachées aux hommes'. In this sense, it can mean 'perception d'objets chimériques', 'imagination vaine, idée sans fondement réel', synonymous with 'hallucination'.[3] From a bourgeois point of view the 'reality' of the poet's visions is uncertain, but in the absence of a guarantee as to the meaning of external phenomena, these visions are much more valid than any claims of an 'objective reality'. As Baudelaire writes in 1859: 'Ces choses, parce qu'elles sont fausses, sont infiniment plus près du vrai'.[4] This salutary ambiguity is maintained in the phrase 'les inventions d'inconnu', suggesting that the *inconnu*, the site of a re-motivated poeticity, is not to be observed outside the poet, but rather created within him. However, this internal source of poeticity must be presented as if it were somehow universal, in order to preserve the necessary poetic illusion of authenticity.[5]

Like Baudelaire, Rimbaud also re-motivates the notion of authorial superiority by claiming that poetic insight into these creations/visions

---

[1] folio, p.88.
[2] folio, p.88.
[3] *Grand Dictionnaire Universel du XIXe Siècle*, 15: 1113.
[4] *Salon de 1859*, VII, 'Le Paysage' (O.C.II: 668).
[5] folio, p.93.

is not available to everyone: 'il faut être fort, être né poète, et je me suis reconnu poète'.[1] Yet if poetry is only experienced by a privileged few, it loses the degree of universality without which poetic essence cannot claim to be beyond dispute. Rimbaud solves the problem with the notion of the soul, beginning with that of the poet: 'il cherche son âme, il l'inspecte, il la tente, l'apprend'; 'il arrive à l'inconnu! Puisqu'il a cultivé son âme, déjà riche, plus qu'aucun!'.[2] Since the poet's visions are presented as 'objective', there is a link between the poet's soul and the collective soul. In this way the poet is said simply to enjoy superior sensitivity to something which is both fundamental to all and yet inaccessible to most: 'Le poète définirait la quantité d'inconnu s'éveillant en son temps dans l'âme universelle'.[3]

Recalling Baudelaire's 'Projets de préface', Rimbaud also rejects the reductive, formulaic poetic forms which represent the now abandoned world view. Greek poetry articulated a 'Vie harmonieuse',[4] and as Pierre Sauvanet explains, rhythm was not just an aesthetic notion, but a fundamental Truth, external to man and a universal constant: 'Avec Platon, le rythme apparaît comme une puissance d'ordre, la puissance d'un ordre à la fois cosmique et social'.[5] Thanks to this belief in universally meaningful order, the poetic idea is understood and shared by everyone. Rimbaud compares this to the blind faith of the Middle Ages, which produced texts he deems unpoetic thanks to uninspired obedience to a fallacious formal guarantee of poeticity: 'De la Grèce au mouvement romantique – moyen âge – il y a des lettrés, des versificateurs'. Secure faith leads to sham poetry; the certainty of God and a stable poetic idea produce only: 'prose rimée, un jeu, avachissement et gloire d'innombrables générations idiotes'.[6] Whereas in Greece 'vers et lyres *rythment l'Action*', Rimbaud now situates Poetry beyond this purely rhythmic evidence, as a mysterious given: 'La Poésie ne rythmera plus l'action; elle *sera en avant*'.[7] The poetry he announces will not be a product of

---

[1] Letter of 13 May 1871 (folio, p.84).
[2] folio, pp.88 and 89.
[3] folio, p.92.
[4] folio, p.87.
[5] 'Ordre et chaos ou du rythme en philosophie', *Ritm* 1 (1991), 125-33; p.126.
[6] folio, p.87.
[7] folio, pp.88 and 92; Rimbaud's italics.

predictable formal techniques, but rather, form will have to respond to the *évidence* of the poetic visions which precede and influence it.

Since Poetry now exists independently of formal restrictions, Rimbaud insists: '*Les Misérables* sont un vrai poème'.[1] Just as poetry is possible in prose, verse is no guarantee of poetry. Introducing the verse poem 'Le Cœur supplicié', Rimbaud teases Izambard with the question: 'Est-ce de la poésie?', as if the octosyllables and *abaaabab* rhyme scheme were insufficient proof.[2] Since *voyance* involves a willingness to embrace 'toutes les formes d'amour, de souffrance, de folie', the poet is no longer formally partial. He will study the *inconnu*, and 'si ce qu'il rapporte de *là-bas* a forme, il donne forme; si c'est informe, il donne de l'informe'.[3] Yet in the metrical verse of 1870-71, the formless can only disrupt the verse mould, and thereby acquires negative connotations, disturbing verse harmony as 'unpoetic' discord. For example, 'Les Poètes de sept ans', perhaps also written in May 1871, implies that Poetry is above all a way of feeling, of responding to the world before a word is written. The divine guarantee is rejected – 'Il n'aimait pas Dieu' (l.48) – in favour of 'la Liberté ravie' (l.32) and 'Vertige, écroulements' (l.61) recalling the 'écroulements d'eaux au milieu des bonaces' and the disintegration of order ('Le Bateau ivre', l.51). Traditional poetic form also crumbles, with the appearance of Rimbaud's first F6 line (l.33) along with three C6, two P6 and eleven D6 lines, yet this can only be seen in terms of a rebellion against order. The 1872 poems, however, remove the metrical framework which characterizes non-canonical forms as disorder, and express the poet's visions without reductive pre-conceptions as to the inherent poetic superiority of certain privileged forms over others. As we shall see, this experiment with a formally inclusive poetics ultimately proves impossible to maintain, as the poetic idea, rather than successfully embracing the poetic potential of the formless, threatens to disappear completely.

---

[1] folio, p.92.
[2] Letter of 13 May 1871 (folio, p.84).
[3] folio, p.91; Rimbaud's italics.

5
A Formally Inclusive Poetics

It is generally agreed that 'L'histoire d'une de mes folies' described in *Une saison en enfer* (1873) refers to the poetic activity of the Spring and Summer of 1872.[1] The narrator tells us: 'le printemps m'a apporté l'affreux rire de l'idiot', relating his descent into madness after rejecting absolute aesthetic values: 'Un soir, j'ai assis la Beauté sur mes genoux. – Et je l'ai trouvée amère – Et je l'ai injuriée'.[2] With a capital 'B' this notion of absolute Beauty maintains the universal analogy which provides for Hogarth 'les principes de la nature d'après lesquels nous sommes déterminés à regarder certaines formes comme belles et gracieuses, et d'autres comme laides et désagréables'.[3] This corresponds to the principle upheld by Banville in 1872, that certain verse forms are inherently more beautiful, more poetic than others: 'il faut connaître tous [les rythmes] qu'ont employés nos prédécesseurs, et qui ont été construits conformément à des lois éternelles, et ne pas les remplacer inutilement par d'autres qui ne les valent pas'.[4] For him, non-canonical structures are aesthetically worthless. They are a product of 'l'empirique fantaisie du premier venu, en dehors de toute harmonie musicale', a remark echoing Baudelaire's dismissal of fantasy as a threat to Poetry.[5]

This formal tyranny perpetuates the reductive *forme/informe* distinction of the universal analogy according to which the irregular is deemed unpoetic in comparison to canonical form. The poet of 1872, however, declares this poetic illusion at an end: 'Rien de rien ne m'illusionne' ('Bannières de mai', l.23). For Rimbaud, *forme* and *informe* are no longer aesthetic opposites: 'si ce qu'il rapporte de *là-bas* a forme, il donne forme; si c'est informe, il donne de l'informe'. The idea of exclusive Beauty must, therefore, be replaced by one of

---

[1] See, for example, Cornulier, *Théorie du vers*, p.251, or *Rimbaud, Œuvres*, ed. by Suzanne Bernard and André Guyaux, Paris: Garnier, 1981, pp.470-71.
[2] folio, p.177.
[3] *Analysis of Beauty*, 1753; *Analyse de la Beauté*, 1991, p.45. See also pp.88-89 of the present study.
[4] *Petit Traité*, p.166.
[5] ibid., p.158, and *Salon de 1859*: 'la fantaisie est vaste comme l'univers multiplié par tous les êtres pensants qui l'habitent. Elle est la première chose venue interprétée par le premier venu' (O.C.II: 644-45). See also pp.102-03 of this study.

inclusive beauty in which all structures have equal poetic potential, with no absolute dichotomy between poetic *forme* or unpoetic *informe*. In 1873 Rimbaud compares this project to a series of *couacs*, which denote, as Mario Richter observes, 'un son faux et discordant, un faux accord dans un contexte prétendu harmonieux'.[1] More precisely, the fallacious notion of harmony underlying aesthetic exclusivity will now be rendered meaningless.

The narrator of *Une saison en enfer* rejects all social and religious absolutes, returning to his pre-Christian roots: 'Je n'ai jamais été de ce peuple-ci; je n'ai jamais été chrétien; [...] je ne comprends pas les lois; je n'ai pas le sens moral [...]. Oui, j'ai les yeux fermés à votre lumière. Je suis une bête, un nègre'.[2] In 'Mauvais sang' he considers his pagan forefathers with whom he shares 'l'idolâtrie et l'amour du sacrilège'.[3] This contradictory statement resumes the poet's delicate task: he will sacrilegiously denounce accepted notions of Poetry and Beauty, but he is simultaneously unable to escape an idolatrous need for some sort of divine image, anything but the canonical ones: 'Ah! je suis tellement délaissé que j'offre à n'importe quelle divine image des élans vers la perfection'.[4] His indiscriminating openness towards any divine image suggests a willingness to see Poetry in anything, allowing any form the potential for structural perfection. As he admits in 'Alchimie du verbe': 'Je finis par trouver sacré le désordre de mon esprit'.[5]

This formal inclusivity accompanies the fresh look at nature announced in 'Le Bateau ivre'. Like Baudelaire in his essay on Hugo, the narrator is similarly dissatisfied with the restrictive interpretation of scientific certainties in terms of the divine:

Mais n'y a-t-il pas un supplice réel en ce que, depuis cette déclaration de la science, le christianisme, l'homme *se joue*, se prouve les évidences, se gonfle du plaisir de répéter ces preuves, et ne vit que comme cela! Torture subtile, source de mes divagations spirituelles. La nature pourrait s'ennuyer peut-être![6]

---

[1] 'Echos baudelairiens dans le prologue d'*Une saison en enfer* de Rimbaud', *Parade Sauvage* 15 (1998): 86-90; p.89.
[2] folio, p.182.
[3] folio, p.178.
[4] folio, p.181.
[5] folio, p.194.
[6] folio, p.200.

Whereas, like Baudelaire in 'La Pipe', the poet of 'Oraison du soir' sat contentedly in the 'impalpables voilures' of his tobacco-smoke (1.4), the narrator rejects the veil of illusion which man constructs around him: 'N'est-ce pas parce que nous cultivons la brume! [...] Et l'ivrognerie! et le tabac! et l'ignorance! et les dévouements!'.[1] Instead he declares: 'Je vais dévoiler tous les mystères: mystères religieux ou naturels'.[2] The result is the projection of an interior vision onto an external object: 'Je m'habituai à l'hallucination simple; je voyais très-franchement une mosquée à la place d'une usine'. The azure sky becomes: 'une mer de flammes et de fumée', 'des calèches sur les routes du ciel' or 'des plages sans fin couvertes de blanches nations en joie'.[3] Like Baudelaire's clouds, nature provides raw material for a wide variety of poetic visions, and recalling 'Les Fenêtres', Rimbaud's narrator comments: 'A chaque être, plusieurs *autres* vies me semblaient dues'.[4]

Wondering, 'Puis-je décrire la vision', the narrator realizes: 'Les hallucinations sont innombrables'.[5] Since his visions replace the universal analogy, they refuse the verse form closely associated with it, a form which takes metrical *nombre* as its principle. As the boat discovered in 'Le Bateau ivre', fresh poetic visions resist expression in the *nombre* of metre and rhyme. The 1872 poems, therefore, hinder our perception of the *nombre* which we anticipate in a poetic text, creating an impression of formlessness which recreates for the reader, on a formal level, the sort of interpretative dilemmas experienced by the poet. As we hunt for a form constantly submerged in the *informe* our faith in form as a reliable guarantee of poeticity is increasingly challenged. Anticipating our natural reaction to a poetics of the formless, the texts constantly resist reduction to familiar, regular forms, forcing us to scrutinize our accepted notions of the poetic.

From alexandrine to dodecasyllable

The metrical issues raised by only sixty-four dodecasyllables, in just two 1872 poems, 'Qu'est-ce...' (24) and 'Mémoire' (40), have inspired much insightful commentary, from Cornulier and Bobillot in

---

[1] folio, p.200.
[2] folio, p.186.
[3] folio, pp.194, 182, 194 and 203.
[4] folio, p.197; Rimbaud's italics.
[5] folio, pp.185 and 186.

particular. These dodecasyllables are striking for their unprecedented concentration of rhythmically problematic structures. Eleven lines from 'Qu'est-ce...' and twelve from 'Mémoire' are F6, F7 or M6; these two poems feature four of the five F7 lines and seven of the eight F6 lines of the whole Rimbaldian corpus. Furthermore, all four F6 and M6 lines in the 1871 poems can be scanned 8/4,[1] whereas in 1872 at least nine F6, F7 or M6 lines refuse this scansion, the last defence before slipping into a resolutely non-metrical framework.[2] Of the other lines, eleven are C6 and two P6, categories ignored by Cornulier and Bobillot. This gives a total of thirty-seven metrically problematic lines, leaving regular alexandrines in the minority, with the D6 category affecting a further eleven. Only four lines from 'Qu'est-ce...' and around twenty from 'Mémoire' can be read as a standard 6+6 alexandrine.

Such 'dérèglement soigneusement réglé de la métrique de l'alexandrin'[3] means that the reader is unable to apprehend the lines' syllabic equivalence, as the anticipated metrical markers are lost. Throughout both poems, the pre-existent metrical structure is submerged in unpredictable rhythms. For Cornulier, then, the poems are non-metrical:

Certes, il peut y avoir là des divisions rythmiques évidentes; mais du moment qu'elles ne délimitent pas des *segments métriques*, c'est-à-dire contribuant par leur quantité syllabique à l'isométrie, elles ne déterminent pas une *mesure*, ne sont pas *métriques*.[4]

Bobillot agrees that most lines are 'parfaitement non-métriques'.[5] They depart from the sacred alexandrine model, the guarantee of poeticity defined by its rigidity:

Nous ne reconnaissons, désormais, de mètre proprement dit que lorsque l'équivalence de vers à vers se mesure à une structure abstraite, transcendante [...] indifférente à

---

[1] For Cornulier , 'en complément ou au lieu de la composition 6 + 6 malmenée ou absente, le rythme 8-4 (ou 4-4-4, ou 3-5-4) fonctionne comme substitut de la mesure de base' ('Sur la métrique des "premiers" vers de Rimbaud', *Parade Sauvage Colloque* 2 (1990), 4-15; p.11).
[2] Cornulier, 'Métrique du vers de 12 syllabes chez Rimbaud', p.157.
[3] Cornulier, *Art poétique*, p.91.
[4] *Art poétique*, p.161; and *Théorie du vers*, p.256.
[5] 'Le clinamen d'Arthur Rimbaud', p.97.

tous les énoncés qu'elle pré-détermine, et, en droit, indépendante de l'articulation syntaxico-accentuelle concrète [...] immanente à chaque énoncé singulier.[1]

Bobillot explains, 'le "vers" était le lieu élu de la prédétermination', and the traditional alexandrine is 'doublement *pré-déterminé*: par une mesure abstraite (le 'mètre'), par une prosodie spéciale (le 'syllabisme')'.[2] Yet in 'Qu'est-ce...' and 'Mémoire', Rimbaud retains only isosyllabism, which resists intuitive perception of its regularity thanks to the variety of dodecasyllabic combinations therein. The disoriented reader must resort to counting the syllables in order to confirm this isosyllabism, losing formal certainty in an impression of formlessness. For Bobillot, this represents 'la *liquidation métrico-prosodique*', since unpredictably rhythmed isosyllabism subverts the metrical definition of the alexandrine: '12 syllabes, certes, mais il n'est pas certain que ces vers se perçoivent comme égaux entre eux; autre dissociation, donc: *le nombre n'est pas le mètre*'.[3] This disappearance of metre is confirmed by the relative paucity of D6 lines, whose function is precisely metrical disruption; without metre, they lose their relevance. Similarly, there are now few first- or seventh-syllable accents, since the metrical accents which they might undermine have vanished. Adjacent accentuation no longer disturbs the metre, but creates a staccato effect between semantically loaded monosyllables. In 'Mémoire', the accentual emphasis on internal syllables, accompanied by Pv and Cv *contre-rejets*, supersedes the line-final accent so that we can no longer be sure where one line finishes and the next begins:

leur livre de maro / quin rouge! Hé<u>las</u>, <u>Lui</u>, <u>comme</u>	(l.21)
meut ses <u>bras</u>, <u>noirs</u>, et *<u>lourds</u>*, / et <u>frais</u> sur<u>tout</u>, <u>d'herbe</u>. *<u>Elle</u>*	(l.6)

For Cornulier, the disappearance of metre is equivalent to the disappearance of the poetic line itself. His hardline stance, which over-simplifies the poetic potential of the verse/prose dichotomy upon which our poets capitalize, nonetheless highlights how rhythmical stability vanishes without regular *coupes*:

---

[1] 'Entre mètre et non-mètre: le "décasyllabe" de Rimbaud', *Parade Sauvage* 10 (1994), 29-44; p.29.
[2] 'Vers, prose, langue', *Poétique* 89 (1992), 71-91; pp.90 and 72; Bobillot's italics.
[3] ibid., pp.74 and 75; Bobillot's italics.

La disparition de la mesure dans certains vers est la disparition du vers-même en ce qu'il a à cette époque d'essentiel. C'est par un euphémisme trompeur que certains critiques parlent, à ce sujet, de 'rythmes impalpables'; car cette expression voile la disparition même du rythme strictement métrique: le vers impalpable, c'est la prose.[1]

The obliteration of metre, Bobillot confirms, is a rejection of the impersonal poetic order which it represents, the formal regularity which no longer guarantees poeticity:

Le mètre est cette commune mesure abstraite et transcendante au moule de laquelle tout énoncé poétique devrait, pour être reçu, se conformer – énoncé, par là même, immédiatement communautaire et ne relevant d'aucun 'sujet' particulier.[2]

The remaining rhythms, therefore, are entirely contingent, unpredictable, which requires a constant effort on the reader's part:

Le rythme est cet incessant travail, immanent et concret, grâce auquel tout énoncé poétique, ne se conformant à aucun moule preéxistant [...] ne s'offrant pas, non plus, comme le moule potentiel d'autres énoncés, préserve l'éphémère de sa singularité.[3]

Metrical *nombre* disappears while syllabic *nombre* remains. In this sense the prophecy of the *voyant* is fulfilled, with poems still 'pleins du *Nombre*', yet a *nombre* which becomes almost unrecognizable, remaining one step ahead of the reader.[4] Thus Rimbaud's remark 'La vieillerie poétique avait une bonne part dans mon alchimie du verbe' might suggest that he retains the traditional poetic notion of regularity, yet shifts it from a metrical to a syllabic level.[5] This regularity is practically imperceptible in the rhythmical haze, and the dodecasyllables of 1872 give the impression of formlessness while nevertheless retaining regular form as a sort of horizon which the reader senses without ever being able to perceive it clearly. As we shall see, the 1872 poems exploit our anticipation of, and search for, regularity as a poetic constant, demanding we interrogate the hitherto unquestioned assumption that it guarantees poeticity.

---

[1] 'Métrique du vers de 12 syllabes chez Rimbaud', p.162; Cornulier's italics.
[2] 'Le vers la lettre – des "rimes grammatiques" au "poème littéral"', *Ritm* 3 (1992): 45-76; p.76.
[3] ibid., p.76.
[4] folio, p.92; Rimbaud's italics.
[5] folio, p.194.

The decasyllable

The same rhythmical uncertainty-within-regularity characterizes the 1872 decasyllables. 'Tête de faune', possibly of May 1872, has also provoked much detailed metrical criticism. In a thorough historico-metrical analysis, Marc Dominicy suggests that: 'la métrique de *Tête de faune* annonce les 10-syllabes déstructurés que Rimbaud composera entre mai et juillet 1872'.[1] Like the dodecasyllables, although the poem is isosyllabic, it is emphatically heterometric. Bobillot asks: 'Dans le 10-syll., n'y a-t-il, de métrique, que l'articulation 4+6 – comme, dans le 12 –, il n'y a, *stricto sensu*, de métrique, que le 6+6?'[2] and the first stanza can be scanned more or less traditionally: 4+6, 4+6, 4-6, 4+6. Yet the second stanza demands mostly 5/5 scansion, 'cette innovation romantique':[3] 5+5, 5-5, 5+5, 6-4 (4+6?), and the final stanza continues the uncertainty: 5+5, 6+4 (4+6?), 6+4, 6+4 (4+6?). Cornulier confirms that 4/6 and 5/5 are 'des mètres composés radicalement différents' which present 'des combinaisons de longueurs qui n'ont rien de commun'.[4] This rhythmical unpredictability obscures poetic form in apparent formlessness, as metrical regularity disappears:

> Une telle hésitation, mettant en balance deux modes de scansion, risque fort, pour le moins, de remettre en cause le statut de pur 'mètre' […]. Le 4-6 rimbaldien, au même titre que son 5-5, serait donc d'emblée, seulement – et au mieux –, *quasi-métrique*; en aucun cas, 'métrique' *stricto sensu.*[5]

Without metre, the reader must search for rhythmic reading strategies, none of which can be definitive. Dominicy suggests that the *contexte métrique* of stanza two might impose a 5+5 *coupe* in line 8, the C5 creating 'une violente discordance syntaxique',[6] while Bobillot

---

[1] '*Tête de faune* ou les règles d'une exception', *Parade sauvage* 15 (1998), 109-88; p.178.

[2] 'Entre mètre & non-mètre: le "décasyllabe" chez Verlaine', in *Verlaine à la loupe*, ed. by Jean-Michel Gouvard and Steve Murphy, Paris: Champion, 2000, pp.179-200; p.185.

[3] 'Entre mètre et non-mètre: le "décasyllabe" de Rimbaud', p. 31. On the date of the text, see p.37.

[4] 'L'invention du "décasyllabe" chez Verlaine décadent: le 4-6, le 5-5, le mixte et le n'importe quoi', in *Verlaine à la loupe*, pp.243-89; p.245.

[5] 'Entre mètre et non-mètre: le "décasyllabe" de Rimbaud', p.33.

[6] '*Tête de faune* ou les règles d'une exception', p.160.

considers 'une lecture purement "accentuelle", et, partant, résolument non-métrique'.[1] 'Tête de faune' features the same sort of natural imagery as many of the 1872 poems, and just as 'la feuillée incertaine' (l.2) suggests the hesitations of the observer of nature, so too the heterometrical form is similarly uncertain. The poet's interpretative uncertainties before natural phenomena are reflected, therefore, in formal uncertainty for the reader, a technique developed in the other 1872 decasyllables: 'Plates-bandes...', 'Jeune ménage' and 'Comédie de la soif' (V).

'Comédie de la soif' (V) begins 5-5, 5+5, 5+5, yet soon topples into 6+4, 4+6, 5+5, before presenting a line which resists any canonical scansion, with accents possible on only the third and seventh syllables:

> Expirer / en ces viole / ttes humides (1.7)

'Jeune ménage' presents the same mixture of 4+6, 5/5 and 6/4 lines, with three more 3-7 *coupes*, although the second example might allow a recuperative 6-4 scansion:

Pas de pla / ce: des coffrets / et des huches	(l.2)	(3-7 or 7+3)
Plusieurs en / trent, marrai / nes mécontentes	(l.9)	(3-7 or 6-4)
Puis y re / stent! le ména / ge s'absente	(l.11)	(3-7 or 7-3)

Similarly, 'Plates-bandes...' augments the 4/6, 5/5, 6/4 selection with 3/7 or 7/3 lines, the 3/7 rhythm occasionally reinforced by internal rhyme:

Plates-ban / des d'amaran / tes jusqu'à	(l.1)
La Juliett / e, ça rappe / lle l'Henriette	(l.13)
Bavardag / e des enfants / et des cages.	(l.20)
Au poison / des escargots / et du buis	(l.22)
Boulevart / sans mouvement / ni commerce	(l.25)

All these lines resist *coupes* after the fourth, fifth and sixth syllables, as recognizable metrical *forme* vanishes in the *informe* and the poet pushes the reader's perception of regularity beyond canonical norms. Regularity no longer defines the text as a rhythmical *évidence*, but

---

[1] 'Entre mètre et non-mètre: le "décasyllabe" de Rimbaud', p.33.

rather, hovers on the edge of perception, demanding constant effort on the reader's part in a search for the recurrent formal principles which, until now, have been a given of the poetic text.

Other metres

Rimbaud also engages his reader in this search for poetically meaningful form in other, less common metres such as the hendecasyllable.[1] Although it admits *coupes* of 5/6, 6/5, 4/7 or 7/4, tradition dictates that they should not be mixed in the same poem, since regularity of the *coupe* is required to compensate for the unfamiliar syllabic count. Of course, in 'Larme' and 'Est-elle almée...', Rimbaud mixes them all, confusing the reader rhythmically on both syllabic and metrical levels. Cornulier observes of the lines:

Ils n'ont pas de mètre réel, ils n'ont qu'une métrique de papier, un nombre total non accessible à la perception, obligeant le lecteur à les lire comme des vers, et le privant en même temps du sentiment de la mesure.[2]

In 'Michel et Christine' the 3/8 divisions, like 3/7 in the decasyllable, transgress the limit of recognizable form:

Zut alors / si le soleil quitte ces bords!	(l.1)
Dans les sau / les, dans la vieille cour d'honneur	(l.3)
Fuyez l'heu / re des éclairs supérieurs	(l.10)
Blond troupeau, / quand voici nager ombre et soufre	(l.11)

Eight syllables is the maximum, however; the absence of 2/9 or 9/2 *coupes* supports Cornulier's observation that nonasyllables are conspicuously absent from the 1872 texts.[3] He suggests that eight syllables represents our 'capacité métrique'; since the isosyllabism of lines of up to eight syllables is perceptible intuitively, they need no fixed caesura. Lines of over nine syllables, however, require regular *coupes* which facilitate our perception of isosyllabism.[4] Therefore, by

---

[1] Michèle Aquien notes: 'un vers assez ancien, mais utilisé en France de manière irrégulière' (*Dictionnaire de poétique*, Paris: Librairie Générale Française, p.143).
[2] 'Mètre "Impair", métrique "Insaisissable"? Sur les "derniers vers" de Rimbaud', in *Le Souci des apparences*, ed. by Marc Dominicy, Brussels: Editions de l'Université, 1989: pp.75-91; p.81.
[3] 'Métrique du vers de 12 syllabes chez Rimbaud', p.163.
[4] *Théorie du vers*, p.18.

extending the limit of the *coupes* to eight syllables in 'Michel et Christine', Rimbaud pushes the reader to the very limits of perception of the formal regularity by which the poetic text is recognized.

Whereas in lines of more than eight syllables the impression of regularity is undermined by a lack of internal measure, shorter lines must be subverted in a different way, by the disturbance of isosyllabism itself. Indeed, Cornulier shows that all 1872 lines of over eight syllables are isosyllabic, whilst several shorter lines feature one syllable more or less.[1] This technique disrupts perceptible regularity more noticeably, often with just one problematic line per poem:

(a 6 amid 5s)	Et visible à l'œil nu	('Âge d'or', 1.15)
(a 6 amid 5s)	et blêmi, justement!	('Entends comme…', 1.20)
(a 6 amid 5s)	Et se mêle au Cédron	('Le loup criait…', 1.12)
(an 8 amid 7s)	Qu'à sa mort, pourtant, ô mon Dieu!	('Honte', 1.19)[2]

In contrast to the hazy rhythmic uncertainty in the *vers composés*, this technique is indeed 'visible à l'œil nu'. It disturbs the isosyllabism, easily perceptible in these *mètres simples*, with a *faux accord* and confounds poetic regularity with a line formally irreconcilable with its neighbours.

This insertion of a *vers faux* is a common feature of the 1873 versions of 1872 poems quoted in *Une saison en enfer* where, as Cornulier observes: 'Rimbaud augmente, en retouchant ses poèmes, la dose d'irrégularité métrique'.[3] 'Chanson de la plus haute tour', reduced to a refrain and two stanzas, remains pentasyllabic except for the line:

De cent sales mouches (5) → Des sales mouches (4)

In 'Faim', the altered line 9 retains its seven syllables, yet line 12 becomes octosyllabic:

Pains couchés aux vallées grises! (7) → Pains semés dans les vallées grises. (8)

---

[1] See *Théorie du vers*, pp.258-59.
[2] For a comprehensive study of these lines, see Bobillot, 'Rimbaud et le "vers libre"', *Poétique* 66 (1986), 199-216; p.202.
[3] 'Métrique du vers de 12 syllabes chez Rimbaud', p.164.

'Le loup criait…' features among its heptasyllables the following line:

> Et se mèle au Cédron. (6)

Similarly, while certain variants of 'L'Eternité' retain the penta-syllable, line four loses two syllables and two new lines added to the fifth stanza feature three and four syllables:

> Avec le soleil (5)   →   Au soleil (3)
>
> Le Devoir s'exhale (5)   →   Votre ardeur (3)
>   Est le devoir (4)

The amputation of two syllables, the most explicit of these examples, obliterates any notion of meaningful isosyllabism, and leaves us with a poem which staunchly refuses the syllabic regularity traditionally associated with 'poetic' value.

As the poet abandons familiar poetic form in order to embrace the poetic potential of the *informe*, we are led to wonder: in the absence of a stable aesthetic hierarchy, are we to see all these structures as equally poetic? Rimbaud shows us the importance of context to the question, with poems where line-lengths are mixed, but in recurrent strophic patterns, such as 'Comédie de la soif' I (7/2/7/7/7/7/7/7) and II (6/5/6/5), and 'La Rivière de Cassis' (11/5/11/5/11/5, 11/7/11/7/11/7). Heterosyllabism seems acceptable when used in predictable, recognizable patterns, but transgressive in isolation, inviting reflection on these units' poetic value. Are the *vers faux*, then, really *informes*? Surely the hexasyllabic *vers faux*, in an alexandrine, would be seen as a traditional hemistich? In the following couplet from 'Michel et Christine', diaeresis – correct in the first case and permissible in the second – would give two alexandrines:

> Cette religi-euse / après-midi d'orage
> Sur l'Europe anci-enne / où cent hordes iront! (ll.19-20)

Yet the syllabic context, however imperceptible, is hendecasyllabic. If we are to respect the regularity which we expect of a poetic text, we must resist the temptation towards recognizable poetic form which these 'alexandrines' represent. The form traditionally seen as poetic must thereby be rejected as disruptive, as notions of *forme* and *informe* are reversed. The regular becomes irregular, and vice versa, revealing the ultimate relativity of aesthetic values and the importance of context to the notion of poeticity.

Similarly, the monosyllabic *rejets* of 'Honte', 'n'aura / Pas' (ll.1-2) and 'son / Nez' (ll.5-6), give octosyllabic sense-units at odds with the heptasyllabic lines. In terms of the canon so fiercely guarded by Banville, it is the octosyllabic units which are more 'poetic', yet in 'Honte' they are seen as transgressive, destabilizing a regularity made from unfamiliar line-lengths. Bobillot suggests manipulating the line-final *e féminin* in order to compensate for the only tetrasyllable amid the pentasyllables of the revised 'Chanson de la plus haute tour' (1873):

> Au bourdon farouch (5)
> →   *e* Des sales mouches. (5)[1]

However, as Murphy observes:

> Si l'on peut donc, par diverses astuces, réduire ou augmenter le nombre de syllabes de certains vers pour effectuer une 'rectification' métrique, de telles opérations ne font que mettre en évidence le caractère spontanément amétrique de ces vers.[2]

Although this constant compensation for structural discrepancies provides us with an enjoyable challenge, it ultimately provides no answers; the search for rhythm leads only to an endless questioning. If the *informe* is as poetic as *forme*, irregularity as poetic as regularity, the stability of these very notions vanishes. Syllables might be added or removed without detriment to the text's poeticity. 'La Rivière de Cassis' features a line identical to one from the earlier octosyllabic 'Les Corbeaux', except for the removal of one syllable. Now, however, they are both equally poetic, according to their respective syllabic contexts:

> (8) Les chers corbeaux délici-eux!   ('Les Corbeaux', l.6)
> (7) Chers corbeaux délici-eux!   ('La Rivière de Cassis', l.16)

---

[1] 'Vaches, mouches, figures: *Les reparties de Nina, Chanson de la plus haute tour, Chanson de la plus haute tour*', *Parade Sauvage* 14 (1997): 19-32, p.24.
[2] Champion edition, p.728, note 18.

Despite this instability, however, the reader of poetry nevertheless retains a certain faith in order, since, as Baudelaire argued, it is a fundamental requirement of the poetic mind. It is this faith that the texts challenge, constantly provoking a search for an order which eludes us time and again.

'Bonne pensée du matin', for example, is the most formally iconoclastic poem of 1872, and tests our faith in regularity to the limit. Despite the recurrent four-line stanzas there is no syllabic or metrical constant: 9/8/8/6, 9/8/10/4, 9/9/8/6, 8/8/8/6, 6/8/8/12.[1] Without a constant, we cannot see the lines as either *forme* or *informe*. We cannot ascertain their poetic value without knowing against which measure to read them, and this is the difficulty of Rimbaud's inclusive poetics: our constant uncertainty as to the lines' formal significance. Cornulier highlights 'l'à peu près complète liberté' of the poem as all impression of *forme* is lost.[2] For Bobillot, 'par défaut de pression métrique faisant critère', the text inspires an irresolvable formal questioning, 'une tentative sans précédent pour piéger la lecture dans un dispositif instable qui l'invite tour à tour à choisir la prosodie contre la métrique, la métrique contre la prosodie, sans qu'on puisse s'arrêter à un parti satisfaisant'.[3] In the revised version of 1873, this inconsistency is increased by further disfiguring the octosyllables; while some altered lines still allow octosyllabic scansion (ll.7, 9, 10, 13-15, 18), others appear to lose or gain a syllable quite arbitrarily:

(8) Vers le soleil des Hespérides   →   (7) Au soleil des Hespérides
(8) Vénus! laisse un peu les amants   →   (9) Vénus! quitte un instant les Amants
(8) Pour que leurs forces soient en paix. → (7) Que leurs forces soient en paix

In search of compensatory 'poetic' regularity, and echoing the 'élisions naturelles' proposed by Bernard and Guyaux,[4] Michel Murat suggests that an octosyllabic constant appears if we ignore each pronounced feminine 'e':

Les ennéasyllabes (v.1,5,9,10) et le décasyllabe (v.7) qui se glissent dans les octo-syllabes, sont pris dans un jeu parodique: si on les lit comme des vers, ils sont faux et

---

[1] Scansion confirmed by Bobillot, 'Rimbaud et le "vers libre"', p.202.
[2] 'Métrique du vers de 12 syllabes chez Rimbaud', p.157.
[3] 'Rimbaud et le "vers libre"', p.207.
[4] See their edition of Rimbaud's *Œuvres*, p.436.

dérythmés; pour qu'ils soient justes, il faut les lire comme s'ils étaient de la prose: l'évidence du vers est rétablie au prix de cette transgression.[1]

This scansion works in several lines, before faltering at line 11 where a pronounced 'e' is required:

> Où la richess[e] de la ville

Here, 'e'-elision provides only a heptasyllable, as our attempt to restore regularity is confounded. Yet Murat's idea of reading the lines 'prosaically' in order to restore their verse qualities is attractive, as Rimbaud pits two poetic traditions – isosyllabism and the counted 'e' – against each other in irresolvable tension. As if to taunt us, the poem ends on a perfect alexandrine, its rhythmic equilibrium and phonetic patterns providing welcome relief after our search:

> *En* attendant *l*e bain / d*ans l*a <u>m</u>er, à <u>m</u>i*d*i.   (1.20)
> ã a ã d ã l   d ã *l*a <u>m</u>   a <u>m</u> i *d* i

Yet since the *contexte métrique*, seen by Cornulier as vital to the perception of metre, contains no other alexandrines, the status of what was once an unquestionable guarantee of poeticity is now uncertain. Throughout the poem, syllabic regularity is only possible if we sacrifice the modes of pronunciation which, traditionally, contribute to this very regularity. If it is only by the transgression of one code that the reader can adhere to another, the value of the regularity which we try to achieve is undermined. Rimbaud compounds the difficulties of our search for recognizably poetic form by defamiliarizing certain vowel sequences. They no longer act as a signpost towards regularity, but rather, as obstacles to a coherent rhythmical reading, drawing us into an irresolvable dilemma.

Syllabic uncertainty

Rimbaud ensures that the reader searching for rhythm is constantly drawn into contradicting canonical norms, as reliable values of syllabic interpretation are lost. In 'Plates-bandes...' the decasyllabic context demands an unnatural diaeresis:

---

[1] 'A propos de *Mouvement*', *Parade Sauvage* 4 (1986): 69-77; p.71.

– Je sais que c'est Toi, qui, dans ces **li-eux**   (l.3)
  1   2   3   4   5   6   7   8 9 10

Yet since the first four lines present strongly marked *coupes* of 3-7, 6+4, 5+5 and 4+6, there is no regular metrical context, and the syllabic requirement cannot be felt intuitively. The reader is obliged both to count syllables and then to dislocate the vowel sequence in order to provide the formal regularity which we assume the poetic text demands. Rhythmical regularity can only be achieved by creating a syllabic *faux accord*. In 'Bonne pensée du matin', where the *contexte métrique* is uncertain, Murat's reading, without the 'e' *caduc*, also requires unnatural synaeresis to provide an octosyllable:

Ils prépar [ent] les lambris pré**cieux**   (1.10)
  1   2 3   4   5   6   7 8

Restoring both the 'e' and correct diaeresis would give a decasyllable, albeit 3-7 or 7+3:

Ils prépa / rent les lambris / préci-**eux**
  1   2 3   4   5   6   7   8 9 10

However, there is no other decasyllable in the immediate metrical context, and once again, the traditionally correct interpretation is sacrificed to a regularity whose poeticity we are increasingly tempted to doubt. Lastly, 'Le loup criait...' features two problematic lines among its heptasyllables:

(6? 7?)   Les salades, les fr**ui**ts   (1.5)
(7? 8?)   Ne mange que des vi**ol**ettes   (1.8)

These can be forced to fit the metre with unnatural diaeresis ('fru-its') and synaeresis ('violettes') although in the chaotically heterosyllabic context of the other 1873 poems, the poetic value of isosyllabic regularity, which we pursue via these *entorses*, is far from certain.

    It is not just metrical instability that creates problems. The poet treats similar units inconsistently, creating what Bobillot calls 'élasticité métrico-prosodique'.[1] In 'Plates-bandes...', stanza three begins with correct diaeresis on substantive use of 'ion', with synaeresis on 'anciennes':

> – Calmes maisons, anc*iennes* passi-**ons!**   (1.9)
>   1   2   3 4   5 6 7 8 9 10

The very next line, however, providing a *rime pauvre* for the ear if not the eye, demands synaeresis on both 'io' elements in order to fit the decasyllable:

> Kiosque de la Folle par affection.   (1.10)
>   1   2 3 4 5 6 7 8 9 10

Not only does this immediately contradict the previous line, but also a *rime léonine* is confounded by the incorrect synaeresis: [i-ɔ̃/ jɔ̃]. We could compensate by expanding 'anciennes' with diaeresis, and contracting 'passions' to increase the rhyme strength to [sjɔ̃]:

> – Calmes maisons, anci-ennes pa**ssions!**
> Kiosque de la Folle par affe**ction.**

Yet the reader simply compensates for the poet's own transgression of the syllabic norm with another transgression, pronouncing 'passions' as if it were an imperfect verb rather than a noun. The challenge to accept the poetic potential of the *informe* leads us into an irresolvable dilemma. This inconsistency is maintained throughout the poem:

> Charmante station du chemin de fer (1.14)   Réuni-**on** des scènes infinie (1.27)
>   1   2 3 4 5 6   7 8 9 10   1 2 3 4   5   6 7 8 9 10

In other texts, incorrect synaeresis features in 'millions' ('Comédie de la soif', 1.42), 'questions' ('Âge d'or', 1.5), 'violette' ('Fêtes de la faim', 1.22, 'Comédie de la soif', 1.74, 'Le loup criait...', 1.8) and 'patience' ('Chanson de la plus haute tour', 1.13). As Banville states, 'ieu' requires diaeresis in polysyllabic adjectives, such as 'supéri-eurs' and 'délici-eux'.[2] Rimbaud, however, uses synaeresis in 'furieux'

---

[1] See 'Rimbaud et le vers libre', p.203, and also 'Elasticité métrico-prosodique chez Apollinaire: Une lecture formelle des *Colchiques*', *Poétique* 84 (1990): 411-33.
[2] *Petit Traité*, p.37.

('Qu'est-ce pour nous...', l.13), 'religieuse' ('Michel et Christine', l.19), 'sérieusement' ('Jeune ménage', l.12) and 'vicieux' ('Âge d'or', l.29). The following line is doubly infuriating, since traditional diaeresis would give a dodecasyllable, albeit F6, if pronounced according to tradition:

> Les passi-**ons** mortes / des chevaliers errants   ('La Rivière de Cassis', l.11)

This is yet another example of the poet tempting his reader to restore one constant, the correct diaeresis, at the expense of another, the hendecasyllabic context.

Incorrect diaeresis provides the temptation to resolve the nonasyllable which concludes 'Qu'est-ce...' on the obliteration of both metre and isosyllabism. For Murphy this constitutes a 'perturbation métrique délibérée': 'l'effondrement en quelque sorte terminal prend la forme d'une perte de forme strophique, syllabique et rimique'.[1] Given the poet's disrespect for syllabic norms elsewhere, we might be tempted to create a dodecasyllable with ridiculous diaeresis:

> Ce n'est ri-**en**! / j'y su // -is! j'y su- / is toujours!   (l.25)

Of course, since not even Rimbaud splits diaeresis at the caesura or other *coupes*, such a line is totally implausible; for Cornulier: 'il ne fonctionne pas comme mètre: hors mètre, hors strophe, hors rime, c'est un non-vers'.[2] Yet the very possibility of such an interpretation demonstrates how far Rimbaud manages to stretch our expectations of a rhythmic 'norm' beyond traditional barriers of *forme* and *informe*. Furthermore, this is the only line to feature nine syllables, the missing link in the leap detected by Cornulier between octo- and deca-syllables; it exists, therefore, just beyond the edge of our rhythmical perception as the notion of poetic form vanishes completely.

This syllabic uncertainty plays an important role in the creation of interpretative irresolvability, and allows the poet to write a truly formless text. In the decasyllabic 'Plates-bandes...', syllabic inconsis-

---

[1] Champion edition, pp.870-71.
[2] 'Mètre "impair", métrique "insaisissable"? Sur les "derniers vers" de Rimbaud', p.79.

tency is pushed to the point of absurdity. 'Juliette' (l.12) first features diaeresis:

Ombreux et très-bas de la Ju li - ette.
1   2   3   4   5 6 7 8 9 10

On first reading the next line, we will naturally assume consistency within the same word, pronouncing 'Juliette' with diaeresis. The same diaeresis would then also apply to 'Henriette', equally trisyllabic and ending in 'iette'. This provides twelve syllables, contravening the decasyllabic context, but is all the more tempting since an *alexandrin romantique* is produced with two consecutive *coupes italiennes*; the 'e' *caducs* lend a pleasing rhythmic *bercement* and the first and third segments rhyme with an internal *rime léonine*:

– La Juli-ett / *e*, ça rappell / *e* l'Hen ri - ett / [*e*]
1   2 3 4   5 6 7   8   9   10 11 12

Although other poems feature metrically unique lines, such as the final 'alexandrine' of 'Bonne pensée du matin', in this context the 'alexandrine' is transgressive. Again we are disappointed, obliged to sacrifice a pleasingly recognizable 'poetic' segment in order to maintain an unstable, imperceptible isosyllabism. This isosyllabism is only possible with awkward synaeresis on both words, contradicting the precedent set only one line previously and creating disturbing internal inconsistencies. The line now becomes:

– La Juliette, ça rappelle l'Henriette
1 2 3 4 5 6 7 8   9 10

As Murphy remarks, this reinforces 'le brouillage de la perception d'un poème isonumérique plus qu'isométrique', necessitating 'un décompte syllabique laborieux'.[1] Thus we pursue a provocative and highly problematic regularity, searching for solutions to a formal conundrum which tests to the limit our faith in the equation 'poetry = formal regularity'.

---

[1] Champion edition, p.865.

In line 8 of the same poem the absurdity of this search for regularity reaches its peak, as two identical words, placed side by side, must be interpreted differently if we respect the syllable count:

> Troupes d'oiseaux! o iaio, iaio!...
> 1 2   3   4   5

Again, we assume that identical sequences are to be scanned consistently. Yet synaeresis on all four 'ia' and 'io' provides only nine syllables; diaeresis on either both 'ia' or both 'io' gives eleven, and diaeresis on all four provides thirteen.[1] Only one of the four can carry diaeresis, yet we are thereby obliged to contradict this interpretation on its twin. Furthermore, we can choose between all four without any one being more appropriate than the other, as the regularity of poetic form seems entirely arbitrary, and thereby meaningless. Significantly, it is bird-song that the reader is required to interpret, yet again reflecting on a formal level the irresolvable dilemma of the interpretation of natural phenomena. Indeed, the line itself is formally irresolvable in that it resists reduction to one formal realization. By placing four potential scansions in competition, none of which can be definitive, Rimbaud achieves the creation of the *informe*. This provokes us into an active search for a poetic rhythm which now refuses to be realized, confirming what Bobillot calls: 'une toute autre conception du *rythme*, comme résultante concrète des séries de tensions qui s'établissent, à chaque ligne, entre les différents modes de scansions qui y sont, simultanément, à l'œuvre'.[2]

In the 1873 versions, the poems' resistance to formal realization increases. In 1872, line 19 of 'L'Eternité' features two examples of incorrect synaeresis; in 1873, 'avec' is replaced by 'et', obliging the reader to make a choice:

(5) Nul orietur	→	(5) Pas d'*orietur*
(5) Science avec patience	→	(?) Science et patience

---

[1] Murphy comments: 'Il s'agit d'un jeu sur des hiatus dans un poème où les occurrences de la combinaison *i* + *voyelle* jouent systématiquement sur le choix entre synérèse et diérèse' (Champion edition, p.862). Bobillot also highlights the problem, in 'Rimbaud et le "vers libre"', p.206.

[2] 'Le vers la lettre – des "rimes grammaticales" au "poème littéral"', p.72.

Synaeresis on both will give four syllables, diaeresis on both, six, but five are required, as Bobillot notes: 'le vers peut aussi bien être de 4, 5 ou 6 syllabes, et seule la "pression métrique" fait critère'. Solving the syllabic problem means inconsistency within the line, and besides, how do we decide which element should receive which treatment? Bobillot imagines the reader 'pratiquant indifféremment et arbitrairement la synérèse ici, la diérèse là'.[1] If our decision is entirely inconsequential, the notion of meaningful form in poetry disappears, since neither solution seems more significant than the other. Thus the line, resisting the imposition of one definitive form, is perfectly formless.

The altered refrain of 'Chanson de la plus haute tour' features a similar example of what Bobillot calls 'le brouillage numérico-prosodique':[2]

(5) Ah! Que le temps vienne   →   (?) Qu'il vienne, qu'il vienne,
(5) Où les cœurs s'éprennent.   →   (6) Le temps dont on s'éprenne.

With six syllables required, synaeresis on both 'ien' gives five, diaeresis on both, seven. Once again, if an interpretative decision is made, the result can only be seen as arbitrary and meaningless. The line refuses formal realization, and the notion of poetically meaningful *nombre* reaches breaking point, challenging the reader to accept a poetics in which aesthetic value might exist independently of constant formal values. Just as the poems inspire a search for rhythmic regularity, they also problematize the notion of poetic harmony, fulfilling the *voyant*'s prediction of poems 'toujours pleins du *Nombre et de l'Harmonie*'.[3]

The search for harmony

The problematization of form is compounded by erosion of the rhyme scheme, with a dramatic decrease in *rimes riches* (27, or 9.2%) and *léonines* (5, or 1.7%), and a rise in *rimes pauvres* (51, or 17.3%).[4]

---

[1] 'Rimbaud et le "vers libre"'; both quotations: p.203.
[2] 'Vaches, mouches, figures', p.23.
[3] folio, p. 92.
[4] Highlighting the caution with which purely statistical analyses should be treated, my results differ slightly from those obtained by Danielle Bandelier, who counts: 1.17% *léonines*, 7.64% *riches*, 48.2% *suffisantes*, 23.5% *pauvres*, 15.8% *assonances*, 3.5%

The 1872 poems are also remarkable for eighty-four approximate or problematic rhymes, thirty-six rhymes relying only on consonance or assonance, and twenty-three lines which rhyme with no other. Bobillot sees in certain rhymes a mixture of 'hypertraditionalisme graphique et manquement absolu aux exigences d'homophonie', giving symmetry for the eye but not for the ear:

restent / justement	('Entends comme brame', ll.17-20)
ti*ll*euls / ha*ll*ali / spirituel*l*es / grosei*ll*es	('Bannières de mai', ll.1-4)
fer / verger	('Plates-bandes...', ll.14-15)[1]

The eighty-four approximate rhymes defy graphemic convention with mixtures of singular and plural, masculine and feminine, and rhymes for the ear alone:

chers / mer	('Comédie de la soif', ll.31-32)
pure / pourritures	('Mémoire', ll.25-28)
clairevoies / envoie / matois	('La Rivière de Cassis', ll.13-17)
bruyère / vert	('Larme', ll.2-4)
vie / midi	('Bonne pensée du matin', ll.18-20)
soir / gares	('Larme', ll.10-12)
blême / Bethléem	('Jeune ménage', ll.21-23)
étang / flottants	('Comédie de la soif', ll.50-52)
or / Nord	('Comédie de la soif', ll.59-60)
vienne / s'éprennent	('Chanson de la plus haute tour', ll.5-6)
voix / moi	('Âge d'or', ll.1-3, 21-23)
génies / fournit	('Jeune ménage', ll.5-7)
remplira / rat	('Jeune ménage', ll.18-20)
n'aura / gras	('Honte', ll.1-3)
les / railway	('Michel et Christine', ll.14-16)

This can seem gratuitous, as if Rimbaud were unable to resist asymmetry at every opportunity; indeed, in his notes to the rhyme 'pure / pourritures' ('Mémoire', ll.25-28), Murphy observes: 'Rimbaud semble avoir écrit *pourriture* avant d'ajouter le *s* terminal'.[2]

---

rimes nulles ('Les rimes de Verlaine et de Rimbaud', in *Arthur Rimbaud: Poesia e Avventura: actes du colloque de Grosseto, 11-14 sept. 1985*, ed. by Mario Matucci, Pisa: Pacini, 1987, pp.181-88; p.182).
[1] 'Le vers la lettre – des "rimes grammatiques" au "poème littéral"', p. 56.
[2] Champion edition, p. 830.

Similarly, in a manuscript version of 'Comédie de la soif', the eventual rhymes, 'filleule / gueules' (ll.37-39) and 'plages / sauvage' (ll.41-43), both match perfectly: 'filleule / gueule', 'plages / sauvages'.[1] Yet since most rhymes preserve harmony for the ear if not for the eye, such irregularities seem almost acceptable compared to the frequent consonantal or assonantal rhymes, and the pure non-rhymes. Faced, then, with the constant threat of unpoetic disorder, the reader comes to accept what is traditionally discordant as a possible source of an evolving poetic harmony. For instance, the surfeit of harmony in 'La Rivière de Cassis' (stanza two) gives six successive masculine rhymes in /ã/, in *ababab* with the *a* rhymes spelled 'an' and the *b* rhymes 'en', suggesting that poetic harmony is possible beyond the restrictive canonical prescriptions.

In the lyrical setting of 'Ophélie', nature seemed a mysterious source of poetic meaning: 'On entend dans les bois lointains des hallalis' (l.4). 'Bannières de mai', however, announces a swansong:

> Aux branches claires des tilleuls
> Meurt un maladif hallali. (ll.1-2)

Just as meaning in nature disappears, rhyme harmony also falters, as mostly consonantal rhymes (stanza one) give way to the highest concentration of non-rhymes in all the poems. In 'Larme', all sorts of echoes complicate our search for harmonic correspondences:

ll.1,3,5,7	villageoises / noisetiers / **Oise** / colocase	[vi*ll*ageoises]
ll.2,4,6,8	bruyère / vert / couvert / suer	↑
ll.9,11,13,15	auberge / perches / vierges / coquillages	↓
ll.10,12,14,15,16	soir / gares / mares / coquillages / boire	[coqui*ll*ages]

For Jean-Louis Aroui, 'Larme' obliterates the rhyme as 'Qu'est-ce...' does the metre: 'Rimbaud écrit ici un texte où il détruit systématiquement les différentes règles constitutives de la rime'. However, although rhyming regulations are transgressed, harmony is not altogether destroyed, existing in potential: 'D'une certaine façon, la rime tend vers un état de perfection (rime = similarité phonique ET graphique), sans jamais réussir à s'y maintenir continuellement'.[2]

---

[1] ibid., p.696.
[2] 'Rimbaud: les rimes d'une *Larme*', *Parade Sauvage* 13 (1995), 24-44; pp.24 and 26.

Thus harmony, much like rhythm, becomes an active process on the reader's part and indeed, they complement each other. The blurring of rhyme blocks our intuitive perception of isosyllabism, drawing us into a simultaneous hunt for both, as if, somewhere in these structures, regular rhythms and harmonies were to be found, but not in conventionally recognizable form.

Danielle Bandelier, commenting on Rimbaud's 'appauvrissement de la rime', observes: 'l'anticipation de la rime [...] ôte elle aussi aux dernières syllabes le privilège de l'homophonie'.[1] Homophony, therefore, although erased from the line-end, is still possible elsewhere, and it is the possibility of such harmonies that fuels our faith in the texts' poeticity. Bernard Meyer, for example, interprets internal echoes as a sort of poetic compensation for apparently unpoetic, 'prosaic', irregularities:

Absence de régularité rythmique, enjambement et rupture interne, rimes inexistantes ou pauvres contribuent à donner parfois au poème l'allure de la prose. Toutefois, parallèlement aux rimes, on trouve un réseau assez dense de récurrences sonores qui renforce au contraire l'allure poétique du texte. Tous les vers présentent au moins une allitération et une assonance.[2]

The poet, blurring recognizable poetic *forme*, leaves us with a choice between the poetic potential of the *informe* and elusive, problematic rhythms and harmonies. Disturbed by a lack of poetically familiar form, we invariably search elsewhere for the reassuring rhythmic and harmonic regularity which was hitherto associated with poeticity.

In pentasyllabic lines the absence of rhyme strikes the reader all the more. 'L'Eternité' features only *rimes pauvres* and *suffisantes*, with four consonantal rhymes, and 'Âge d'or' features seven problematic rhymes, five cases of consonance and two non-rhymes. It is in 'Âge d'or' that the poet admits:

> Ces milles questions
> Qui se ramifient
> N'amènent, au fond,
> Qu'ivresse et folie   (ll.5-8)

---

[1] 'Les rimes de Verlaine et de Rimbaud: l'aventure poétique de la contestation du vers', p.187.
[2] *Sur les 'Derniers vers'.Douze lectures de Rimbaud*, Paris: L'Harmattan, coll. 'Poétiques', 1996, p.199.

The formal inclusivity of the 1872 poems has clearly led to an endless questioning of the poetic significance of form; Bobillot asks, for example: 'quel peut être, *aujourd'hui*, le sens de la *forme* appelée "rime"?'.[1] The poetic potential of the formless was seen in the 'Lettre' as an exciting and necessary part of the re-generation of Poetry, but the enthusiastic 'ivresse' soon gives way to 'folie'. Without the stable measuring system by which poetic meaning can be gauged, the poet, like the 'planche folle' of 'Le Bateau ivre' (l.78), cannot long maintain a poetics in which no form is more significant than any other. With hindsight, in *Une saison en enfer*, he admits the ultimate impossibility of a poetics of the formless, heralding the re-motivation of poetic exclusivity at work in *Illuminations*.

Failure of an inclusive poetics

'Alchimie du verbe' opens with the remark: 'Depuis longtemps je me vantais de posséder tous les paysages possibles'.[2] Without the universal analogy, external phenomena can be interpreted as the poet sees them, embracing the infinite possibilities of his poetic visions: 'J'ai créé toutes les fêtes, tous les triomphes, tous les drames. J'ai essayé d'inventer de nouvelles fleurs, de nouveaux astres, de nouvelles chairs, de nouvelles langues'.[3] As we have seen, this required formal inclusivity, creating what Bobillot calls: 'une conception radicalement neuve du beau, résultant d'une prise en compte plurielle, et discordante, sans exclusivité'.[4] However, the lack of an aesthetic hierarchy, a stable guarantee as to values of poeticity, has led to madness, and the poet declares: 'Je dois enterrer mon imagination et mes souvenirs!'.[5]

He concludes the account of his folly by recognizing the importance of a notion of beauty to any aesthetic project: 'Cela s'est passé. Je sais aujourd'hui saluer la beauté'.[6] Beauty is no longer invited to sit on the poet's knee, but rather, he acknowledges it from a certain distance. One absolute Beauty, whose value is eternally fixed,

---

[1] 'Le vers la lettre – des "rimes grammatiques" au "poème littéral"', p.56; Bobillot's italics.
[2] folio, p.192.
[3] folio, p.203.
[4] 'Vaches, mouches, figures', p.32.
[5] folio, p.203.
[6] folio, p.198.

is detrimental to poetry, leading to a handful of restrictive, predictable forms. Yet beauty has now lost its capital letter. This implies that it is no longer absolute, recalling Baudelaire's post-illusory remark: 'L'esprit du vrai poète doit être ouvert à toutes les beautés'.[1] The poetic idea cannot survive without some notion of beauty, since if anything can be Poetry, then Poetry is nothing, it is invalid as an aesthetic concept. As Robert M. Pirsig remarks: 'If you can't distinguish between good and bad in the arts they disappear. There's no point hanging a painting on the wall when the bare wall looks just as good'.[2] For Poetry to exist, therefore, some sort of qualitative difference between *forme* and *informe* must be restored.

Without a formal guarantee of poeticity, the *voyant* also loses confidence in his 'objective' visions, losing all sense of external and internal stability: 'Connais-je encore la nature? me connais-je?'.[3] 'Bannières de mai' recalls the Baudelairean crisis of 'Le *Confiteor*...'; in the first stanza the poet describes his personal interpretation of nature:

> Le ciel est joli comme un ange.
> L'azur et l'onde communient. (ll.7-8)

However, in the second stanza nature is absolute again, as the poet rejects the interpretative instability of *le moi* in the hope of a return to constant, inherent value:

> Que par toi beaucoup, ô Nature,
> – Ah moins seul et moins nul! – je meure. (ll.15-16)

This bears a striking resemblance to the despair of the 'bateau ivre', which ends its poetic adventure with a similar cry: 'Ô que ma quille éclate! Ô que j'aille à la mer' (l.92). Like Baudelaire's prose poet, the poet concedes another defeat in his interpretative duel with nature: 'A toi, Nature, je me rends' (l.20).

---

[1] *Salon de 1859*, V, 'Religion, histoire, fantaisie' (O.C.II: 630). See also page 118 of the present study.
[2] *Zen and the Art of Motorcycle Maintenance. An Inquiry into Values*, 1974; London: Vintage, 1991, p.219.
[3] folio, p.182.

Just as he loses his grip on his *moi*, so too the poet doubts of his reality for others: 'ceux que j'ai rencontrés *ne m'ont peut-être pas vu*'. Faith in his insight into the collective soul falters, and unlike the poet of 'A une heure du matin', he cannot even pray for salvation from the depths of the *gouffre*: 'Peut-être devrais-je m'adresser à Dieu. Je suis au plus profond de l'abîme, et je ne sais plus prier'. Overwhelmed by the dizzying infinity of interpretative possibilities, the poet admits: 'Ma santé fut menacée. La terreur venait'.[1] Doubting the poeticity of his visions, he also loses confidence in the language used to express them, as if he has lost the shared system of reference, repeating: 'Je ne sais même plus parler', *'Je ne sais plus parler!'*.[2] Interpretative and expressive crises, then, go hand in hand.

The dead-end at which the poet has arrived can be read allegorically in the two dodecasyllabic poems of 1872. Cornulier sees 'Qu'est-ce...' as 'violemment anti-métrique', a revolt against form beginning with an alexandrine which is soon overwhelmed. The poem's 'fonction anti-métrique' is clear: 'faire chercher (en vain) une métrique défaillante'. In comparison, 'Mémoire' is 'a-métrique' from the outset, its non-metrical dodecasyllables demonstrating 'une liberté acquise, le métrique baignant presque naturellement dans le non-métrique comme une image nette dans le flou'.[3] Indeed, in the first three sections of 'Mémoire', metre seems but a distant memory, as the poem opens with 'L'eau claire; comme le sel des larmes d'enfance', recalling the 'enfant accroupi plein de tristesses' (l.95) of 'Le Bateau ivre'. Yet the sixteen lines of the last two sections feature twelve stable alexandrines, suggesting a return to the metrical framework reminiscent of the drunken boat's longing for a return to the parapets. Now aboard a similar vessel, a stranded 'canot', the poet cries:

> Jouet de cet œil d'eau morne, je n'y puis prendre,
> ô canot immobile! oh! bras trop courts! ni l'une
> ni l'autre fleur   (ll.33-35)

Unable to impose a course on the waters, he contemplates more natural images reminiscent of the interpretative dilemma: 'la poudre des saules qu'une aile secoue' (l.37) echoes 'Les saules frissonnants'

---

[1] folio, pp.182, 187, 191 and 197; Rimbaud's italics.
[2] folio, pp.188 and 202; Rimbaud's italics.
[3] All quotations from 'Métrique du vers de 12 syllabes chez Rimbaud', pp.165-67.

of 'Ophélie' (1.11), and 'Les roses des roseaux dès longtemps dévorées' (1.38) recalls both the reeds of 'Ophélie' (1.12) and the boat 'Dévorant les azurs verts' ('Le Bateau ivre', 1.23). It seems that formal liberation has now run its course; having begun with two C6 lines, a P6 line and an F6 line, the poem ends with three perfectly metrical 6+6 alexandrines and a subtly reinforced rhyme: '**secoue** / quelle **boue**' (ll.37-40).

Furthermore, although the first two lines begin with capital letters, confirming the versificatory *forme*, the only other capitals throughout the poem follow completed sentences anywhere within the line. In line 6 a new sentence even begins at the twelfth syllable, the traditional point of syntactic closure, as the lines' extremities disappear in the *informe*. However, the last four lines begin with a capital, the fourth coming, syntactically, mid-sentence as the poet admits his stasis:

> Mon canot, toujours fixe; et sa chaîne tirée
> Au fond de cet œil d'eau sans bords, – à quelle boue? (ll.39-40)

Despite the poet's attempt to abandon metrical form, in a humble 'canot', like the 'bateau frêle' ('Le Bateau ivre', 1.96), there comes the inevitable return to order, to the chains of the 'haleurs' ('Le Bateau ivre', 1.2). In this way 'Qu'est-ce...' and 'Mémoire' narrate the same inescapable cycle as that of 'Le Bateau ivre': the rebellion against order, 'Sanglots de tout enfer renversant / Tout ordre' ('Qu'est-ce...', ll.3-4), the *ivresses* of liberation, and finally the realization of a need for some sort of order. Yet Rimbaud's poetic journey is far from over, and the return to beauty with a little 'b' offers a solution to the poet's dilemma in much the same way as Baudelaire's prose poems. *Illuminations* re-motivates the notion of exclusivity necessary to the survival of the poetic idea in a form which refuses fixity, constantly in movement towards a promised absolute, the realization of which is perpetually deferred.

6
Restoring Poetic Mystery

Since the date of composition of *Illuminations* has provoked much debate, it would be imprudent to argue that all the texts follow both the 1872 poems and *Une saison en enfer*, but the coherence of their thematic and formal characteristics suggest nonetheless a resolution of the problems explored in these two works.[1]

Exclusivity re-defined

'Jeunesse IV' expresses the aesthetico-religious dilemma explored in *Une saison en enfer*: 'Tu en es encore à la tentation d'Antoine. L'ébat du zèle écourté, les tics d'orgueil puéril, l'affaissement et l'effroi'. Thus the inclusive poetics of the *voyant* is resumed, from initial euphoria and pride to eventual fear and collapse. As he has discovered, if anything can be poetic then Poetry itself disappears, since everything is already Poetry, and the poet and his work are rendered obsolete. Yet the poet offers a solution, resolving: 'tu te mettras à ce travail: toutes les possibilités harmoniques et architecturales s'émouvront autour de ton siège'.[2] This is both a liberation and a restriction; the new poetics will allow for all formal possibilities, yes, but only those which are harmonic and architectural, and not those which are inharmonious and un-architectural. This recognizes that, in order for Poetry to exist, certain structures must be seen to be unpoetic. It is against these that the aesthetic value of the poetic can be measured. The simultaneous liberation and restriction comes again in 'Solde' as the narrator promises: 'toutes les énergies chorales et orchestrales', not all energies, but only those which are choral and orchestral. Again the musical metaphor asserts the value of the poetic over the inharmonious, the very concept of which the 1872 poems rejected.

---

[1] André Guyaux suggests a compromise: 'S'il est un problème chronologique, sa solution est relativement simple: les *Illuminations* chevauchent la *Saison en enfer*. Ou si l'on préfère, la *Saison* interrompt et coupe la composition, d'ailleurs nécessairement décousue, fragmentée elle aussi, des *Illuminations*' (*Rimbaud. Œuvres*, Paris: Garnier, 1981, lxii).

[2] Both quotations: folio, p.237.

This, then, is the key to Poetry's survival: the maintenance of the distinction between poetic notions of harmony and the unpoetic *faux accord*. 'Matinée d'ivresse' restores the idea of poetic intoxication so common in Baudelaire, and with it the necessarily inharmonious state from which it offers an escape, echoing 'La Chambre double', as the narrator declares: 'Ce poison va rester dans toutes nos veines même quand, la fanfare tournant, nous serons rendu à l'ancienne inharmonie'.[1] Crucially, this disharmony is seen as unartistic, as familiar notions of art are restored. Whereas, in the drafts of *Une saison en enfer*, Rimbaud had written: 'l'art est une sottise', 'Villes I' restores art to its rightful place, above nature in the hierarchy of aesthetic values: 'Les parcs représentent la nature primitive travaillée par un art superbe'.[2] As we have seen, Baudelaire reaches the same conclusion in 1861, celebrating the artistic imagination which brings order to nature, 'un amas incohérent de matériaux'.[3]

However, this re-motivation of formal exclusivity must not allow formal values to become fixed, and so the poet acknowledges a fundamentally poetic structural sensibility without prescribing what forms 'the poetic' will henceforth take. This is the same awareness that allows Baudelaire, after 1860, to write sonnets in forms outside canonical norms, whilst still fulfilling poetic notions of order: QTTQ ('L'Avertisseur') or TTQQ *aaa bbb cdcc dcdd* ('Bien loin d'ici'). In contrast to the former poetics, restricted to a handful of privileged, iconic forms which caused the dangerous stagnation of poetry, this notion of an underlying yet indefinite formal principle will be able to survive inevitable aesthetic evolution. New forms will not be dismissed, but rather, welcomed as fresh incarnations of this poetic principle, articulated via recurrent musical metaphors such as the 'musique savante' of 'Conte'.[4] Echoing the *constellation savante* of Baudelaire's post-illusory poetry, this suggests an acknowledgement of the artificial nature, and ultimate vanity, of aesthetic values.

In 'Vies II' the poet is a musician who has found 'quelque chose comme la clef de l'amour', or 'la clef de cette parade sauvage' in

---

[1] folio, pp.217-18.

[2] Draft quotation from *Œuvres complètes*, Paris: Gallimard, 'Bibliothèque de la Pléiade', 1971, p.171; 'Villes I' quotation from folio, p.223.

[3] *L'Œuvre et la vie d'Eugène Delacroix* (O.C.II: 752).

[4] folio, p.212.

'Parade'.[1] In the context of recurrent musical terminology these keys might denote the clef which opens and defines the stave upon which musical notation is placed, dividing pitch into only twelve notes. Like the seven colours into which the infinitely nuanced spectrum appears to divide, these twelve units are an approximation, imposed by the artistic mind. Sounds whose pitch does not correspond to these divisions seem cacophonous to the ear accustomed to this artificial system. Of course, this is not their 'real nature' since, as the poet has discovered, musical and poetic artifice corresponds to no transcendent 'reality'. Yet within this artistic context according to which harmony is produced, anything else seems inharmonious and anti-architectural. This re-motivation of the poetic validity of artificial aesthetic values demonstrates the importance of context, of an interpretative framework, banished from the 1872 poems, from within which the poetic value of forms might be judged.

Similarly, in 'Villes I' the enormous dome of the 'Sainte-Chapelle' is 'une armature d'acier artistique'.[2] The 'armature', an architectural skeleton, can also mean a musical key signature placed after the clef, defining the relationship between the following notes. Thus the poet of *Illuminations* posits a framework which restores the artificial musical distinction between harmony and discord, the poetic distinction between *forme* and *informe*. Yet neither clef nor key signature prescribe the precise nature of the music to be written, providing simply an underlying structural principle according to which the aesthetic value of the piece is defined. Thanks to the restoration of a salutarily non-prescriptive notion of context, poetry might once again be written without reduction to predictable formulae.

This 'quelque chose comme la clef de l'amour' reminds us of 'Le Bateau ivre', where formal poetic evolution can be seen in terms of the fermentation of 'les rousseurs amères de l'amour' (1.28). This process of structural alteration is echoed as the prince of 'Conte' yearns for 'd'étonnantes révolutions de l'amour'. Like the poet of 1872, he dismisses Beauty, destroying all that is beautiful around him, just as the poet obliterated all notion of poetic regularity: 'Quel saccage du jardin de la beauté!'. Yet try as he might, the prince cannot destroy beauty, which keeps coming back, in the same way that the

---

[1] folio, pp.215 and 213 respectively.
[2] folio, p.223.

narrator of *Une saison en enfer* admits the impossibility of poetry without beauty, little 'b'. A solution comes in the figure of the genie:

Un Génie apparut, d'une beauté ineffable, inavouable même. De sa physionomie et de son maintien ressortait la promesse d'un amour multiple et complexe! d'un bonheur indicible, insupportable même![1]

This quotation contains two essential points about poetic form as it appears in *Illuminations*. Firstly, the genie promises ineffable beauty and 'un amour multiple et complexe': not restricted to one form, but multiple, resisting one fixed incarnation; not the simple regularity of metrical verse, but a complex form, the poeticity of which does not strike the reader, but which must actively be sought. Secondly, the 'amour' suggests that the fermentation of love, or the evolution of poetic form, is finally reaching a conclusion. However, the poem concludes: 'La musique savante manque à notre désir', indicating that in the present time, such a revelation is impossible. It establishes the anticipation of this future revelation; the promise is announced, yet we cannot reach it, and this is crucial to the survival of the poetic idea. Just as Baudelaire's prose poet feels only disappointment on arrival in 'Déjà!', so too *Illuminations* defers indefinitely our arrival at the anticipated state of formal resolution. This constant evolution must be believed to lead to a glorious final state, in which the poet and his reader must place their faith, even if they suspect it to be a mere illusion. Poetic form is henceforth multiple, complex, elsewhere. Like the marvellous worlds depicted in *Illuminations*, it resists fixity, ensuring the survival of poetic mystery by its resistance to both reductive, static definitions and our comprehension.

Formal problematization

The urban model plays as prominent a role in the formal complexity of *Illuminations* as it does in *Le Spleen de Paris*. 'Les Ponts' provides a 'bizarre dessin' unlike any structural pattern ever seen, described yet again in musical terms: 'Des accords mineurs se croisent, et filent, des cordes montent des berges'.[2] Similarly, in 'Métropolitain', 'viennent de monter et de se croiser des boulevards

---

[1] All quotations: folio, p.212.
[2] folio, p.221.

de cristal'.[1] The recurrence of the verb *croiser* recalls Baudelaire's 'villes énormes' and the 'croisements de leurs innombrables rapports'.[2] Both collections of prose poetry, therefore, articulate a formal principle based on a complex system of *croisements*, a similarity which extends to the theme of enormity, such as in 'Villes I' whose 'acropole officielle outre les conceptions de la barbarie moderne les plus colossales', presenting 'dans un goût d'énormité singulier toutes les merveilles classiques de l'architecture'.[3]

The reader is constantly confronted with bizarre, unrecognizable constructions, unpredictable juxtapositions, strange correspondences which seem to obey a mysterious logic, a structural principle which eludes us, or which we are not yet ready to comprehend. In the futuristic setting of 'Villes I', 'le haut quartier a des parties inexplicables'; the poet explains: 'pour l'étranger de notre temps la reconnaissance est impossible', since 'la loi doit être tellement étrange'. In 'Ville', 'tout goût connu a été éludé dans les ameublements et l'extérieur des maisons aussi bien que dans le plan de la ville' without the recognizable, obsolete forms of the past: 'vous ne signaleriez les traces d'aucun monument de superstition'.[4] In 'Villes II' it is the music which is unfamiliar: 'Des châteaux bâtis en os sort la musique inconnue', like the 'mélodies impossibles' of 'Soir historique' or the 'bandes de musique rare' of 'Vagabonds'.[5] In 'Matinée d'ivresse' the poet cries: 'Hourra pour l'œuvre inouïe et pour le corps merveilleux, cette fois!', the poet of 'Phrases' yearns for 'un "luxe inouï"' and a mysterious 'voix impossible', whilst 'Mouvement' presents 'les lumières inouïes'.[6] In 'Vies I', having played 'les chefs-d'œuvre dramatiques de toutes les littératures', the poet proclaims: 'Je vous indiquerais les richesses inouïes', and in 'Solde', announces:

A vendre les applications de calcul et les sauts d'harmonie *inouïs*. Les trouvailles et les termes *non soupçonnés*, possession immédiate,
　　Élan insensé et infini aux splendeurs *invisibles*, aux délices *insensibles* [...].[7]

---

[1] folio, p.231.
[2] 'A Arsène Houssaye' (O.C.I: 276).
[3] folio, p.223.
[4] folio, pp.223-24 and 221-22.
[5] folio, pp.225, 239 and 226
[6] folio, pp.217, 241 and 218-19.
[7] folio, pp.215 and 234; my italics.

Thus the structural principle of *Illuminations* defies recognition. The recurrence of the adjective 'inouï', in particular, supports the notion of a new kind of music, governed by an unfamiliar 'clef' and 'armature'. Formally challenging and provocative, this structural principle will protect poetic form from the dangerous rut of predictability.

Just as form eludes us thanks to its constant novelty, *Illuminations* also presents forms in perpetual process, refusing to settle, like the clouds in which the Baudelairean prose poet finds inspiration. For example, 'Being beauteous' describes another large structure, 'un Etre de Beauté de haute taille', which seems, 'comme un spectre' or the Baudelairean *fantôme*, to herald a return to the previous notion of absolute Beauty.[1] However, the image is in constant movement, made to 'monter, s'élargir et trembler', as the flesh breaks open and the colours dance. Recalling Baudelaire's admiration for Méryon's cityscapes with their 'prodigieux échafaudages des monuments en réparation', the 'Vision' is only 'sur le chantier', under construction, in a process of becoming, resisting the final resolution which would be its undoing.[2] Indeed, as Pirsig concludes in his 'Inquiry into Values': 'With Quality as a central undefined term, reality is, in its essential nature, not static but dynamic'.[3] Thus the poet of 'Ville' observes 'des spectres nouveaux roulant à travers l'épaisse et éternelle fumée de charbon', intangible forms constantly in movement.[4] 'Villes II' shows 'une mer troublée par la naissance éternelle de Vénus' and the constant rebirth of the icon of absolute Beauty suggests exactly this dynamic quality of aesthetic values and poetic forms.[5] 'Being beauteous' concludes with the birth of just such a new form: 'nos os sont revêtus d'un nouveau corps amoureux'. 'D'un', we notice, and not 'du', since form is no longer definitive but open to constant change. In the same way, the structural revolution of prose poetry means that Poetry too is 'revêtu d'un nouveau corps amoureux', as the formal markers of poeticity undergo a necessary, salutary evolution without excluding the possibility of others.

In the present, therefore, form can only be in process, yet the poet nevertheless promises a future moment where form is perfected and

---

[1] All quotations from folio, p.214.
[2] *Salon de 1859*, VII, 'Paysage' (O.C.II: 666). See also page 114 of this study.
[3] *Zen and the Art of Motorcycle Maintenance*, p.287.
[4] folio, p.222.
[5] folio, p.225.

resolved. 'Génie' anticipates the coming of a wondrous figure: 'Il est l'amour, mesure parfaite et réinventée', as if the fermentation of the 'rousseurs amères de l'amour' had finally come to an end. In a rhythmical context, 'mesure' denotes 'la division du temps en plusieurs parties égales', the regular metrical mould which pre-exists the verse mould of the old poetics.[1] In 'Un cœur sous une soutane', this rhythmic regularity is synonymous with the naïve, idealistic *élan* of lyrical poetry, as the love-struck narrator tells us: 'mon cœur [...] bat la mesure dans ma poitrine'.[2] 'Génie', however, promises a post-rhythmic future, just as in 'A une raison' the poet declares: 'Un coup de ton doigt sur le tambour décharge tous les sons et commence la nouvelle harmonie'.[3] One tap alone does not constitute a rhythm, and the usual rhythmical function of the drum is subverted, just like poetic rhythm. The poetic endeavour is no longer the creation of rhythm in time, but rather, the problematization of rhythm, and the anticipation of a future state of harmonic perfection embracing, of course, 'tous les sons' in a resolution which is impossible in the present time of poetry.

Thus the genie promises 'la terrible célérité de la perfection des formes et de l'action', 'l'abolition de toutes souffrances sonores et mouvantes dans la musique plus intense' via a rapid process of release and liberation:

Ô fécondité de l'esprit et immensité de l'univers!
Son corps! Le dégagement rêvé, le brisement de la grâce croisée de violence nouvelle![4]

This 'dégagement' recalls that of 'Solde' and 'l'occasion, unique, de dégager nos sens' which offers not only 'toutes les énergies chorales et orchestrales' but also, equally importantly, 'leurs applications instantanées'. 'Phrases' begins with the anticipation of a future point at which 'le monde sera réduit en un seul bois noir'.[5] Yet the poems never depict our arrival at this future point which remains but a dream: 'Rêve intense et rapide de groupes sentimentaux avec des êtres de tous

---

[1] Larousse, *Grand Dictionnaire Universel du XIX Siècle*, 11: 126.
[2] folio, p.25.
[3] folio, p.217.
[4] folio, pp.243-44.
[5] 'Solde': folio, pp.243 and 233; 'Phrases': folio, p.218.

les caractères parmi toutes les apparences'.[1] This is the unique formal dynamic of *Illuminations*, an evolution via the marvellous and the unrecognizable, promising a resolution which must necessarily remain on the horizon, safely beyond reach. In the same way our appreciation of the poems' form itself requires an understanding of the mechanisms by which the recognition of apparently familiar poetic markers is both encouraged and obstructed by the poet.

The search for rhythm

Illuminations continues to provoke a wide range of reactions as critics grapple with the problem of interpreting poetic form in the absence of recognizable verse structures. A recurrent critical theme is the anachronistic belief that regular rhythm is still somehow vital to the texts' poeticity. Max Ribi, quoting Marmontel's maxim, 'Le rythme est essentiel à la poésie', believes the poetic value of rhythm is guaranteed by precisely the kind of Hugolian universal analogy rejected in the 'Lettre du voyant':

Le rythme est une hantise de tout être vivant, une sensation universelle qui semble refléter un ordre suprème et mystérieux de toute vie, un ordre que nous ne cessons de poursuivre. De même, le rythme est à la base de toute expression [...]. Ce rythme est enseigné à l'être par les manifestations immuables de l'univers, astronomiques aussi bien que biologiques [...] sensation très puissante qui ne peut pas ne pas faire songer chacun de nous à un balancier régulateur universel, idéal.[2]

For Ribi, then, assonance is 'un élément rythmique de premier ordre', 'un outil rythmique essentiel' in a prose text 'où le mètre fait défaut'.3 He finds many examples of Aristotle's tetrapartite 'perfect sentences', 'adaptation d'un principe universel', which provide 'une constante rythmique toute aussi puissante que la rime et le mètre'.[4]

This conviction that the poet feels the need to compensate for the lack of metre in order to make the texts poetic pervades much formal criticism of *Illuminations*. G. M. Macklin, for example, suggests that 'poetic' rhythm is created in 'Solde' 'by placing the "à vendre" cry in a consistently prominent position so that it creates a rhythmical pulse

---

[1] 'Veillées II' (folio, p.227).
[2] *Essai d'une Rythmique des Illuminations d'Arthur Rimbaud*, Zurich: Uto, 1948, p.49.
[3] ibid., pp.22, 27 and 23.
[4] ibid., pp.62-63.

and regularity so important in the prose poem where rhyme and verse form have been surrendered'.[1] For Nathaniel Wing, line-initial verbal anaphora in 'Nocturne vulgaire' is 'underscored by the dashes which function as rhythmic notation',[2] and in 'A une raison' David Ducoffre sees 'tout un travail de balancement mélodique' and 'un intense souci d'harmonie structurelle'.[3] This insistence on a drive towards fixed order maintains the value system of the obsolete verse/prose dichotomy which, as the poet knows, is detrimental to the poetic idea since it restricts poeticity to the predictable and the formulaic. Yet this value system and the obsession with vague rhythmical notions still dominate critical discourse. Insisting, '"Veillées I" must surely rank as verse rather than prose', Charles Chadwick suggests: 'Rimbaud has given it a rhythm of a fluid kind by creating a series of balanced elements', as if, in the absence of regular rhythm, there must at least be some kind of poetic rhythm in evidence. Likewise, in 'Marine' and 'Mouvement', texts with 'not the slightest trace of any regular pattern of either rhyme or rhythm', Chadwick observes instead 'a flexible kind of rhythm'. In 'Fleurs', he suggests, 'Rimbaud makes an obvious use of alliteration and assonance to lift his text out of the domain of ordinary prose'.[4]

The search for regularity as clues to a text's poeticity is the very principle which Rimbaud exploits in the 1872 poems. In *Illuminations* he plays a similar game thanks to a series of rhythmically foregrounded segments which tempt the reader towards the poetic interpretation of recognizable form while simultanously resisting reduction to fixed regularity. André Guyaux draws our attention to a number of apparently 'metrical' segments in liminal, or more commonly, terminal, position:

(8)	J'ai embrassé l'aube d'été.	('Aube')
(8)	Au réveil il était midi.	('Aube')
(8)	Voici le temps des Assassins.	('Matinée d'ivresse')
(10)	Départ dans l'affection et le bruit neufs!	('Départ')
(12)	Arrivée de toujours, qui t'en iras partout.	('A une raison')

---

[1] 'Aspects of the Rimbaldian Prose Poem: Pattern and Disorder in the *Illuminations*', *Orbis Litterarum* 45:3 (1990), 248-72; p.255.
[2] *Present Appearances: aspects of poetic structure in Rimbaud's 'Illuminations'*, University of Mississippi, Romance Monographs, 1974, p.124.
[3] 'Lecture d'"A une Raison"', Parade Sauvage 16 (2000), 85-100; pp.87, 90 and 97.
[4] *Rimbaud*, London: The Athlone Press, 1979, pp.97 and 101.

(12)	La musique savante manque à notre désir.	('Conte')
(12)	C'est aussi simple qu'une phrase musicale.	('Guerre')
(12)	J'ai seul la clef de cette parade sauvage.	('Parade') [1]

These segments attract our attention not only by their positional *mise en relief*, but also by their often provocatively hermetic content which invites further reflection and closer study. Indeed, since these phrases resist reduction to stable semantic interpretation, many critics search for possible meaning in their form. Once our eye is attuned to the possibility of reassuringly poetic meaning in the challenging forms of *Illuminations*, it is drawn to other segments within the body of certain texts. Guyaux gives the following examples:

(12)	– Était-ce donc ceci?	
	– Et le rêve fraîchit.	('Veillées I')
(12)	Ton cœur bat dans ce ventre où dort le double sexe.	('Antique')
(12)	Il nous a connus tous et nous a tous aimés.	('Génie')
(12)	Il y a une horloge qui ne sonne pas.	('Enfance III') [2]

The aesthetic value of these 'lines' is problematic, and invites reflection on their poetic significance in the context of the search for meaningful form. The crux of the issue seems to revolve around the thorny issue of intentionality: are they a conscious strategy on the poet's part, or a product of our over-imaginative yearning for reliable guarantees of poeticity? As Guyaux remarks:

Il y a pourtant dans les *Illuminations* des vers égarés, incorporés, incrustés – on ne sait comment les désigner, car ce ne sont pas véritablement des vers – des phrases ou parties de phrases qui prennent, comme par hasard – mais il n'y a pas non plus de hasard – la mesure d'un vers.[3]

This is the challenge which the poet of Illuminations sets his reader: in the absence of metre and rhyme, are we able to resist the temptation to see these segments as formally meaningful, signifying a poetic authorial intention? Or can we accept them as products of hasard, and if so, does this cancel their poetic value? Perhaps the poetic can now be born of chance? If poetry can admit chance over authorial

---

[1] Taken from *Poétique du fragment: Essai sur les Illuminations de Rimbaud*, Neuchâtel: A la Baconnière, 1985, p.159.
[2] *Poétique du fragment*, p.159.
[3] *Duplicités de Rimbaud*, Paris: Champion, 1991, p.165.

intention, then is the source of poeticity the reader's eye, the gaze of the Baudelairean 'être spirituel'? Does this not challenge our faith in stable notions of poeticity, the idea that we might 'see poetry' in a structure in which the poet himself had not? Exploiting this uncertainty, these segments take us on a search for meaningful rhythm and an elusive, provocative poet, who forces us to scrutinize our own critical gaze and its role in creating the poeticity of a text.

Unfortunately, critical response to the challenge has been restricted to arguments about whether or not these segments actually count as 'verse', as if, were we to ascertain their 'metrical' nature, the problem of authorial intention and poeticity would simply be solved. Having identified the prose poet's 'rhythmic strategies' in the perennial critics' favourite, 'Phrases V', Chadwick proclaims: 'short though the text is, it deserves to rank as verse rather than prose, thanks to these opening and closing alexandrines and to the regular rhythm'.[1] Yet the 'metrical' status of the lines in question is not so obvious:

> J'ai tendu des cordes / de clocher à clocher
> des chaînes **d'or** d'étoile / à **étoile**, et je danse

The first 'line' is clearly F6, and so, in a verse context, rhythmically problematic. In prose, without the necessary metrical context, it is not certain that such a segment would strike the reader immediately as a rhythmical *évidence*, although the 3/3 balance of the second 'hemistich' does compensate for the 5/7 imbalance. As for the second 'line', the syntactic accents of a prosaic reading suggest that a 4+5+3 rhythm imposes itself much more strongly than a 6+6 rhythm, especially given its D6 quality. Thus these problematic, unstable rhythms appear to lead the reader towards meaningful form, yet ultimately disappoint, as the regularity of which we sense the promise is confounded.

The most notorious proponent of these *segments métriques* is Antoine Fongaro, who devotes an entire monograph to what he calls 'l'opération de dissection arithmétique', analysing and classifying liminal and terminal segments, 'dodécasyllabes intérieurs', 'autres segments traditionnels', 'mesures impaires' and 'les "vers" de

---

[1] *Rimbaud*, p.101.

quatorze syllabes'.[1] Should a segment correspond to the metrical mould, hallowed 'alexandrine' status is without hesitation bestowed upon it:

Et, presque chaque nuit, aussitôt endormi   ('un alexandrin régulier')

et du reste descend en face du talus   ('un alexandrin indiscutable')

Dans le ciel de tempête et les drapeaux d'extase
Il nous a connus tous et nous a tous aimés   ('deux alexandrins réguliers')

Le haut étang fume continuellement   ('un étonnant "alexandrin" comme il y
                                                                                                                                    en a chez Verlaine et chez Mallarmé')[2]

This appropriation of versificatory terminology pervades much critical analysis of *Illuminations*. Chadwick sees in certain dodecasyllables 'the rhythm of a classically balanced alexandrine' and Guyaux sees 'un parallélisme métrique' in the following alliteration and assonance:

Promène-toi, la nuit, // *en* m<u>ou</u>v*ant* / <u>d</u>o<u>u</u>cem*ent*   ('Antique')
    m   ã **m** <u>u</u> ã   <u>u</u> **m** ã

In the final line of 'A une raison', Ducoffre sees 'un pseudo-alexandrin régulier s'autorisant de l'élision du [e] dans "Arrivée"', highlighting 'la force métrique de cette phrase, le quasi surgissement de l'alexandrin', 'la somptueuse construction métrique du poème' and 'un jeu savant d'imbrications métriques'.[3] Roger Pensom sees the coincidence of syntactic accent with alliterative or assonantal patterns as an 'équivalence métrique et phonétique', although he acknowledges: 'Il existe bien sûr des équivalences métriques et phonétiques dans nos textes, mais ces traits communs au vers et à la prose ne suffisent évidemment pas à définir le poème en prose'.[4]

Unsurprisingly, this confusion of metrical and rhythmical properties in the name of Poetry is emphatically rejected by Cornulier:

[1] 'Segments métriques dans la prose d'"Illuminations"', Presses Universitaires du Mirail-Toulouse, 1993, p.11.
[2] 'Segments métriques dans la prose d'"Illuminations"', pp.28-29.
[3] 'Lecture d'"A une Raison"', pp.89, 96, 92 and 95.
[4] 'Le poème en prose: de Baudelaire à Rimbaud', *French Studies* 56:1 (2002), 15-28; p.26.

A force de n'étudier le rythme que dans le vers, on en vient naturellement à confondre fait rythmique et fait métrique, et à perdre de vue la notion même de mesure. Et paradoxalement, ce que le vers y perd, la prose y perd aussi, quand on s'amuse à la tronçonner en morceaux dont on compte les syllabes sur les doigts de la main comme si on analysait des vers.[1]

In a detailed critique of Fongaro's study, Cornulier observes: 'Fongaro omet de préciser qu'il range apparemment sous le nom d'alexandrins plusieurs formes rythmiques dont le nombre total numérique est 12'.[2] Fongaro's eager eye brushes aside a multitude of accentual and rhythmical irregularities in his haste to find poeticity in recognizable form. Cornulier demonstrates the metrical implausibility of only a small selection of his findings, such as:

L'**eau est** grise et bleue, / large comme un bras de mer	(hiatus, *e surnuméraire*)
moi pressé de trouver / le **lieu et** la formule	(hiatus)
La musique savante / manque à notre désir	(*coupe épique*)
J'ai seul la clef de cett / **e** parade sauvage	(F7)
Arrivée de toujours, / qui t'en iras partout	(*e surnuméraire*)
C'est aussi sim / ple qu'**u** // **ne** phra / se musicale	(F7, C6, although 4/4/4)

Taking as his cue the 1872 poems, where regularity is hardly a stable guarantee of poeticity, Fongaro takes liberties with highly irregular and inconsistent synaeresis and diaeresis, *coupes épiques* and conveniently disappearing *e caducs*. He even suggests that his observations might provide clues as to possible dates of composition, 'les textes les plus "versifiés" ayant la plus grande possibilité d'être les premiers en date'. The proof of the texts' poeticity, then, is seen to spring from these formal techniques: 'Il va de soi que [...] la présence de mesures syllabiques analogues aux mesures de la versification abonde plus ou moins dans la prose dite "poétique"'.[3]

Addressing the problem of these segments' 'real' value, Cornulier highlights 'le rôle de la disposition typographique dans la détermination du rythme des textes lus'.[4] Many texts present short paragraphs

---

[1] *Théorie du vers*, p.287.

[2] 'Illuminations Métriques: Lire ou faire des vers dans la prose à Rimbaud', in *Rimbaud 1891-1991. Actes du colloque d'Aix en Provence et de Marseille*, ed. by André Guyaux, Paris: Champion, 1994, pp. 103-23; p.113.

[3] 'Segments métriques dans la prose d'"Illuminations"', both quotations, p.51.

[4] 'Des vers dans la prose', *Poétique* 57 (1984), 76-80; p.80.

uncommon in prose, separated by blanks in the manner of verse stanzas: 'Enfance III-V', Départ', 'A une raison', 'Phrases', 'Veillées I, III', 'Aube' and 'Dévotion'. This fuels critical speculation as to their poetic value, and Rimbaud's presentation of other texts as mere 'prose' disappoints many critics, who re-arrange them in what they feel to be more pleasingly poetic quasi-versificatory patterns. Ribi cuts 'Fleurs' up into *vers libre*, rhythmical segments following each syntactic pause marked with punctuation.[1] Fongaro even corrects Ribi's effort, as if his own version might be more poetic, applying the same process to 'Antique', 'Royauté', 'Les Ponts', the second section of 'Being beauteous' and 'Phrases V'.[2] Likewise Roger Little, inspired by 'the a-b-b-a rhymes of the first "quatrain"', restructures the fourteen lines of 'Sonnet' in *vers libre*.[3] Guyaux isolates the following grammatically and syllabically symmetrical sentence from 'H' as if, although C6, both parts were alexandrines:

Sa solitude est **la** / mécanique érotique,
sa lassitude, **la** / dynamique amoureuse.[4]

Likewise, Ducoffre finds two symmetrical 'alexandrines' (both F7) in 'A une raison':

Ta tête se détourn / e: le nouvel amour!
Ta tête se retourn / e, – le nouvel amour![5]

Finally, Fongaro even sees 'Marine' and 'Mouvement' as 'l'exemple du découpage de la prose en segments mesurés', as if Rimbaud had simply hacked up a prose text; indeed, Guyaux too succumbs to temptation, arranging 'Marine' in prose, just 'pour voir'.[6]

Although Fongaro's ingenuously enthusiastic rhythmical study has been much maligned, we must not forget that such speculation is initially stimulated by recurrent, provocative *mise en relief* of these segments. To state categorically, as Jean-Louis Aroui does in his

---

[1] *Essai d'une Rythmique des Illuminations d'Arthur Rimbaud*, pp.61-62.
[2] 'Segments métriques dans la prose d'"Illuminations"', pp.19-23.
[3] *Rimbaud: Illuminations*, London: Grant & Cutler, 1983, pp.26-27.
[4] *Duplicités de Rimbaud*, p.162.
[5] 'Lecture d'"A une Raison"', pp.86-87.
[6] 'Segments métriques dans la prose d'"Illuminations"', p.11; *Duplicités de Rimbaud*, p.177.

rejection of Fongaro's analysis, that: 'la prose de Rimbaud n'est rien d'autre que de la prose' is to do a great injustice to the subtle rhythmical problematization at work in *Illuminations*.[1] Surely, despite the rhythmical gymnastics of Henri Meschonnic's reading, an article from *Le Monde* is 'rien d'autre que de la prose'. *Illuminations*, however, deals with the very uncertainty of knowing just what features make certain literary forms poetic, and as such deserves analysis of the ways in which this uncertainty is exploited. For instance, not only are the most obvious 'metrical' segments foregrounded in liminal or terminal position, separated from the rest of the text by blanks or a new paragraph, but they also contain alliterative and assonantal patterns which the reader will be tempted to interpret as poetic. The very sentence articulating the temptation of both poet and reader to believe in the poetic significance of order presents both a quasi-metrical rhythm and repetitive phonetic devices:

> Tu <u>en</u> es <u>en</u>core / *à* la tent*a*tion d'<u>Ant</u>o*i*ne. ('Jeunesse' IV)
> t   t   t   [d]   t
>   ã   ã   ã   ã
>   a   a   a   a

This tempts the reader to see an example of recognizably poetic form, although the line's 'verse' appearance is arguable since it demands the incorrect synaeresis [jɔ̃]. Thus the leaning towards perfect regularity is confounded and the arrival at fixed poetic form deferred. Other segments display similar phonetic arrangements which facilitate the perception of quasi-metrical accents or *coupes*:

> **Arr**ivée de *tou*j*ou*rs, / qui *t*'en **iras** part*ou*t   ('A une raison')
> **a r i**   *t u*   *u r i t*   **ira**   **ar** *tu*

> J'**ai** em*b*rassé / l'au*b*e d'été   ('Aube')
> **e**   *b*   **e**   *b*   **e e**

> L'éclairage revient / à l'ar*b*re de *b*âtisse   ('Veillées II')
> **ra** ə ə   a   **ar** *b* ə ə *b* **a**

> C'<u>est</u> l'<u>aim</u><u>ée</u> **ni** *tour*m<u>en</u> / *tan*te **ni** *tour*m<u>en</u>t<u>ée</u>.   ('Veillées I')
> <u>e</u>   <u>e</u> **m** <u>e</u> **ni** *tur* **m** *ã*   *tãt*   **ni** *tur* **m** *ãt* <u>e</u>

---

[1] *Parade Sauvage* 13 (1995), 156-59; p.158.

La musique savante / manque à notre désir   ('Conte')
 a m zi   a ã   m ã   a   zi

Il **nous a** connus *tous* / et **nous a** *tous* aimés   ('Génie')[1]
  nuz a   *tus*   e **nuz a** *tus* e   e

moi pressé de trouver / le lieu et la formule   ('Vagabonds')
      e   e l l e l   l

Ton cœur bat **dans** ce ventre / où dort le double sexe   ('Antique')
              ã   ã   u d   d u

Un cheval détale / sur le turf suburbain   ('Jeunesse I')
     al   al   yr   yr y b yr b

It is as if the reader's eye, like Baudelaire's in 'Obsession', is being tempted to submit to its fundamental desire for poetically meaningful order. As Guyaux remarks, 'dès qu'il y a reflet du vers dans la prose, présence intruse, consciente ou non, le rythme et le sens de la phrase penche irrésistiblement de ce côté'.[2] Yet as Cornulier argues, 'l'alexandrin cesse d'être évident dès qu'on cesse de le chercher'.[3] Whereas the drunken boat yearned for the 'anciens parapets' (l.84) of regular verse structure, *Illuminations* offers only 'de frêles parapets',[4] an unstable, flimsy *fantôme* of the former poetic, formal certainties. Like the 'horloge qui ne sonne pas' of 'Enfance III', which no longer fulfils its anticipated sonorous function, verse fragments no longer ring out with the same accentual certainty. Rhythmical recognition is thus both encouraged and hindered, destabilizing traditionally 'poetic' forms and confounding resolution.

In metrical verse, the author's poetic rhythmical intentions are thought to be guaranteed by the visual evidence of regular form. In its absence, critics enthusiastically hunting for values of poeticity find themselves obliged to insist that the rhythms they find in the prose texts are the result, neither of chance, which they believe to be the very antithesis of Art and Poetry, nor even less, of their own eager

---

[1] The chiastic effect of 'connu tous [...] tous aimés' adds to the 'poetic' appearance of the sentence, just as in the following example from 'Vies II': 'une campagne aigre au ciel sobre [...] l'air sobre de cette aigre campagne' (folio, p.215).

[2] *Poétique du fragment*, p.161.

[3] 'Illuminations Métriques: Lire ou faire des vers dans la prose à Rimbaud', p.117.

[4] 'Les Ponts' (folio, p.221).

imagination, but rather, of an authorial poetic intention which is unwisely assumed to be stable. The image of the author occurs repeatedly in prose poetic critical discourse, implied in the expressions 'travail', 'souci', 'volonté' (Fongaro), 'supervision', 'expression', 'creation' (Chadwick), and 'orchestrate', 'beautifully handled' (Nick Osmond).[1] Stamos Metzidakis argues: 'Poems most often have the textual shape they have because their creators, for whatever reasons, feel that this shape is the only one possible for them to have'.[2] In a poetic context, then, the responsibility for non-metrical rhythm is seen to lie with the writing subject, as Meschonnic argues: 'Le lien entre le rythme et le sujet vient de ce que j'entends par pensée poétique une invention du rythme, au sens ou le rythme n'est plus une alternance formelle mais une organisation du sujet'.[3]

The reader's faith in the poet is satirized in 'Soir historique', with its 'touriste naïf', 'à sa vision esclave', for whom 'la main d'un maître anime le clavecin des prés'.[4] The innocent observer, like Hugo with his universal analogy, sees authorial intention behind the apparent musicality of nature, just as the critic who restricts poeticity to his own, outdated agenda believes in the authorial guarantee. Thus Chadwick, exasperated by the texts' referential obscurity and formal problematization, declares: 'on ne reçoit nulle part [...] l'impression d'un écrivain qui travaille son texte', the figure of the author disappearing with reliable, comfortably recognizable form.[5] Ribi insists that 'la volonté rythmique nous est inévitablement imposée par le poète', and Fongaro asks, rhetorically: 'Est-il nécessaire d'avertir que le point de vue à adopter ici est, de toute évidence, celui de Rimbaud lui-même?'.[6] Offering Fongaro tentative support, Ducoffre suggests: 'il semble donc néanmoins que son travail corresponde exactement à la formule du calcul rimbaldien':

---

[1] *Illuminations*, ed. by Nick Osmond, London: The Athlone Press, 1976; pp.138-39.
[2] *Understanding French Poetry: Essays for a New Millenium*, New York: Garland, 1994, viii.
[3] *Politique du rythme, politique du sujet*, Lagrasse: Verdier, 1995, p.9.
[4] folio, p.239.
[5] Quoted in Macklin, 'Aspects of the Rimbaldian Prose Poem: Pattern and Disorder in the "Illuminations"', pp.268-69.
[6] *Essai d'une Rythmique des Illuminations d'Arthur Rimbaud*, p.65; 'Segments métriques dans la prose d'"Illuminations"', p.4.

Sans prétendre que l'ardent génie du poète maîtrisait, mûrissait tous les membres rythmiques de ses écrits en prose, nous soutenons que cette découverte d'une esthétique littéraire nouvelle reposant sur les imbrications variées de différents segments métriques fut bien le fait de Rimbaud, qu'il les élaborait sciemment.[1]

Yet in *Illuminations*, the issue of elusive rhythm is not solved, but rather, complicated by an equally elusive poet figure who by turns affirms and denies his poetic authority.

The poet as guarantee

Critical assumptions as to an authorial intention which might guarantee the poeticity of these unfamiliar forms are perfectly understandable since *Illuminations*, like *Le Spleen de Paris*, situates the source of meaning firmly within the figure of a poet who shuts the window on unstable external 'reality' in favour of personal/universal poetic visions. The unfolding drama of the open/closed window can be read throughout Rimbaud's work. In 'Un cœur sous une soutane' (1870) the idealistic young poet, his heart beating a regular rhythm, projects the universal analogy through the poetic window and onto nature: 'j'écoutais battre mon cœur plein de Thimothina, et mes yeux se plongeaient dans l'azur du ciel, entrevu par la vitre supérieure de la fenêtre'.[2] Similarly, in the early 'Première soirée', nature is observed through the window:

> Et de grands arbres indiscrets
> Aux vitres jetaient leur feuillée (ll.2-3)

By 'Les Chercheuses de poux', however, the poetic window, the *croisée* reflecting the poem's own *rimes croisées*, has been opened. Suddenly, the nature viewed beyond no longer seems part of universal harmony, but rather, a 'fouillis', jumbled and disordered. This is represented metrically by seventh-syllable accentual disruption:

> Elles assoient l'enfant devant une croisée
> Grande ouverte où l'air bleu / <u>baigne</u> un fouillis de fleurs (ll.5-6)

---

[1] 'Lecture d'"A une Raison"', p.98.

[2] folio, p.33.

The window remains open in the inclusive poetics of 1872, as in 'Jeune ménage': 'La chambre est ouverte au ciel bleu-turquin' (l.1), yet in *Illuminations* it is firmly closed again.

In 'Vagabonds', for example, a poetic reality different from that of the previous poetics is projected through the window: 'Je [...] finissais par gagner la fenêtre. Je créais, par delà la campagne traversée par des bandes de musique rare, les fantômes du futur luxe nocturne'.[1] This new reality is characterized by yet more mysterious 'musique rare' and intangible, spectral forms. It is also through his window that the narrator of 'Ville' observes forms in constant process: 'de ma fenêtre, je vois des spectres nouveaux roulant à travers l'épaisse et éternelle fumée de charbon'.[2] In 'Nocturne vulgaire' the uneven thickness of the glass distorts that which is seen through it, deforming the old poetic window in favour of the poet's own visions: 'dans un défaut en haut de la glace de droite tournoient les blême figures lunaires, feuilles, seins'.[3] Thus the poet can be seen as the source of a new poetic reality, and poetry as the process by which he shares this reality with the reader.

Since the 'Lettre du voyant', the poet has been re-defined as a privileged observer/creator of poetic visions which must be shared with the rest of humanity. In the prologue to *Une saison en enfer* the narrator considers 'la clef du festin ancien', declaring: 'La charité est cette clef'.[4] By sharing with us his text the poet performs an act of charity, as in 'Matinée d'ivresse' where the poet, succumbing like Baudelaire's prose poet to an illusory *ivresse*, tells us: 'Nous savons donner notre vie tout entière tous les jours'.[5] In the same poem the expression 'Ô *mon* Bien! Ô *mon* Beau!' recalls its Baudelairean equivalent: 'J'ai trouvé la définition du Beau, – de mon Beau', as the poet's conception of Beauty transcends the personal and assumes an air of universality.[6] Similarly, the poet is no longer confined to the body or mind of one subject, but becomes multiple; in 'Enfance IV' he assumes the roles of 'saint', 'savant' and 'piéton', highlighting his transcendence of the merely personal. As Hiroo Yuasa observes: 'On

---

[1] folio, p.226.
[2] folio, p.222.
[3] folio, p.230.
[4] folio, p.177.
[5] folio, pp.217-18.
[6] 'Fusées' X (O.C.I: 657).

ne peut pas dire lequel de ces "Je" est le plus authentiquement proche de son vrai "Je"; car, étant donné le décentrement de l'identité subjective, aucun d'entre eux n'est plus "vrai" que l'autre'.[1] The poet, then, abandons personality and partiality for the role of a universal being, privileged spokesman for a poetic reality, like the miraculous central character of 'Génie'.

Indeed, this figure can be seen as a poetic 'genius' as well as 'genie' since, as Claude Abastado points out, this is a familiar topos: 'Considérer le génie comme une raison supérieure qui régit à la fois la création de l'écrivain et le jugement de l'amateur est un point exprimé par les poéticiens du XVIIe siècle'.[2] The genie embodies a 'mesure parfaite et réinventée, raison merveilleuse et imprévue', and 'mesure', in its other, non-musical sense, can mean: 'moyen d'évaluation [...] de comparaison et de juste appréciation'.[3] The poet, then, is the privileged judge of poetic value, and Pirsig comes to a similar conclusion after lengthy investigation of sources of absolute value when he remembers the Sophists' maxim: 'Man is the measure of all things'.[4] Thus the poet is the centre of the formal processes at work in *Illuminations*, as in 'Jeunesse IV': 'toutes les possibilités harmoniques et architecturales s'émouvront *autour de ton siège*'.[5]

'Génie' concludes with the wondrous communion of mankind and the genie who has become absolute ('Ô Lui et nous'), elevated to a position from which he might provide a measure, a universal poetic constant. Significantly, perhaps, communion of poet and mankind comes in possibly the most obviously 'metrical' segment of the collection: 'Il nous a connus tous et nous a tous aimés'.[6] Multiplicity is resolved in unity in a sentence recalling the iconic alexandrine rhythm which, as critical reaction to the texts demonstrates, is an enduring symbol for faith in a commonly shared hierarchy of poetic values. Similarly, the collection's other unproblematic segment, 'Ton cœur bat dans ce ventre où dort le *double* sexe', also articulates the

---

[1] 'La Tentative du "je-autre" ou l'approche de l'inconnu', in *Rimbaud Multiple*, ed. by Alain Borer, Gourdon: D. Bedou et J. Touzot, 1986, pp. 228-44, p.241.
[2] 'La notion de génie', in *Mythes et rituels de l'écriture*, Brussels: Editions Complexe, 1979, pp.30-45; p. 34.
[3] Larousse, *Grand Dictionnaire Universel du XIXe Siècle*, 11: 121.
[4] *Zen and the Art of Motorcycle Maintenance*, p.252.
[5] folio, p.237; my italics.
[6] folio, p.244.

resolution of duality in unity in a fleeting echo of the alexandrine, the former guarantee of poetic perfection.[1] Yet although the source of poetic meaning is this 'universal' poet himself, he must remain, like Baudelaire's prose poet, as mysterious and inscrutable as the divine Creator whose authority he replaces. If the secret of poeticity is revealed, Poetry is finished, and so although the *Illuminations* re-motivate the poet's superior insight, they also, necessarily, problematize this very authority, creating a salutary veil behind which Poetry can be re-mystified.

The poet, therefore, constantly teases his reader with the unfamiliar, claiming only he holds the key to its meaning. In 'Parade' he declares: 'J'ai seul la clef de cette parade sauvage', yet there the poem ends, and we are denied access to a key which, we are nevertheless assured, does exist. In the hermetic 'H' the reader is left baffled by a final, provocative: 'Trouvez Hortense', which has inspired endless critical curiosity and countless hypotheses.[2] The poet of 'Guerre' dreams of a war 'de logique bien imprévue', recalling the mysterious 'logique de l'Absurde' of 'Les Dons des Fées', and suggesting that the reader must now come to terms with a new, unpredictable poetic logic which defies our reason.[3] The poem ends with the declaration: 'C'est aussi simple qu'une phrase musicale', but nothing is less simple for the mystified reader than this 'phrase musicale' which appears from out of nowhere, like the 'musique savante' which closes 'Conte'. Indeed, this is as problematic as Baudelaire's use of the same adjective in his playfully provocative *dédicace*: 'le miracle d'une prose poétique, musicale sans rythme et sans rime'.[4] Yet thanks to the poet's insistence on the simplicity of infinitely problematic issues, the reader baffled by the texts' formal enigmas is never allowed to lose faith completely in the possibility of solving the mystery of their poeticity.

The poet is not always omniscient, however, and he occasionally renounces his authority, mystifying his reader all the more. Recalling the recurrent 'à quoi bon' of *Le Spleen de Paris*, he admits in 'Villes II': 'la loi doit être tellement étrange, que je renonce à me faire une

---

[1] 'Antique', folio, p.214; my italics.
[2] folio, pp.213 and 240.
[3] folio, p.235 and Baudelaire, O.C.I: 307.
[4] O.C.I: 275.

212 Rhythm, Illusion and the Poetic Idea

idée des aventuriers d'ici', and: 'Impossible d'exprimer le jour mat produit par le ciel immuablement gris, l'éclat impérial des bâtisses, et la neige éternelle du sol'.[1] In 'Vies II', the poet has found 'quelque chose comme la clef de l'amour', but does not elucidate. Indeed, perhaps he too is unsure of the status of what he has found, since the 'quelque chose comme' indicates an interpretative uncertainty similar to that which Baudelaire claims in his *dédicace*: 'quelque chose (si cela peut s'appeler *quelque chose*) de singulièrement différent'.[2] 'Après le déluge' ends on a note of mystery for poet and reader alike: 'la Reine, la Sorcière qui allume sa braise dans le poet de terre, ne voudra jamais nous raconter ce qu'elle sait, et que nous ignorons'.[3] In the light of such authorial uncertainty, therefore, the poetico-rhythmical intentionality assumed by so many critics to provide the key to the texts' poeticity is far from stable and must be approached with the necessary awareness of its problematic nature.

Thus poetry becomes, as in Baudelaire's prose poems, a matter of the reader's faith in absolute values of poeticity around which the text creates a necessary veil. 'Aube' shows a child, echoing perhaps the child-poet who closes 'Le Bateau ivre', in pursuit of the intangible, the goddess of the dawn. In an attempt to see the Truth, the child strips away the veils which preserve her mystery: 'je levai un à un les voiles', just as all formal veils were stripped away in 1872. However, when all the veils have been removed, as in Baudelaire's 'Les Métamorphoses du vampire', nothing is left. The poet must now, having stripped Poetry down to its fundamental *vide*, restore the protective veils, and indeed, the poem finishes on this very act: 'je l'ai entourée aves ses voiles amassés'.[4] Both goddess and child then collapse together just as, during the re-veiling process of *Illuminations*, Poetry and the poet become inextricably linked.

Yet if there is nothing more to poetry than a conscious veiling of what everyone agrees to be a fiction, poetry loses the sense of instability, doubt and hope upon which, as we have seen, it thrives. The poetic endeavour must henceforth be re-defined as both the restoration of the veil and the promise of its imminent lifting which

---

[1] folio, pp.224 and 223.
[2] O.C.I: 276.
[3] folio, pp.215 and 208.
[4] folio, p.228.

might reveal, not the *vide*, but the sort of wondrous new harmony promised in 'A une raison'. Poetry is now a kind of anticipation, tempting the reader with a revelation which the poet must constantly defer by problematizing both his own presence and the rhythms of which he is believed to be the guarantee. Poetry requires the figure of the poet in order to confirm its poeticity, and yet he must remain just out of sight. And so *Une saison en enfer* presents a narrator revelling in his presence-absence, teasing the reader: 'Il n'y a personne ici et il y a quelqu'un', or: 'Je suis caché et je ne le suis pas'.[1] The poeticity of *Illuminations* resides in precisely this irresolvability, the constant questioning which stirs the reader's faith. As Cornulier concludes, on the matter of the metrical segments: 'Le problème est en effet ici d'avoir, ou de n'avoir pas, la "bonne foi" d'Antoine Fongaro'.[2] This is a faith which Rimbaud, like Baudelaire before him, both puts to the test yet never allows us to lose, saving the poetic idea from obsolescence thanks to a similar mystification of the rhythmical and authorial concepts according to which it is usually understood.

---

[1] folio, pp.186-87.
[2] 'Illuminations Métriques: Lire ou faire des vers dans la prose à Rimbaud', p.117.

PART THREE. MALLARMÉ

7
Towards an External Ideal

The Mallarméan equivalent of Baudelaire's capitulation to 'la vorace Ironie' can be seen in his well documented and much discussed spiritual crisis of spring 1866, where he realizes the fictional status of both absolute values and the poetic Ideal. In the preceding years the young poet proves a fervent aesthetic idealist, aiming in his verse to reflect that absolute Beauty towards which poetry is believed to point. When Mallarmé loses his faith in an external, transcendent absolute, he does not abandon verse, but rather, celebrates its value as a glorious symbol of an Ideal whose source is the poetic imagination. The theoretical difficulties tackled by Baudelaire and Rimbaud as to the necessary universality of this Ideal are explored in Mallarmé's critical writings, where a mischievous ambiguity is maintained between notions of authorial personality and impersonality. On the value of poetic rhythm, there is similar ambiguity between the impression of regularity in nature, which appears to structure human consciousness and pre-exist the poem, and an artificial regularity imposed on the world by the poetic gaze which must, at the same time, appear common to all. Mallarmé, therefore, uses canonical verse forms to project a fictional poetic Ideal, as formal harmony and discord create, in the 1880-90s, a salutary tension acknowledging the instability of the illusion. Yet poeticity is not simply equated with regularity, and Mallarmé preserves the mystery of Poetry with the appearance of 'Un Coup de dés' which, like his predecessors' prose poems, leads the reader on a necessarily irresolvable search for poetic constants.

Although much useful statistical research has been carried out on the Mallarméan alexandrine, analysts have so far avoided any serious attempt to interpret their metrical observations thematically in the way Graham Robb's *Unlocking Mallarmé* imaginatively explores the poet's choice of rhyme words.[1] Jean-Michel Gouvard's study of Mallarmé's early alexandrines amply demonstrates their metrical

---

[1] London: Yale University Press, 1996.

originality yet does not explore their symbolic importance to his poetics.[1] In *Théorie du vers*, Mallarmé is the only poet to whom Cornulier does not devote a whole chapter. Observing a total of seven FM6 or F7 lines, all presenting the *mesure de substitution* 4/4/4, and twenty-two C6 and eighteen P6 lines, which feature only five and six *alexandrins romantiques* respectively, Cornulier states: 'Il faudrait expliquer pourquoi la mesure 4-4-4 s'impose dans les vers où la mesure 6-6 est empêchée par la propriété F6 ou M6, mais pas dans ceux où elle est empêchée par la propriété C6'.[2] Yet the potential for thematic interpretation within the context of Mallarmé's poetic development goes unfulfilled.

In an article of 1999 Cornulier proposes 'quelques observations éparses' on Mallarmé's versification which reveal only that:

La versification du poète mûr dans ses vers officiels est, malgré quelques traits de modernité mesurée dans le traitement de l'alexandrin, d'un classicisme et d'une sobriété remarquables si on la compare aux productions contemporaines des poètes (non ringards), et par rapport à l'ensemble de la production de Mallarmé lui-même.[3]

In contrast, it would seem, to the progression observed in Baudelaire and Rimbaud, where caesural infringement, accentual hiatus and *rejets* gradually become both more ostentatious and more frequent, the general view of the late Mallarmé is that of a champion of versificatory restraint. Indeed, Cornulier offers only the most perfunctory of conclusions, in deference to the accepted image of a poet imitating an Absolute Poem by using rigorously regular structures: 'il vise haut'.[4] Yet such an over-simplification bypasses the necessary contradictions of Mallarméan verse theory and practice. For example, his only F6 and F7 lines, the most metrically rebellious of all, both feature in poems from the 1890s. They are surely more than just 'quelques traits de modernité', since unprecedented in the poet's career and antagonistic to the image of the late Mallarmé as a guardian of verse perfection. In an effort to bridge this gap between formal and

---

[1] 'L'alexandrin de Mallarmé et la poésie française (1850-1865)', *Cahiers du Centre d'Études Métriques* 4 (1999), 89-137.
[2] *Théorie du vers*, pp.193-94, and Cornulier's appendix pp.291-93.
[3] 'Remarques sur la métrique de Mallarmé', *Cahiers du Centre d'Études Métriques*, 4 (1999), 69-88; p.82.
[4] ibid., p.82.

thematic analysis, let us begin with the importance of poetic rhythm to Mallarmé in the years leading up to his crisis, in order to familiarize ourselves with the formal techniques through which, after 1866, the verse mould becomes the privileged site of projection of a fictional poetic Ideal.

An Absolute Rhythm

In contrast to both Baudelaire and Rimbaud, for whom the genre comes late, Mallarmé writes nine prose poems in 1864, alongside his verse: not an irreversible thematic and formal shift, but rather, two different yet complementary viewpoints, analogous to Baudelairean faith and irony.[1] Like the poet of 'A une heure du matin' who prays for 'la grâce de produire quelques beaux vers',[2] Mallarmé considers in his prose poems the problem of maintaining faith in the traditional poetic correspondence between verse rhythm and an external, transcendent absolute. Set in a time where Beauty and rhythm are a mere anachronism, they assert the poetic value of that which might seem obsolete but which, as in 'Les Fenêtres', harks back to the 'ciel antérieur où fleurit la Beauté' (1.32). 'Frisson d'hiver' articulates the poet's love of things past, and in 'Le Phénomène futur' the 'Montreur des choses Passées' presents contemporary society with a vision of absolute Beauty. This 'Femme d'autrefois', whose hair suggests 'quelque folie, originelle et naïve', inspires the disillusioned poets with *ivresse*, renewing their faith in an absolute towards which to strive. Disenchanted with society 'à une époque qui survit à la beauté', they remain nevertheless 'hantés du Rythme', clinging to their aesthetic idealism and faith in an Absolute Rhythm.[3] Although this Rhythm remains necessarily unattainable, the poets' faith in its existence is restored and verse composition – we assume, since the text does not make it explicit – is resumed.

This assumption finds corroboration in the three literary prose poems of 1864, grouped in 1865 as the 'Symphonie littéraire', where

---

[1] These are the first six poems of 'Anecdotes où poèmes' (*Divagations*) and the triptych 'Symphonie Littéraire', of which a manuscript exists entitled 'Trois poèmes en prose' (*Œuvres Complètes*, ed. by Henri Mondor and G. Jean-Aubry, Paris: Gallimard, coll. 'Bibliothèque de la Pléiade', 1945; p.1544) (hereafter 'O.C., 1945').

[2] Baudelaire, O.C.I: 288.

[3] *Igitur. Divagations. Un coup de dés* (Paris: Gallimard, coll. 'Poésie', 1976), pp.70-71 (hereafter *Div.*).

the poet, abandoned by his Muse, bemoans in prose his inability to write satisfactory verse. In the Gautier text, sterility is again seen as a condition of the modern age, and verse elevated to absolute status thanks to its rhythms. Like the Baudelaire of 'La Muse malade', the poet addresses his 'Muse moderne de l'Impuissance, qui m'interdis depuis longtemps le trésor familier des Rythmes'. Indeed, just as Baudelaire, re-motivating poetic mystery in 1861, couches its guarantee in a rhythmic *être spirituel*, the poet evokes verse, the highest form of art, in terms of both spirituality and rhythm: 'Tout mon être spirituel, – le trésor profond des correspondances, l'accord intime des couleurs, le souvenir du rythme antérieur, et la science mystérieuse du Verbe, – est requis'. Familiar characteristics of the poetic illusion are present, from the 'harmonie surnaturelle' to the 'ineffable équilibre' by which the poet's faith is restored and, like the Baudelairean drug-taker, the poet exclaims: 'je me perds en la divinité'. Furthermore, as in the other prose poems, poetic rhythm is 'antérieur', belonging to a past time of faith, a motif repeated in the hommage to Baudelaire: 'Le rythme de ce chant ressemble à la rosace d'une ancienne église'. The rhythmic illusion also features in the tribute to Banville, where the poet, prone to *ennui* and unable to reach 'les cieux spirituels', senses that: 'l'âme rythmique veut des vers'.[1] The rhythmic nature of the human soul supports the poetic illusion, reinforcing the necessary superiority of verse, whose metre both satisfies an innate human requirement and points towards an ideal Rhythm in a glorious transcendent realm.

In terms of this aesthetic hierarchy, it is not the prose poems themselves that constitute the 'Symphonie littéraire', but rather, the verse works of the poets mentioned since, as Larousse explains: 'La symphonie est la plus pure manifestation du génie musical; elle est l'idéal de l'art, le poème par excellence'.[2] For Mallarmé, in 1865, verse's privileged position at the top of the aesthetic hierarchy is maintained thanks to the regular metrical rhythms by which it is closer to the unattainable Absolute Rhythm than the irregular, contingent form of prose. Yet as Bertrand Marchal explains, it is this artistic idealism that ultimately leads to Mallarmé's metaphysical crisis.[3] This

---

[1] All quotations: *Div.*, pp.343-47.
[2] *Grand dictionnaire universel du XIXe Siècle*, 14: 1317.
[3] See *La Religion de Mallarmé*, Paris: José Corti, 1988, pp.45-67.

crisis is preceded by three consecutively composed poems of the mid-1860s, the 'Scène d'Hérodiade', the 'Faune' and the 'Ouverture', which explore the poet's relationship with the unattainable Ideal. On a formal level, both harmony and discord assume symbolic value as the poet points towards this aesthetic absolute whilst simultaneously maintaining the distance necessary for his Ideal to remain unrealised.

Hérodiade

Referring to 'Hérodiade' in late 1864, Mallarmé states his intention to depict *'non la chose, mais l'effet qu'elle produit'*.[1] Recalling Baudelaire's early faith in absolute aesthetic values and his reservations about sculpture, this seems to imply that the effect produced by an object is absolute.[2] The poet's task is to recreate in language 'the' effect of the object on the observer, situating his early poetics firmly within the interpretative stability of the universal analogy. Similarly, he intends to predict and control the poem's effect on the reader, leaving nothing to chance. Whereas Baudelaire later sees the irony of 'The Philosophy of Composition', exploiting the discrepancy between intention and effect in his prose poems' mystification of Poetry, the young Mallarmé takes Poe literally, telling Cazalis: 'Le poème inouï du Corbeau a été ainsi fait'.[3] He criticizes des Essarts's 'Élévations', which falls short of absolute sound/sense correspondence since certain words can be changed, 'sans que le sens du vers change'.[4] Thus he sets as his poetic goal the model which Banville demands for verse in 1872: 'une composition dont l'expression soit si absolue, si parfaite et si définitive qu'on n'y puisse faire aucun changement, quel qu'il soit, sans la rendre moins bonne et sans en atténuer le sens'.[5]

Mallarmé applies the same musical metaphor to 'Hérodiade' as he does to the masterpieces of Gautier, Baudelaire, and Banville: 'toutes ces *impressions* se suivent comme dans une symphonie', comparing

---

[1] *Correspondance complète 1862-1871. Suivi de Lettres sur la Poésie 1872-1898*, ed. by Bertand Marchal, Paris: Gallimard, coll. 'Folio Classique', 1995, p.206; Mallarmé's italics (hereafter *Corr. fol.*).
[2] See *Salon de 1846* (O.C.II: 487) and pages 117-18 of the present study.
[3] Letter of 7? January 1864 (*Corr. fol.*, p.161).
[4] Letter of 18 February 1865 to Eugène Lefébure (*Corr. fol.*, p.224).
[5] *Petit Traité*, p.5.

his poem to a musical masterpiece.[1] Explaining the intended effects of
'L'Azur' to Cazalis, he suggests that pure Poetry, the aesthetic Ideal,
requires a certain rhythmical regularity: 'Ç'a été une terrible difficulté
de combiner, dans une juste harmonie, l'élément dramatique, hostile à
l'Idée de Poésie pure et subjective, avec la sérénité et le calme des
lignes nécessaires à la Beauté'.[2] Since drama, or surprise, disturbs
metre, this serenity might correspond to a regular metrical *bercement*.
This clearly echoes Baudelaire's hommage to the aesthetic absolute,
'La Beauté', where Beauty tells mankind, in a perfect 6+6 sonnet: 'Je
hais le mouvement qui déplace les lignes' (l.7). According to the
aesthetic hierarchy of the universal analogy, where regularity is more
beautiful than irregularity since it is closer to the absolute, the Idea of
pure Poetry is projected via harmonious, metrical verse. However,
'Hérodiade' presents a mixture of both regularities and irregularities,
since it is vital, in order for the absolute to remain just that, that pure
Poetry cannot be written, only suggested.

Acknowledging the necessarily elusive nature of his Ideal,
Mallarmé describes the poem as 'un Rêve qui ne verra peut-être
jamais son accomplissement'.[3] In this context, I propose an allegorical
reading in which Hérodiade represents the aesthetic Ideal who senses
yet resists the artist's approach, protecting her 'mystère vain' (l.75)
from his profane human gaze: 'je ne veux rien d'humain' (l.82).[4] The
similarities between the princess and the aesthetic absolute of
Baudelaire's sonnet support this comparison between Hérodiade and
the artist's Ideal. She is 'immortelle' (l.65), 'belle affreusement' (l.66)
and 'sculptée' (l.82) like the 'rêve de pierre' ('La Beauté', l.1), and
just as Baudelaire's Beauty displays 'la blancheur des cygnes' (l.6),
Hérodiade later becomes 'un cygne cachant en sa plume ses yeux',
'cygne légendaire et froid, mélancolique' ('Ouverture', ll.92-94). The
'Scène' develops at length two images from the sonnet, the mirror and
the heroine's eyes, with their 'clarté mélodieuse' (l.92):

---

[1] Undated letter of January 1865 (*Corr. fol.*, p.220); Mallarmé's italics.
[2] Letter of 7? January 1864 (*Corr. fol.*, p.161).
[3] Letter of 15 January (*Corr. fol.*, pp.220-21).
[4] The text used is the 'Fragment d'une étude scénique ancienne d'un poème
d'Hérodiade' sent to the *Parnasse contemporain* in 1869 (*Œuvres Complètes*, ed. by
Bertrand Marchal, Paris: Gallimard, coll. 'Bibliothèque de la Pléiade', 1998, pp.142-
46) (hereafter O.C., 1998).

De purs miroirs qui font toutes choses plus belles:
Mes yeux, mes larges yeux aux clartés éternelles! (ll.13-14)

The princess is both horrified by and satisfied with her virginal purity: 'J'aime l'horreur d'être vierge' (l.103), refusing to be touched by the nurse (ll.53-55) or the future lover she denies: 'un mortel devant qui [...] Sortirait le frisson blanc de ma nudité' (ll.97-99). The alteration of 'devant' (1871) to 'selon' (1887) indicates that the lover she fears is not just a passive witness to the revelation of her nudity, but rather, an actor in this unveiling, such as the very artist who attempts to compose his perfect poem. The princess-poem must resist this artist-lover, since she will die if she is unveiled:

Prophétise que si le tiède azur d'été,
Vers lui nativement la femme se dévoile,
Me voit dans ma pudeur grelottante d'étoile,
Je meurs!   (ll.100-3)

The artistic Ideal must remain unattainable; were the artist able to attain his absolute poem, it would cease to be an absolute.[1] This poem, therefore, is necessarily unwritable, and the prudent artist must allow the Ideal to elude unveiling. The drama of the artist's movement towards his Ideal and her resistance to his advances is played out in the very form of the poem.

Mallarmé tells Cazalis of his 'sujet effrayant, dont les sensations, quand elles sont vives, sont amenées jusqu'à l'atrocité, et si elles flottent, ont l'attitude étrange du mystère'.[2] The Ideal is horrifying when perceived too clearly, and mysterious when kept *insaisissable*, just as formally: 'mon Vers, il fait mal par instants et blesse comme du fer!'. The capital 'V' suggests that some alexandrines approach Ideal status, and in terms of the aesthetic hierarchy this implies a surfeit of symmetry and harmony. However, it is only 'par instants' that *les vers* approach *le Vers*, as the tension between veiling and unveiling of the Ideal runs the length of the poem. The 'Scène' contains 110 perfectly balanced 6+6 lines out of 134, yet this rhythmical symmetry alone is surely not enough to elevate *le vers* towards *le Vers*. A possible source

---

[1] Graham Robb reaches the same conclusion in his discussion of 'Le Nénuphar blanc' (*Unlocking Mallarmé*, p.149). It is also in this book that Robb suggests the useful notion of versificatory drama, which I apply throughout Part Three.

[2] Letter of January 1865 (*Corr. fol.*, p.220).

of increased regularity is the line-end, where the metrical mould and the rhyme coincide. Indeed, the poem features only three *rimes pauvres*, with twenty-five *riches*, nine *léonines* and three rhymes reinforced over two syllables:

d'hiver	épris	me voir
de fer (ll.11-12)	débris (ll.19-20)	miroir (ll.27-28)

There is no synaeresis/diaeresis imbalance at the rhyme, and two rhymes in adjacent couplets are reinforced over three syllables:

se dévoile	et je veux
grelottante d'étoile (ll.101-2)	mes cheveux (ll.103-4)

In the second example the similarity between the palato-alveolar fricatives 'j' and 'ch', voiced and voiceless, allows the harmony to quiver between *léonine* and trisyllabic, suggesting a higher plane of symmetry without quite reaching it. It is here that Hérodiade insists: 'J'aime l'horreur d'être vierge' (l.103), yet the rhyme harmony creeps back down the line, fixing the symmetry more firmly and taking the lines closer towards the structural Ideal, as if the artist were defying her resistance. Indeed, the first and last couplets spoken by Hérodiade feature a *rime léonine*, encasing her speech in a preciously rich framework as the poet toils towards his goal despite her protestations.

Rhyme symmetry is reinforced rhythmically by a number of isosyllabic rhymes as metre and harmony coincide:

manières / crinières	(ll.25-26)	offerte / déserte	(ll.85-86)
métal / natal	(ll.39-40)	lumière / première	(ll.89-90)
enfance / défense	(ll.41-42)	calices / délices	(ll.97-98)
lointaine / fontaine	(ll.49-50)	dévoile / d'étoile	(ll.101-2)
fureur / terreur	(ll.63-64)		

Yet the most subtle way in which rhyme harmony is reinforced is by phonetic similarities sown the length of the rhyming hemistich, a more sustained, complex version of the Baudelairean rhyme reinforcement catalogued by Chesters:[1]

---

[1] See *Some Functions of Sound-Repetition in 'Les Fleurs du Mal'*, pp.12-29.

/ oubl*ié* d*es* pR*o*phètes
/ mouR*a*nts, s*es* tR*i*stes fêtes, (ll.9-10) (4 patterns: /u/, /i/, /e/ and 'R')

/ stérile d*u* métal,
/ joyaux d*u* m*u*r natal, (ll.39-40)   (2 or 3 patterns: /dy/ and /m/ and the final /y/)

/ selon qui, d*es* calices
/ aux farouches d*é*lices, (ll.97-98) (2 patterns: /de/ and /a/)

/ *en* ma cou*ch*e, reptile
/ *en* la *ch*air inutile (ll.105-6)   (3 patterns: /ã/, /a/ and '*ch*')

/ ô nourri*ce d*'hiver,
/ *d*e pierr*es* et *d*e fer (ll.11-12)   (3 or 4 patterns: 'rr', '*d*', *e caduc* and 'v / f')

/ aux exi*l*s, *et j*'effeuille,
/ dont *le* j*et* d'*eau* m'accueille, (ll.17-18)   (4 patterns: /o/, /l/, /e/ and '*j*')

/ en ses bout*eill*es closes,
/ aux vi*eill*ess*es* d*e* roses (ll.29-30)   (3 patterns: /s/, '*eill*' and *e caduc*)

/ offe*rt*s et, *le* d*i*rai-je?
/ enco*re* sac*ri*lège, (ll.57-58)   (4 patterns: /r/, /i/, /l/, and schwa / *e caduc*)

n*ée* / *en d*es sièc*les* malins
m*é*chanc*eté* / d*es* ant*res* sibyllins! (ll.95-96) (5: /e/, /ã/, /d/, /s/, and *e caduc* + '*s*')

/ blanc *d*e m*a* nu*d*ité,
/ tiè*de* azur *d*'été, (ll.99-100)   (3 patterns: /d/, /a/ and /y/)

/ *d*e ta pâ*le* cla*rt*é,
/ brû*les d*e chast*eté*, (ll.107-8)   (5 patterns: /d/, /l/, /a/, /r/ and *e caduc* / schwa)

/ en son c*a*l*me d*ormant
/ reg*a*rd d*e d*i*a*mant.. (ll.115-16)   (4 patterns: /a/, /d/, /r/ and *e caduc*)

/ s*a*is-tu p*a*s un pays
/ *ait* les reg*a*rds haïs (ll.123-24)   (2 patterns: '*ai*' and /a/)

/ *le* myst*Er*e *et* vos cris,
/ sup*r*E*mes* *et* meu*rt*ris (ll.131-32)   (5 patterns: /m/, /t/, /ɛ/, /r/ and '*et*')

Such assonantal and alliterative patterns point towards the ideal princess-poem which shimmers on the horizon of possibility, yet remains just beyond the poet's reach.

This attention to structural echoes extends to numerous internal rhymes. Hérodiade asserts her virginity with the image of a mirror reflecting her beauty, a symmetry represented formally:

> Héro*di*a*d*e / au clai*r* // *r*egard / *de di*amant... (1.116)
> *d* i-a *d*e   *r* // *r*   *de d* i-**a**

Although the undermined caesura challenges the 6+6 symmetry of the line, symmetry is recuperated – even increased – by the 4+4+4 rhythm, which retains the sense of balance with greater complexity. The chiastic pattern makes of the caesura the mirror in which pure beauty is reflected, as symmetrical metre becomes the privileged symbol of Hérodiade's self-sufficient beauty. This regular metre is phonetically reinforced in the following lines:

> Et regard**ant** en vous, / vrai**ment**, avec terreur;
> Mais pour**tant** adorable / au**tant** qu'une immort*elle*,
> O mon en**fant**, *et* b*elle* / affreuse**ment** *et* t*elle*   (ll.64-66)

Every *accent mobile* is a nasal /ã/ and the last line features identical vowels on the fourth, fifth and sixth syllables of each hemistich, reinforced by the *rime batelée* /ɛl/. This attention to rhythmic and harmonic correspondences shows the poet working towards his aesthetic Ideal, yet through a number of emphatic irregularities his Ideal is simultaneously allowed to elude him and protect her perfect, indivisible unity.

The most striking examples are the one M6, three C6 and three P6 lines, four of which refuse 4/4/4 resolution:

> A me peigner / noncha // lamment / dans un miroir.   (1.28)
>
> Le blond torrent / de mes // cheveux / immaculés   (1.4)
> Descendre, à travers ma / rêverie en silence   (1.21)
> Je me crois seule en ma / monotone patrie   (1.113)
>
> Comme des feuill / es sous // ta glace / au trou profond   (1.48)
> Mais, horreur! des soirs, dans / ta sévère fontaine   (1.50)
> Métaux qui donnez à / ma jeune chevelure   (1.93)

Gouvard, confirming 'l'originalité et la précocité de l'œuvre de Mallarmé pour ce qui est de sa contribution à la rénovation de l'alexandrin', highlights these lines' disruptive value in suitably musical terms: 'ces alexandrins étaient perçus comme excessivement dissonants dans la première moitié des années 1860, par les lecteurs de l'époque'.[1] All these lines are spoken by Hérodiade, who resists the regular rhythms through which the poet tries to approach her. Indeed, the very first line she speaks is C6, reinforced by a *rime batelée* which emphatically announces her resistance to rhythmical regularity:

> Reculez.
> Le blond torrent de mes / cheveux immaculés   (ll.3-4)

The poem also features seven seventh-syllable accents which destabilize the rhythmical equilibrium, such as the very line in which Hérodiade rejects the revelation of her ideal nudity:

> Sortirait le frisson / blanc de ma nudité   (1.99)

Similarly, when she asserts the purity of her hair, the word 'vierge' comes on the seventh syllable, as her insistence on her untouched virginity confounds the artist's rhythmical strategy:

> Mais de l'or, à jamais / vierge des aromates   (1.37)

At the rhyme position, eight rhythmically problematic *rejets* disrupt the site of verse harmony:

glace / D'horreur	(ll.5-6)	d'obscures / Épouvantes	(ll.70-71)
vertu / Funèbre	(ll.31-32)	dévorée / D'angoisses	(ll.73-74)
désolée / Des songes	(ll.47-48)	je veux / Vivre	(ll.103-4)
réprime / Ce geste	(ll.54-55)	Des ondes / Se bercent	(ll.122-23)

Thus the Ideal resists precisely at the point where the artist tries to fix her in verse, and the strongly reinforced rhyme 'et je veux / mes cheveux' is itself disrupted by the *rejet* 'Vivre'.

This disruptive *enjambement* can also highlight metrically redundant phonemes over the *entrevers* of a feminine rhyme: 'glace / D'horreur' (ll.5-6), 'd'obscures / Épouvantes' (ll.170-1). For Michael Temple, the *e caduc*, 'that most shadily absent of letters and essentially silent of syllables' represents 'a crepuscular presence', 'the

---

[1] 'L'alexandrin de Mallarmé et la poésie française (1850-1865)', pp.131-32 and p.127.

very shadow of poetry', 'the indeterminate extra of language which Stéphane exhorts us to breathe, or to hear breathing, in poetry'.[1] By manipulating the syntax in order to emphasize this traditionally silent syllable, the poet allows the suggestion of the *indicible* on the horizon of the poem's structures, just beyond the iconic poetic *nombre*, twelve. This reinforces the notion that verse can only go so far towards the Ideal, which must be allowed to remain within sight, yet out of reach. Of course, this side-effect of *enjambement* is hardly without precedent, but it does accompany the first appearance of Hérodiade herself, in 'Les Fleurs', underlining its relationship with the figure who will, in the 'Scène', come to embody the poetic Ideal:

> Et, pareille à la chair de la femme, la rose
> Cruelle, Hérodiade en fleur du jardin clair   (ll.10-11)

It is mid-line that this *e caduc* hovers most delicately on the edge of perception, as the caesural pause separates it from a following vowel. The 'Scène' features five such hiatal caesuras.[2] In each case, there is irresolvable tension between the elision which would cancel out the pause, and a pause which might encourage pronunciation of the 'e'. In two consecutive examples, the second hemistich begins on a new line, leaving the e hanging on the blank page after the caesura:

Sont immortels. O femme, / un baiser me tûrait	(l.7)
Que je les hais, nourrice, / et veux-tu que je sente	(l.33)
Nourrice, suis-je belle? /	
Un astre, en vérité	(l.52)
Mais cette tresse tombe... /	
Arrête dans ton crime	(l.53)
Et ta sœur solitaire, / ô ma sœur éternelle	(l.110)

The poem's final rhyme, 'rêveries / pierreries' (ll.133-34), also captures the *indicible* within the verse artifice of pronouncing both schwa. Although the second is pronounced in normal speech [pjɛrəri], the first is not [rɛvri], yet metrical convention not only brings it into

---

[1] *The Name of the Poet: onomastics and anonymity in the works of Stéphane Mallarmé*, University of Exeter Press, 1995, pp.149-50.

[2] Clive Scott proposes the term 'hiatal e' for such a technique at any point in the line ('Mallarmé's Mercurial E', *Forum for Modern Language Studies* (1998) 34: 1, 43-55) although he does not explore its use at the caesura.

existence but also fixes it in a *rime léonine*.[1] Thus the verse mould helps the artist pursue his Ideal by allowing the suggestion of the *indicible* on the horizon of poetic form.

Finally, the example 'obscures / Epouvantes' highlights not only the 'e' but also the 's', the grammatical marker of plurality to which Mallarmé, in his studies of language and the formal properties of the signifier, is particularly sensitive. In a note from 1895, meditating on these 'signes éteints', which are graphically present yet silenced, Mallarmé ponders the mystery of 's', which, like 'la loi mystérieuse de la rime',[2] or the Ideal itself, manages to reconcile plurality and singularity:

> Aucune juvénile simplification en effet ne me persuadera [...] que n'existe [...] un rapport, oui, mystérieux, on entend bien, par exemple entre cet *s* du pluriel et celui qui s'ajoute à la seconde personne du singulier, dans les verbes, exprimant lui aussi, non moins que celui causé par le nombre une altération ..... quant à qui parle .....
>
> *S*, dis-je, est la lettre analytique; dissolvante et disséminante, par excellence [...] j'y trouve l'occasion d'affirmer l'existence [...] d'une secrète direction confusément indiquée par l'orthographe et qui concourt mystérieusement au signe pur général qui doit marquer le vers.[3]

In the *contre-rejet* 'obscures', this silent 's' is stressed, underlining the plurality which, without the *enjambement*, would go unpronounced. The rhyming commonplace 'paradis / jadis' (ll.83-84) is similarly re-motivated, as the second 's' disrupts the harmony of the rhyme if pronounced. The reader, therefore, is torn: in the first example, between syntactically necessary *enjambement* and sacrificing the 's' to the rhyme harmony; in the second, between rhyme harmony and correct pronunciation. In both examples the 's', when pronounced, is incompatible with the verse harmony through which the poet hopes to approach his Ideal. Harmony is confounded by the marker of a plurality antagonistic to the wholeness of the poetic Ideal, indicating that the re-arrangement of linguistic multiplicity in verse can never quite reach perfect unity, despite the poem's surfeit of harmonic correspondences.

---

[1] See Gabriel Surenne, *French Pronouncing Dictionary*, Edinburgh: Oliver & Boyd, 1880.

[2] 'Solennité' (*Div.*, p.234).

[3] *Div.*, pp.385-86.

At the poem's conclusion, however, Hérodiade admits that, despite her protestations, she nevertheless anticipates the approach of something unknown, as yet unrealized: 'J'attends une chose inconnue' (l.130). Perhaps her staunch refusal of the artist-lover is a lie (ll.129-30). Hérodiade is not just an immortal Ideal, but also a human, a reticent child about to enter adolescence, anticipating the inevitable loss of her purity. Significantly, this loss of purity is compared to the very fall of unity into multiplicity dramatized in the examples above:

> Jetez-vous les sanglots suprêmes et meurtris
> D'une enfance sentant parmi les rêveries
> Se séparer enfin ses froides pierreries.   (ll.132-34)

The indivisible whole of the virgin's perfection is threatened, perhaps by the approach of the lover who will unveil her. In poetic terms, this also implies the artist's possession of his Ideal, a disaster which is explored allegorically in the first draft of the 'Faune'.

'Le Faune, Intermède héroïque'

Despite Mallarmé's epistolary allusions to the link between the 'Scène' and the 'Intermède' of 1865, and their many thematic and lexical similarities, they have inspired little comparative commentary.[1] This likeness is highlighted in their very first lines: the nurse exclaims: 'Tu vis! ou vois-je ici l'ombre d'une princesse?', just as the faun wonders: 'J'avais des nymphes! Est-ce un songe?'. Both texts begin, therefore, with the possibility that Hérodiade and the nymphs might not actually exist, a possibility which, read allegorically in the context of the artist's relationship with his Ideal, becomes more insistent as Mallarmé reworks the 'Faune' after 1866 and his crisis of faith in absolute values. For the moment, however, the nymphs do exist, appearing like Hérodiade as real characters. The faun's narration of his possession of the nymphs can be read as the Ideal's fall into impurity and plurality, as the faun transgresses the sacred boundary between artist and Ideal which is fundamental to aesthetic idealism.

---

[1] With the exception of the short paper by Jean-Louis Backès, 'Hérodiade et le faune', in *Mallarmé: actes du colloque de la Sorbonne du 21 novembre 1998*, ed. by André Guyaux, Paris: Presses de l'Université de Paris-Sorbonne, 1998, pp.133-44.

When the faun first spies the nymphs, their 'encolure / Immortelle' (ll.59-60) recalls the untouchable Hérodiade, 'Immortelle' (l.65).[1] As they escape, they become a single collective noun with a singular verb, preserving the wholeness of the 'pierreries' which Hérodiade feels beginning to separate ('Scène', ll.132-34):

> Et la troupe, du bain ruisselant, disparaît
> Dans les cygnes et les frissons, ô pierreries! (ll.62-63)

The parallels with Hérodiade's own evasion of the artist are emphasized by the alterations made in the 'Improvisation' of 1875, recalling the 'blond torrent' of her hair (l.4) and her eyes with their 'clarté mélodieuse' (l.92):

> Et le splendide bain de cheveux disparaît
> Dans les *clartés* et les frissons, ô pierreries! (ll.66-67, my italics)

The seizure of the nymphs is presented as the fall of unity into plurality. When the faun first takes them, 'sans les désenlacer' (l.67), they are united 'parmi l'extase d'être deux', the delicious, mysterious union of multiplicity in unity which pre-occupies Baudelaire.[2] By ravishing the nymphs, the faun spoils this indivisible unity:

> Mon crime fut d'avoir, sans épuiser ces peurs
> Malignes, divisé la touffe échevelée
> De baisers que les dieux avaient si bien mêlée (ll.78-80)

Compared to the defiled nymphs, Hérodiade is a 'reptile / Inviolée' (ll.105-6). Whereas she refuses the nurse's kiss (l.7) and 'cette main encore sacrilège' (l.58), their hair is 'échevelée / De baisers', the adjective underlining the disorder brought to their formerly divine unity. The nymphs, therefore, suffer the fate which Hérodiade resists; in 1875, 'séparé' replaces 'divisé', echoing even more explicitly her loss of unity: 'une enfance sentant […] Se séparer enfin ses froides pierreries' ('Scène', l.134). Indeed, in the 1865 text Iane experiences a similar fall into adolescence, 'une enfance qui s'enfuyait' (II, l.8). Just

---

[1] The text used is that of the *copie manuscrite* (O.C., 1998, pp.153-59).
[2] See 'Tout entière', for example, or 'Victor Hugo' (O.C.II: 137-38).

as Hérodiade feels 'les sanglots suprêmes et meurtris' of an impending fall into impurity, it is these sobs of submission which excite the faun: 'des sanglots dont j'étais encore ivre!' (1.88). The nymphs' flight at precisely the moment of possession reinforces the notion that the Ideal must never be attained, or it simply vanishes.

However, the faun's memories of his exploits bolster his confidence that he might possess other nymphs:

> Je suis content! Tout s'offre ici: de la grenade
> Ouverte, à l'eau qui va nue en sa promenade   (ll.91-92)

This image of the opened pomegranate henceforth comes to symbolize the pursuit of the Ideal and the indefinite deferral of its capture, as Mallarmé tells Lefébure of 'ce mot sombre, et rouge comme une grenade ouverte, Hérodiade'.[1] In the 'Scène', the same rhyme recurs as the evening brings about the inevitable opening:

> Au matin grelottant de fleurs, ses promenades,
> Et quand le soir méchant entr'ouvre ses grenades! (ll.65-66)

The role of verse form in the artist's pursuit of this Ideal is highlighted by Mallarmé's later amendment to the line: 'Et quand le soir méchant a coupé les grenades', since the metrical framework is governed by rhythmical *coupes*. Mallarmé tells Jules Huret in 1891 of 'la merveilleuse science du vers, l'art suprême des coupes', and refers in 1892 to 'la prosodie, rimes et coupes'.[2] Indeed, the image of the faun making his flute from the reeds progresses through successive drafts as:

> Que je venais casser les grands roseaux domptés
> Par ma lèvre   (1865, ll.22-23)

> Que je cassais en deux l'un des roseaux domptés
> Par le chanteur   (1875, ll.26-27)

> Que je coupais ici les creux roseaux domptés
> *Par le talent*   (1876, ll.26-27)[3]

---

[1] Letter of 18 February 1865 (*Corr. fol.*, p.226).
[2] 'Enquête sur l'évolution littéraire' (*Div.*, p.391) and 'Théodore de Banville' (*Div.*, p.157).
[3] Mallarmé's italics.

The second version reflects formally how the alexandrines, 'les creux roseaux', are broken in two, as 'deux' and 'l'un', opposite poles of the plurality and unity dichotomy, are brutally separated by the caesural *coupe*. Ianthé also uses the verb *couper* in reference to the 'grands roseaux' of the flute:

> L'homme, sa rêverie interdite te brise,
> Les coupa pour verser en eux ses chants sacrés. (II, ll.28-29)

These metrical 'roseaux' echo the 'joncs' where Iane's nudity is unveiled: 'je tremblai, sans voile, dans les joncs' (II, ll.7-9), and as the faun describes how he made his flute, the trembling reeds recur: 'Joncs tremblant avec des étincelles' (l.21). The faun's art, therefore, is linked to the dangerous unveiling of the nymphs, an analogy made explicit by Iane herself: 'Les femmes sont les sœurs des roseaux massacrés' (II, ll.28-30).

The nymphs' unveiling, and resulting fall from perfection into imperfection, are reflected in the poem's versification, which is much more disruptive than that of the 'Scène'. The loss of verse harmony and regularity underlines the poet's distance from his newly defiled Ideal. None of the eight CP6 lines can be resolved as 4/4/4:

Ô feuillage, si tu / protèges ces mortelles	(l.4)
Joncs tremblant avec des / étincelles, contez	(l.21)
Aux ivresses de sa / sève?	
Serais-je pur?	(l.33)
Dans les cygnes et les / frissons, ô piererries!	(l.63)
Je les saisis, sans les / désenlacer, et vole	(l.67)
Par ma lèvre: quand sur / l'or glauque de lointaines	(l.23)
Sans un murmure et sans / dire que s'envola	(l.29)
Des perfides et par / d'idolâtres peintures	(l.51)

Significantly, the most metrically disruptive line in the poem (M6), compounded by an accentually weak *contre-rejet*, comes as Iane decribes the loss of her purity:

> D'une enfance qui s'en / fuyait avec de longs (II, l.8)

Similarly, the line recounting the faun's seizure of the nymphs, heralding the impending division of their unity, is C6 as the caesura visibly divides a coherent syntactic unit:

Je les saisis, sans les / désenlacer, et vole   (1.67)

The 'Intermède' also features a much higher proportion of D6 lines
than the 'Scène', forty-two compared to sixteen, of which no fewer
than seventeen feature a post-caesural adjective. Certain monosyllabic
examples contain echoes of the Ideal's lost purity, from nudity to
swan-like whiteness and purity:

> Ouverte, à l'eau qui va / *nue* en sa promenade   (1.92)
> N'était que les sanglots / *blancs* de cette buveuse   (II, 1.21)
> Une âme de cristal / *pur* que jette la flûte   (III, 1.75)

A similar effect is created in the following variant:

> Et la voix naît des joncs / *vierges*, que nous n'osâmes [1]

Indeed, the 'Intermède' contains more seventh-syllable accents than
the 'Scène'. The sound of Iane playing the flute creates 'une mélodie à
sept notes', a number which, in the wake of Baudelaire's 'Les Sept
vieillards', can be seen to represent the fall of the Ideal and a loss of
faith in poetic *nombre*. Mallarmé's awareness of the figure's symbolic
value can be seen in the 1866 alteration of 'plus las cent fois' to 'sept
fois' ('Las de l'amer repos...', 1.4). In the 'Faune', it is the ravished
nymph who plays this seven-note melody, and the seventh-syllable
accents formally disrupt the alexandrines whose perfect 6+6 symmetry
has been spoiled. With the fall of the Ideal into plurality, metrical
nombre also falters, with an echo, in 'seul', of Hérodiade's necessary
solitude which the artist must respect:

> N'est-ce pas moi qui veux / *seul*, et sans tes douleurs   (1.78)

Similarly meaningful accentual jolts occur at the first syllable, as
'Vaine!' (1.49), 'L'homme' (II, 1.28) and 'L'art' (III, 1.54) dramatize
the possible vanity of verse form in the face of the defiled Ideal. There
is also a hexa-accentual line, unprecedented but for the point at which
the 'Pitre châtié' rebels against verse artifice and rejects the safety of
the poetic window, as 'enjambé' also suggests metrically transgressive
enjambement:

---

[1] O.C., 1998, p.832.

J'ai, Muse, – moi, ton pitre – / enjambé la fenêtre   ('Le Pitre châtié', l.3)

The hexa-accentual line from the 'Faune' itself precedes a mono-syllabic *rejet*, making of the rhythmically disruptive sequence an emphatic 'mélodie à sept notes':

> Pardon, à toi, pardon! – /
> Ô folle, viens! Ne tarde
> Plus!   ('Intermède' II, l.36)

Fittingly, rhythmically problematic *enjambement* also leaps from eight cases in the 'Scène' to twenty-one in the 'Intermède', with five monosyllabic, adjectival *contre-rejets*: 'clair / Rubis' (ll.1-2), 'closes / Paupières' (ll.101-2), 'longs / Fleuves' (II, ll.8-9), 'noire / Source' (II, ll.14-15) and 'frais / Vent' (III, ll.46-47). Also common are the noun/adjective model: 'rameaux / Nubiles' (ll.5-6), 'délice / Farouche' (ll.71-72), 'peurs / Malignes' (ll.78-79), 'grenade / Ouverte' (ll.91-92), 'voix / Seules' (II, ll.26-27), 'douleurs / Amères' (III, ll.78-79); compound nouns: 'confidents / Des fuites' (ll.42-43), 'éclair / De haines' (ll.73-74), 'piscine / Des sources' (III, ll.79-80); and verbal constructions: 'Ne tarde / Plus' (II, ll.36-37), 'nous n'osâmes briser' (III, ll.59-60). The disruptive force of these techniques is all the more powerful since the rhymes of the 'Intermède' prove noticeably richer than those of the 'Scène', with more *rimes riches* and twice as many *léonines*. The strongest reinforced rhyme, '**avanie** / ma **manie**' (III, ll.51-52) creates tension just as the faun intends to 'briser des joncs mauvais' (l.50). Similarly, two consecutive *rimes léonines*, 'fatal / natal' and 'n'osâmes / nos âmes' (ll.57-60) reinforce the harmonic unity just as he refers to the 'joncs unis, que nous n'osâmes / Briser'.

The drama of unity and plurality played out at the *entrevers* in the 'Scène' is reflected in the rhyme: 'Vénus / pieds nus' (ll.97-98). In order to create a satisfying *rime léonine* [enys], 'nus' would require incorrect pronunciation of its 's'. Conversely, if we compensate by pronouncing [veny / pje ny] the 's' is lost, as we sacrifice the very marker of plurality in order to reconcile the rhyming elements in an artificial unity. The status of this present-absent 's' is also uncertain in the *contre-rejet* 'bleus / Et verts' (ll.10-11); the syntax encourages us to pronounce it, whereas the rhyme [lø] urges against this option. In line one the very word 'nymphes', which embodies this unity/duality drama, precedes a pause marked by blank space:

J'avais des nymph*es*!
              Est-ce un songe? Non: le clair

However, if we pause, the *e caduc* required by the metre is lost; we must instead pronounce both 'e' and 's', ignoring the pause in favour of liaison to the 'Est-ce', which itself echoes the 's' whose status is unstable. The *e indicible*, a suggestion of the necessarily intangible absolute, is echoed elsewhere by *enjambement* of feminine rhyme: 'mouss*e* / Vaine' (ll.48-49), 'délic*e* / Farouche' (ll.71-72), 'clos*es* / Paupières' (ll.100-1), 'noir*e* / Source' (II, ll.14-15), 'tard*e* / Plus' (II, ll.36-37) and 'avid*e* / D'ivresse' where the chiastic 'v-i-d-e-d-i-v' envelops the phantom syllable, foregrounding its necessarily present-absent status on the periphery of metrical *nombre*.

The duality-unity tension also features in certain additions to the 1876 version of the poem. Recalling Ianthé's comparison of the sisters to reeds, duality is resolved in the faun's 'jonc vaste et jumeau' (l.43), symbolic of the art by which he attempts to conjure up a vision of the nymphs. Similarly, at the poem's conclusion the nymphs are finally united in a singularity as 'couple' and 'ombre', addressed as 'tu':

Ouvrir ma bouche à l'astre efficace des vins!
Couple, adieu; je vais voir l'ombre que tu devins. (ll.109-10)

However, there is no such resolution in the rhyme, which is tantalizingly close to a *rime léonine*. This invites reflection, since Mallarmé could easily have closed the poem on a pleasingly harmonious 'de vins / devins'. Yet it is precisely the 's', grammatical marker of plurality, which confounds the resolution in poetic unity, as verse harmony still proves a long way from perfect wholeness.

As the poem nears its conclusion the faun succumbs to the illusion that he might ultimately possess 'la grande Vénus' (l.97), an illusion made more explicit throughout the drafts: 'Si!...' (1865, l.100), 'Si je la...' (1875, l.104), 'Je tiens la reine!' (1876, l.104). The isolated 'Si!' of the 'Intermède' can also be seen as the seventh note in the diatonic scale, announcing the imminent arrival of the next 'do' which provides a perfect cadence with the previous one. In an excellent study of Mallarmé's basic knowledge of music theory, Heath Lees highlights 'the straining of *si* towards *ut*', suggesting that 'si' 'loses all its meaning if it does not fulfil itself in taking that small upward semitone, to what is now called "the tonic"'.[1] Thus the faun yearns to possess the goddess via the musical metaphor of resolution in perfect harmony, but wisely decides to approach his Ideal only in a dream: 'Dormons: je puis rêver à mon blasphème / Sans crime'(ll.103-4). His crime was to divide the nymphs' unity (l.78), and so, realising this possession is impossible in reality, he allows them to return to the dream-space where they might be imagined at a safe distance. Similarly, whereas the faun seized the nymphs – 'Je les saisis' (l.67) – Mallarmé's next project is an 'insaisissable ouverture', which firmly restores the necessary distance between the poet and his Ideal while nonetheless straining towards it thanks to the poem's unprecedented harmonic richness.[2]

'Ouverture d'Hérodiade'

Here the nurse foretells Hérodiade's impending loss of purity, at the 'Lever du jour dernier qui vient tout achever' (l.88).[3] The room contains the sensual aroma of roses (l.30) whose *ivresse* Hérodiade had rejected ('Scène', ll.32-34) and the mixture of sexual and textual imagery in 'le lit aux pages de vélin' (l.59) announces both the lover's possession of the princess and the artist's possession of his Ideal. Indeed, in his correspondence Mallarmé claims to have glimpsed the 'Poème dans sa nudité', as if it were a woman, and at times the reference blurs, as if Hérodiade and the poem were one: 'Je reviens à *Hérodiade*, je la rêve si parfaite que je ne sais seulement si elle existera jamais'.[4] However, as at the end of the 'Faune', this Ideal is allowed to remain a dream, and the moment of possession is situated safely in an imaginary future beyond the poem. The textual nature of the consummation is underlined by the '*plis* jaunes de la pensée' and '*toile* encensée' (ll.41-42, my italics), the imminent revelation of 'Le vieil éclat voilé du vermeil insolite' (l.49) depending on rhythmical patterns, both poetic and penetrative:

---

[1] '...depuis Wagner, la poésie'. Mallarmé and the All-Embracing Word Work', in *Situating Mallarmé*, ed. by David Kinloch and Gordon Millan, Oxford: Peter Lang, 'French Studies of the Eighteenth and Nineteenth Centuries', vol. 10, 2000, pp.13-32; pp.23 and 21.
[2] Letter of 5 December 1865 to Cazalis (*Corr. fol.*, p.259).
[3] The text used is the second version, to which, as Marchal observes, corrections might have been made at any point between 1866 and 1898 (O.C., 1998, pp.137-39).
[4] Letters of 3 January 1866 (*Corr. fol.*, p.280) and 24 April 1866 (*Corr. fol.*, p.295).

Par les trous anciens et par les plis roidis
Percés selon le rythme et les dentelles pures   (ll.44-45)

It is rhythm, piercing Hérodiade's mystery, that will release the incense from the heart of the censer in which it is enclosed, and as Mallarmé later insists, the poet enjoys a privileged relationship with rhythm, 'suivant l'instinct de rythmes qui l'élit'.[1] Furthermore, this rhythm appears to be regular, like 'les dentelles pures' which suggest the symmetrical, repetitive patterns of lacework, 'Cet unanime blanc conflit / D'une guirlande avec la même' ('Une dentelle s'abolit', ll.5-6). Sure enough, the 'ouverture musicale'[2] presents the most preciously rich structures so far in Mallarmé, as the surfeit of harmony heralds the unveiling of the Ideal. A number of emphatic irregularities, though, ensure that the poet's arrival at this absolute poem is also, necessarily, deferred.

The poem features an unprecedented concentration of phonetic correspondences. It boasts the most emphatic trisyllabic rhyme so far ('évocati-on / incantati-on', ll.39-40) and the highest percentage of *rimes léonines* in the three poems: 34% compared to 9% ('Scène') and 19% ('Faune'). Many of these are grouped consecutively:

abandon		insolite	
brandon		acolyte	
mausolée		splendeurs	
désolée	(ll.11-14)	demandeurs	(ll.49-52)

évocati-on		année	→	heurée
incantati-on		damnée	→	pleurée
pensée		ombre, pas		
encensée		indicible pas		
refroidis		salarie		
roidis	(ll.39-44)	tarie		
		glacier		
		l'acier	(ll.69-76)	

The intricate system of phonetic correspondences observed in the 'Scène' is taken to new extremes in the 'Ouverture', reinforcing the following rhyming hemistichs:

---

[1] 'Le Mystère dans les Lettres' (*Div.*, p.274).
[2] Letter of 28 April 1866 to Cazalis (*Corr. fol.*, p.297).

/ **et** s<u>a</u>c<i>r</i>ifi<u>c</u><u>a</u>trice,
/ **du** n<u>é</u>nuph<u>a</u>r, <u>c</u>aprice (ll.5-6)   (5 patterns: /**e**/, /<u>a</u>/, /k/, /r/ and /**f**/)

/ f<u>a</u>ta<i>l</i>e se r<u>é</u>signe,
/ <i>l</i><u>a</u> p<i>l</i>ume ni <i>l</i>e <u>c</u>ygne (ll.9-10)   (4 patterns: /<u>a</u>/, /<i>l</i>/, /ə/, and /<u>s-z</u>/)

/ g<i>r</i>**and** ouv<i>er</i>t, c<u>e</u> vitrail.
/ **en** un cad<i>r</i><u>e</u>, attirail (ll.19-20)   (4 patterns: /r/, /ã̃/, /<u>ə</u>/ and 'it / tti')

/ <u>à</u> <i>l</i>'iv<u>oi</u><i>r</i>e fermé
/ <i>l</i>'<u>a</u>rgent n<u>oi</u>r p<u>a</u>rsemé (ll.27-28)   (4 or 5 patterns: /<u>a</u>/ and /<u>wa</u>/, /<i>l</i>/, /r/, and /ə/)

/ **et** <i>l</i>es dentEl<i>l</i><u>es</u> pures
/ par ses bEl<i>l</i><u>es</u> guipures (ll.45-46)   (4 patterns: /**e**/, /<i>l</i>/, /ɛ/ and *e caduc* + silent 's')

/ <i>l</i>e vieil éc<i>l</i><u>a</u>t v<u>oi</u>lé,
/ **en** ces <u>a</u>ppe<i>l</i>s celé! (ll.47-48)   (3 patterns: /<i>l</i>/, /**e**/, and /<u>a</u>/)

bassins // *an*ciens <u>se</u> r<u>é</u>signe.
/ **in**cohér*en*te, <u>s</u>igne (ll.57-58)   (6 patterns: /ẽ̃/, /ã̃/, /e/, /<u>s</u>/, /r/ and /ə/)

/ n'*a* p<i>l</i>us <i>l</i><u>e</u> cher grimoire,
/ *à la* déser<u>te</u> moire, (ll.61-62)   (4 patterns: /*a*/, /<i>l</i>/, /**er**/ and /r/, and /<u>ə</u>/)

/ <u>en</u>dorm<i>i</i>s. L'avait-il?
/ <u>en</u> son plais<i>r</i> subtil, (ll.63-64)   (3 patterns: /<u>ã</u>/, /i/ and 'ai')

/ mais au c<u>a</u>d<i>r</i>an de fer
/ suspen<i>d</i>*an*t Lucifer, (ll.67-68)   (2 patterns: /d/ and /<u>ã</u>/)

/ pr<u>é</u>s<u>age</u> *et* mauvais rêve!
/ le vit<u>rage</u> s'<u>é</u>lève (ll.81-82)   (3 patterns: /r/, 'age' and /e/)

/ d*e* tR<u>i</u>s<u>te</u> **c**Répu<u>s</u>cule   (5 patterns: /ə/, 'R', /i/, /<u>s</u>/, /k/)
/ la <u>ci</u>R*e* qu<i>i</i> R**e**cule! (ll.85-86)   (internal rhyme: [s-i-r-e-k-i-r-e])

/ av<u>an</u>t sa <i>f</i>uite <u>an</u>tique
/ et <i>f</i>roid, mél<u>an</u>colique, (ll.93-94)   (2 patterns: /<u>ã</u>/ and /<i>f</i>/)

Two couplets push this phenomenon to its limit, as correspondences extend all the way back along the line. The first features three pre-caesural patterns: '*l*', '<u>t</u>' and '*i*' and four post-caesural patterns: '**au**', '<u>pa</u>' or '<u>a</u>', '*l*' and *e caduc* or schwa:

> L<u>a</u>men<u>t</u>ab<i>l</i>e! <i>l</i>e <i>l</i><u>i</u><u>t</u> // **au**x p<u>age</u>s d*e* vé<i>l</i>in,
> T<u>e</u><i>l</i>, inu<u>ti</u><i>l</i>e et si // c<i>l</i>**au**st<u>ra</u><i>l</i>, n'est p<u>as</u> <i>l</i>e <i>l</i>in! (ll.59-60)

The second couplet is remarkable for both its phonetic and rhythmical symmetry:

> A l'heur / e d'agon*ie* // **et** *d*e lu*t*t / es funèbres!
> Et, forc / e *d*u s*i*lence // **et** *d*es noir / es *t*énèbres   (ll.53-54)

Both lines are metrically 2/4//3/3, with a bisyllabic noun or adjective at syllables two to three, nine to ten and eleven to twelve, and with pronounced *e caduc* at the third and tenth syllables and elided 'e' at the caesura; their phonetic symmetry comes from the recurring '*d*' falling on the fourth and eighth syllables, the '**et**' at the seventh, and the '*i*'s of the first hemistich. Finally, one chiastic example of verse symmetry recalls the 'Hérodiade au clair regard de diamant' of the 'Scène' (1.116), reinforcing the caesura in which letters are mirrored:

> **De** qu*i* *l*e *l*ong regret / **et** *l*es t*i*ges **de** qu*i*   (1.35)
> də k*i* *l*ə *l*   e / e *l*e i ə də k*i*

The later changes made to the 'Ouverture' reinforce this drive towards perfection; two *rimes léonines* are altered to rhyme *pour l'œil*, and a *rime suffisante* is strengthened:

passé	→	**passé**
effacé	→	lassé (ll.55-56)

année	→	heurée
damnée	→	**pleurée** (ll.69-70)

antique	→	**allée**
mélancolique	→	**allée** (ll.93-94)

The final few lines, the only section extensively reworked, present a dizzying concentration of phonetic correspondences wherein the poet comes as close as possible to self-reflecting lines without slipping into the meaningless accumulation of sound over sense:

> La rougeur de ce temps // prophétique qui pleure
> Sur l'enfant, exilée // en son cœur précieux
> Comme un cygne cachant // en sa plume ses yeux,
> Comme les mit le vieux // cygne en sa plume, allée
> De la plume en détresse, // en l'éternelle allée
> De ses espoirs, pour voir // les diamants élus
> D'une étoile, mourante, // et qui ne brille plus!

The highly artificial system of phonetic echoes, with the consecutive line-initial 'Comme' and 'De', or the repetition of 'plume' and 'cygne', almost defies analysis in the indivisible complexity of its dazzling poetic *éclat*. The first three lines all present a regular 3/3//3/3 metre, a quasi-incantatory rhythm with internal rhyme on many of the accents, as if the nurse's prophecy of the rhythmic penetration of the Ideal were coming true. It recalls an earlier *rythme monotone*, when the nurse foresees a similar victory and resignation; here the rhythm is accentuated by a sort of chiastic *rime batelée* and the nasal [ɛ̃]:

> Fatidi / que, vaincu, // monoton / e, lassé,   [as-e]
> Comme l'eau / des bass*ins* // anci*ens* / se résigne. (ll.56-57) [e-as]

Such intricate phonetic patterns are mentioned in 'Solennité' (1887), which contains *en filigrane* references to the Hérodiade/faun drama, such as: 'le voile de la Déesse', 'Vénus', the idealized 'Vers' and the 'hymen' which appears in the 1875 'Faune'. Mallarmé praises the resplendent rhymes of Banville's *Le Forgeron*:

[…] la rime ici extraordinaire parce qu'elle ne fait qu'un avec l'alexandrin qui, dans ses poses et la multiplicité de son jeu, semble par elle dévoré tout entier comme si cette fulgurante cause de délice y triomphait jusqu'à l'initiale syllabe.[1]

However, any drive towards the Ideal must be accompanied by irregularities which maintain a healthy distance, and despite the poem's closing *feu d'artifice*, with the prodigious extension of harmony over two consecutive *rimes enjambées* 'allée / De […] allée / De', the poem ends on the whimper of the humble *rime suffisante* [ly]. Although relatively tame compared to the 'Faune', in terms of metrical disruption, the 'Ouverture' contains twenty-two D6 and two C6 lines:

> Loin du lit vide qu'un / cierge obscurci cachait   (l.31)
> Par la clepsydre à la / goutte obscure damnée   (l.70)

Several adjacent accents also ensure that the text maintains the necessary distance from perfection, with nine at first syllable position, five at seventh, and two mid-line. Recalling the 'Faune', where echoes

---

[1] *Div.*, p.233.

of the Ideal disrupt rhythmic regularity at the seventh syllable, it is the swan, whose purity recalls Hérodiade herself, that breaks the rhythm:

Comme les mit le vieux / *cygne* en sa plume, allée   (l.93)

Similarly, the following hexa-accentual line dramatizes the presence-absence of the princess and her 'ombre' as the *e caduc* is variously elided, pronounced or problematized by the hiatal caesura:

Que, délaissée, elle erre, / et, sur son ombre, pas   (l.71)

The present-absent princess also appears at the *entrevers*. As the nurse foretells her imminent undoing, *enjambement* encourages pronunciation of the *e surnuméraire*: 'signe / Lamentable' (ll.58-59). Also, the correction of 'caprice / Inutile' to 'caprice / Solitaire' (ll.6-7), with the chiastic [r-i-s-*e*-s-i-r] around the *e*, highlights its metrically transgressive presence all the more. The alteration of 'chant d'étoile' to 'quelque étoile' allows the elided schwa to flutter on the edge of perception. Mallarmé's *poésies de jeunesse* highlight his sensitivity to the matter with 'quelqu'aigle' ('Pan', l.90) and 'Quelqu'oiseau' ('Causerie d'adieu', l.19). Anxious to underline the metrically necessary elision, the young poet defies the correct spelling in case the 'que' seems *de trop*.[1] This very uncertainty is later exploited in an amendment to 'Dame…' (1896): 'Ni brise quoique, avec' (l.6). In order to satisfy the metre, the conjunction must be pronounced [kwak] despite the following comma, which indicates a pause encouraging the pronunciation [kwa-kə]. Another addition to 'Dame…' dramatizes the schwa by placing it at the metrically obligatory caesural pause: 'quelque / apparence' (l.11). If we pause, the schwa provides a transgressive thirteenth syllable, and so the line exists in a state of irresolvable metrical tension thanks to the presence-absence of the poetically *indicible*.

The drama of multiplicity and unity at work in the 'Scène' and the 'Faune' is also played out in the 'Ouverture' in the instability of 's' at the rhyme:

---

[1] Larousse confirms: 'Cet adjectif [quelque] ne subit l'élision que devant les mots *un, une*; ce serait une faute d'écrire *quelqu'autre circonstance, quelqu'utile conséquence*; il faut mettre *quelque autre, quelque utile*, bien que dans la prononciation on ne fasse pas du tout sentir l'*e*.' (*Grand Dictionnaire Universel du XIXe Siècle*, 13: 514).

plis / Inutiles avec les yeux ensevelis   (ll.23-24)
         z   z   z   z

The /z/ phoneme of the *entrevers* liaison is picked up three times in the following line, amplifying the echo until 'ensevelis', contrary to the anticipated rhyme [liz], breaks rather than continues the sequence, leaving the potential resolution of plurality in unity unrealised thanks to precisely the 's', symbol of plurality. A similar effect occurs later:

sur son ombre, pas / Un ange accompagnant son indicible pas! (ll.71-72)

The exclamation mark alerts us to an irony present in the rhyme drama, and we hesitate between liaison of 'pas', tightly bound to the following noun, and respect for the rhyme harmony which causes a discordant hiatus at the *entrevers* [pa œ̃]. The first 'pas', then, is literally 'indicible', only an 'ombre', caught in the irresolvable hesitation between two conflicting readings.

The thematics of duality and unity also features on a subtle graphological level. The first draft of the 'Ouverture' already contains the following correspondence:

à *l*a *l*une
s'effeui*ll*e l'une   (ll.33-34)

Not only are the two 'l's graphologically reconciled in the single phoneme 'll', summarized by the following 'l'une', but their individuality also dissolves in the shift in pronunciation from /l/ to /j/. In the second draft, two other such adjustments are made in consecutive lines (ll.15-18):

/ un chant d'étoile, mais	→	/ de que*l*que étoi*l*e, mais	[l + l]
/ ne scintilla jamais.		/ ne scinti*ll*a jamais.	[ll]
/ ancienne! supplice!		/ ancienne! su*pp*lice!	[pp]
/ de la rougeur complice!	→	/ de la *pourp*re complice!	[p + p]

This culminates in the play between all the single and double 'l's of the final reworked lines and the last two words: 'bri*ll*e p*l*us' (l.96). In this way, plurality-unity tension is visible in the alphabet itself, the original elements of multiplicity which form the basis of so many languages, 'imparfaites en cela que plusieurs'.[1]

In conclusion, Mallarmé's early faith in an external Ideal guarantees the poetic value of harmony and regularity over discord and irregularity. The poet, aiming to approach a necessarily unrealizable perfection in his verse, is intellectually exhausted by his 'travail rigoureux sur le vers'.[2] As he tells Cazalis in the oft-quoted letter of 28 April 1866 detailing his spiritual crisis, it is 'en creusant le vers à ce point' that Mallarmé realizes the ultimate vanity of poetry which, in the absence of an external absolute realm, corresponds to no transcendent reality.[3] However, although the fallacious verse mould no longer mirrors a universal rhythmic Truth, the discovery of the 'Néant' does not inspire him to reject verse. On the contrary, Mallarmé's poetic career is henceforth dedicated to celebrating 'La Gloire du Mensonge, ou le Glorieux Mensonge',[4] which echoes Baudelaire's similarly post-illusory 'Amour du mensonge'. Yet it is precisely the illusory nature of the poetic Ideal that poetry must not admit, and the re-location of the Ideal within man necessitates, as for Baudelaire and Rimbaud, the complementary illusion of its universality. Whereas these poets explore the problem in prose poetry, Mallarmé has written both verse and prose poems from early on, and so the genre lacks for him the irreversible, revolutionary force of *Illuminations*. Rather, it is in his critical articles and correspondence that Mallarmé mystifies the figure of the poet and the nature of rhythm. For the rest of his career he maintains the illusion of poetic universality while simultaneously admitting – so subtly, in fact, that this crucial point might often escape the reader – that it is nothing more than a salutary fiction. Whilst mystifying the nature of Poetry,

---

[1] 'Crise de vers' (*Div.*, p.244).
[2] Marchal, *La Religion de Mallarmé*, p.46.
[3] *Corr. fol.*, p.297.
[4] *Corr. fol.*, p.298.

Mallarmé re-motivates the value of the verse mould abandoned by many of his contemporaries, as harmony and discord come to articulate the irresolvable tension at the heart of his self-consciously fictional Ideal.

8
Protecting a Poetic Fiction

The internal Ideal

Following the collapse, in 1866, of Mallarmé's faith in external absolutes, the Ideal does not disappear but, like 'Dieu et notre âme', transforms into a 'Rêve qu'[on] sait n'être pas', absolute yet fictional.[1] The 1875-76 alterations to the 'Faune', where the faun concludes that the nymphs should only be approached in a dream, foreground the henceforth unstable status of this dream. In the 'Improvisation' (1875) the nymphs gain a capital letter, becoming absolute in the very first line: 'Ces Nymphes'. However, whereas the faun of 1865 did not doubt their existence, he now admits: 'Mon doute, loin ici de finir, se prolonge' (l.4). Although his wish 'je les veux émerveiller' (l.1) supposes a real, external object, all that remains by line two is an impalpable haze in the air. The possible source of this haze, the 'pudeur ordinaire de roses' (1875, l.7), or the 'faute idéale de roses' (1876), underlines the nymphs' thematic links with Hérodiade, 'la rose / Cruelle' ('Les Fleurs', ll.10-11), the poetic Ideal which is now but a dream. Indeed, the poem's allegorical re-location of this Ideal in the artistic imagination is supported by the alteration of 'Est-ce un songe?' (1865, l.1) to 'Baisais-je un songe?' (1875, l.3), echoing the 'baiser' which Hérodiade feared would spoil her purity.

This uncertainty is compounded by tension in the verse fabric itself (l.1). Although it matches the tone of the *églogue* genre, the placement of the object pronoun before the modal verb strikes the reader as odd. Mallarmé could easily have written 'veux les', since the poem features other C6 lines, yet his decision actually reinforces the caesura; what is more straightforward than the assertion: 'Ces Nymphes, je les veux'? However, this implies a concrete exernal object which the faun might grasp, and the reinforced verse mould is thereby linked to faith in the Ideal. However, as we read over the caesural pause to the following infinitive, 'perpétuer' (1876), the sense of the phrase is no longer quite so evident, and the status of the nymphs' existence is called into question along with the rhythmical fabric of the line.

---

[1] Letter of 28 April 1866 to Cazalis (*Corr. fol.*, pp.297-98).

Whereas the 1865 nymphs left a palpable mark on the faun, the 'morsure / Féminine' (ll.39-40) becomes in 1875 the less certain 'morsure / Mystérieuse' (ll.40-41). The nymphs' existence is now simply a matter of faith for the faun who, with no concrete proof, has only the 'visible et serein souffle artificiel / De l'inspiration' (ll.21-22), his 'chant crédule' (l.47) which might stir his belief. Following the disappearance of the external Ideal, poetry too becomes a 'chant crédule', a 'feinte' (l.58) by which the artist might promote his dream of the internalized Ideal. This internalization is made explicit in 'Quand l'ombre menaça...', as poetic idealism takes refuge in a 'Rêve' (l.2) following the collapse of the external absolute. The poet declares: 'Il a ployé son aile indubitable en moi' (l.4), yet this re-location of the Ideal in *le moi* risks the dangers faced by the Baudelairean prose poet. Since *le moi* is an insufficient guarantee of the poetic authenticity of an internal Ideal, it requires a notion of universality, as if the poet possessed a heightened sensitivity towards that which is shared by everyone. Therefore, recalling Rimbaud's solution to the problem with the figure of the 'génie', 'Quand l'ombre menaça...' ends on precisely the same word, celebrating the role of poetic genius in presenting a fictional poetic Ideal as if it were a universal Truth inherent to all mankind: 'Que s'est d'un astre en fête allumé le génie' (l.14). Although this 'astre' is usually seen as the earth, it also recalls Hérodiade herself, whose beauty makes her 'Un astre, en vérité' ('Scène', l.52), underlining the privileged relationship between artistic genius and the newly internalized Ideal.

The fall of the external Ideal brings down with it the universal analogy according to which there is only one absolute way of seeing the world, but if there exist as many ways of seeing the world as there are observers – recalling Baudelaire's concerns over *la fantaisie* – the poet's 'rêve' lacks the necessary universality. Thus, as in Rimbaud's 'Lettre du voyant', the poet finds himself obliged to argue that his way of seeing is, in fact, the only one possible. This issue is tackled in the only prose poem of the 1870s, 'Un spectacle interrompu' (1875), where the poet writes of the need for 'un journal qui remarque les événements sous le jour propre au rêve':

Artifice que la *réalité*, bon à fixer l'intellect moyen entre les mirages d'un fait; mais elle repose par cela même sur quelque universelle entente: voyons donc s'il n'est pas, dans l'idéal, un aspect nécessaire, évident, simple, qui serve de type.[1]

Reality is an artifice, yet one which owes its success to 'quelque universelle entente', a shared agreement which the 'rêve' must now assume. The poet rejects reality in favour of his own poetic interpretation of events: 'Je veux, en vue de moi seul, écrire comme elle frappa mon regard de poète, telle Anecdote'.[2] Yet the pitfalls of *le moi* are skilfully avoided in the conclusion, where the poet insists that his interpretation is not a simple *fantaisie*, but rather, the Truth to which others are blind and to which he enjoys privileged access, 'étonné de n'avoir pas senti, cette fois encore, le même genre d'impression que mes semblables, mais serein: car ma façon de voir, après tout, avait été supérieure, et même la vraie'.[3] Naturally, the poet's fellows must be seen as his 'semblables', as if the only difference between him and them were his privileged insight into a Truth imperceptible, yet not completely alien, to them.

In 'La Déclaration foraine' the poet fulfils his 'devoir' of sharing this insight with the assembled crowd, offering a 'représentation' of his companion.[4] They can all see her standing on the table, just as we can all see the natural world in which we live, but the fair-goers seem to need the poet to describe what it is they see. As the poet explains, this requires recourse to 'quelque puissance absolue', an illusion of universality which might reinforce 'l'authenticité du spectacle'. Suggesting the fragility of this illusion, his pronouncement is 'rien que lieu commun d'une esthétique', recalling Baudelaire's passion for the 'lieu commun' expressed in 1859.[5] This commonplace might easily be a mere 'rien', and it is on this uncertainty between universality and vanity that Mallarmé's post-illusory poetry thrives. The poet himself tells his companion: 'il faut proclamer quelque chose fût-ce la rêverie', the typically Mallarméen imperfect subjunctive suggesting the tension between possibility and certainty upon which poetry must not conclude. This is also expressed by the woman's mysterious

---

[1] *Div.*, p.80; Mallarmé's italics.
[2] *Div.*, p.80.
[3] *Div.*, p.83.
[4] All quotations: *Div.*, pp.85-91.
[5] *Salon de 1859*, I, 'L'Artiste moderne' (O.C.II: 609). See also page 103 of this study.

'Peut-être!' which closes the poem, and this instability underlies many deceptively clear Mallarméan statements on the nature of the poetic idea.

In 1867, for example, Mallarmé insists: 'Il n'y a que la Beauté; – et elle n'a qu'une expression parfaite, la Poésie'.[1] Although this follows his crisis of faith by a year, he still insists that there is only one absolute Beauty, and Poetry, its only possible expression, also enjoys absolute status. Unlike Baudelaire, who declares in 1859: 'l'esprit du vrai poète doit être ouvert à toutes les beautés', or Rimbaud, who admits in *Une saison en enfer* to the need for a non-absolute notion of beauty, Mallarmé maintains that there can be only one, and that it is absolute.[2] Yet this apparently simple declaration brushes over a myriad of problems, such as the characteristics of the Poetry which expresses absolute Beauty. If Poetry can exist in verse or prose, the insistence on the singularity of 'une expression parfaite' leaves us wondering what recognizably poetic features are shared by these formally diverse texts, later pushed beyond recognizable limits with 'Un Coup de dés'. Sure enough, we are told that Poetry is to be recognized by its rhythm, but following the collapse of the universal analogy, this is a rhythm upon whose origin, meaning and definition the poet constantly refuses to conclude.

The ambiguous status of rhythm

In 1884 Poetry retains its capital 'P'. Notions of authenticity and spirituality are still *en jeu*, and Mallarmé still seems to insist that it articulates one absolute meaning:

La Poésie est l'expression, par le langage humain ramené à son rythme essentiel, du sens mystérieux des aspects de l'existence: elle doue ainsi d'authenticité notre séjour et constitue la seule tâche spirituelle.[3]

Yet although the singular 'du sens mystérieux' suggests one fixed meaning, the infuriatingly vague 'des aspects de l'existence' implies a plurality of ways of seeing, an 'aspect' being an object's 'forme

---

[1] Letter of 14 May to Cazalis (*Corr. fol.*, p.344).
[2] Baudelaire: *Salon de 1859*, V, 'Religion, histoire, fantaisie' (O.C.II: 630) and Rimbaud: folio, p.198.
[3] Letter of 27 June 1884 to Léo d'Orfer, *Correspondance*, ed. by Henri Mondor and Lloyd James Austin, Paris: Gallimard, 11 vols, 1959-1985; 2: 266 (hereafter *Corr.*).

extérieure, manière de paraître aux regards'.[1] Indeed, in this passage, typical of Mallarmé's later writings for its wide scope for contradictory readings, the form of poetry is just as problematic as its object. As always, Poetry is linked to rhythm, and this passage is usually read as articulating Mallarmé's firm belief in one essential rhythm underlying language, which pre-exists Poetry's appropriation of it. However, the possessive 'son' could just as easily refer not to 'le langage humain', but to 'la Poésie'. This would imply that the essential rhythm is not that of language, but of Poetry itself, threatening the usual critical assumption that this rhythm corresponds to any sort of reality beyond that of a fictional Poetry alone. Besides, the suggestion that this essential rhythm really does exist under the surface of language sits uneasily with Mallarmé's loss, in 1866, of faith in external absolutes. It is possible, then, that this mysterious essential rhythm – which goes conveniently undefined – belongs only to the Poetry which Mallarmé knows to be a pure fiction.

Despite his lucid account of Mallarmé's poetic fictions, Marchal often seems to imply that the poet believes in a rhythmic constant in man which corresponds to regular rhythms in nature:

> Le rythme, en somme, est à l'origine de l'homme et de la vie [...]. Ce rythme, cette pulsation originelle, c'est justement ce qui, pour le poète, rattache l'homme au cycle de la nature [...] il reste ainsi en l'homme un instinct rythmique, qui conserve le secret de l'âme humaine.[2]

Yet Mallarmé remains carefully unclear on the fundamental question of the origins of this apparent regularity, and in 'L'Ecclésiastique' (1886) parodies 'un naturalisme absolu ou naïf', 'un contact avec la Nature immédiat, net, violent, positif, dénué de toute curiosité intellectuelle'.[3] It is by no means certain that the human rhythmic constant, this preference for order and regularity, imitates an essentially cyclical nature. In 1891, Mallarmé tells Huret: 'les choses existent, nous n'avons pas à les créer; nous n'avons simplement qu'à en saisir les rapports', yet these 'rapports' are not necessarily pre-

---

[1] Larousse, *Grand Dictionnaire Universel du XIXe Siècle*, 1: 756.
[2] *La Religion de Mallarmé*, p.188.
[3] *Div.*, pp.96-97. This recalls Rimbaud's 'Soir historique', where the 'touriste naïf' believes that 'la main d'un maître anime le clavecin des prés' (folio, p. 239). See also page 207 of the present study.

existent poetic *correspondances* within nature itself. They might be the 'rapports' between nature and the human mind which itself projects a model of order onto objects, creating their meaning. Indeed, the seizure of these 'rapports' alone does not constitute poetry, but rather: 'ce sont les fils de ces rapports qui forment les vers', as if the poeticity of the 'rapports' lay in their arrangement by the poetic mind. Thus the 'rapports' reflected in verse might represent not a pre-existent pattern in nature, but the projection of an internal poetic model onto otherwise irregular external phenomena.

In 1894 the same formula re-appears in a more problematic form which seems to confirm these suspicions. The omission of 'en' suggests that the 'rapports' in natural phenomena do not simply pre-exist the gaze:

La Nature a lieu, on n'y ajoutera pas [...]. Tout l'acte disponible, à jamais et seulement, reste de saisir les rapports, entre temps, rares ou multipliés; d'après quelque état intérieur et que l'on veuille à son gré étendre, simplifier le monde.[1]

Here the precise link between nature and the 'rapports' is left frustratingly unspecified. The lack of hyphen in 'entre temps' hints that these 'rapports' are to be observed in the intervals of a rhythm, yet 'd'après quelque état intérieur' suggests that this rhythm lies not in nature, but rather in the poetic imagination. This imagination attempts to smooth out irregularities in external structures, 'simplifier le monde', in order to satisfy its own internal preferences, 'à son gré'. Indeed, correspondences are presented not as an external *évidence*, but rather, a product of poetic language: 'Le tour de telle phrase ou le lac d'un distique, copiés sur notre conformation, aident l'éclosion, en nous, d'aperçus et de correspondences'.[2] They are hatched within man, according to some internal structural model, as the 'nous' once again unites the poet and his fellows and lends an illusion of universality to the poetic imposition of rhythm on phenomena.

In a note to the same text, with another ambiguous 'en', Mallarmé states: 'Au vers impersonnel ou pur s'adaptera l'instinct qui dégage, du monde, un chant, pour en illuminer le rythme fondamental et rejette, vain, le résidu'.[3] The instinct which teases this rhythm out

---

[1] 'La Musique et les Lettres' (*Div.*, pp.356-57).

[2] ibid., (*Div.*, p.355).

[3] ibid., (*Div.*, p.368).

from the world does not simply correspond directly to metrical verse; it must adapt itself, suggesting that the correspondence between verse and the 'chant' cannot be taken for granted. Furthermore, we wonder: does the 'rythme fondamental' belong to the 'monde' or the 'chant'? Again the referent of 'en' is frustratingly, yet necessarily, ambiguous, as Mallarmé refuses to answer, hinting at the fundamental impossibility of knowing. Thus the notion of verse as a reflection of regularity in the world is far from unproblematic. Maybe this essential rhythm exists in the world, below the surface, awaiting discovery by the poetic eye; maybe it is simply a product of an artificial 'chant', which creates mystificatory 'confusions / Fausses' between 'La beauté d'alentour' and the faun's 'chant crédule' (1876, ll.46-47), as the poetic gaze projects meaningful order onto the world. Since we can never know for sure, it is up to Poetry both to acknowledge and to exploit this very irresolvability.

In 1896 Mallarmé alludes to the possibly fictional status of rhythm in the expression 'quelques rêves, comme la mesure à quoi tout se réduit'.[1] The regular poetic 'mesure', like the Ideal itself, may well be a 'rêve', an internal Truth created by the poet who craftily presents it as an external force pre-existing his insight, 'suivant l'instinct de rythmes qui l'élit'.[2] This ambiguity can be seen in 'Igitur', which Marchal sees as 'le passage [...] du rêve d'absolu à la reconnaissance définitive de la fiction'.[3] Here the rhythms of the body, usually seen as regular, like the beating heart or the blood 'aux rythmiques sanglots' in Baudelaire's 'La Fontaine de sang' (l.2), seem by turns regular and irregular. On the one hand, 'l'ombre n'entendit dans ce lieu d'autre bruit que le battement régulier qu'elle reconnut être celui de son propre cœur', 'c'était elle-même qui scandait sa mesure'; on the other, 'son heurt redevient chancelant comme avant d'avoir la perception de soi: c'était le scandement de ma mesure'; 'maintenant qu'il avait la notion de lui-même, le bruit cessa, et redevint ce qu'il était, chancelant'.[4] References to irregular scansion and measure suggest that the relationship between verse and natural rhythms, even within the human body, is not simply an unproblematic reciprocal regularity.

---

[1] 'Le Mystère dans les Lettres' (*Div.*, p.275).
[2] ibid., (*Div.*, p.274).
[3] *La Religion de Mallarmé*, p.92.
[4] *Div.*, pp.58-59, 60, 50-51, 60.

When Mallarmé tells Vittori Pica in 1886: 'je crois tout cela écrit dans la nature',[1] he is careful to present any 'proof' of rhythmical regularity in nature not as an incontrovertible Truth, but as a belief, since *je crois que* is certainly not the same as *c'est un fait que*. He also neglects, conveniently, to speculate on the identity of the author. *Écrit par qui?* we might reasonably ask, yet the poet's silence on the matter reminds us that this uncertainty as to the origin of rhythm is the very condition for the existence of Mallarméan poetry. Similarly, when he tells Huret: 'le monde est fait pour aboutir à un beau livre', he avoids any pronouncement as to who made the world in the first place. Surely, if God made the world, and we see evidence of regular rhythm in nature, we are simply back to the universal analogy. However, in light of the ambiguities observed so far as to the origins of poetic and natural rhythm, the world might equally be seen as written by the poetic imagination. As in Baudelaire's 'La Soupe et les nuages', where God creates the clouds only to offer them up for interpretation by the poet, the source of meaning no longer necessarily lies exclusively with the creator of the object.[2]

This mystification of the nature of poetic rhythm pre-occupies the poet at a time when the rhythmical extends to include the irregular, unpredictable forms of *vers libre*. Since metrical verse is seen to peddle an obsolete universal analogy through redundant regular rhythms, *vers libre* is welcomed by Mallarmé's fellows for replacing what they see as a fallacious, oppressive universality and for recognizing the value of individual poetic expression. Imagining their frustration with metre, Mallarmé tells Huret:

N'est-ce pas quelque chose de très anormal qu'en ouvrant n'importe quel livre de poésie on soit sûr de trouver d'un bout à l'autre des rythmes uniformes et convenus là où l'on prétend, au contraire, nous intéresser à l'essentielle variété des sentiments humains![3]

However, since 'il n'y a que la Beauté, – et elle n'a qu'une expression parfaite', Poetry must remain an absolute. Therefore, where his contemporaries imagine a wide variety of human sentiments, Mallarmé argues that poetic sentiment springs from a common source,

---

[1] Letter of 27 November 1886 (*Corr.* 3: 73).
[2] Baudelaire O.C.I: 350. See also pages 116-17 of the present study.
[3] 'Enquête sur l'évolution littéraire' (*Div.*, p.389).

such as 'l'instinct de ciel en chacun'.[1] Thus, throughout the 1880s and 1890s, he demands impersonality in poetry, an impersonality which maintains the universality of the poetic Ideal, flying in the face of the trend for individualism. Yet in keeping with the constant ambiguity in Mallarméan poetics over the nature of rhythm – universal Truth or personal poetic fiction? – the poet who argues for impersonality is also, mischievously, the poet *par excellence* of the proper name, simultaneously piercing the illusion of universality with the suggestion of its illusory status.

Impersonality and individuality

Marchal confirms the importance of impersonality to the notion of universality in reference to 'la divinité qui n'est que le type impersonnel (et par là universel)'.[2] In his final published article, Mallarmé insists that man's mystery is common to all: 'Il doit y avoir quelque chose d'occulte au fond de tous, je crois décidément à quelque chose d'abscons, signifiant fermé et caché, qui habite le commun'.[3] However, the sarcastic tone of this reply to Proust, and the use of 'il doit y avoir' and 'je crois' rather than a simple *il y a*, suggests that what Marchal calls 'ce principe rythmique', 'ce rythme constitutif de l'homme' might simply be another Mallarméan fiction.[4] In order to create the illusion of this rhythmic essence, the soul, seen in 1866 as a pure invention, is presented as the site of this rhythm. Mysteriously intangible, it is a matter for faith and conjecture which conveniently resists proof and analysis; in 1887 Mallarmé affirms 'une âme ou bien notre idée (à savoir la divinité présente à l'esprit de l'homme)', whose necessarily rhythmical qualities are later highlighted in a reference to 'l'âme, ou notre rythme'.[5]

The poet, therefore, must sacrifice his individuality and express instead the universal, in order for rhythm to be seen as an absolute Truth and not simply 'un indéracinable sans doute préjugé d'écrivain'.[6] Thus, in May 1867, as he explores his post-crisis poetics,

---

[1] 'La Musique et les Lettres' (*Div.*, pp.365-66).
[2] *La Religion de Mallarmé*, p.301.
[3] 'Le Mystère dans les Lettres' (*Div.*, p.274).
[4] *La Religion de Mallarmé*, p.188.
[5] 'Crayonné au théâtre' (Div., pp.177-78); letter of 15 November 1896 to Émile Dodillon (*Corr.* 8: 288).
[6] 'Crise de vers' (*Div.*, p.250).

Mallarmé abandons *le moi* and his name, declaring: 'je suis maintenant impersonnel, et non plus Stéphane que tu as connu, – mais une aptitude qu'a l'Univers Spirituel à se voir et à se développer, à travers ce qui fut moi'.[1] In his later correspondence Mallarmé thanks other poets for the countless volumes sent to him, such as Adolphe Retté, who is congratulated on 'des coups d'archet impersonnels et purs'.[2] Thanking Émile Verhaeren for 'Les Soirs', he writes:

L'ouvrier disparaît (ce qui est absolument la trouvaille contemporaine) et le vers agit: un sentiment avec ses sursauts ou son délice s'y rythme tout seul et devient le vers, sans que quelqu'un l'impose brutalement et de son fait![3]

The *vers* seems to erase the figure of its author who might jeopardize the impersonality of its rhythm. Indeed, for Meschonnic, rhythm is a product of the subject: 'Si le sens est une activité du sujet, si le rythme est une organisation du sens dans le discours, le rythme est nécessairement une organisation ou configuration du sujet dans son discours'.[4] As we have seen, in the post-illusory poetry of both Baudelaire and Rimbaud, the hunt for poetically meaningful rhythm inevitably becomes a search for an elusive author who refuses to provide precisely this guarantee. Similarly, for Mallarmé, as is well known, the subject must erase himself from his work, since 'l'œuvre pure implique la disparition élocutoire du poète'.[5] The illusion of a universally coherent 'tout' is a product of this necessary impersonality: 'admis le volume ne comporter aucun signataire, quel est-il: l'hymne, harmonie et joie, comme pur ensemble groupé dans quelque circonstance fulgurante, des relations entre tout'.[6]

This illusion of impersonality is vital to the defence of a regular poetic rhythm, and the two provide mutually supportive fictions. On Verlaine, Mallarmé mentions a 'type impersonnel dont se réclame quiconque fit de beaux vers', seen in emphatic capital letters as 'LE POÈTE', as if, just as there can be only one *Livre*, *Beauté* or *Poésie*,

---

[1] Letter of 14 May 1867 (*Corr. fol.*, p.343).
[2] Letter of May 1893 (*Corr.* 6: 99).
[3] Letter of 22 January 1888 (*Corr.* 3: 167).
[4] *Critique du rythme*, p.71. Also quoted in Marchal, *La Religion de Mallarmé*, p.491.
[5] 'Crise de vers' (*Div.*, p.248).
[6] 'Le livre, instrument spirituel' (*Div.*, p.267).

there could also be only one author.[1] Praising Banville, Mallarmé admires 'l'épuration, par les ans, de son individualité en le vers' which allows the appearance of 'une métrique absolue'. This asserts 'le principe qui n'est que – le Vers!' and the text exists 'hors de tout souffle perçu grossier'.[2] This 'souffle' is frequently applied to the personal poetry which, for Mallarmé, threatens the fiction of an absolute poetic idea. 'Crise de vers' sums up the *vers-libriste* endeavour: 'tout individu apporte une prosodie, neuve, participant de son souffle'.[3] We know from the 'Faune' that the flute's melody, which produces the poetic 'chant crédule' (1.47) and the illusion of an external Ideal, is 'Le visible et serein souffle artificiel / De l'inspiration' (1876, ll.21-22). The visible 'souffle' required to play the flute allows its artifice, and thus its ultimate vanity, to be perceived. The poet, therefore, must prevent the perception of his 'souffle', 'remplaçant la respiration perceptible en l'ancien souffle lyrique ou la direction personnelle enthousiaste de la phrase'.[4] Indeed, 'Feuillet d'album' echoes the 'Faune', as the girl asks the poet if she might 'Ouïr se révéler un peu / Le bois de mes diverses flûtes' (1.4). The poet, however, refuses to reveal 'ce vain souffle que j'exclus' (1.9). It is for allowing the perception of its 'souffle' that Mallarmé rejects *vers libre* as a glorification of the poet's individuality to the detriment of a Poetry which must, in contrast, be seen to obey a universal, eternal constant.

The 'crise de vers' results, Mallarmé tells Huret, from contemporary artists' 'inexpliqué besoin d'individualité'.[5] By proudly taking the writing subject, *le moi*, as sole guarantee of the poeticity of its rhythm, 'la notation émotionnelle proportionnée' denies the universal rhythmic Truth of the impersonal *Soi* which Poetry demands.[6] Dismissing the genre, he employs the metaphor of simplistic, melodic, 'musical' poetry which he himself abandoned in 1865, yet which remains, in the 1880s, a fertile source of mystificatory terminology for the champions of *vers libre*. In 1887 Rodolphe Darzens is 'congratulated' on 'une musique propre qui n'est autre que

---

[1] 'Enquête sur Verlaine' (*Div.*, p.396).
[2] 'Solennité' (*Div.*, pp.233-34).
[3] *Div.*, p.246.
[4] 'Crise de vers' (*Div.*, p.249).
[5] *Div.*, p.389.
[6] Letter of March 1893 to Charles Bonnier (*Corr.* 6: 65).

la phrase conduite par le rythme sentimental intérieur [...] le solo d'un instrument exquis et qui est vous-même'.[1] Interestingly, the only alteration which Mallarmé makes to his 'Faune' before publication in 1887 affects precisely this 'solo' (l.45):

> Rêve avec un duo / que nous amusions   (1875)
> Rêve, en un long solo, / que nous amusions   (1876)
> Rêve, dans un solo / <u>long</u>, que nous amusions (1887)

The semantic consequences of the correction, if any, are slight. On a formal level, however, the syntactic and metrical accents no longer coincide at the sixth syllable, as the very word 'long' makes the sense unit one syllable too long for the metrical mould. Moreover, the poem's strongest rhyme 'am**usi-ons** / conf**usi-ons**' falls from trisyllabic to *pauvre*; the diaeresis in 'amusions' contracts, which leaves only the nasal to rhyme, strictly speaking: [yzjɔ̃ / yzi-ɔ̃]. If the preciously rich rhyme can be read as a symbol of the universal 'rapports' which impersonal poetry seeks to foreground, its erasure by a transgressive individual 'solo' dramatizes the antagonism between *vers libre* and metrical verse. Indeed, it is the personal quality of the faun's art that reveals his dream of an Ideal to be a pure fiction. This naïve, 'musical' poetry symbolizes in the 1880s a *vers libre* detrimental to the illusion of universality upon which Poetry's survival as an absolute depends. Mallarmé tells Adrien Mithouard, with implicit criticism, of his 'L'Iris exaspéré': 'quant aux vers, ce sont ceux d'un rêveur très particulier et d'un musicien, dont l'instrument est personnel et rare'.[2] Just as the faun's 'chant' aims 'aussi haut que l'amour se module' (l.48), so too *vers libre* is a 'modulation individuelle' which leaves Poetry open to the objection that it is a mere personal fantasy rather than an essential universal Truth.[3]

This individual music thus contradicts absolute Music, the structure which, Mallarmé insists, underlies all things and provides metrical verse with its rhythmical guarantee. In 'Crise de vers' he allows *vers libre* only a very specific place in the current versificatory climate: 'Toute âme est une mélodie, qu'il s'agit de renouer; et pour

---

[1] Letter of 11 October 1887, *Corr.* 5: 283.
[2] Letter of 4 June 1895 (*Corr.* 7: 220).
[3] 'La Musique et les Lettres' (*Div.*, p.352).

cela, sont la flûte ou la viole de chacun'.[1] The flute features as he describes *vers libre* to Huret: 'chaque poète allant, dans son coin, jouer sur une flûte, bien à lui, les airs qu'il lui plaît'.[2] In the mid-1860s poems, as Mallarmé's musical metaphor evolves from simple melodies of phonetic patterns towards the silent structural notion, the 'flûte' and 'viole' symbolize an outdated poetics. In 'Don du poème' as the poet takes his frail new poem to his wife, 'la berceuse' (1.9), for resuscitation, her voice recalls the 'viole et clavecin' (1.11) of yore. In 'Sainte' the 'viole' goes unplayed, situating its sounds far in the past, 'jadis avec flûte ou mandore' (1.4) as poetry becomes 'Musicienne du silence' (1.16). Thus the poetry of the faun-flautist and the *vers-libristes* corresponds to the 'sonorités élémentaires' of instrumental music which, Mallarmé argues, is only one personal manifestation of a universal principle, 'l'ensemble des rapports existant dans tout, la Musique'.[3]

This musical principle recurs in 1893 with yet another conveniently ambiguous reference to rhythm: 'Musique dans le sens grec, au fond signifiant Idée ou rythme entre des rapports'. Again, it is impossible to say whether this rhythm pre-exists our gaze, inherent in the world, or whether it is a product of our poetic ordering faculties. The result of this rhythm is 'l'au-delà magiquement produit par certaines dispositions de la parole'; 'produit', not *atteint, entrevu* or *reflété*, but 'produit', and so this absolute Music actually creates the illusion of a fictitious transcendent *ailleurs*.[4] In the same year Mallarmé refers directly to this very veiling function: 'Y a-t-il mieux, à une gaze ressemblant que la Musique!'.[5] Thus by erasing the poet's individuality, suggesting that the poet simply enjoys heightened sensitivity to a universal absolute, Mallarmé places a veil over what he has known, since 1866, to be 'le Rien qui est la vérité'.[6]

However, just as the origins of rhythm remain necessarily ambiguous, in the hesitation between the personal *je crois* and the impersonal *il y a*, so too the demand for impersonality is counter-balanced throughout Mallarmé's work by the personal. In 1885, he

---

[1] *Div.*, p.244.
[2] *Div.*, p.388.
[3] 'Crise de vers' (*Div.*, p.250).
[4] Letter of 10 January 1893 to Edmund Gosse (*Corr.* 6: 26).
[5] 'Les fonds dans le ballet' (*Div.*, p.199).
[6] Letter of 28 April 1866 to Cazalis (*Corr. fol.*, p.298).

informs Verlaine of this paradoxical project: 'mon travail personnel
qui je crois, sera anonyme, le Texte y parlant de lui-même et sans voix
d'auteur'.[1] Indeed, alongside his demands for impersonality, Mallarmé
is also the poet of the proper name, as Michael Temple demonstrates
in *The Name of the Poet*, exploring the numerous ways in which the
poet's personality and signature are written into the text.[2] Whereas the
poems of the 1880s onwards are anonymous, with either no title, or a
simple generic description such as 'Hommage', 'Eventail', 'Prose',
'Chanson', 'Feuillet d'album', 'Billet' or 'Petit air', the 1887 edition
of verse is published under the highly personal title *Les Poésies de
Stéphane Mallarmé*. And whereas Mallarmé tells Deman in 1891,
preparing the edition entitled simply *Poésies*: 'Le vers n'est très beau
que dans un caractère impersonnel, c'est-à-dire typographique', the
only edition published in his lifetime (1887) is a facsimile of his own
handwritten manuscript, the most personal presentation possible.[3]

Like Rimbaud's 'génie', the Mallarméen poet is at once *un* and
tout thanks to 'l'apparence qu'on est pour soi tout'.[4] In 'De Même',
the church choir 'évoque, à l'âme, l'existence d'une personnalité
multiple et une, mystérieuse et rien que pure', stirring his faith in this
illusion.[5] This ambiguity between universality and individuality is
inextricably linked to the question of poetic form thanks to
Mallarmé's frequent recourse to the terms when discussing *vers libre*.
Regularity can be seen to reflect that fictional rhythm 'inherent' in
nature, which is disturbed, like the alexandrine disrupted by the faun's
'solo long', by irregularities articulating the personal, *le moi*
constantly at odds with *le Soi*.

Regularity and irregularity

Underlining the link between authorial impersonality and formal
regularity, Mallarmé tells Huret of his admiration for the Parnassians,
'amoureux du vers très strict, beau par lui-même', 'absolus serviteurs
du vers, y sacrifiant jusqu'à leur personnalité'. The alexandrine is thus
presented as an impersonal force: 'l'alexandrin, que personne n'a

[1] Letter of 16 November 1885; 'Autobiographie' (*Div.*, p.374).
[2] Exeter University Press, 1995.
[3] Letter of 7 April 1891 (*Corr.* 4: 219).
[4] 'L'Ecclésiastique' (*Div.*, p.97).
[5] *Div.*, p.292.

inventé et qui a jailli tout seul de l'instrument de la langue'.[1]
However, in yet another contradiction, Mallarmé suggests elsewhere
that: 'd'intentions pas moindres, a jailli la métrique aux temps
incubatoires'.[2] Here metre is said to have sprung not miraculously
'tout seul' from language, as if it were the underlying 'rythme
essentiel', but from the poetic intention which strives to 'à son gré
étendre, simplifier le monde',[3] projecting artistic regularity onto
linguistic disorder. The same ambiguity underlies two highly similar
pronouncements on poetic form, where the regular units constantly
presented as necessary to poetry seem to impose themselves on the
poet from outside before he groups them together:

> Similitude entre les vers, une régularité durera parce que l'acte poétique consiste à
> voir soudain qu'une idée se fractionne en un nombre de motifs égaux par valeur et à
> les grouper; ils riment: pour sceau extérieur, leur commune mesure qu'apparente le
> coup final.[4]

However, given Mallarmé's frequent suggestion of the instability of
what we see when we observe the world, the status of the verb 'voir',
which constitutes the first part of the process, is not wholly
straightforward. Rimbaldian visions, in particular, are inventions
which are presented as if they were discoveries, and the status of
rhyme here maintains this ambiguity. Just as rhyme was proof of
underlying meaning for Hugo and a product of chance for Baudelaire,
its significance here depends on whether we read the verb 'voir' as
discovery or creation. This possibility – that what the poet sees, 'out
there', is actually a poetic creation – remains ambiguous in the second
passage:

> Le fait poétique lui-même consiste à grouper rapidement, en un certain nombre de
> traits égaux, pour les ajuster, telles pensées lointaines autrement et éparses; mais qui,
> cela éclate, riment ensemble, pour ainsi parler. Il faut donc, avant tout, disposer la
> commune mesure, qu'il s'agit d'appliquer; ou le Vers.[5]

---

[1] All quotations: *Div.*, pp.390-91.
[2] 'Crise de vers' (*Div.*, p.245).
[3] 'La Musique et les Lettres' (*Div.*, p.357). See also page 252 of the present study.
[4] 'Crise de vers' (*Div.*, p.246).
[5] Letter of March 1893 to Charles Bonnier, *Corr.* 6: 65.

Here the verb 'voir' disappears, as if the poetic endeavour were simply the gathering of otherwise disparate thoughts, 'lointaines autrement et éparses', contrary to their natural state. Yet the rhyme suggests that what had appeared unnatural is, in fact, proof of inherent meaning waiting to burst forth upon discovery by the happy artist: 'cela éclate'. The 'commune mesure' features in both passages, caught in this ambiguity between its correspondence to the 'real' nature of an external idea, and its imposition on an irregular reality. In the face of this instability as to the 'true' meaning of metre, metrical regularity creates the illusion of a pre-existent universal rhythmic Truth, threatened by the personal *vers libre*, and thus requiring constant re-motivation.

Regularity, then, is exploited to reflect Poetry's possibly fictional universality, and in 1891 Mallarmé tells Huret: 'Toutes les fois qu'il y a effort au style, il y a versification'.[1] As Larousse observes, style refers to the 'manière particulière à un artiste' which lends the work 'un cachet particulier, individuel',[2] which might appear to sit more easily alongside Mallarmé's thoughts on *vers libre*. Yet in a pronouncement of 1893, versification suggests a certain symmetry, or order: 'au moins faut-il de la symétrie, ou pluralité de rapports, entre différents gestes libres, pour constituer, je crois, une versification'.[3] Once again the fiendish 'je crois' puts us on our guard, and the 'ou' creates another ambiguity: are 'symétrie' and 'pluralité de rapports' synonymous, or are they two different possible definitions of versification? Whichever interpretation we choose, it seems that whenever a poet thinks he is expressing his individuality, he actually leans towards certain patterns of order which satisfy a universal aesthetic notion. Indeed, Dujardin refers to 'le rythme et les assonances d'un vers libre', as the vehicle of individual expression imports those ordering techniques for which the rejection of metrical verse is supposed to express distaste.[4] In this way order is presented as a universal artistic value, but Mallarmé simultaneously hints that the artifice of symmetry belongs only to the 'Rêve', that its value is purely fictional. Igitur considers 'cette inquiétante et belle symétrie de

---

[1] *Div.*, p.389.
[2] *Grand Dictionnaire Universel du XIXe Siècle* 14: 1158.
[3] Letter of 2 April 1893 to Charles Bonnier (*Corr.* 6: 73-74).
[4] *Mallarmé par un des siens*, p.192. See also page 13 of the present study.

la construction de mon rêve', and in 1893 Mallarmé mentions a 'symétrie, comme elle règne en toute édifice, le plus vaporeux, de vision et de songes'.[1] Nonetheless he repeats in 1894: 'le vers est tout, dès qu'on écrit. Style, versification s'il y a cadence'.[2] Since 'cadence' can signify both rhythmical regularity and rhyming harmony, the versification presented as a universal Truth is doubly symmetrical, horizontally at the caesura and vertically at the rhyme.

However, regular metrical verse comes under criticism for precisely this tiresome regularity, the eternal return of the 'commune mesure' which provokes the revolution of the *vers-libristes*. Mallarmé tells Camille Mauclair that 'le nombre fixe, lequel frappé uniformément et réel devient insupportable autrement que dans les grandes occasions'.[3] He tells Huret: 'on est surtout las du vers officiel; ses partisans même partagent cette lassitude', a diagnosis which Albert Mockel, among others, confirms: 'écœuré que j'étais du ronron lourd et monotone de l'alexandrin [...] qui rampe sur ses douze pattes et s'articule en hémistiche'.[4] Indeed, Mallarmé himself tells Cazalis of the 'bercement continu des vers que j'omets un peu par lassitude'.[5] However, in 'Crise de vers' he still refers to the alexandrine as 'le joyau définitif' or 'fleur', the same imagery applied to the floral Hérodiade, or to the 'Ouverture', 'joyau magnifique', in 1865.[6] The 'cadence nationale', therefore, requires protection from the *ennui* it provokes, the 'lassitude par abus', if the mutually supportive fictions of regular rhythm and external Ideal are to survive the present crisis of faith.[7]

Despite the general lassitude, Mallarmé argues, with typical emphasis on his 'indéracinable sans doute préjugé d'écrivain', for the value of this alexandrine which represents a universal poetic Ideal: 'je ne vois, et ce reste mon intense opinion, effacement de rien qui ait été beau dans le passé, je demeure convaincu que dans les occasions

---

[1] *Div.*, pp. 49 and 'Planches et feuillets' (*Div.*, p.227).
[2] 'La Musique et les Lettres' (*Div.*, p.351).
[3] Letter of 9 October 1897 (*Corr.* 9: 289).
[4] *Div.*, p.389, and Mockel's letter quoted by Dujardin in *Mallarmé par un des siens*, pp.170-71.
[5] Letter of May 1893 (*Corr.* 6: 87).
[6] *Div.*, p.242 and letter of 5 December 1865 to Cazalis, *Corr. fol.*, p.259.
[7] 'Crise de vers' (*Div.*, p.243).

amples on obéira toujours à la tradition solennelle'.[1] In 1891 he
assigns 'un canon [...] officiel' only to 'les grandes cérémonies', and
in 1894 re-iterates that 'l'alexandrin dans toute sa tenue' should be
reserved for 'les grandes occasions'.[2] Since 'le vers officiel ne doit
servir que dans des moments de crise de l'âme', Mallarmé proposes a
mixture of rhythmically irregular and regular alexandrines. The former
allow the individual soul room for 'personal' expression, whereas the
latter provide comfort, a reassuring sense of universal regularity when
the individual suffers a metaphysical crisis, like Baudelaire retreating
from the *gouffre* as his artistic liberty overwhelms him: 'Ah! ne jamais
sortir des Nombres et des Etres!' ('Le Gouffre', l.14). Each rhythmic
extreme is equally untenable, since eternal regularity provokes only
ennui, and absolute liberty inspires either terror or madness, such as
that caused by Rimbaud's plunge into the *informe* of 1872.

As Baudelaire realizes, both symmetry and surprise are henceforth
necessary to metrical verse in order to prevent meaningless monotony.
Mallarmé's own formula for the same idea comes in 1893:

Un ensemble versifié convie à une idéale représentation: des motifs d'exaltation ou de
songe s'y nouent entre eux et se détachent, par une ordonnance et leur individualité.
Telle portion incline dans un rythme ou mouvement de pensée, a quoi s'oppose tel
contradictoire dessin: l'un et l'autre [...] la figure, que demeure l'idée.[3]

The verbs *se nouer* and *se détacher* describe the rhythmical motifs
tending either towards or away from the verse mould, with
individuality ascribed to irregularities within an impersonal
'ordonnance'. In 1891 Mallarmé describes his most irregular poem,
the 'Après-midi d'un faune' which for David Hillery is 'as
rhythmically extraordinary as anything Verlaine ever wrote',[4] as
precisely this juxtaposition of the personal, expressed in familiar
musical terms, and the impersonal, used only sparingly:

J'y essayais, en effet, de mettre, à côté de l'alexandrin dans toute sa tenue, une sorte
de jeu courant pianoté autour, comme qui dirait d'un accompagnement musical fait

---

[1] ibid., (*Div.*, p.244).
[2] 'Enquête sur l'évolution littéraire' and 'La Musique et les Lettres' (*Div.*, pp.352 and 393).
[3] 'Planches et feuillets' (*Div.*, p.227).
[4] *Music and Poetry in France: from Baudelaire to Mallarmé*, Berne: Peter Lang, 1980, p.58.

par le poète lui-même et ne permettant au vers officiel de sortir que dans les grandes occasions.[1]

Yet the simple juxtaposition of regular and irregular lines is intended only as one stage on the road to renovation, and Mallarmé tells Huret of a marvellous future hybrid line, resolving both 'la constriction parnassienne' and *vers libre*, since 'les deux efforts peuvent se compléter'.[2] In a letter rich in echoes of Hérodiade, the artistic Ideal, Mallarmé enthusiastically suggests that Rodenbach might have achieved this very feat with 'Les Vies encloses':

Un miracle, ce livre: une symphonie, frisson à frisson pas même, de toute la pureté en jeu, quand une vision, vierge ou seulement lucide par quelques rapports à tout survivant, se replie en soi – jamais poésie miroita, autant, d'absolu; [...] Quant au vers, cher ami, ce délice de toute minute, se succède-t-il assez fluide, avec un trait inné de chant, divinement, sans qu'on subisse aucune répétition de la mesure: ceci est inouï et glorifie à point l'alexandrin, rien d'autre n'étant plus nécessaire.[3]

As Cornulier has demonstrated, the perception of equality between isometrical lines depends less on the rhymes which unite them than on metre.[4] Yet if this metrical regularity inspires only lassitude, a succession of dodecasyllables is needed whose metre is obscured by unpredictable structures which differ from line to line. Thus, Mallarmé claims, regularity will be perceived, not directly thanks to an eternally repetitive 6+6, but thanks to a more intangible isosyllabism within which the metre goes out of focus: 'dans la multiple répétition de son jeu seulement, je saisis l'ensemble métrique nécessaire'.[5] In this way, as Michel Collot observes: 'le mètre est devenu pour la poésie moderne un horizon: un point de repère, certes, mais mobile et jamais atteint'.[6] Regularity must be almost imperceptible, fluttering on the edge of the reader's consciousness, and in 'Crise de vers', Mallarmé praises those who defend the alexandrine by undoing the metre whilst maintaining rigorous isosyllabism:

---

[1] 'Enquête sur l'évolution littéraire' (*Div.*, p.393).
[2] *Div.*, p.391.
[3] Letter of March 1896 (*Corr.* 8: 80).
[4] See 'La rime n'est pas une marque de fin de vers', *Poétique* 46 (1981): 247-56.
[5] 'Planches et feuillets' (*Div.*, p.226).
[6] 'Rythme et mètre: entre identité et différence', *Protée* 18:1 (1990), 75-80, p.78.

Les fidèles à l'alexandrin, notre hexamètre, desserrent intérieurement ce mécanisme rigide et puéril de sa mesure; l'oreille, affranchie d'un compteur factice, connaît une jouissance à discerner, seule, toutes les combinaisons possibles, entre eux, de douze timbres.[1]

However, the exact number of these 'combinaisons possibles' also requires careful mystification, since if the number of rhythmical and accentual possibilities for the dodecasyllable is finite, the line might not be able to cater for the personal expression of a possibly infinite number of individuals, and the illusion of a glorious future alexandrine reconciling *tout* in *un* collapses.

Mallarmé, therefore, tells Huret: 'le volume de poésie future sera celui à travers lequel courra le grand vers initial avec une infinité de motifs empruntés à l'ouïe individuelle', a formal mixture of both the personal and the impersonal.[2] He insists that this *vers futur* will be able to express the infinity of individual *nombres*, recalling the religious conundrum of the miraculous resolution of infinite multiplicity in unity.[3] In the interview with Huret, Mallarmé insists: 'avec la merveilleuse science du vers, l'art suprême des coupes, que possèdent des maîtres comme Banville, l'alexandrin peut arriver à une variété infinie, suivre tous les mouvements de passion possible'.[4] However, in his correspondence, Mallarmé allows the veil to slip, telling Georges Polti of 'le vers (dont les combinaisons de rythme ne sont pas à l'infini)' and informing Henri de Régnier:

Je ne crois pas les combinaisons neuves du vers, depuis sa retrempe, infinies; et vous avez la chance et l'honneur d'en avoir façonné un nombre d'inoubliables, de vraiment délicieuses, telles que l'alexandrin ne nous les avait pas fait connaître encore.[5]

For Mallarmé, while poets await the arrival of the miraculous *vers futur*, reminiscent of the totalizing harmony of *Illuminations*, the rhythmical possibilities of the alexandrine must be pushed beyond their traditional boundaries while retaining the dodecasyllabic horizon of regularity. It is in this light that tension between regularity and

---

[1] *Div.*, p.242.
[2] All quotations: *Div.*, p.390.
[3] Mentioned in Baudelaire's essay on Hugo (O.C.II: 137-38). See also page 22 of the present study.
[4] *Div.*, p.391.
[5] Letter of 29 April 1888 (*Corr.* 3: 190).

irregularity in Mallarmé's later alexandrines can be read. It represents formally the tension between the impressions of impersonality and universality necessary to the poetic illusion, and the subtle admission that this might be nothing more than a fiction, a vain artifice manipulated by an individual poet. Inscribed on both a rhythmic and a harmonic level, this dramatizes the instability of both the ultimate value of poetic form and the status of the external/internal poetic Ideal.

9
The Internal Ideal and Poetic Form

The Mallarméan alexandrine (1880-1890s)

As Laurent Jenny observes, Mallarmé is 'moins attaché au vers strict qu'à son principe'.[1] This principle is now simply dodecasyllabic rather than metrical, and the recurrence of the number twelve throughout Mallarmé's work underlines its importance to his poetics. In 1869, for example, he describes 'le vers' as a 'système agencé comme un spirituel zodiaque', exploiting the correspondence between the iconic *nombre* of verse perfection and the divisions imposed on the celestial dome by human consciousness.[2] Thus the origin of this principle might be a purely internal poetic instinct; in *Les Dieux antiques*, Mallarmé declares of the twelve labours of Heracles: 'le nombre en a été fixé par les poètes', just as 'l'Olympe et ses Douze Dieux' represents 'une œuvre d'art inspirée par un goût de la symétrie'.[3] As we now know, this symmetry might be nothing more than a 'rêve', and the 'correspondance profonde' which Marchal sees 'entre l'ordre cosmique et le tréfonds de l'âme humaine' might not necessarily originate in the exterior, but rather, in the internal poetic drive for order.[4] The French alphabet 'avec ses vingt-quatre signes'[5] may correspond to the syllabic total of an alexandrine couplet, but this number is far from absolute and, like Rimbaud's musical principle in *Illuminations*, reflects a human construct rather than an external Truth.[6] Thus the ultimate value of the dodecasyllable is as unstable as

---

[1] 'Mallarmé: musique, espace, pensée', *Po&sie* 85 (1998), 115-22; p.117.

[2] 'Fragments et notes' (*Div.*, p.378).

[3] O.C., 1945, pp.1186 and 1181.

[4] *La Religion de Mallarmé*, p.286.

[5] 'Fragments et notes' (*Div.*, p.378)

[6] Indeed, in this case the 24 letters are a deliberate Mallarméan fiction. Grevisse observes that the first French alphabet comprised only 23 letters, increasing to twenty-five in 1762 with the separation of 'j' and 'i', and 'v' and 'u'. Only in the twentieth century was 'w' added, taking the total to 26 (*le bon usage, grammaire française*, 13th edition, rev. by André Goosse, Paris: Duculot, 1993, p.85).

that of both rhythm and language; it is the flimsy illusion of inherent meaning that Mallarmé exploits in order to project the fictional poetic Ideal as if it did indeed correspond to some external reality.

Having understood the fictional status of the poetic Ideal and the fragility of verse rhythm, Mallarmé defends the alexandrine in two ways. Firstly, he simply uses it less frequently; in the 1880s roughly half of his published poems are in alexandrines, a figure which falls to only three from seventeen in the 1890s. Secondly, he protects it from monotony with infrequent yet emphatic irregularities, and no poem in alexandrines after 'Sur les bois oubliés...' (1877) is free from metrical disruption. The 1880s alterations to 'Le Guignon' alone add one M6, one C6 and two P6 lines to the version of 1862, with a third P6 line rewritten:

> Aux fauves séraphins / du Mal! Ces baladins
> Mais eux, pourquoi / n'endo // sser pas, / ces baladins (1.59)
>
> Quand chacun a sur eux / vomi tous ses dédains
> Quand en face tous leur / ont craché les dédains   (1.61)
>
> La plupart ont râlé / dans des ravins nocturnes
> La plupart râla dans / des défilés nocturnes   (1.10)
>
> Les poètes savants / leur prêchent la vengeance
> Les poètes bons pour / l'aumône ou la vengeance   (1.52)
>
> S'ils pantèlent, c'est sous / un ange très-puissant
> Leur défaite, c'est par / un ange très puissant   (1.13)

The 1880s poems feature a further six P6 lines of any period, as well as twenty-seven D6 lines. Strikingly, it is during the 1880s, as the verse mould comes to symbolize the Ideal's illusory universality, that the first Em6 line, the most metrically disruptive of Mallarmé's career so far, appears.

'La chevelure vol...' begins with eight perfect 6+6 alexandrines, just as in 1897 Mallarmé congratulates Camille Mauclair on his mixture of fluidity and regularity: 'vous allez jusqu'à en recomposer un rythme librement à côté! il est vrai, employant le nombre fixe au début, pour donner l'intonation'.[1] This use of metrical regularity to

---

[1] Letter of 8 October 1897 (*Corr.* 9: 289).

donner le ton, or *donner le la*, recalls the faun of 1876 'qui cherche le *la*', aiming for 'Trop d'hymen' (1.34), perhaps a surfeit of metrically identical lines. In the context of the 'mélodie à sept notes' which disturbs metre on the seventh syllable, the search for *la*, the sixth note, reflects the search for the sixth syllable which 'disappears' as monotonous metre is erased by rhythmical innovation. Since too much metrical regularity would inspire lassitude – and scepticism – jeopardizing the poetic value of the metre used to project the fictional Ideal, *le la* is emphatically undermined at line nine:

> Une nudité de / héros tendre diffame

Echoes of Hérodiade are unmistakable in the 'héros', completed by the '**diad**ème' (1.3), and the reference to 'nudité'. Placed, in the Deman edition, directly after the 'Scène' and the 'Après-midi', which dramatize the artist's relationship with his Ideal, the poem describes a 'chevelure' recalling that of Hérodiade. As Marchal suggests, the woman to whom the sonnet is originally addressed, in 'La Déclaration foraine', is 'moins une femme réelle [...] qu'un archétype de femme', 'cette idée qui est en quelque sorte la compagne idéale du poète'.[1] Indeed, the narrator refers to her as 'notre pensée', as if she were an internal idea common to all.[2] It is striking that vocabulary associated with the drama of Hérodiade appears in Mallarmé's later alexandrines at several points of tension between regularity and irregularity. Since, as I have argued, this drama can be read as an allegorical exploration of the very nature of the poetic Ideal, such echoes at sites of metrical tension highlight the instability of both the Ideal itself and the self-consciously flimsy veil of verse which partly obscures its purely fictional status.

For example, Hérodiade also haunts the Em6 lines of the 1890s. 'Remémoration d'amis belges' features the line:

> Que se dévêt / pli se // lon pli / la pierre veuve (1.4)

The metrically transgressive 'selon' recalls that applied in the 'Scène' to the lover-artist 'selon qui [...] Sortirait le frisson blanc de ma

---

[1] *La Religion de Mallarmé*, pp.265-66.
[2] *Div.*, p.91.

nudité' (ll.97-99). The 'pierre veuve' recalls the adamant 'je ne veux rien d'humain' of the asexual Hérodiade, 'sculptée' (1.82), like the 'rêve de pierre' of Baudelaire's 'La Beauté' (1.1). In the 'Ouverture' the statuesque 'vierge' is imagined to be unveiled by the textual/sexual 'plis', and the verb *se dévêtir* alludes to the same undressing and revelation of nudity. In 'Crise de vers' the sanctity of the alexandrine is threatened by the partial tearing of the veil as the 'plis' recur: 'une inquiétude du voile dans le temple avec des plis significatifs et un peu sa déchirure'.[1] Elsewhere these 'plis' are synonymous with rhythm: 'intervention du pliage ou le rythme, initiale cause qu'une feuille fermée, contienne un secret, le silence y demeure'.[2] Regular rhythm falters, therefore, amid suggestions of the possible vanity of a verse form which corresponds to no external Ideal.

In 'Le Tombeau de Charles Baudelaire', the preposition 'selon' recurs in another Em6 line. This too echoes Hérodiade, 'de vols partis costumée et fantôme' ('Ouverture', 1.29), whose impending 'Noces' are suggested by the verb *découcher*:

Dont le vol selon le / réverbère découche   (1.8)

Tellingly, 'selon' also precedes the problematically present-absent *e indicible* in an 1896 correction to 'Dame...': 'selon quel*que* / apparence' (1.11). Here Hérodiade's 'ombre' is present in the image of the 'rose [...] cruelle ou déchirée', removing her 'blanc habit de pourpre', 'Pour ouïr dans sa chair pleurer le diamant' (ll.2-4) in an echo of the princess's own 'sanglots' ('Scène', 1.132) and 'clair regard de diamant' ('Scène', 1.116). The *clin d'œil* to the veil over the Ideal is even more explicit in the 1887 original: 'Même du voile lourd de parfums se délace' ('Méry', 1.3).

The 'ombre' of Hérodiade also lurks in other unprecedented irregularities of the 1890s, the F6 and F7 alexandrines which Cornulier passes off as 'quelques traits de modernité mesurée'.[3] In the 'Tombeau' to Verlaine comes the sole F6 line:

Nubiles plis / l'astre // mûri / des lendemains   (1.7)

---

[1] *Div.*, p.240.
[2] 'Le Livre, instrument spirituel' (*Div.*, p.268).
[3] 'Remarques sur la métrique de Mallarmé', p.82.

Again this irregularity suggests the possible vanity of verse as the 'plis' echo the futile 'plis / Inutiles' ('Ouverture', ll.23-24) and the imminent consummation of the nubile Hérodiade's purity in 'le lit aux pages de vélin' (l.59). Furthermore, the 'astre mûri' recalls both the nurse's reply when Hérodiade seeks confirmation of her beauty: 'Un astre, en vérité' ('Scène', l.52), and the image of the princess as a ripened fruit, 'précoce avec terreur' (1887, l.64). Similar echoes surround the F7 line of the 'Tombeau de Charles Baudelaire':

Contre le marbr / e vain // ement de Baudelaire(l.11)

Since Mallarméan poetry exploits the tension between the personal and the universal, this text, like many others, can be read both as a highly specific *poème de circonstance* and simultaneously, in more general terms, as poetry about Poetry. Thus the 'marbre de Baudelaire' also provides another echo of the statuesque Hérodiade who, with the nymphs, haunts the next two lines: 'Au voile qui la ceint absente avec frissons / Celle son Ombre même' (ll.12-13). The verb *ceindre* and the 'Ombre' recall the faun's desire to unveil the nymphs' image which resists him: 'A leur ombre arracher encore des ceintures' (1865, l.52). This 'Ombre' also recalls the first line of the 'Scène', which establishes from the outset the uncertain presence-absence of Hérodiade: 'Tu vis! ou vois-je ici l'ombre d'une princesse?' (l.1). Finally, the 'frissons' echo the 'frisson blanc de ma nudité' (l.99) which Hérodiade is loathe to reveal. At such sites of formal tension, this abundance of vocabulary from the small yet highly charged Mallarméan *réseau* subtly inscribes the drama of the (possibly) fictional Ideal.

A number of MCP6 lines from the 1880s and 1890s also echo this drama. Firstly, the M6 line from 'Toujours plus souriant...' echoes in its blood, sighs and swooning the deadly, heady sexual act which Hérodiade refuses, preserving the mystery of the Ideal:

Soupirs de sang, / or meur // trier, / pâmoison, fête! (l.2)

In 'Le vierge, le vivace...', the absolutized 'Cygne' (l.14), echoing the princess-swan, becomes a 'Fantôme' with 'son pur éclat' (l.12). The C6 line recalls the immobilization by which Hérodiade might become a statue, and the 'froideur stérile' ('Scène', l.39) of her 'rêve' (l.51) is echoed in the 'songe froid':

Il s'immobilise au / songe froid de mépris (l.13)

In 'Le Pitre châtié', the virgin Hérodiade, whose beauty and chastity are both linked to death in the 'Scène' (ll.8 and 108), lurks in the following P6 line:

Mille sépul / cres pour // y vierg / e disparaître (l.8)

In the 'Scène', as Hérodiade applies the adjective 'vierge' to the unsullied purity of her hair, it resists the metre with a disruptive seventh-syllable accent:

Mais de l'or, à jamais / vierge des aromates (l.37)

Similar echoes abound in the D6 lines, as common words in rhythmically problematic positions underline their importance to the drama of Hérodiade. In 'Le Pitre châtié', for instance, the mysterious 'Yeux' echo Hérodiade's 'yeux comme de purs bijoux' ('Scène', l.86); the 'lacs', which creates accentual hiatus, recalls the water metaphors extended throughout the 'Scène' and the 'Ouverture', and the clown's 'simple ivresse' echoes that of the perfumes which Hérodiade rejects (ll.33-35):

Yeux, lacs avec / ma simple // ivress / e de renaître (l.1)

The D6 line of 'Une négresse...' recalls the apprehensive princess's nudity, the Truth about the poetic Ideal which must not be revealed:

Contre la nudité / peureuse de gazelle (l.9)

In the 'Hommage' to Wagner, the adjective preceding the caesura recalls the 'clarté mélodieuse' of Hérodiade's eyes ('Scène', l.93), as the rhyme-word echoes Mallarmé's mid-1860s epistolary comments on his quest to transfer his 'rêve' to the written page:

Entre elles de clartés / maîtresses a jailli (l.10)

Finally, the incipit 'Ô si chère de loin...' resumes perfectly the relationship between the artist and his necessarily distant Ideal. Although the poem is ostensibly personal, featuring the name of its addressee, Méry Laurent, in line 2, it is also full of echoes of the impersonal, universal Ideal, reminiscent of the *un/tout* reunion in 'La Déclaration foraine' where the personality or impersonality of the poet's companion is ambiguous: 'toute femme, et j'en sais une'.[1] The D6 line contains three echoes of Hérodiade, 'la rose / Cruelle' ('Les Fleurs', ll.10-11), who fears 'le tiède azur d'été' ('Scène', l.100):

La même rose / avec // le bel / été qui plonge (l.7)

The rhyme-verb is also applied both to the swan's unhappy introversion ('Ouverture', l.14) and the nymphs' escape from the faun (1875, l.32). Indeed, the third *b* rhyme 'prolonge / La même rose' (ll.6-7) recalls the faun's desire to 'perpétuer' his nymphs (1876, l.1). The artist's relationship with the 'rêve' of his Ideal underlies the whole poem, especially since *prolonger* echoes the faun's doubt as to the nymphs' very existence: 'Mon doute, loin ici de finir, se prolonge' (1875, l.4). Moreover, the rhyming of 'songe' and 'mensonge' ('Ô si chère de loin...', ll.2-3) underlines the possibility that this 'rêve' might now be nothing more than a fiction, but a fiction which verse regularity – here rhyme harmony – helps nonetheless to perpetuate.

Echoes of the drama of the Ideal also feature in a number of first- and seventh-syllable accents, such as the 'Yeux, lacs' which begins the revised 'Pitre châtié' with rhythmical hiatus. Similarly, in 'La chevelure vol...', Hérodiade, the 'astre, en vérité' ('Scène', l.52) disrupts the metre:

Celle qui ne mouvant / <u>astre</u> ni feux au doigt (l.10)

In 'Une négresse...' the 'Triste fleur' or 'naïve enfant' ('Scène', l.76, l.79), 'précoce' like a ripe fruit ('Scène', 1887, l.64), also disturbs:

Veut goûter une enfant / <u>triste</u> de fruits nouveaux (l.2)

Hérodiade's solitude is emphasized in the 'Scène': 'Triste fleur qui croît seule' (l.76), 'Ô charme dernier, oui, je le sens, je suis seule!' (l.117). This solitude, the necessary inviolability of the poetic Ideal, is echoed by two seventh-syllable adjectives of the 1880s, both following key nouns in her drama, the 'pli' and the deadly 'baiser':

---

[1] *Div.*, p. 85.

Dispose plus qu'un pli / <u>seul</u> sur le mobilier   ('Hommage', à Wagner, l.2)
Tout bas par le baiser / <u>seul</u> dans tes cheveux dite ('O si chère de loin…', l.14)

Indeed, the hair to which this kiss is applied recalls both the 'cheveux immaculés' which symbolize Hérodiade's unspoiled purity ('Scène', l.4) and the 'touffe échevelée / De baisers' that the faun's passion defiles (1865, ll.79-80).

Similar examples dominate the few adjacent accents of the 1890s. The alteration to 'Méry Sans trop d'aurore…' both erases the referential personality of the proper name 'Méry' in general impersonality, and disturbs the rhythmical regularity:

<u>Dame</u>
      sans trop d'ardeur / à la fois enflammant   (l.1)

In 'Remémoration d'amis belges' the dawn echoes the ominous 'Lever du jour dernier qui vient tout achever' ('Ouverture', l.88), and the fatal, murderous tone is echoed in the adjective 'défunt'. Also, the verb 'multipliant' recalls the tension between singularity and multiplicity which underlies the drama of Hérodiade and the nymphs:

<u>Brug</u>es multipliant / <u>l'aube</u> au défunt canal (l.10)

Similarly, the example from the 'Tombeau' to Verlaine, suggesting the mourning of an immaterial entity, reflects the death of the external Ideal which is re-motivated, in verse, as a self-conscious fiction:

Cet immatériel / <u>deuil</u> opprime de maints   (l.6)

These echoes of Hérodiade at points of rhythmical problematization inscribe into verse form the drama central to Poetry: the antagonism between regularity and irregularity, representing the fundamental instability of the illusion of a universal poetic Ideal. If this Ideal is a mere fiction, the veil of verse is all in vain, and a series of disruptive syllables from the 1860s onwards underlines precisely the vanity of a verse artifice whose regularity corresponds to no external reality.

The vanity of verse
    The fundamental vanity of the poetic Ideal is suggested by the nurse's reference to 'le mystère vain de votre être' which Hérodiade guards so fiercely ('Scène', l.75). This vanity is consistently inscribed

at first- and seventh-syllable position as Mallarmé's verse proclaims its own 'Glorieux Mensonge'. The trend begins as early as 1865, in the 'Faune', where three line-initial accents feature key terms in the drama of the Ideal:

> Vaine!
>   Mais dédaignons / de vils traîtres!
>   Serein   (I, l.49)
> L'homme, sa rêverie / interdite te brise   (II, l.28)
> L'art, quand il désigna / l'un des faunes élus   (III, l.54)

As verse rhythm is disrupted the ultimate value of poetic art is called into question: does it reflect a pre-existent reality, or is it simply a vehicle for the poet to project a vain fictional Ideal? In the 'Ouverture' another seventh-syllable accent suggests the possible *nullité* of verse:

> De la voix languissant, / nulle, sans acolyte   (l.50)

In the 1870s amendments to the 'Faune', where doubt as to the external reality of the Ideal becomes more explicit, similar examples of semantically loaded accentual disruption multiply. This is most significant in the lines:

> Rêve, en un long solo, que nous amusions
> La beauté d'alentour par des confusions
> Fausses entre elle-même et notre amour crédule   (1876, ll.45-47)

The 'Rêve' in which the poetic Ideal takes refuge proves incompatible with metre, providing a rhythmical jolt, just as the 'amour crédule' reflecting the artist's self-conscious projection of this 'Rêve' relies on 'confusions' whose *fausseté* is also underlined by the monosyllabic *rejet*. The final line, with its illusion of reuniting duality in singularity, is doubly disruptive:

> Couple, adieu; je vais voir / l'ombre que tu devins   (1876, l.110)

The two rhythmically problematic words articulate the poles of the dilemma, duality and singularity, and their incompatibility with regular form highlights the vanity of the verse mould which attempts their resolution in a miraculous poetic Ideal.

This vanity is also implied in the seventh-syllable accents added to the 'Faune' in 1875. In the first example the faun wonders whether what he thought was a nymph might have been an illusion:

Comme brise du jour / <u>vain</u>e dans ta toison   (l.13)

Just as the breeze creates a vain illusion of the nymphs, so too verse creates an equally vain illusion of the poetic Ideal. The seventh syllable recalls Mallarmé's only F7 line, where the same word places the usually *indicible* 'e' at the same position: 'vain / ement'. In the second example the faun's music is explicitly revealed as pure artifice:

L'invisible et serein / <u>souffle</u> artificiel   (l.21)

Here the faun's 'souffle' which, as we have seen, undermines the illusion of universality necessary to the convincing projection of the fictional Ideal, also disturbs the impersonal metrical mould with the personal. As the illusion of impersonality falters, so too does the metrical regularity, as the verse mould and the artist's 'souffle' prove incompatible.

When Mallarmé returns to Hérodiade in 1898, the 'Noces' continue the trends established in his later alexandrines. Alongside highly balanced lines feature one Em6, five M6, four C6 and five P6 lines, of which ten resist a 4/4/4 rhythm:

Parle ou bien faut-il que / l'arcane messéant   ('Finale' I, l.24)

Nimbe là-bas / très glo // rieux / arrondissant   ('Prélude' I, l.2)
Que cette pièce / héré // ditair / e de dressoir   ('Prélude' I, l.10)
Un selon de chers pre / ssentiments inouï   ('Finale' I, l.15)
Peut-être que / cet [te] att // iranc /e du désastre   ('Finale' I, l.17)
A cet arrêt / surna // turel / que ce n'est point   ('Finale' I, l.20)

Comme emblème sur une / authentique nourrice   ('Prélude' III, l.29)
Affres que jusqu'à leur / lividité hérisse   ('Prélude' III, l.30)
Évanoui comme un / séculaire plumage   ('Scène Intermédiaire', l.3)
Tandis qu'autour / de son // sachet / de vieille faille   ('Scène Intermédiaire', l.7)

Aussi peut-être hors / la fusion entre eux   ('Prélude' I, l.5)
Immobilisés par / un choc malencontreux   ('Prélude' I, l.6)
Comme une cime dans / ses ténèbres hostile   ('Finale' I, l.9)
A dire excepté par / une bouche défunte   ('Finale' I, l.25)
N'accorde comme dans / la plus riche des couches   ('Finale' II, l.5)

The key words 'vain', 'nul' and 'faux' appear at crucial points, both at
the metrical *points de repère* – caesura, rhyme – and in counterpoint:

Vains les nœuds éplorés, / la nitidité fausse   ('Prélude III', l.17)
A quel psaume de nul / antique antiphonaire   ('Prélude III', l.1)
Dans l'hésitation / vaine à prendre congé   ('Scène intermédiaire', l.6)
Dans sa gaine debout / nulle de firmament   ('Finale II', l.27)

Finally, the 'Rien qui est la vérité' is increasingly inscribed in line-
initial position during the 1890s, underlining the suspicion already
expressed in 'La Déclaration foraine', that verse form is 'rien que lieu
commun d'une esthétique':

(1865)   Rien, ni le vieux jardin reflété par mes yeux ('Brise marine', l.4)
(1865)   Rien.
          Je les veux!
          Mais si ce beau couple au pillage ('Faune', l.8)
(1891)   Rien qu'un battement aux cieux ('Eventail', l.2)
(1893)   Rien, cette écume, vierge vers ('Salut', l.1)
(1896)   Rien, au réveil, que vous n'ayez ('Rien, au réveil…', l.1)

In 'Eventail', it is from the 'logis très précieux' (l.4) – the preciosity
of verse artifice? – that the 'futur vers se dégage' (l.3), articulating
'Rien qu'un battement aux cieux', a possibly vain verse rhythm.
Indeed, as many critics have observed, the 'Rien' of 'Salut' opens the
Poésies with the emphatic assertion of the *vide* underlying the poetic
fiction contained therein. Thus the vanity of the 'vierge vers',
assimilating Hérodiade and verse in the same way as the 'nymphes-
roseaux' ('Faune', 1865, II, l.30), is announced at the outset. Since the
Ideal is pure fiction, the verse mould corresponds to no external Truth;
the value of poetic form is henceforth unstable, and for the poet and
his reader, as for Baudelaire and Rimbaud, poetry becomes a matter of
faith. Two complementary poems of the 1870s, omitted from
Mallarmé's published collections, provide allegorical insight into two
opposing reactions to the *nombre* of verse and its dependence on our
faith.

In 'Dans le jardin' (1871), the poet's widow doubts that a
transcendent heavenly realm exists, denying the 'faux Éden' (l.8). As
if her loss of faith in an external absolute causes her to lose faith in
verse, her doubts assail her 'Quand des heures Midi comblé jette les
douze' (l.3). Indeed, her rejection of the afterlife is articulated in two

irregular lines in which the metrical *douze* is disturbed by two sorts of accentual hiatus:

> Tu mens. Ô vain climat / <u>nul</u>! je me sais jalouse
> Du faux Eden <u>que</u>, <u>triste</u>, / il n'habitera pas.   (ll.7-8)

Again, this 'nul' at the seventh syllable, disrupting the metrical *point de repère*, asserts the vanity of a verse mould which peddles a purely fictional Ideal. Clear echoes of Hérodiade, such as the garden, the flowers and the rhyme 'calices / délices' (ll.13-14) which also features in the 'Scène' (ll.97-98), highlight the relevance of what is firstly a *poème de circonstance* to the bigger Mallarméan picture.

In 'Sur les bois oubliés...' (1877), the dead woman calls to her lover from the afterlife. Midday is replaced by midnight, the iconic poetic hour of 'Igitur' at which the hero attempts to overcome *le hasard*: 'Il jette les dés, le coup s'accomplit, douze, le temps (minuit)'.[1] The relevance of midnight, with its *douze coups*, to the drama of Hérodiade is inscribed throughout Mallarmé's work. In the 1887 edition the nurse implies that Hérodiade's purity will be lost at midnight, when the *douze coups* are achieved: 'Tombera, le minuit, ce dédain triomphant' (l.79); just as she is 'dévorée / D'angoisse' ('Scène', ll.73-74), the 'Sonnet en -ix' begins with 'L'Angoisse, ce minuit'; and it is echoes of the princess, such as 'clarté' (l.12), 'impératrice enfant' (l.13) and 'des roses' (l.14), that illuminate the midnight darkness (l.6) of 'Victorieusement fui...'.

In 'Sur les bois oubliés...', unlike in 'Dans le jardin', the vanity of twelve, the iconic poetic *nombre*, is ignored: 'Sans écouter Minuit qui jeta son vain nombre' (l.5). The poem is metrically regular, and the ghost explains that this refusal to acknowledge the vanity of the poetic *douze* is crucial to the appearance of her absolutized 'Ombre' (l.8). It is as if, in order to conjure up her phantom, her lover must re-motivate his faith in rhythm, just as the poet and his reader must put their faith in verse regularity if the projection of the fictional Ideal is to succeed. However, the ghost also tells her lover:

> Pour revivre il suffit qu'à tes lèvres j'emprunte
> Le souffle de mon nom murmuré tout un soir   (ll.13-14)

---

[1] *Div.*, p.66.

The verb *murmurer* echoes the opening, in 1875, of the Hérodiade-fruit: 'Chaque grenade éclate et d'abeilles murmure' ('Faune', 1.96), suggesting the imminent revelation of the Ideal. However, the 'souffle' recalls the faun's breath, and that of the individual *vers-libristes*, which is detrimental to Mallarmé's poetic fiction. In this poem, it is only to the individual poet that the 'Ombre' appears, whereas, as we have seen, the Mallarméan poet must hide this 'souffle' in order to create the illusion that this vision might be seen, not just by the poet alone, but by all mankind. Yet this is Mallarmé's final poem in alexandrines to feature no metrical irregularities, as the rest of his career dramatizes formally the constant tension between the illusion of poetic absolutes and its ultimate vanity. From the 1870s onwards Mallarmé comes increasingly to use the sonnet form, the very icon of absolute poetic constants, as a privileged symbol of this self-conscious 'Glorieux Mensonge'.

The sonnet and the Ideal

Since poetic regularity no longer reflects a stable universal analogy, but rather, generates its own perpetually unstable meaning, David Scott suggests that the Mallarméan sonnet is 'an effective means of imposing significant order on the arbitrary phenomena of the universe'.[1] Of course, it does not correspond to any external aesthetic Ideal, but our poetic conditioning invites us to interpret the sonnet as the pinnacle of aesthetic beauty. Roger Pearson, for example, admires 'that most sacred of poetic constellations, the Sonnet', as Michel Sandras enthuses: 'Le sonnet c'est l'Idéal'.[2] The young Mallarmé shares this enthusiasm, and on the eve of beginning his 'Ouverture' tells Heredia: 'je crois, à la joie rythmique qui me balançait, quand je relisais ce soir vos sonnets, que je me remettrai facilement à l'œuvre'.[3] Indeed, the form's structural unity provides an effective support for the projection of the dodecasyllable as a poetic principle, and in 1891 Mallarmé tells Ernest Raynaud: 'Le sonnet reste le refuge absolu de l'alexandrin'.[4]

---

[1] *Sonnet Theory and Practice in Nineteenth-century France: Sonnets on the Sonnet*, University of Hull Publications, 1977, p.73.
[2] *Unfolding Mallarmé: The Development of a Poetic Art*, Oxford: Clarendon Press, 1996, p.270 and *Lire le poème en prose*, Paris: Dunod, 1995, p.187.
[3] Letter of 30 December 1865 (*Corr. fol.*, p.272).
[4] Letter of 17 January 1891 (*Corr.* 4: 184).

It is striking that between 1876 and 1897, every new poem in alexandrines is a sonnet. Even more striking, given Mallarmé's Baudelairean experiments with the form from 1858 to 1868, is the overwhelming shift to that which Banville proclaims in 1872 to be the only regular sonnet: *abba abba ccd ede*.[1] Just as Mallarmé claims there are a convenient twenty-four letters in the alphabet, so too Banville's value judgement, or rather, imposition, contradicts historical evidence. As we know, the tercet pattern *ccd eed* is more common by far than *ccd ede* throughout the sixteenth and seventeenth centuries, contradicting Banville's choice of regular iconic form.[2] It would be unwise to suggest that Banville's stipulation alone inspired Mallarmé's later fondness for this form, but his adherence to a poetic constant raised to 'absolute' status by authorial rhetoric rather than empirical evidence certainly situates his sonnet practice within the context of the self-consciously fictional poetics observed thus far.

The value of the Banvillian form is demonstrated by the two sonnets discussed above. 'Dans le jardin' expresses in rhythmically problematic alexandrines the loss of faith in transcendent absolutes, and this is also reflected in the rhyme scheme, as the quatrains diverge from the model in which we must put our faith: *abab abab*. However, this is the last poem in which a crisis of faith is articulated explicitly, and as 'Sur les bois oubliés...' (1877) calls for a restoration of faith in the versificatory veil, it does so in Banville's 'absolute' form. 'Le Tombeau d'Edgar Poe' (1876), where the poet becomes 'Le Poète' (1.2), obeys the same rhyme scheme, from which Mallarmé's QQTT sonnets never again deviate. 'Plusieurs sonnets', which for François van Lære is 'véritablement le "saint des saints" du recueil', opens with 'Quand l'ombre menaça...', proclaiming the value of the 'Rêve' (1.2) in the Banvillian form which corresponds to the simultaneously absolute yet illusory status of the dream.[3] From this point onwards, the Deman edition features only sonnets, seventeen in all, of which fifteen are Banvillian, the sonnet form inscribed at the very head of the collection, in 'Salut', as an unstable poetic fiction.

---

[1] *Petit Traité*, p.195. Pearson makes a similar observation (*Unfolding Mallarmé*, pp.157-58).
[2] See pages 64-65 of the present work.
[3] 'L'ordonnance d'un livre de vers', in *Mallarmé ou l'obscurité lumineuse*, ed. by Bertrand Marchal and Jean-Luc Steinmetz, Paris: Hermann, 1999, pp.221-28; p.226.

Mallarmé's alterations to two 1860s sonnets in the 1880s attest to his dedication to this form. 'Le Pitre châtié' depicts the hapless artist cutting a window in the 'mur de toile' – echoing the Baudelairean prose poet's fatal mistake – only to realize that the revelation of 'la nudité [...] pure' (ll.10-11) must be avoided at all costs. Thus the poem, like 'L'Amour du mensonge' or 'Le Masque', celebrates the 'fard' (l.14) of poetic artifice, the veil over the 'pièce principale ou rien'.[1] Fittingly, it is re-worked to present a Banvillian rhyme scheme in which the rhyme strength is also consistently increased:

quais	[k ɛ]	a		renaître	[n ɛtr]	a
pénètre	[n ɛtr]	b		évoquais	[k ɛ]	b
fenêtre	[n ɛtr]	b		quinquets	[k ɛ]	b
quinquets	[k ɛ]	a		fenêtre	[n ɛtr]	a
traître	[ɛtr]	b		traître	[r ɛtr]	a
appelais	[l ɛ]	a		mauvais	[ov ɛ]	b
galets	[l ɛ]	a		innovais	[ov ɛ]	b
hêtre	[ɛtr]	b		disparaître	[r ɛtr]	a
nouveau	[o]	c		irrité	[ite]	c
tyrannie	[ni]	d		nudité	[ite]	c
assainie	[ni]	d		nacre	[akr]	d
l'eau	[o]	c		passiez	[asje]	e
peau	[o]	c		sacre	[akr]	d
génie	[ni]	d		glaciers	[asje]	e

Certain new *rimes léonines* recall the drama of Hérodiade, as if, in order to project this fictional poetic Ideal, an increase in rhyming harmony were required to strengthen the veil. The 'nudité', for example, echoes that of the princess's 'rêve épars' ('Scène', l.51). The 'glaciers', which feature in 'Le vierge, le vivace...' as 'Le transparent glacier des vols qui n'ont pas fui' (l.4), recall Mallarmé's discovery of 'le Beau' as a glorious fiction, as he tells Cazalis of his journey to 'les plus purs glaciers de l'Esthétique'.[2]

Two 1868 drafts and the definitive version of 'Quelle soie aux baumes de temps' (1887) display a similar genesis:

---

[1] 'La Musique et les Lettres' (*Div.*, p.356).
[2] Letter of 13 July 1866 (*Corr. fol.*, p.310).

Temps	[tã]	a	venue	[ny]	a	temps	[tã]	a
venue	[ny]	b	temps	[tã]	b	s'exténue	[ny]	b
nue	[ny]	b	nue	[ny]	a	nue	[ny]	b
détends	[tã]	a	détends	[tã]	b	tends	[tã]	a
tentures	[tyr]	c	avenue	[ny]	a	méditants	[tã]	a
seul	[sœl]	d	j'entends	[tã]	b	avenue	[ny]	b
sépultures	[tyr]	c	nue	[ny]	a	nue	[ny]	b
linceul	[sœl]	d	contents	[tã]	b	contents	[tã]	a
vagues	[vag]	e	vagues	[vag]	c	sûre	[syr]	c
vagues	[vag]	e	vagues	[vag]	c	morsure	[syr]	c
cheveux	[vø]	f	cheveux	[vø]	d	amant	[amã]	d
naître	[ɛtr]	g	renaître	[ɛtr]	e	touffe	[tuf]	e
Être	[ɛtr]	g	Être	[ɛtr]	e	diamant	[amã]	d
désaveux	[vø]	f	désaveux	[vø]	d	étouffe	[tuf]	e

Both quatrains and tercets show a steady progression from irregular to canonical form: the four quatrain rhymes of the first *sonnet libertin* are reduced to two in the second version, finally arranged in *rimes embrassées* in the third, with the last four rhymes becoming *croisées* only in the third version. Furthermore, the new *rime léonine* 'amant / diamant' evokes the drama of Hérodiade 'au clair regard de diamant' ('Scène', l.116) who refuses any lover. Indeed, her 'ombre' haunts the whole poem, from the nude form in the mirror (stanza one) to the 'trous de drapeaux' (l.5) which recall the 'trous anciens' of 'Percés selon le rythme et les dentelles pures' ('Ouverture', ll.44-45). Similarly, the drama of the faun and his unstable 'rêve' of the nymphs is suggested by the 'morsure' (l.10), calling to mind his 'morsure / Mystérieuse' (1875, ll.40-41), and the 'touffe' (l.12) which echoes the 'touffe échevelée / De baisers' (1875, ll.83-84) whose unity is defiled, requiring restoration by poetic artifice.

As if in recognition of the fact that the Banvillian form is not the only possible iconic form, Mallarmé simultaneously favours a 'mode primitif du sonnet', 'usité à la Renaissance anglaise', which first appears in 1887 with 'La chevelure vol...' and features a further eight times in the collection.[1] Since the 'ombre' of Hérodiade is a constant presence in the poem, the notion of 'Renaissance' might refer to the death of the external Ideal and its rebirth as an internal fiction. Indeed,

---

[1] 'La Déclaration foraine' (*Div.*, p.89).

these sonnets are mostly heptasyllabic, corresponding to what Virginia La Charité sees as 'the number which symbolizes perfect order'.[1] Furthermore, each quatrain of this form presents *rimes croisées*, which might represent formally the restoration of the poetic window through which this Ideal is projected. The *croisée* is certainly a recurrent Mallarméan synonym for *fenêtre*, appearing in 'Les Fenêtres' as the idealist poet flees 'à toutes les croisées' (l.25) and 'Ses purs ongles...', where the 'défunte nue en le miroir' (l.12), suggesting Hérodiade and the *vide* of the Ideal, is seen 'proche la croisée au nord vacante' (l.9). Mallarmé's affection for the image is demonstrated by his embellished translation of Poe's 'The Sleeper', as the poet mourns the death of his love:

All Beauty sleeps! – and lo! where lies	Toute Beauté dort: et repose, *sa croisée*
Irenë, with her Destinies!	*ouverte au ciel*, Irène avec ses Destinées.[2]

The importance of the *croisée* in projecting the Ideal as if it were a universal Truth is highlighted in 'Notes sur le théâtre' (1887), where the actor's personality disappears as he is seen 'à travers la croisée, impersonnel comme l'être vu de dos [...] dans un au-delà de vitrage et son cadre'.[3] Adherence to these fixed forms, therefore, is an effective method of surrendering authorial individuality to the fiction of poetic Beauty's universality.

In the early prose poem 'Frisson d'hiver' the poet also asserts the value of the antique with recurrent reference to the *croisées*. Hérodiade is present-absent, as ever, as the poet contemplates the mirror: 'je suis sûr que plus d'une femme a baigné dans cette eau le péché de sa beauté; peut-être verrais-je un fantôme nu si je regardais longtemps'.[4] Indeed, the suggestion that the naked phantom might be glimpsed as the poet himself looks in the mirror supports the notion of an internal Ideal whose source is the poetic imagination. In order to project this Ideal the verse poet requires recognizable formal symbols which might be imagined to correspond to a poetic reality, but in the prose poem – used in the 1860s to express a certain loss of rhythmic

---

[1] *The Dynamics of Space: Mallarmé's Un Coup de dés jamais n'abolira le hasard*, Lexington, Kentucky: French Forum, 1987, p.127.
[2] O.C., 1945, p.202; my italics.
[3] O.C., 1945, pp.343-44.
[4] *Div.*, p.73.

faith – the rhythmically disillusioned poet notices spiders' webs on the 'croisées', as if symbolizing the obsolescence of the verse window. Like the lover of 'Sur les bois oubliés…' whose deceased companion urges him to ignore the vanity of *nombre* – 'Sans écouter Minuit qui jeta son vain nombre' (l.5) – the poet attempts to ignore the worn-out appearance of these windows: 'Ne songe pas aux toiles d'araignées qui tremblent au haut des grandes croisées'.[1] Thus our faith in the ultimately vain verse mould requires constant and conscious re-motivation in the absence of any external Ideal. The poet's staunch adherence to fixed sonnet forms allows him to posit poetic constants which become inextricably linked with fictional notions of absolute Beauty. Since its form is defined by the rhyme scheme, Robb notes that the sonnet, 'plus que toute autre forme "sérieuse", met en relief la rime'.[2] Indeed, the artifice of rhyme comes to assume prime importance in the projection of Mallarmé's internal poetic Ideal, although it proves to be both the illusion's crowning glory and, ultimately, its downfall.

Rhyme and the Ideal

In 'La Déclaration foraine' the poet tells his companion that without the general agreement of the crowd, she might not have found his poetic performance so 'irréfutablement' convincing, 'malgré sa réduplication sur une rime du trait final'.[3] Thus it seems that the rhyme contributes greatly to the poetic illusion of external ideal values, especially when foregrounded in a terminal couplet, as in the Elizabethan sonnets. Following his 1866 crisis of faith, Mallarmé's rhymes become increasingly richer as the illusion of meaningful 'rapports' inherent in language is inscribed into verse form. The rhyme is vital in constructing a 'Glorieux Mensonge' over the 'Rien qui est la vérité' and in May 1866 Mallarmé tells Cazalis of the alterations made to his poems before sending them to the *Parnasse contemporain*:

Sentant que, (bien qu'aucun de ces poèmes n'ait été en réalité conçu en vue de la Beauté, mais plutôt comme autant d'intuitives révélations de mon tempérament, et de la note qu'il donnerait, et que par conséquent je ne dusse pas les retoucher avec mes

---

[1] *Div.*, p.74.
[2] *La poésie de Baudelaire et la poésie française 1838-1852*, p.310.
[3] *Div.*, p.91.

principes actuels,) plusieurs cependant étaient trop imparfaits, même au point de vue Rythmique, pour les publier tels, je consacrai des nuits consécutives à les corriger.[1]

Mallarmé's 'principes actuels', as explained in the April letters to Cazalis, aim to glorify the fiction of an absolute Beauty, and many of the corrections made to these poems concern the rhyme scheme. Indeed, almost every altered rhyme becomes *léonine*:

'Le Sonneur':	idé**al**	idé**al**	
(ll.10-11)	lili**al**	→ fé**al**	*suffisante* [al] → *léonine* [e-al]
'A un pauvre':	écl**aircie**	écl**aircie**	
(ll.8-12)	ambro**isie**	→ in**ertie**	*pauvre* [i] → *léonine* [ɛr-si]
'Epilogue':	stéril**ité**	stéril**ité**	
(ll.7-8)	désert**é**	→ vis**ité**	*suffisante* [te] → *léonine* [i-te]
	ra**vie**	ra**vie**	
(ll.17-18)	leur **vie**	→ sa **vie**	*suffisante* [vi] → *léonine* [a-vi]
'Tristesse d'été':	ténéb**reux**	lang**oureux**	
(ll.2-4)	poud**reux**	→ am**oureux**	*suffisante* [rø] → *léonine* [u-rø]
	fiév**reux**	peu**reux**	
(ll.6-8)	poud**reux**	→ heu**reux**	*suffisante* [rø] → *léonine* [ø-rø]
'Les Fleurs':	mens**onge**	fi-**ole**	
(ll.22-24)	r**onge**	→ éti-**ole**	*suffisante* [ɔ̃ʒ] → *léonine* [i-ɔl]

These preciously rich rhymes serve to project the illusion of mysterious correspondences in language, a veil around the fictional Ideal, and in 1887 Mallarmé mentions precisely this 'loi mystérieuse de la Rime, qui se révèle avec la fonction de gardienne'.[2]

Rhyming richness is also important on a strictly formal level. Cornulier argues a polemical metrician's stance: that the principal function of rhyme is to define stanzaic superstructures, and not to 'chime', confirming the line-end, since metre itself fulfils this role.[3] However, the *vers futur* predicted by Mallarmé must, in order to prevent lassitude, erase the sensation of metre whilst retaining on the

---

[1] Letter of 21 May 1866 (*Corr. fol.*, p.304).
[2] 'Solennité' (*Div.*, p.234).
[3] 'La rime n'est pas une marque de fin de vers', p.254.

horizon the hazy impression of isosyllabic equivalence which supports the regularity/universality analogy. Therefore, in the absence of metre, it is the rhyme which confirms isosyllabism at the line-end, allowing it to remain on the horizon, at the edge of the reader's perception. In the 1880-90s, rhythmically problematic *enjambement* almost disappears from the alexandrines, from five (1880s) to three (1890s) and two ('Noces'), as if, in order to compensate for the problematization of internal metre, a stable rhyme were required to maintain this vague impression of isosyllabism.

Many metrically problematic poems include prodigiously rich rhymes, illustrating this function of line-final harmony. The 'Hommage' to Wagner features three D6 lines and the *rime léonine* '**mobilier** / **pilier** / **millier** / fam**ilier**' (ll.2-7); the disappearing rhythmical certainty of 'Le Tombeau de Charles Baudelaire', with its F7, Em6, M6 and C6 lines, is recuperated by the rhymes '**rubis** / An**ubis** / s**ubis** / p**ubis**' (ll.2-7) and '**frissons** / pér**issons**' (ll.12-14); the Em6, P6 and three D6 lines of 'Dame...' are tempered by the rhymes 'enfl**ammant** / di**amant**' (ll.1-4), '**et lasse** / dé**lace**' (ll.2-3), '**gentiment** / sent**iment**' (ll.5-8) and '**année** / spont**anée**' (ll.9-10); and 'Mes bouquins refermés...' closes the Deman edition with a total of ten *vers léonins* which compensate for the P6 and two D6 lines: '**génie** / b**énie** / n**énie** / d**énie**' (ll.2-7), '**de faulx** / paysage **faux**' (ll.5-8), '**régale** / **égale**' and 'parf**umant** / éperd**ûment**' (ll.11-13). And so the collection ends with the poet confessing his desire for the absent Ideal in terms strongly reminiscent of Hérodiade, the *grenade précoce*:

> Ma faim qui d'aucuns fruits ici ne se régale
> Trouve en leur docte manque une saveur égale:
> Qu'un éclate de chair humain et parfumant!   (ll.9-11)

The sempiternal Mallarméan 'peut-être' ends the collection on the ambiguity of the poet's relationship with a possibly illusory 'rien', to which the extent of his devotion is unsure:

> Je pense plus longtemps peut-être éperdument
> A l'autre, au sein brûlé d'une antique amazone.   (ll.13-14)

The poem's multiplication of *rimes léonines* dramatizes one final time the instability of both the poet's attitude towards his poetic Ideal and the value of rhyming richness. Just as the poet himself wavers between total belief and ironic distance, so too the illusion of inherent meaning created by rhyme is far from stable. Indeed, as Robb remarks: 'the richer the rhyme, the more the coupling of two words will appear due to chance', 'the more it reminds us that language is riddled with arbitrary or spurious connections, coincidental harmonies'.[1] Thus in the absence of external, pre-existent absolute values, rhyme harmony becomes deliciously fragile, quivering in the tension between external and internal sources of meaning upon which Mallarmé also refuses to conclude when discussing rhythm and the Ideal.

Alterations made to the 'Faune' between 1875 and 1887 reflect the henceforth unstable value of rhyme harmony. The following rhyme comes as the faun asserts the value of his musical artifice by which he might conjure up the illusion of the nymphs' presence:

> L'invisible et serein souffle artificiel
> De l'inspiration, qui regagne le ciel.   (1876, ll.21-22)

The rhyme marries poetic artifice and the sky where the Ideal is usually projected. As we have seen, the illusion is punctured by the faun's 'souffle' which, on the seventh syllable, disturbs metrical impersonality. The illusion is also punctured by the rhyme. It appears graphemically symmetrical, and as the first rhyme unit is pronounced, the diaeresis [si-ɛl] awaits resolution in a *rime léonine* which might lend weight to the illusion. However, synaeresis on the second unit [sjɛl] confounds our expectation, leaving only a *rime suffisante*; yet the possibility of greater harmony is not lost, quivering on the edge of the reader's perception in the phonetic similarity between [i] and [j]. A similar example comes in:

> Lys! et l'un de vous tous pour l'ingénuité.
>
> Autre que ce doux rien par leur lèvre ébruité,
> Le baiser [...].   (1876, ll.37-39)

The first line suggests yet again the similarity between the universal and the personal, in the familiar *un*/*tous* motif. Just as the faun's art is a 'chant crédule' (l.47), the first rhyme unit underlines the 'ingénuité'

---

[1] *Unlocking Mallarmé*, pp.36 and 29-30.

necessary in order to succumb to this illusion, and the diaeresis [y-ite] suggests imminent resolution in trisyllabic rhyme harmony. Of course, this is disappointed by the synaeresis [ɥite] of the second unit, and although a *rime léonine* survives, the suggestion remains of a higher plane of correspondence towards which the rhyme strains without achieving it completely.

In the third example, the only alteration made to the 'Faune' in 1887, 'Rêve, en un long solo' becomes:

> Rêve, dans un solo long, que nous amusions
> La beauté d'alentour par des confusions   (ll.45-46)

Here, as we have seen, the trisyllabic rhyme [yzi-ɔ̃] becomes *pauvre* as the diaeresis contracts, a result of the metrical disturbance: [yzjɔ̃].[1] Once again the richer rhyme harmony is not lost altogether, but remains in potential, unrealized, at once present and absent. In these three examples, rhyming instability accompanies the faun's discussion of his art, as Mallarmé both encourages and tests our faith in, or our ability to succumb to, a glorious poetic fiction maintained in the 1880s by increasingly rich rhymes.

After its 1870s slump to only five cases, the number of *rimes léonines* rises in the 1880s to forty-five, with a similarly high total of forty-five maintained throughout the 1890s. Trisyllabic rhymes also increase from one (1870s) to six (1880s) and three (1890s), such as:

battement / **délicatement**	('Autre éventail', ll.6-8)
de lavandes / **me la vendes**	('Chansons bas', II, ll.1-3)
l'y tri-er / **vitri-er**	('Types de la rue', V, ll.2-4)
gentiment / **sentiment**	('Dame...', ll.5-8)
mes divers / **et d'hivers**	('Salut', ll.5-7)
hormis l'y taire / **militaire**	('Petit air (guerrier)', ll.1-3)

Reinforced rhymes also increase over the same period: over two syllables, from four (1870s) to sixteen (1880s), twelve (1890s) and eight ('Noces'); and over three syllables from one (1870s) to six (1880s) and two (1890s). Furthermore, the rhymes are foregrounded during these years by their use in shorter lines. One of the first

---

[1] For the metrical implications of this variant, see page 258 of the present study.

octosyllabic poems of the 1880s is the 'Prose', in which the instability of the rhyming veil is at its most obvious, matching similar ambiguity in the content. The poem's generic title refers to a form of latin hymn doubly reminiscent of Mallarmé's later conception of the alexandrine. As Lloyd James Austin observes, such hymns were reserved for 'les grandes solennités', and featured no repetitive metre: 'on y observe seulement le nombre des syllabes, sans avoir égard à la quantité prosodique'.[1] Within octosyllabic quatrains in *rimes croisées*, any rhythmical combinations were possible, prompting Larousse to reject 'ces poésies informes' as 'un art tout à fait primitif'.[2] Rhythmical repetition is thus avoided, with the isosyllabic equivalence confirmed at the rhyme, whose prodigious harmony is unequaled in Mallarmé's entire *œuvre*: no *rimes pauvres*, three *suffisantes*, ten *riches*, nine *léonines*, four trisyllabic and two tetrasyllabic rhymes, with six pairs further reinforced by preceding echoes:

léonine	*3-syllables*	*reinforced*
sais-tu	la science	par la science
vêtu (ll.2-4)	patience (ll.5-7)	ma patience (ll. 5-7)
on dit	spirituels	se para
approfondit (ll.14-16)	rituels (ll.6-8)	sépara (ll.26-28)
été	monotone ment	litige
Eté (ll.18-20)	étonnement (ll.42-44)	la tige (ll.37-39)
chacune	par chemins	nous nous taisons
lacune (ll.25-27)	parchemins (ll.50-52)	pour nos raisons (ll.38-40)
se para		pleure la rive
sépara (ll.26-28)		ampleur arrive (ll.41-43)
de voir		son jeu monotonement
devoir (ll.30-32)		mon jeune étonnement (ll.42-44)

---

[1] 'Mallarmé, Huysmans et la *Prose pour des Esseintes*', in *Essais sur Mallarmé*, ed. by Malcolm Bowie, Manchester University Press, 1995, pp.92-132; p.120.
[2] *Grand Dictionnaire Universel du XIXe Siècle*, 13: 281; 'Sauf une exception ou deux, c'est le vers de huit syllabes qui est toujours employé, et la strophe ordinaire est de quatre vers à rimes croisées'.

taisons
raisons (ll.38-40)   *4-syllables*

la rive   de visions
arrive (ll.41-43)   devisions (ll.22-24)

aïeul   désir, Idées
glaïeul (ll.54-56)   des iridées (ll.29-31)

Except for 'ce qu'on fait rance / cette conférence', these are
Mallarmé's only two tetrasyllabic rhymes.[1] Despite the surfeit of
harmony of this *feu d'artifice*, the rhyme 'de visi-ons / devisi-ons'
highlights the self-conscious artifice of the illusion. It is unique in
Mallarmé for transgressing the correct monosyllabic interpretation of
'ions' as an imperfect verb ending.[2] Mallarmé scrupulously observes
this rule elsewhere, correcting 'amusi-ons' in the 1887 'Faune', yet he
leaves it untouched in 'Prose'. He even uses the correct synaeresis on
an identical verb form, 'promenions' (l.9), highlighting the fault with
intra-textual tension. Since the rhyme would otherwise merely be
pauvre, this demonstrates the artificiality of a precious rhyme made
possible only by breaking another rule of verse. The tension between
the two highlights the instability of a poetry which articulates a flimsy,
fictional Ideal, a notion also explored in the poem's content.

Indeed, the mysterious figure of 'cette sœur sensée et tendre' (l.33)
might usefully be read as an 'ombre' of Hérodiade, the phantom of the
poetic Ideal with which the poet strolls in the fantastical garden.[3]
Sororal and horticultural motifs are, after all, common in both the
'Scène' and the 'Faune', and the instability of this poetic Ideal is
dramatized in the very lines announcing the problematic rhyme 'de
visi-ons / devisions':

> Oui, dans une île que l'air charge
> De vue et non de visions   (ll.21-22)

---

[1] *Vers de circonstance* (O.C., 1998, p.316).
[2] For this rule of prosody, see Banville, *Petit Traité*, p.38.
[3] Other suggestions as to her possible identity include: 'l'héroïne d'un roman
d'Alexandrie', 'la lectrice idéale', 'une Idée de la poésie', 'la conscience du poète',
'sa patience', 'son inspiration', sa 'science', 'sa race', Méry Laurent, the poet's sister
Maria, 'la conscience du poète', 'toutes les femmes chantées par Mallarmé'; overview
by Austin ('Mallarmé, Huysmans et la *Prose pour des Esseintes*', p.130, note 87).

This is reminiscent of the illusion of the nymphs' presence which the air creates for the waking faun: 'Leur incarnat léger, qu'il voltige dans l'air' (1876, l.2). The problematic status of what we see in natural phenomena, explored in the previous chapter, revolves around the ambiguity between 'vue', which implies straightforward observation, and 'visions', which suggests creation or imagination. The necessarily irresolvable tension between the two notions, which Mallarmé maintains throughout his career, is reflected in the formally problematic nature of the 'de visions' rhyme itself.

This tension is maintained in certain corrections brought to two *terza rima* of the 1860s for inclusion in the 1887 edition. On the one hand, the following triplets are modified to extend their *léonine* harmony to all three units:

'Le Guignon':	brisés	[ize]		effacés	[ase]
	gueusés	[ze]	→	assez	[ase]
	éternisés	[ize]		cuirassés	[ase] (ll.53-57)
'Aumône':	horizons	[izɔ̃]		baisons	[ɛzɔ̃]
	prisons	[izɔ̃]	→	maisons	[ɛzɔ̃]
	feuillaisons	[zɔ̃]		feuillaisons	[ɛzɔ̃] (ll.5-9)

On the other, the rhyme 'terne / citerne / prosterne' of 1862 ('Le Guignon, ll.26-30) is subtly undermined in 1887 by the addition of an 's' to 'ternes'. Thus the marker of plurality, at odds with the singularity synonymous with verse harmony, punctures the 'Glorieux Mensonge' of rhyme as its strength increases elsewhere in the same poem.

Similar tension is present in the 'Noces d'Hérodiade' (1898). Just as, in the 'Ouverture', rhyme harmony is reinforced to suggest the *élan* towards the Ideal, the 'Noces' continue the rhyming trend of the 1880-1890s with a surfeit of phonetic correspondences. They contain only one *rime pauvre*, and twenty-one *léonines*, which are particularly foregrounded in the 'Cantique' on the tetrasyllabic lines which close each hexasyllabic stanza:

Aussitôt re**descend**	
Incan**descent**	(ll.3-4)

Toutes dans un **frisson**	
A l'uni**sson**	(ll.7-8)

> Que vous le surpassiez
>   Tous ô glaciers   (ll.23-24)

Numerous unfinished lines contain at least the rhyming word, as if the rhyme scheme provided the cornerstone of the composition process, and all diaeresis at the rhyme is symmetrical: 'inou-ï / épanou-ï' ('Finale' I, ll.15-16), 'né-ant / messé-ant' ('Finale' I, ll.33-34). The poem also features a number of reinforced rhymes over two and three syllables, such as: '**déçus / dessus**' ('Finale' I, ll.7-8), '**jardins / incarnadins**' ('Finale' I, ll.11-12), '**à foison / pâmoison**' ('Prélude' I, ll.21-22).

Most strikingly of all, the 'Noces' display many examples of the correspondences between rhyming hemistichs which were pushed to extremes in the 'Ouverture':

I   / à *l*a *l*angue ro*i*die
    / et v*a*c*a*nt *i*ncendie (ll.3-4)   (3 patterns: /a/, /l/, /ã/)

    / *l*a fus*io*n **en**tre eux
    / *l*e choc ma*l*en**co**treux (ll.5-6)   (4 patterns: /l/, /a/, /õ/ and /ã/)

    / *d*ont *l'* *ab*and*on* d*él*a*b*re
    / **et** *l*e tors can*dél*a*b*re (ll.7-8)   (6 patterns: /d/, /õ/, /l/, /ab/, /ã/, /e/)

    / **de** *s*ouve*n*ir au *s*oir
    / d*i*tai*r*e **de** d*r*e*ss*oir (ll.9-10)   (4 or 5 patterns: /də/, /d/ and /ə/, /s/, /i/, /r/)

    / à bouch*e* puis *l*es vautre
    / qu'on goût*e* *l'*un à *l'*autre (ll.23-24)   (4 patterns: /a/, /u/, /l/ and /ə/)

    / *t*aci*t*u*r*n*e*, pou*r*quoi
    / et s'*ét*e*r*nis*e* coi (ll.25-26)   (4 patterns: /t/, /s/, /r/ and /ə/)

III   / *pl*aci*d*e am**ba**ssadeur
    / *pl*at nu *d*an*s* *s*a *spl*endeur (ll.19-20)   (6 patterns: /p/, /l/, /a/, /s/, /d/ and /ã/)

    / géant *qu*i les a*tt*ache
    / **et** fa*t*i*d*i*qu*e panache (ll.13-14)   (5 patterns: /e/, /k/, /i/, /a/ and /t/)

    / to*r*s*es* *s*u*r* *l*e *l*inon
    / en *l*e *s*igne que non (ll.15-16)   (5 patterns: /r/, /s/, /ə/, /l/ and /i/)

    / en *m*aint épars *fil*et
    / et *m*a*léfi*que lait (ll.35-36)   (6 patterns: /m/, /e/, /a/, /fl/, /i/ and /l/)

VI / n<u>e</u> mon*t*a *p*as *pl*us haut
/ dont *l*<u>e</u> ca*p*rif s<u>u</u>rsaut (ll.3-4)   (7 patterns: /<u>ə</u>/, /õ/, /t/, /a/, /p/, /l/ and '<u>u</u>')

/ de p<u>eu</u>*r* de se d*i*ssoudre
/ l'intér*ieu*re foudre (ll.5-6)   (4 patterns: /ə/, /<u>œ</u>/, /r/ and /i/)

/ où ta cécit<u>é</u> poind,
nat / urel que ce n'<u>est</u> point (ll.19-20)   (4 patterns: /t/, /a/, /s/ and /<u>e</u>/)

/ *Ch*ange*a*nt   en   non*ch*al<u>oi</u>r
/   <u>a</u>vant de *ch*<u>oi</u>r (ll.39-40)   (3/4 patterns: '*ch*' and '*ge*', /ã/ and /a/)

/ *de* s<u>e</u>s rêv*es d*é<u>ç</u>us
/ <u>et</u> ré*gn*<u>e</u>r par-*de*ssus (ll.7-8)   (5 patterns : /d/, /ə/, /s/, /<u>e</u>/ and /r/)

/   j*ar*d<u>in</u>s
/ amb*r*és, <u>in</u>c*arn*ad<u>in</u>s (ll.11-12)   (3 patterns: /a/, /r/ and '<u>in</u>')

/   *pir*<u>e</u> baiser
/   d<u>e</u> *pr*éci*s*er (ll.27-28)   (5 patterns: /p/, /i/, /r/, /<u>ə</u>/ and /e/)

VII / qui *p*ass / <u>e</u> *l*<u>e</u> *pr*<u>e</u>mier   (5 patterns: /p/, /a/, /l/, /<u>ə</u>/and /r/)
/ *p*oud*r*eus / <u>e</u> du *p*a*l*mier (ll.3-4)   (2/4, *coupe italienne*, bisyllabic rhymes)

/ la *pl*us *r*iche *d*es couc*h*es   (9 patterns: /l/, /p/, /r/, /i/, '*ch*', schwa
/ *q*ue *d*es *pr*émices *l*ouc*h*es (ll.5-6)   or mute '*e*', /d/, /e/ and /k/)

/ sur *ell*e étince-la
/   ce*ll*e-là (ll.11-12)   (2 patterns: /s/ and '*ell*')

/ de <u>s</u>'off*r*ir en fe-stin
/ le <u>s</u>eigneu*r* clande-stin (ll.15-16)   (4 patterns: /ə/, /<u>s</u>/, /r/ and /ã/)

/ *si* le tranchant l*uci*de
/   s*ui*ci*de* (ll.21-22)   (3 patterns: /s/, /i/ and /y/)

/ <u>or</u>*d*onné pa<u>r</u> son geste
/ a*d*<u>or</u>able *et* funeste (ll.25-26)   (5 patterns: '<u>or</u>' and /<u>r</u>/, /d/, /n/, /e/ and /a/)

As 'Finale II' draws to a close, the symmetrical patterns occupy two
hemistichs (ll.27-28):

D*a*ns sa <u>g</u>a*i*n*e d*ebout // *nu*l*l*e de fi*r*Ma*M*e*nt*   (/ã/, /a/, /<u>en</u>/, /ə/, /u/, /ny/,
A p<u>ei</u>n*e* *l*a M*i*nu*t*e // *i*noub*l*i-ab*l*e*M*e*nt*   /b/, /l/, /i/, /M/)

The whole piece is framed by two isosyllabic *rimes léonines*, 'l'éblouissant / arrondissant' ('Prélude' I, ll.1-2) and 'dénie / génie' ('Finale' II, ll.33-34), but within this prodigiously rich rhyme scheme feature the inevitable problematic rhymes. In 'Finale I' the anticipated [li] rhyme of 'avilis' (l.31) is confounded by 'lys' (l.32). In 'Prélude III' the [ly] rhyme 'absolus / plus' (ll.11-12) is disturbed by the *rejet* 'Insoumis' (l.13), which demands liaison with the *contre-rejet* 'plus', in order to avoid the hiatus [ply' ɛ̃sumi]. Yet again it is the 's', formal marker of the drama of *nombre* in both 'Scène' and 'Faune', which disrupts verse harmony, confounding the resolution of multiplicity in ideal unity towards which the rhyme strains.

The rhyming veil is also undermined by Mallarmé's frequent use of preciously rich rhyme as a humorous device. Indeed, only the *Vers de circonstance* rival 'Prose' for the intensity of its rhyming artifice, with huge numbers of *rimes riches*, *léonines* and beyond. Mallarmé exploits both rich rhyme on proper names and rhyming diaeresis in order to achieve comic effects:[1]

Portalier / porte alliez	(p.259)	initi-a / Missi-a	(p.275)
déranger / Béranger	(p.271)	dédi-a / Hérédi-a	(p.280)
a de laine / Madeleine	(p.274)	Jou-y / ou-ï	(p.328)

In many of these examples, a large part of the humour comes from the contortions to which we imagine the figure of the poet trying to subject the rhyme words. For instance, when a *rime léonine* is created thanks only to two awkward *enjambements*, the rhyming richness seems absurdly forced, as in 'Chansons bas II':

> **ce sil /**
> Osé [...] hypocrite s'il /
> En tapisse   (ll.2-5)

Such *enjambement* is frequently used in the shorter lines to undermine the illusion of rhyme harmony. As the octo- and hepta-syllabic lines multiply in the 1880-1890s, so too does *enjambement*, including three

---

[1] André Guyaux highlights the similarly comic effect of the matching diaeresis in 'Prose': 'de visi-ons / devisi-ons' ('Jeux de rimes et jeux de mots dans les poésies de Mallarmé', in *Stéphane Mallarmé: Actes du colloque de la Sorbonne du 21 novembre 1998*, ed. by André Guyaux, Paris: Presses de l'Université de Paris-Sorbonne, 1998, pp.191-200; p.193). In all my examples, the page numbers refer to O.C., 1998.

other Cv *contre-rejets* which draw attention to the awkward syntax thanks only to which the rhyme harmony is possible:

Sans même s'enrhumer **au**
Dégel, ce gai siffle-litre   ('Types de la rue', III, ll.2-3)

Quel sépulcral naufrage (**tu**
Le sais, écume, mais y baves)   ('A la nue…', ll.5-6)

Par son chant reflété jusqu'**au**
Sourire du pâle Vasco   ('Au seul souci…', ll.13-14)

In the *Vers de circonstance* the absurdity of this technique is pushed to the limit with such implausible *contre-rejets* as:

A toutes jambes, Facteur, **chez l'**
Editeur […] Quai Saint-Mi**chel**   (p.266)

Porteurs de dépêche **allez vi-**
Te […] 8 rue **Halévy**.   (p.268)

Julie ou Bibi du M**esnil** […]
Ne méprisez ni le **nez ni l'**
Hommage ému   (p.300)

Such rhymes allow the poet's 'souffle' to be clearly perceived, as we imagine him awkwardly contorting language in order to create these unnatural 'rapports' into which, in their natural state, they do not fit. This recalls the ambiguity maintained in those passages, analyzed in chapter eight, where the status of such 'rapports' in nature is equally problematic, wavering between discovery and imposition. The Mallarméan rhyme scheme encapsulates perfectly this fundamental instability, hinting at its own illusory status with both emphatic disruptive techniques and its own formal preciosity. The possibility that the correspondences observed in language are due simply to chance, rather than to any inherently meaningful 'rapports', highlights the possible vanity of a poetics whose value is based on harmony and regularity.

In 1897, however, the relationship between poeticity and regularity becomes even more unstable as Poetry suddenly appears in a text resembling neither verse nor prose, nor even *vers libre*. 'Un Coup de dés' dramatizes as never before the problematic status of what we see both in the world and in a text, confronting us with an interpretative dilemma which continues to stir and resist critical curiosity over one hundred years after its publication. The text's formal ambiguities provide insight into the mechanisms by which meaning is generated, as semi-recognizable forms demonstrate the importance of *nombre* in creating poetic order from apparent disorder, Poetry in the face of 'le Rien qui est la vérité'. 'Un Coup de dés' will provide a fitting conclusion to the present study; although it proclaims loud and clear the ultimate Truth of *le Hasard*, the value of poetic artifice is nonetheless gloriously re-affirmed.

A formal conundrum

Just as Baudelaire and Rimbaud challenge the formal canon with prose poetry, 'Un Coup de dés' contradicts the illusion of 'poetic' regularity maintained in Mallarmé's verse and criticism. In his epistolary discussion of the poem, Mallarmé is at pains to affirm, with his customary *je crois*, that rhythm must correspond to the object which it aims to reflect:

Je crois que toute phrase ou pensée, si elle a un rythme, doit le modeler sur l'objet qu'elle vise et reproduire, jetée à nu, immédiatement, comme jaillie en l'esprit, un peu de l'attitude de cet objet quant à tout.[1]

The rhythm of a phrase must reproduce the effect of the object, an effect which is both universal: 'quant à tout', and internal to the human mind: 'comme jaillie en l'esprit'. Similarly, Mallarmé tells Gide: 'le rythme d'une phrase au sujet d'un acte ou même d'un objet n'a de sens que s'il les imite'.[2] This notion of modelling a rhythm on an object, and imitating the impression which it creates, recalls 'Un spectacle interrompu', where the poet's way of seeing constitutes a useful illusion in support of Poetry's universality. As we have seen, we might imagine the rhythm of metrical verse to be 'modelled' on the fictional poetic Ideal of universal regularity. Yet as Mallarmé highlights in the preface, the rhythm of 'Un Coup de dés' is not that of 'traits sonores réguliers ou vers'.[3] What is the object, then, which this formally revolutionary text might be seen to imitate?

---

[1] Letter of 8 October 1897 to Camille Mauclair (*Corr.* 9: 288).
[2] Letter of 14 May 1897 (*Corr.* 9: 196).
[3] *Div.*, p.405.

Although the poem contains numerous references to concrete objects, and critics see in the layout of certain double pages a boat, or a feather, for example, we cannot be sure that the object in question is so simple. In the preface Mallarmé states that the poem's irregular form represents 'subdivisions prismatiques de l'Idée', or 'quelque mise en scène spirituelle exacte'.[1] Thus the object is an Idea raised to absolute status, and the adjective 'spirituelle' recalls the link made between this adjective and the poetic by both Baudelaire and Mallarmé. The preface ends with the deceptively simple affirmation: 'la Poésie – unique source', as if Poetry itself were the source of the rhythms of the text. Indeed, in contrast to the ambiguity of the 'Anecdotes ou poèmes' in prose, the word 'POÈME' dominates the title page in 1898, and the preface refers to the 'Poème ci-joint'. This leaves no doubt as to the text's fundamentally poetic nature, and the reader is left wondering how, exactly, the poetic idea is to be recognized in 'Un Coup de dés'.

Although it is guaranteed by the generic title, we are unsure as to how the text imitates Poetry, as to where its poeticity resides. The adjective 'exacte', applied to the 'mise en scène spirituelle', signifies 'ce qui ne s'écarte pas de la vérité', yet it is precisely the 'vérité' of Poetry that escapes us.[2] In 'Notes sur le théâtre' (1886-1887), the adjective features as the universal 'soi' is acknowledged to be a 'rêve' or 'rien':

> [...] n'existe à l'esprit de quiconque a rêvé les humains jusqu'à soi rien qu'un compte *exact* de purs motifs rythmiques de l'être, qui en sont les reconnaissables signes: il me plaît de les partout déchiffrer.[3]

Rhythmical motifs are the recognizable signs of this 'soi', Mallarmé insists, and while it is unclear whether they are regular or irregular, they nonetheless form a 'compte exact'. In what form, we wonder, might the 'rêve' or the 'Idée' of Poetry be recognized? Congratulating Vielé-Griffin on *Les Cygnes*, Mallarmé uses the same epithet again:

---

[1] ibid., p.405.
[2] Larousse, *Grand Dictionnaire Universel du XIXe Siècle*, 7: 1172.
[3] O.C., 1945, p.345; my italics.

Vous avez superbement le sens poétique; et en particulier l'instinct de la chose mystérieuse appelée poème, depuis son jet initial mêlant entre eux avec bonheur plusieurs beaux motifs *exacts*.[1]

Here these 'beaux motifs exacts' refers to irregular *vers libre*, yet they correspond to the nature of a poem. In the following remark of 1894, however, it seems to be regular verse which is 'exact', *selon* Mallarmé: 'Le vers, selon moi, se précise où il en est aujourd'hui, il revient, à travers toutes les flottaisons, indéformé, essentiel, exact'.[2] As ever, we can only speculate on the aspects of poeticity common to texts presenting such diverse formal characteristics, and 'Un Coup de dés' itself offers much scope for such an interrogation.

This constant undecidability as to the precise formal definition of the poetic is symbolized by the term 'subdivisions prismatiques de l'Idée'. The prism is not an original poetic metaphor; Hugo, for instance, refers to 'le prisme de la poésie'.[3] However, in view of the fortuitous homonym *verre*/*vers* exploited in 'La Déclaration foraine' – 'comme symétriquement s'ordonnent des verres d'illumination peu à peu éclairés en guirlandes'[4] – the prism is a usefully ambiguous mystificatory tool. As Pearson notes, a prism divides pure light into the seven colours of the rainbow.[5] In a way this reflects the division of the Idea into a number of equal motifs, on which Mallarmé insists in 'Crise de vers'.[6] However, as Larousse reveals, a prism is also a 'cause d'illusion'.[7] The equal bands of the rainbow are nothing more than imaginary boundaries imposed by the human eye on an infinite spectrum which it is unable to apprehend otherwise. The pure light ray achieves the resolution of infinity in pure singularity, and the prism, therefore, symbolizes not a fictional poetic value which we believe to be inherent in order, but rather our tendency to impose *nombre*,

---

[1] Letter of 7 April 1887 (*Corr.* 3: 102); my italics. See Guy Michaud, *Message poétique du symbolisme*, vol. II, 'La révolution poétique', Paris: Nizet, 1947, pp.361-62 for further information on *Les Cygnes*.
[2] Letter of 7 February 1894 to Charles Guérin (*Corr.* 6: 214).
[3] Larousse, *Grand Dictionnaire Universel du XIXe Siècle*, 13: 167 (no reference given for source text).
[4] *Div.*, p.86.
[5] *Unfolding Mallarmé*, p.264.
[6] 'L'acte poétique consiste à voir soudain qu'une idée se fractionne en un nombre de motifs égaux', (*Div.*, p. 246). See also page 261 of the present study.
[7] *Grand Dictionnaire Universel du XIXe Siècle*, 13: 167.

regular divisions, on this spectrum. Thus we are encouraged to scrutinize our way of seeing, and 'Un Coup de dés' challenges the reader with structures which contradict the anticipated regularity of the poetic Idea. Whereas versification was defined in 1893 as symmetrical – 'au moins faut-il de la symétrie, ou pluralité de rapports, entre différents gestes libres, pour constituer, je crois, une versification' – the asymmetrical blanks surrounding the text now fulfil the same function: 'la versification en exigea'.[1]

The form of 'Un Coup de dés' is indeed a prism in which regularity, at first sight, escapes our eye. However, this dice-throw is an invitation to play with *nombre*, to which several critics have successfully responded. Since the sense of the poem has resisted their interpretative faculties, critics bemused by what La Charité calls a 'crisis of semantic stability'[2] have turned to the form in the search for meaning. Mitsou Ronat, insisting on the most accurate reproduction possible for her edition, as if the meaning depended on it, assures us: 'dans cette forme gît naturellement, le sens (ou l'un des sens) du poème'.[3] Ronat claims that 'le poème entier repose sur un calcul', recalling another meaning of 'exact'.[4] Sure enough, she imagines this calculation to be based on the 'nombre d'or', twelve, 'le nombre de positions métriques du maître-vers alexandrin'.[5] Pearson agrees, in a thorough and imaginative exploration of the poem: 'impossible not to acknowledge, in this poem about the hypothetical throw of at least two dice, that the "profond calcul" governing the text is based on the number twelve'.[6] Thus when confronted with the irregular and un-recognizable, which, as the author implies in the preface, reflects the poetic idea 'exactly', it seems that our natural reaction is to equate this poeticity with a kind of hidden regularity for which we must search.

In her quest for meaning, Ronat finds twelves everywhere, from the 24 sides of paper, whose dimensions measure 3 x 4, to 216 lines with a total of 1224 syllables (both multiples of twelve), from the font sizes of the original text – 60, 36, 24 – to the twelve different kinds of

---

[1] Letter of 2 April 1893 to Charles Bonnier (*Corr.* 6: 73-74), and *Div.*, p.405.
[2] *The Dynamics of Space*, p.136.
[3] 'Cette architecture spontanée et magique', preface to *Un Coup de dés*, ed. by Mitsou Ronat, Paris: Editions Change errant / d'atelier, 1980, pp.1-7; p.1.
[4] 'Qui repose sur un calcul' (*Grand Dictionnaire Universel du XIXe Siècle*, 7: 1172).
[5] 'Cette architecture spontanée et magique', pp.2-3.
[6] *Unfolding Mallarmé*, p.247.

font required. Although La Charité is more cautious about the text's number symbolism, she finds twelve substantives repeated throughout the poem, around which gather twelve corresponding semantic clusters.[1] Ronat also uncovers nineteen quasi-metrical structures, convinced that 'une étude (rythmique) exhaustive révélerait sans doute d'autres régularités', reminding us of the faith of Antoine Fongaro and his similarly thorough study of *Illuminations*.[2] Indeed, as with Rimbaud's text, this search for recognizably poetic verse structures appears to be positively encouraged thanks to the tantalizing segment:

> l'unique Nombre qui ne peut pas être un autre
>
>   Esprit [3]

Invariably remarked upon by commentators, this line represents, for Pearson, 'the one alexandrine in the text'.[4] Its status is not so straightforward, however. The layout certainly foregrounds the dodecasyllabic segment, but the pre-caesural 'qui' seems awkward, and a 4-4+4 scansion would leave the syntactically accentuated 'pas' on an unaccentuable syllable. On the one hand, the line's very content, by raising the iconic *Nombre* of verse to absolute status, seems to confirm the Truth of the poetic *douze*, described elsewhere as 'quelque suprême moule n'ayant pas lieu en tant que d'aucun objet qui existe', and invites us to recognize its form as poetic.[5] Indeed, although the very next word, 'Esprit', suggests that this 'unique Nombre' corresponds not to external reality, but to the mind, it is nevertheless universal, thanks to the capital 'E'. On the other hand, the dodecasyllable skilfully dodges our attempt to impose metrical regularity upon it, indicating that the 'poetic' status of what we recognize as regularity – like the seven colours of light leaving a prism – is far from certain.

---

[1] *The Dynamics of Space*, pp.133-34. Proving the instability of all this, La Charité refutes Ronat's count of twenty-four single pages, blaming 'a misunderstanding of the use of signature sheets' (p.127). However, happily for the reader eager for number significance, La Charité's total, twenty-one, corresponds to the sum of the die.

[2] 'Cette architecture spontanée et magique', p.3.

[3] *Div.*, pp.414-15.

[4] *Unfolding Mallarmé*, p.257. It is strange that the following, much more striking 'alexandrine' escapes his notice: 'caressée / et polie // et rendue / et lavée' (*Div.*, p.416).

[5] 'Solennité' (*Div.*, p.234).

The poem's very title is similarly problematic, the first six syllables giving a perfectly regular hemistich: 'Un Coup de dés jamais', with an approximate internal rhyme on both *accent mobile* and *accent fixe*. However, the rest of the phrase gives seven syllables, the magic twelve confounded only by the etymologically *hasardeux* 'h' of 'hasard', which creates an *e surnuméraire* with 'le' rather than 'l''. In this way, it is the 'e', echoing the *indicible* Ideal which comes increasingly to disturb Mallarméan versification, that confounds our expectations of 'l'unique Nombre', suggesting that the relationship between recognizable form and the poetic Ideal is far from unproblematic. Our tendency to find meaning in regularity is satisfied at the poem's conclusion, where five present participles create a 6+6 'alexandrine', its metrical accents marked by the repetition of the nasal /ã/, with other vocalic echoes in counterpoint: 'veill**ant** do**ut**ant ro**ul**ant / br**i**llant *et* méd**i**tant'. Indeed, the first two participles highlight the dilemma of the reader searching for poeticity. The verb *veiller* recalls 'Sur les bois oubliés…', where the lover who must ignore the vanity of midnight's *douze coups* keeps a similar watch: 'Une veille t'exalte' (1.6). Yet faith in poetic *nombre* is not always easy to maintain, leading us to doubt the significance of forms found in the textual constellation.

Indeed, the stars are a perfect symbol of this search for meaning, exploited by Baudelaire in his post-illusory texts, and the poem's frequent references to constellations and astronomy – 'inclinaison', 'vierge indice', 'élévation ordinaire', 'selon telle obliquité par telle déclivité' – dramatize the reader's own search for recognizable form. Just as the constellations do not exist as a concrete object, but are imagined between their nodal points, so too the implicit object of the poem – Poetry itself – is imagined to lie beyond the meaningful 'rapports' in the text. The astral imagery echoes the illusory seven colours created by the poetic prism:

> vers
> ce doit être
> le Septentrion aussi Nord
> UNE CONSTELLATION
> froide d'oubli et de désuétude [1]

---

[1] *Div.*, p.429.

Where others see poetic twelves in the text, Gardner Davies suggests: 'L'apparition de la dernière étoile de la Constellation consacre le chiffre sept comme un symbole immuable'.[1] Mallarmé capitalizes elsewhere on the astral symbolism of the number, in the 'scintillations sitôt le septuor' of the 'Sonnet en -ix' (1.14) or 'les sept sages qu'on supposait habiter les sept étoiles de la constellation que nous appelons la Grande Ourse', from *Les Dieux antiques*.[2] André Gendre is so taken with the number's symbolism that he even imagines that it structures the *Poésies*: 'Le recueil Deman est accordé au chiffre 7; il comprend 49 pièces qui représentent un total de 1127 vers, soit un multiple de 7'.[3] For Nina S. Tucci, the figure constitutes, in Jungian terms, 'an archetype of the human psyche'.[4] For George A. Miller, on the other hand, the 'significance of the number seven as a limit on our capacities', proven in a number of psychological experiments, is 'only a pernicious, Pythagorean coincidence'.[5] For the author of 'Un Coup de dés', however, any such correspondence between poetry, the stars and *nombre*, whatever its status, might simply be imposed by the insistent poetic gaze, implied by the surreptitious 'ce doit être', sandwiched between 'vers' and 'le Septentrion' in the above quotation.

The 'Si' uttered by the faun features on the eighth double page, articulating both a possibility – 'SI C'ÉTAIT' – and, as Lees puts it, 'the straining of *si* towards *ut*'.[6] This appears to announce imminent resolution, and sure enough 'SI' brings with it another quasi-metrical segment:

SI C'ÉTAIT LE / NOMBRE // CE SE / RAIT LE HASARD [7]

However, the dodecasyllable is resolutely non-metrical, at once F6, Em4 and M8, confounding our anticipation of poetic regularity and

---

[1] *Vers une explication rationnelle du 'Coup de dés'*, Paris: José Corti, 1953, p.168.
[2] O.C., 1945, p.1173.
[3] *Evolution du sonnet français*, p.238.
[4] 'Baudelaire's "Les Sept Vieillards": The Archetype Seven, Symbol of Destructive Time', *Orbis Litterarum* 44 (1989), 69-79; p.71.
[5] 'The Magical Number Seven, Plus or Minus Two', *The Psychological Review* 63:2 (1956), pp.80-97; pp.90 and 96.
[6] '...depuis Wagner, la poésie'. Mallarmé and the All-Embracing Word Work', p.23.
[7] *Div.*, pp.423-25.

forcing us to confront a poetic text which consistently refuses reduction to recognizable forms. Indeed, the line tells us in no uncertain terms that even if *nombre* is apparent, it is all down to chance, and means nothing beyond the text itself. The parenthesis after 'NOMBRE' highlights this:

> EXISTÂT-IL
> autrement qu'hallucination éparse d'agonie [1]

This suggests that *nombre* might only exist as a hallucination, an illusion, and the adjective 'éparse' recalls Mallarmé's claim, of 1893, that: 'Le fait poétique lui-même consiste à grouper rapidement, en un certain nombre de traits égaux, pour les ajuster, telles pensées lointaines autrement et éparses'.[2] The only Truth of *nombre*, then, is that it has no inherent meaning, and its poeticity is simply, to borrow a phrase from the next double page:

> accompli en vue de tout résultat nul
> humain [3]

The juxtaposition of 'nul' and 'humain' suggests the ultimate vanity of the human imposition of order and meaning on *nombre*, yet this is also the very glory of Poetry: the generation of meaning thanks to 'un coup de dés' which allows significance to be attached to the ultimately fortuitous.

Although it corresponds to no poetic form we know of, 'Un Coup de dés' successfully defends the poetic status announced by its author's generic stamp. Unlike certain Baudelairean prose poems, whose challenge to readers' faith in the mystery of poeticity causes some critics to label them unpoetic, 'Un Coup de dés' survives intact, and its poeticity is never questioned. For La Charité, to read the poem is simply 'to experience poetry'; 'the reader inquires into the nature of poetry, [...] discovers the substance of poetry, not the meaning of the poem'.[4] Yet by problematizing the forms previously taken as guarantees of poeticity, the text neither reassures nor reveals, but

---

[1] ibid., p.425.
[2] Letter of March 1893 to Charles Bonnier, *Corr.* 6: 65.
[3] *Div.*, p.427.
[4] *The Dynamics of Space*, pp.150-51.

rather, provokes and disturbs. If the irregular and the unpredictable reflect Poetry 'exactly', we are left unsure as to the relative values of regularity and irregularity. As with *Illuminations*, the deferment of a satisfactory conclusion is Poetry's saving grace, and 'Un Coup de dés' preserves the eternal mystery of the poetic thanks to 'le heurt successif / sidéralement / d'un compte total en formation' which resists the fixity that critics may try to impose on it.[1] We are told, in no uncertain terms: 'RIEN N'AURA EU LIEU QUE LE LIEU', yet this is inscribed in an apparent octosyllable. There follows a mischievous qualification, in yet another dodecasyllable which resists our drive to see it as an alexandrine, thanks to its emphatically C6 and F7, M4 and M8 properties:

EXCEPTÉ PEUT- / ÊTRE U // NE CON / STELLATION [2]

Poetry survives, therefore, in the eternally irresolvable 'peut-être' of poetic form, whose ultimate meaning can never be guaranteed, nor denied, absolutely. Pearson observes:

The stars just happen to be in these positions: the human desire for order has arranged them. Mallarmé's patterning of 'Un coup de Dés' preserves this precariousness, and the reader is caught up in the tension between chaos and order. Just as we may tentatively perceive certain visual shapes in the text [...] so too we may discern numerical patterns and yet wonder if they are really there.[3]

Nothing has taken place, except, perhaps, a poem whose status is as unstable and fragile as the constellations themselves, yet it is these constellations which the poet of Baudelaire's 'Obsession' simply cannot ignore. So too the reader of 'Un Coup de dés', scrutinizing the text for signs of Poetry, is naturally drawn towards those forms which may, or may not – for we can never know – provide the guarantee.

Proving that the 'signes reconnaissables' of Poetry are not the exclusive property of either the irregular or the regular, Mallarmé returns after the iconoclastic formal experiments of 1897 to Hérodiade and the 'traits sonores réguliers ou vers', the 'antique vers' to which

---

[1] *Div.*, p.429.
[2] ibid., pp.426-29.
[3] *Unfolding Mallarmé*, p.252.

he professes his reverence in the preface of 'Un Coup de dés'.[1] As if to continue the theme of the search for poetic significance in *nombre*, 'Les Noces d'Hérodiade' consecrates formally the same iconic poetic numbers as 'Un Coup de dés'. Firstly, the alexandrines display the familiar progression towards the glorious future *un/tout* dodeca-syllable. Although the metrical mould is undone in the EmMCP6 lines, these lines are simultaneously encased, as we have seen, in highly complex phonetic correspondences which reinforce the isosyllabic principle of 'l'unique Nombre'.

As for the sevens, the poem opens with the same line-initial 'Si!..' as that which precedes the faun's dream of possessing 'la grande Vénus' (1865, ll.97-100). Separated from the rest of the text, 'Si' inscribes the whole poem under 'the straining of *si* towards *ut*'.[2] Like 'Un Coup de dés', it leans towards a fictional Ideal which cannot, necessarily, be achieved or understood. Indeed, 'si' structures the poem from its seven parts to the seven stanzas of the 'Cantique'. However, 'Un Coup de dés' has demonstrated the irresolvable 'peut-être' of formal significance based on number symbolism, and as if to introduce a *faux accord* into the illusion, the 'Cantique' features the only occurrence of synaeresis on 'ancien' in all Mallarmé's post-*jeunesse* poetry: 'Les anciens désaccords' (l.15). As Larousse notes, the 'cantique' genre is synonymous with 'naïveté et crédulité', 'des idées fausses, des erreurs ridicules et de puériles superstitions'.[3] This is henceforth the very stuff of poetry, the 'chant crédule' which stirs our faith in a fictional Ideal constantly under threat from the Truth of *le Hasard*. In the search for poetic significance, certain numbers, in certain contexts, appear to connote a fictional perfection necessary to the maintenance of the poetic idea. As these texts problematize these fictional markers of poeticity, we are drawn into searching for them, as if they might eventually provide the key to Poetry. However, as Mallarmé's carefully maintained theoretical and formal ambiguities ensure, the Truth of Poetry, that ineffable object which the rhythms of poetry seem to imitate, will constantly elude us.

---

[1] 'L'antique vers, auquel je garde un culte et attribue l'empire de la passion et des rêveries' (*Div.*, p.407).
[2] Lees, '...depuis Wagner, la poésie'. Mallarmé and the All-Embracing Word Work', p.23.
[3] *Grand Dictionnaire Universel du XIXe Siècle*, 3: 290.

A statement of Mallarmé's poetics can be read in his reaction to a lithograph sent to him by Redon, depicting a 'grand Mage inconsolable et obstiné chercheur d'un mystère qu'il sait ne pas exister, et qu'il poursuivra, à jamais pour cela, du deuil de son lucide désespoir, car *c'eût été* la Vérité!'.[1] Ultimately, there may be no universal mystery, only *le Hasard*, but the Mallarméan *œuvre* creates its own poetic mysteries: the ambiguity maintained over the ultimate value and nature of rhythm; the hesitation to ascribe order in both nature and the text to either discovery or imposition; the tension between the universality or the individuality of the internal Ideal, which replaces the external absolute. Thanks to these ambiguities, Rhythm maintains its privileged link with Poetry, while both concepts consistently elude definition. As Marchal observes: 'toute la question est bien de savoir [...] si [...] de l'autre côté du voile déchiré, il y a quelque chose ou rien'.[2] This is indeed the question, but poetry must constantly defer the answer. Our task as readers of Mallarmé is to explore the necessary irresolvability of the question, to appreciate the techniques by which the textual veil maintains the constant 'peut-être' of the interpretative dilemma. This, after all, is the only answer the poet and his text will give, in order to preserve for ever the rhythmical mystery of 'la Poésie – unique source'.

---

[1] On the lithograph 'Dans mon rêve, je vis au ciel un visage de mystère' (letter of 2 February 1885 to Redon, *Corr.* 2: 280).
[2] 'Les Noces du "Livre"', in *Situating Mallarmé*, ed. by David Kinloch and Gordon Millan, pp.121-42; p. 154.

Conclusion

In the introduction to his *Petit Traité*, Banville insists on the relationship between poetry and religious faith:

Le vers est nécessairement religieux, c'est-à-dire qu'il suppose un certain nombre de croyances et d'idées communes au poète et à ceux qui l'écoutent. Chez les peuples dont la religion est vivante, la poésie est comprise de tous; elle n'est plus qu'un amusement d'esprit et un jeu d'érudit chez les peuples dont la religion est morte.[1]

For Banville, even in 1872, poetry is synonymous only with verse. From within the stable universal analogy, there is no doubt: poetry is rhythmical since it reflects in metre the regular rhythms of God's creation. However, as we have seen, once this analogy disappears, the Baudelairean, Rimbaldian and Mallarméan poets find themselves confronted by a world whose characteristics and significance are no longer guaranteed. If it is to avoid obsolescence, poetry can no longer continue to peddle the universal analogy. In 1861 Baudelaire declares that, since the theological significance of scientific fact is uncertain, the role of poetry cannot simply be 'de fixer plus facilement les découvertes scientifiques dans la mémoire des hommes'.[2] For Rimbaud, such religious stability turns poetry into 'prose rimée, un jeu, avachissement et gloire d'innombrables générations idiotes', fit only for 'des lettrés, des versificateurs'.[3] By coincidence, in texts written within the same twelve months, poetry for Banville has become but a 'jeu' in faithless times, whereas for Rimbaud it is the poetry of religious faith which constitutes a mere 'jeu'. Their choice of similar terms of criticism reflects the instability of a poetic idea upon which, it seems, even poets can no longer agree, an instability to which poetry must somehow now respond. In the event, as we have seen, it is on this very instability that poetry henceforth thrives,

---

[1] *Petit Traité*, p.8.
[2] 'Auguste Barbier' (O.C.II: 145).
[3] Letter of 15 May 1871 to Paul Demeny (folio, p.87).

exploiting the tension and mystery of what Mallarmé later calls 'le doute du jeu suprême' ('Une dentelle s'abolit', l.2).

Like Baudelaire's prose poet exploring the *gouffre*, or the 'Bateau ivre' confronting a world without a distorting interpretative grid, we might expect that the lifting of the veil of religious illusion might finally reveal 'l'être ou le fait tel qu'il existe en dehors de nous'.[1] In the event, our poets all discover that there is no 'fait réel' to be articulated through poetry, and an appropriate reaction to the universal *vide* must be found. For Michel Brix, this 'éclatement de la notion de vérité' means that 'l'œuvre d'art ne cherche pas à rendre témoignage d'une Vérité intemporelle mais seulement de la vérité relative de l'expérience de l'artiste, à un moment et un lieu donnés'.[2] As Gérard Dessons highlights, the poets of *vers libre* devote themselves to precisely this task: 'Le rythme [...] se définit spécifiquement comme l'inscription du sujet dans son discours. [...] Si le rythme est chaque fois unique, comme le discours qui le manifeste, c'est qu'il est issu d'un sujet qui réalise précisément, par le langage, sa propre singularité'.[3] However, as all three of our poets are acutely aware, this is not enough for Poetry. If Poetry is to survive the fall of absolute values, to retain its status as a universal, then as Baudelaire demonstrates, the fantasies of *le moi* are not enough. Hence Rimbaud's insistence, in the 'Lettre du voyant', that his visions really do exist in an external reality, and Mallarmé's argument, in 'Un spectacle interrompu', that his poetic way of seeing the world is, in fact, 'la vraie'.[4] As Banville observes in the passage quoted above, Poetry depends on 'un certain nombre de croyances et d'idées communes au poète et à ceux qui l'écoutent'. It relies on an appearance of universality, and the *bouleversement* of the poetic idea raises the question which our poets must answer: if it is no longer the articulation of faith in pure order, then what is Poetry? If it cannot simply be anything, as Rimbaud discovers in his 1872 poems, by what features, common to all poetic texts, are we to recognize it? All three poets provide a conveniently mystificatory solution in which their readers are encouraged to have faith: Poetry is rhythm.

---

[1] Baudelaire, 'La Corde' (O.C.I: 328).
[2] *Le romantisme français*, Namur: Editions Peeters, 'Collection d'Etudes Classiques', 13, 1999, p.263.
[3] *Introduction à l'analyse du poème*, Paris: Bordas, 1991, p.118.
[4] *Div.*, p.83.

Crucially, however, this rhythm must be neither predictable nor stable. Just as the former inscrutable divinity preserved its absolute status by its very resistance to our senses and our understanding, so too the post-illusory notion of rhythm functions according to a similar principle. Poetry requires a shared belief in absolute values of poeticity which must at the same time elude our critical faculties. If God were to reveal Himself, the realm of religion would shift from unprovable faith to unquestionable Truth, and the need for faith would vanish. However, as Baudelaire maintains: 'Quand même Dieu n'existerait pas, la Religion serait encore Sainte et *Divine*'.[1] The final term, therefore, must always remain one step ahead of us, yet close enough to allow the anticipation of an imminent revelation, an arrival which never comes. This is the poetic value of the eternal *départ* of 'ceux-là seuls qui partent / Pour partir' ('Le Voyage', ll.17-18), the future coming of the marvellous genie in *Illuminations*, or Mallarmé's prediction of a miraculous future dodecasyllable capable of reuniting infinite *nombre* in one. Hence, for the good of Poetry itself, the rhythm of post-illusory texts must also escape us, constantly in process, refusing to settle on simple, predictable forms. If we could all agree on the precise qualities of poetic rhythm, then we would have 'found Poetry', but at the same time Poetry, as 'movement towards' and never 'arrival at', would disappear.

This is not to say, of course, that we cannot have some idea of what makes a poetic rhythm. Indeed, without the tantalizing sense that we know what we are looking for, the pleasure of the interpretative tension we have observed in many of the texts analyzed would also be lost. As Mallarmé argues, the poetic Ideal is fundamentally human, and as such it must respond to the 'immortels besoins' identified by Baudelaire.[2] As the poet of 'Obsession' discovers, the naturally human, poetic response to phenomena is the drive to order: the arrangement of stars into constellations, or the islands of 'Le Bateau ivre' into archipelagoes. However, in a world without the universal analogy there remains an irresolvable question as to the nature of this order, a question exploited by Mallarmé throughout his later career: is rhythm imposed or discovered? Do we arrange *l'informe* into *la forme*, or are we really the sensitive observers of an underlying

---

[1] 'Fusées' I (O.C.I: 649).
[2] 'Projets de préface' (O.C.I: 182).

meaning which pre-exists our gaze? It is precisely this interpretative instability that the post-illusory poetry of Baudelaire, Rimbaud and Mallarmé obliges us to confront, recreating in the drama of form the irresolvable tension of the human condition, like the inescapable 'peut-être' of the Mallarméan constellation.[1]

Neither *Le Spleen de Paris*, *Illuminations* nor 'Un Coup de dés' obeys the recognizably poetic form of metrical verse, and yet we believe that somewhere therein lies a mysterious poeticity awaiting discovery. As the range of critical responses which I have presented shows, we are naturally drawn towards the recognizable, the familiar, those echoes of the regular which convince us we are on the right track. However, whereas under the universal analogy there could be no interpretative instability in verse metre, the presence of so-called metrical segments in these texts is infinitely more problematic. To hold them up as evidence of poetic status, particularly of an authorial poetic intention, is to ignore the irresolvability of the question upon which post-illusory poetry thrives and to which it owes its very existence. Proving our unshakable faith in a connection between the significance of poetic form and the figure of the poet, similar to that between a divine figure and the world, critical debate, particularly on *Illuminations*, has focused almost entirely on the question of whether or not the author intended his text to present these poetic rhythms. To suggest that this matter is resolvable is to misunderstand completely the poetic value of these texts. We are right to search for reassuringly familiar poetic rhythms therein; indeed, their foregrounding seems to encourage this very activity. However, it is crucial that we acknowledge the problematic nature of these rhythmic echoes and of their poetic value. With the appearance of P6 and C6 lines in Baudelaire's 1850s verse, the poetic value of metre itself cannot be taken for granted, and in the prose poetic passages which I have analysed, only very few so-called verse segments fulfil unambiguously metrical criteria. Were we less hasty to ascribe poeticity to regular rhythm, as if the poetic revolution explored in this study had never happened, our reading of post-illusory poetry might progress beyond the restrictions imposed on the poetic idea by the sort of reductive critical anachronisms which our three poets themselves so vigorously reject.

---

[1] 'Un Coup de dés' (*Div.*, p.428).

Yet our faith in rhythm has been fuelled, rather than challenged, by poetic developments in the twentieth century. Although he opens *Alcools* with the ironic 3/3/3/3 alexandrine 'A la fin / tu es las // de ce monde / anci-en' ('Zone', l.1), rejecting the restrictive poetic forms of his ancestors, Apollinaire tells us in 'Les Poètes d'aujourd'hui' (1909) that 'le rythme a pris soudain une importance que les initiateurs, les destructeurs, les révolutionnaires si l'on veut de l'ancienne métrique n'avaient point soupçonnée'.[1] Similarly, while arguing for formal variety in poetry, Paul Claudel rejects the monotonous symmetry of the alexandrine and retains the notion of 'le *rythme* au sens étroit du mot en tant que réglant l'allure de tout un morceau poétique'.[2] It is not only rhythm which remains central to the poetic idea; the notion of mystery which, as we have seen, goes hand in hand with rhythmical problematization, becomes particularly prominent during the twentieth century. For Daniel Leuwers, 'tout décryptage du texte serait un leurre, tant l'irréductibilité du poème est inattaquable', with *Illuminations* or Mallarmé's poetic and critical essays providing a clear model for such developments.[3] The mystery of the poetic text reflects an increasingly inscrutable world, and like Baudelaire's prose poet, Philippe Jacottet sees poetry as 'une manière de parler du monde qui n'explique pas le monde, car ce serait le figer et l'anéantir'.[4] Thus echoes of the interpretative drama which we have explored resound throughout French poetry of the twentieth century, and few are the poets who neither refer to nor cite Baudelaire, Rimbaud and Mallarmé as the starting point for poetic modernity.

As we are faced with ever more unpredictable forms and difficulties of comprehension, our persistent belief in some sort of poetic constant demands further interrogation. How, then, might the foregoing inform our readings of these twentieth-century texts? If poetry is still to be defined by rhythm, what becomes of the relative poetic value of regularity and irregularity? Do the lessons learned from *Le Spleen de Paris* influence, for example, our reaction to Saint-

---

[1] *Œuvres en prose complètes*, vol. 2, ed. by Pierre Caizergues and Michel Décaudin, Paris: Gallimard, coll. 'Bibliothèque de la Pléiade', 1991, p.915.
[2] 'Réflexions et propositions sur le vers français', in *Œuvres en prose*, ed. by Jacques Petit and Charles Galpérine, Paris: Gallimard, coll. 'Bibliothèque de la Pléiade', 1965, p.40.
[3] *Introduction à la Poésie moderne et contemporaine*, Paris: Dunod, 1990, p.118.
[4] *Eléments d'un songe*, Paris: Gallimard, 1961, p.153.

John Perse's foregrounding of metrical fragments in his prose texts? Do they represent, as in Baudelaire, a yearning back to a lost time of faith, or an ingenuous effort, in the terms of Antoine Fongaro, to make prose poetic? Or do they rather challenge our interpretative certainties, recognizing a necessary tension and maintaining the drama which our poets placed at the heart of the poetic idea? Given the lessons learned from this study as to the impossibility of defining Poetry, the development of the musical metaphor also demands closer scrutiny. In modern poetic texts, the notions of rhythm, harmony and melody, and the musical analogy they encourage, are used to refer not only to metre and rhyme, but also to apparently free forms such as Claudel's *Cinq grandes odes*, and yet it seems that in critical discourse they are most often attached to familiar structures, alliterative and assonantal patterns and echoes of a bygone regularity. Surely we should mistrust the common analogy between poeticity and musicality, when our three poets constantly resort to a musical metaphor in reference, not to the straightforward and recognizable, but to the mysterious quality of both poetry and music which resists analysis and definition.

It seems that our inability to define Poetry satisfactorily leads us to scrutinize poetic form for answers, to attempt to define rhythm, as if this were less problematic and more quantifiable. Yet the very indefinability of poetic rhythm is indispensable in protecting the poetic idea against impoverishment. The problematization of this rhythm, the refusal to allow it to be pinned down, functions as a necessary veil over a poetic idea which must remain absolute, universal, mysterious. Perhaps, as Mallarmé declares in 1866, Poetry is but a 'Glorieux Mensonge'; indeed, when the curtain is opened, Baudelaire's 'curieux' is forced to confront the disappointing emptiness of 'la vérité froide' (l.11). However, for Baudelaire, there is always the possibility that the *gouffre* is but a dream, 'le Rêve d'un curieux', whereas for Mallarmé, it is Poetry itself which represents 'Tel vieux Rêve' ('Quand l'ombre menaça', 1.2). The pleasure of post-illusory poetry lies in this very ambiguity, in our appreciation of the strategies by which our faith in Poetry is by turns challenged and restored, the mechanisms which recognize and exploit our desire, as 'êtres spirituels', to believe in a Poetry which constantly escapes us. Like the child of Rimbaud's 'Aube', therefore, we must relish Poetry's re-veiling, and savour the necessary problematization of poetic rhythm which helps to keep this veil in place.

SELECT BIBLIOGRAPHIES

The first bibliography includes general works on poetic rhythm, the prose poem or the musical metaphor, poetic treatises of the nineteenth and twentieth centuries, rhyme dictionaries, etc. It also aims to provide as comprehensive a list as possible of works by Cornulier and other contributors to the *Cahiers du Centre d'Etudes Métriques*, and therefore contains articles on other poets (Verlaine, Apollinaire, Laforgue, Banville, Hugo) which are closely related to metrical matters discussed in the present study.

The next three bibliographies are author-specific, corresponding to parts one, two and three. Where articles by Cornulier or Bobillot, for example, discuss only one poet, the reference is included in the bibliography for that author.

The following abbreviations are used:

P.U.F.	Presses Universitaires de France
C.U.P.	Cambridge University Press
O.U.P.	Oxford University Press

BIBLIOGRAPHY I. GENERAL

Abastado, Claude, *Mythes et rituels de l'écriture*, Brussels: Editions Complexe, 1979.

Allen, W. Sidney, *Accent and Rhythm*, Cambridge: C.U.P., 1973.

Anderson, Stephen R., 'The analysis of French schwa: or, How to get something for nothing', *Language* 58:3 (1982): 534-73.

Aquien, Michèle, *La Versification*, Paris: P.U.F., coll. 'Que sais-je ?', 1990.

--- *La Versification appliquée aux textes*, Paris: Nathan, 1993.

--- *Dictionnaire de poétique*, Paris: Librairie Générale Française, 1993.

Aquien, Michèle, and Honoré, Jean-Paul, *Le Renouvellement des formes poétiques au XIXe siècle*, Paris: Nathan, 1997.

Aroui, Jean-Louis, 'Forme strophique et sens chez Verlaine', *Poétique* 95 (1993): 277-99.

--- 'Poétique des strophes de Verlaine: analyse métrique, typographique et comparative', doctoral thesis, 2 vols., Université de Paris VIII, 1996.

--- 'Nouvelles considérations sur les strophes', *Degrés* 25:104 (2000), e.

Aspley, Keith and Peter France, eds., *Poetry in France: Metamorphoses of a Muse*, Edinburgh University Press, 1992.

Aubertin, Charles, *La Versification française*, Paris, 1898.

Backès, Jean-Louis, *Le Vers et les formes poétiques dans la poésie française*, Paris: Hachette *Supérieur*, coll. 'Les Fondamentaux', 1997.

Banville, Théodore de, *Les Exilés*, Paris, 1867; in *Œuvres poétiques complètes*, ed. by Peter J. Edwards *et al*, 8 vols, Paris: Champion, 1994-2001; vol. 4, 1994.

--- *Petit Traité de Poésie Française*, Paris, 1872; Paris: Charpentier, 1883; Ressouvenances, 1998.

Beaudouin, Valérie, *Mètre et rythmes du vers classique. Corneille et Racine*, Paris: Champion, 2002.

316   *Rhythm, Illusion and the Poetic Idea*

Beaumont, E. M., J. M. Cocking and J. Cruickshank, eds., *Order and Adventure in Post-Romantic French Poetry: Essays Presented to C. A. Hackett*, New York: Barnes & Noble, 1973.

Becq de Fouquières, Louis Aimé Victor, *Traité général de versification française*, Paris: Charpentier, 1879.

Béguin, Albert, *L'Ame romantique et le rêve*, 1937; Paris: José Corti, 1946.

Benloew, Louis, *Précis d'une théorie des rythmes*, Paris: A. Franck, 1862.

Benveniste, Emile, 'La notion de rythme', in *Problèmes de linguistique générale*, vol.1, Paris: Gallimard, 1966: 327-35.

Bernard, Suzanne, *Le Poème en prose de Baudelaire jusqu'à nos jours*, Paris: Nizet, 1959.

Berreur-Avril, Françoise, 'Le rythme et la danse', *Ritm* 3 (1992): 143-61.

Bertrand, Aloysius, *Gaspard de la Nuit*, ed. by Max Milner, Paris: Gallimard, coll. 'Poésie', 1980.

Bertrand, Marc and Geneviève Torlay, *Louis Aragon et Marceline Desbordes-Valmore, Essai de prosodie comparée*, Paris: Publications M.B. et G.T., 1997.

Billy, Dominique, 'La nomenclature des rimes', *Poétique* 57 (1984): 64-75.

--- 'Quelques apports récents à la métrique française', *Bulletin de la Société de Linguistique de Paris* 84:1 (1989): 283-319.

--- 'La rime androgyne. D'une métaphore métrique chez Verlaine', in *Le vers français. Histoire, théorie, esthétique*, ed. by Michel Murat, Paris: Champion, 2000.

--- 'Pour une théorie panchronique des vers césurés', *Cahiers du Centre d'Etudes Métriques* 1 (1992): 2-14.

--- 'Méditation sur quelques nombres', *Cahiers du Centre d'Etudes Métriques* 2 (1994): 5-29.

--- 'Le nombre de la rime', *Degrés* 25:104 (2000), f.

Billy, Dominique, Benoît de Cornulier, and Jean-Michel Gouvard, eds., 'Métrique française et métrique accentuelle', *Langue française* 99, Paris: Larousse, 1993.

Bobillot, Jean-Pierre, 'Le ver(s) dans le fruit trop mûr de la lyrique et du récit', *Procope* 1 (1990): pages unknown.

--- 'Elasticité métrico-prosodique chez Apollinaire: Une lecture formelle des *Colchiques*', *Poétique* 84 (1990): 411-33.

--- 'Recherches sur la crise d'identité du vers dans la poésie française, 1873-1913', doctoral thesis, Université de la Sorbonne nouvelle, Paris IV, 1991; Lille: Atelier National de Reproduction des Thèses.

--- 'Quelque chose comme le rythme existe-t-il ? De la "poésie objective" à la "poésie-action"', *Ritm* 1, 'Rythme et écriture II' (1991): 55-80.

--- 'Vers, prose, langue', *Poétique* 89 (1992): 71-91.

--- 'Référence à la Chanson et *Innovation Prosodique* dans certains vers de Jules Laforgue', *Cahiers du Centre d'Etudes Métriques* 1 (1992): 33-40.

--- 'Le vers la lettre – des "rimes grammaticales" au "poème littéral" (états d'un travail en cours)', *Ritm* 3, 'L'Attente rythmique' (1992): 45-76.

--- 'Entre mètre et non-mètre: le "décasyllabe" chez Verlaine', *Revue Verlaine* 1 (1993): 179-200.

--- 'De l'anti-nombre au quasi-mètre: le "hendécasyllabe" chez Verlaine', *Revue Verlaine* 2 (1994): 66-86.

--- 'A la fin cou coupé', *Poétique* 95 (1993): 301-23.

Bourassa, Lucie, ed., 'Rythmes', special edition, *Protée* 18:1 (1990).

--- *Rythme et sens: Des processus rythmiques en poésie contemporaine*, Montréal: Les Editions Balzac, coll. 'L'Univers des discours', 1993.

Braunschvig, Marcel, *Le Sentiment du beau et le sentiment poétique*, Paris: F. Alcan, 1904.

Brix, Michel, *Le romantisme français*, Brussels: Société des Etudes Classiques, 'Collection des études classiques' 13, 1999.

Broome, Peter and Graham Chesters, *The Appreciation of Modern French Poetry 1850-1950*, Cambridge: C.U.P., 1976.

Brunet, François, 'Musique et poésie dans *Les Stalactites* de Banville', *Bulletin des Etudes parnassiennes* 9 (1987): 3-51.

Campa, Laurence, 'Le Chant des rimes dans *Alcools*: Prolégomènes à une étude statistique des rimes', *Revue des Lettres Modernes* 19 (1996): 127-44.

Campion, Pierre, *La Littérature à la recherche de la vérité*, Paris: Editions du Seuil, coll. 'Poétique', 1996.

Caws, Mary-Ann and Hermine Riffaterre, eds., *The Prose Poem in France: Theory and Practice*, New York: Columbia University Press, 1983.

Celeyrette-Pietri, Nicole, *De Rimes et d'analogies: les dictionnaires des poètes*, Presses Universitaires de Lille, 1985.

Charpier, Jacques and Pierre Seghers, eds., *L'Art poétique*, Paris: Seghers, 1956.

Chérel, Albert, *La Prose poétique française*, Paris: L'Artisan du livre, 1940.

Chetoui, Mohammed, 'Pour une syntaxe intégrée à la poétique: la syntacticométrie', *Cahiers du Centre d'Etudes Métriques* 4 (1999): 138-57.

Chevalier, Jean and Alain Gheerbrant, *Dictionnaire des Symboles*, Paris: Laffont and Jupiter, 1982.

Chevrier, Alain, *Le Sexe des Rimes, Architecture du verbe*, Paris: Les Belles Lettres, 1996.

Collot, Michel, *L'horizon fabuleux*, 2 vols.: I, XIX siècle; II, XX siècle, Paris: José Corti, 1988.

--- *La Poésie moderne et la structure d'horizon*, Paris: P.U.F., 1989.

--- 'Rythme et mètre: entre identité et différence', *Protée* 18:1, (1990): 75-80.

Cornulier, Benoît de, 'Le remplacement d'*e* muet par *è* et la morphologie des enclitiques', in *Actes du Colloque franco-allemand de Linguistique théorique*, ed. by Christian Rohrer, Tubingen: Niemeyer, 1977: 155-80.

--- 'Le vers français classique', *Le Français moderne* 45:2 (1977): 97-125.

--- 'La rime n'est pas une marque de fin de vers', *Poétique* 46 (1981): 247-56.

--- 'Métrique de l'alexandrin d'Yves Bonnefoy: essai d'analyse méthodique', *Langue Française* 49 (1981): 30-48.

--- 'La cause de la rime. Réponse à Jean Molino et Joelle Tamine', *Poétique* 52 (1982): 498-508.

--- *Théorie du vers: Rimbaud, Verlaine, Mallarmé*, Paris: Editions du Seuil, 1982.

--- 'Groupements de vers: sur la fonction de la rime', *Cahiers de Grammaire* 6 (1983): 32-70.

--- 'Musique et vers: sur le rythme des comptines', *Recherches linguistiques* 11 (1983): 114-71.

--- 'Problèmes de métrique française', doctoral thesis, Université d'Aix-en-Provence; Atelier international de reproduction de thèses de l'Université de Lille III, 1984.

--- 'Des vers dans la prose', *Poétique* 57 (1984): 76-80.

--- 'Rime "riche" et fonction de la rime. Le développement de la rime "riche" chez les romantiques', *Littérature* 59 (1985): 115-25.

--- 'Versifier: le code et sa règle', *Poétique* 66 (1986): 191-97.

--- 'Poésies complètes de Victor Hugo: relevé métrique, base de données MS Works 2.0 sur Macintosh', Nantes: Centre d'Etudes Métriques, 1986.

--- 'Pour une grammaire des strophes: Conventions de codage des structures métriques', *Le Français Moderne* 56:3-4 (1988): 223-42.

--- 'Codage et analyses métriques des strophes classiques – l'exemple des *Contemplations*', *Revue des Lettres Modernes*, série Victor Hugo, 2, 'Linguistique de la strophe et du vers', Paris: Minard, 1988: 79-134.

--- 'La Fontaine n'est pas un poète classique; pour l'étude des vers mêlés', *Cahiers du Centre d'Etudes Métriques* 1 (1992): 15-31.

--- 'La *césure* comme frontière sémantique associée: A propos d'une définition de M. Dominicy et M. Nasta', *Cahiers du Centre d'Etudes Métriques* 2 (1994): 84-91.

--- 'Remarques sur la métrique interne de l'alexandrin au XIXe; A propos de la thèse de Jean-Michel Gouvard', Nantes: Centre d'Etudes Métriques, 1994.

--- *Art poétique: notions et problèmes de métrique*, Presses Universitaires de Lyon, 1995.

--- 'Pour mieux lire Verlaine: petit essai d'analyse du 4-6', *L'Ecole des Lettres* 14 (1996): 95-109.

--- 'Sur le pont Mirabeau', *Cahiers du Centre d'Etudes Métriques* 3 (1996): 55-71.

--- *Petit dictionnaire de métrique*, Nantes: Centre d'Etudes Métriques, 1998.

--- 'La place de l'accent, ou l'accent à sa place: position, longueur, concordance', in *Le Vers français: Histoire, théorie, esthétique*, ed. by Michel Murat, Paris: Champion, coll. 'Métrique Française et Comparée', 1999.

--- 'Verlaine, pauvre rimeur: la rime bègue dans 'Caprice'', *Revue Verlaine* 6 (2000): 47-63.

--- 'L'invention du 'décasyllabe' chez Verlaine décadent. Le 4-6, le 5-5, le mixte, et le n'importe quoi', in *Verlaine à la loupe*, ed. by Jean-Michel Gouvard and Steve Murphy, Paris: Champion, 2000: 243-89.

--- *Traité de métrique*, Paris: Belin, forthcoming.

Cornulier, Benoît de, Joëlle Gardes-Tamine and Michel Grimaud, *Linguistique de la strophe et du vers*, La Revue des Lettres Modernes, special edition, 'Victor Hugo' 2, Paris: Minard, 1988.

Deguy, Michel, 'Figure du rythme, rythme des figures', *Langue Française* 23 (1974), 'Poétique du vers français', ed. by Henri Meschonnic: 24-40.

Delas, Daniel, 'On a touché au vers! Note sur la fonction manifestaire du poème en prose au XIXe siècle', *Littérature* 39 (1980): 54-60.

--- 'Silence et rythme', *Ritm* 1 (1991): 11-20.

--- 'Approches du rythme', *Cahiers de sémiotique textuelle* 14 (1988), 'Rythme et écriture': 9-23.

Delente, Eliane, *Le Rythme: Principe d'organisation du discours poétique*, doctoral thesis, Université de Caen: Linguistique française, 1992.

Deloffre, Frédéric, *Le Rythme de la prose: objet et méthodes de l'analyse*, The Hague, 1966.

--- *Le Vers français*, Paris: Société d'édition d'enseignement supérieur, 1969; S.E.D.E.S., 1991.

Dessons, Gérard, *Introduction à l'analyse du poème*, Paris: Bordas, 1996.

Dessons, Gérard, and Henri Meschonnic, *Traité du rythme. Des vers et des proses*, Paris: Dunod, 1998.

Devauchelle, Karine, 'Emergence des vers CPM6 dans la poésie de Théodore de Banville', *Cahiers du Centre d'Etudes Métriques* 4 (1999): 37-68.

Dominicy, Marc, 'Sur la notion d'e féminin ou masculin en métrique et en phonologie', *Recherches linguistiques de Vincennes* 12 (1984): 7-45.

--- ed., *Le Souci des apparences: huit études de poétique et de métrique*, Brussels: Editions de l'Université, 1989.

--- 'On the meter and prosody of French 12-syllable verse', *Empirical Studies of the Arts* 10:2 (1992): 157-81.

Dominicy, Marc, and Christine Michaux, eds., 'Approches linguistiques de la poésie, actes du Colloque International du Cercle Belge de Linguistique 13-15 jan. 2000' *Degrés* 25:104 (2000).

Dominicy, Marc, and Mihai Nasta, 'Métrique accentuelle et métrique quantitative', *Langue Française* 99 (1993): 75-96.

Dorchain, Auguste, *L'Art des vers*, Paris: 1905; 'Libraire des Annales', n.d.

Du Méril, Edelestand, *Essai philosophique sur le principe et les formes de la versification*, Paris: Brockhaus et Avenarius, 1841.

Dupriez, Bernard, 'Disures: le passé et l'avenir du vers français', *Protée* 18:1 (1990): 59-68.

Eigeldinger, Marc, *Lumières du Mythe*, Paris: P.U.F., coll. 'Ecriture', 1983.

Elwert, W. Théodor, *Traité de versification française*, Paris: Klincksieck, 1965.

English, Alan, 'Ambivalence et ambiguité: les limites de la métricité' / '"La volupté de contrarier le lecteur": ambivalence, ambiguité et "indécidabilité" dans la poésie de Verlaine', *Revue Verlaine* 6 (2000): 98-114.

Escal, Françoise, 'Du mètre au rythme: de la suite de danses à la suite de concert', *Ritm* 1 (1991): 35-54.

Filteau, Claude, 'Rythme de tensions et rythme d'intention: à propos du lyrisme moderne', *Protée* 18:1 (1990): 11-19.

Fongaro, Antoine, 'Un vers univers', *Revue des lettres modernes* 13 (1973): 109-18.

Fouché, Pierre, *Traité de prononciation française*, Paris: Klincksieck, 1959.

Fraisse, Paul, *Psychologie du rythme*, Paris: P.U.F., 1974.

Friedrich, Hugo, *Structure de la poésie moderne*, 1956; Paris: Librairie Générale Française, 1999.

Gardes-Tamine, Joëlle, 'A propos de la représentation du rythme', *Travaux du Cercle Linguistique d'Aix-en-Provence* 9 (1991): 15-27.

Gauthier, Michel, *Système euphonique et rythmique du vers français*, Paris: Klincksieck, 1974.

Gendre, André, *Evolution du sonnet français*, Paris: P.U.F., 1996.

Ghil, René, *Traité du verbe*, Paris: Nizet, 1978.

Ghyka, Matila C., *Le Nombre d'Or: rites et rythmes pythagoriciens dans le développement de la civilisation occidentale*, 1931; 2 vols., Paris: Gallimard, vol.1 'Les rites', 1958, vol. 2 'Les rythmes', 1959.

--- *Essai sur le rythme*, 1938; Paris: Gallimard, 1952.

Gouvard, Jean-Michel, 'Métrique et métrico-métrie des poèmes de Jules Laforgue', mémoire de d.e.a. (avec relevé métrique informatisé), Centre d'Etudes Métriques, Université de Nantes, 1991.

--- 'Les mètres de Jules Laforgue: pour une analyse distributionnelle du vers de douze syllabes', *Cahiers du Centre d'Etudes Métriques* 1 (1992): 41-49.

--- 'Frontières de mot et frontières de morphème dans l'alexandrin: du vers classique au 12-syllabe de Verlaine', *Langue Française* 99 (1993): 45-62.

--- 'De la sémantique à la métrique: les "césures" de Verlaine', *Revue Verlaine* 1 (1993): 125-55.

--- 'Sur le statut phonologique de "e": la notion de "e" féminin dans l'alexandrin de Verlaine', *Revue Verlaine* 2 (1994): 87-107.

--- 'Recherches sur la métrique interne du vers composé dans la seconde moitié du dix-neuvième siècle. Pour une analyse distributionnelle systématique', doctoral thesis, Centre d'Etudes Métriques, Université de Nantes, 1994.

--- 'Le vers français: de la syllabe à l'accent', *Poétique* 106 (1996): 223-47.

--- 'Le vers d'*Alcools*', *Littératures contemporaines* 2 (1996): 183-213.

--- 'Métrique et rhétorique: l'alexandrin au 19e siècle', in *Ecriture / parole / discours: littérature et rhétorique au 19e siècle*, ed. by Alain Vaillant, Sainte-Etienne: Editions Printer, 1997: 215-38.

--- *Critique du vers*, Paris: Champion, 2000.

Gouvard, Jean-Michel and Steve Murphy, eds., *Verlaine à la loupe*, Paris: Champion, 2000.

Grammont, Maurice, *Petit Traité de versification française*, 1905; Paris: Colin, 1989.

--- *Le Vers français. Ses moyens d'expression. Son harmonie*, Paris: Delagrave, 1964.

Grimaud, Michel, 'Trimètre et rôle poétique de la césure chez Victor Hugo', *Romanic Review* 70 (1979): 56-58.

--- 'Versification and its discontents: Toward a research program', *Semiotica* 88:3-4 (1992): 199-242.

Grimaud, Michel, and Lawrence Baldwin, 'Versification cognitive: la strophe', *Poétique* 95 (1993): 259-76.

Guichard, Léon, *La Musique et les Lettres en France au Temps du Wagnérisme*, Paris: P.U.F., 1963.

Guilbaud, Jean-Luc, 'L'Alexandrin dans l'œuvre de Guillaume Apollinaire', *Cahiers du Centre d'Etudes Métriques* 3 (1996): 25-54.

Guiraud, Pierre, *La Versification*, Paris: P.U.F., coll. 'Que sais-je?', 1970.

Heugel, Jacques, *Dictionnaire des rimes françaises*, Paris: Editions de 'Psyché', 1941.

Hillery, David, *Music and Poetry in France: from Baudelaire to Mallarmé*, Berne: Peter Lang, 1980.

Holowacz, W., 'Le décasyllabe dans l'oeuvre de Paul Verlaine', mémoire de maîtrise, *Cahiers du Centre d'Etudes Métriques* 3 (1996): 99-122.

Hudson, Margaret Elizabeth, *The Juxtaposition of Accents at the Rime in French Versification*, Philadelphia: University of Philapdelphia, 'Publications of the Series in Romanic Languages and Literatures' 19, 1927.

Hugo, Victor, *Œuvres complètes*, ed. by Jean Massin, 18 vols., Paris: Le Club français du livre, 1967-70; vol. 7.

Ince, Walter, 'Some of Valéry's reflections on rhythm', in *Baudelaire, Mallarmé, Valéry: New Essays in Honour of Lloyd Austin*, ed. by Malcolm Bowie, Alison Fairlie and Alison Finch, Cambridge: C.U.P., 1982: 384-97.

Jacaret, Gilberte, *La Dialectique de l'ironie et du lyrisme dans Alcools et Calligrammes de Guillaume Apollinaire*, Paris: Nizet, 1984.

Jackson, John E., *La Poésie et son autre: essai sur la modernité*, Paris: José Corti, 1998.

Jaffré, Jean, *Le Vers et le poème*, Paris: Nathan, 1984.

Jankélévitch, Vladimir, *La Musique et l'Ineffable*, Paris: Armand Colin, 1961; Paris: Editions du Seuil, 1983.

Jarrety, Michel, *Dictionnaire de Poésie de Baudelaire à nos jours*, Paris: P.U.F., 2001.

Johnson, Barbara, 'Quelques conséquences de la différence anatomique des textes: pour une théorie du poème en prose', *Poétique* 28 (1976): 450-65.

Kastner, Léon Emile, *A History of French Versification*, Oxford: Clarendon Press, 1903; Norwood Editions, 1978.

Kristeva, Julia, *La révolution du langage poétique*, Paris: Editions du Seuil, 1974.

Landais, Napoléon and L. Barré, *Dictionnaire des rimes françaises disposé dans un ordre nouveau d'après la distinction des Rimes en suffisantes, riches et surabondantes, précédé d'un nouveau traité de versification*, Paris: Didier, 1853.

Landry, Eugène, *La Théorie du rythme et le rythme du français déclamé*, Paris: Champion, 1911.

Lanneau, Pierre-Antoine-Victoire Marey de, *Dictionnaire portatif des rimes françaises, rédigé d'après l'Académie*, Paris: Charles Froment, 1850.

Larousse, Pierre, *Grand Dictionnaire Universel du XIXe Siècle*, Paris, 1875.

--- *Nouveau Traité de la versification française accompagné d'exercices d'application*, Paris, 1896.

Le Hir, Yves, *Esthétique et structure du vers français*, Paris: P.U.F., 1956.

Leuwers, Daniel, *Introduction à la Poésie moderne et contemporaine*, Paris: Dunod, 1990.

Lewis, R. A., 'The Rhythmical Creation of Beauty', *Forum for Modern Language Studies* 6 (1970): 103-26.

--- *On Reading French Verse: A Study of Poetic Form*, Oxford: Clarendon Press, 1982.

Long, D. F., *Relevé et analyse métrique des œuvres poétiques non-dramatiques d'Alphonse de Lamartine*, Université de Nantes: Centre d'Etudes Métriques, 1992.

Lusson, Pierre, 'Notes Préliminaires sur le rythme', *Cahiers de Poétique Comparée* 1:1 (1973): 33-54.

--- 'Sur une théorie générale du rythme', in *Change de forme: Biologies et prosodies*, ed. by J.-P. Faye, Paris: U.G.E., coll. '10/18', 1975: 225-45.

--- 'Une méthode d'analyse des rapports texte/musique: application d'une théorie générale du rythme', *Mezura* 13 (1998): 7-45.

Lusson, Pierre and Jacques Roubaud, 'Mètre et rythme dans l'alexandrin ordinaire', *Langue Française* 23 (1974): 41-53.

Martinon, Philippe, *Dictionnaire méthodique et pratique des rimes françaises. Précédé d'un traité sur la versification*, Paris: Larousse, 1905.

Maulpoix, Jean-Michel, *La poésie malgré tout*, Paris: Mercure de France, 1996.

Mazaleyrat, Jean, *Pour une étude rythmique du vers français moderne*, Paris: Lettres Modernes Minard, 1963.

--- *Eléments de métrique française*, Paris: Armand Colin, 1974.

Melançon, Johanne, 'Du rythme musical au rythme poétique', *Protée* 18:1 (1990): 69-74.

Meschonnic, Henri, *Pour la poétique*, 3 vols, Paris: Gallimard, 1970.

--- ed., 'Poétique du vers français', *Langue française* 23 (1974), special edition.

--- 'Fragments d'une critique du rythme', *Langue Française* 23 (1974): 5-23.

--- *Critique du rythme: anthropologie historique du langage*, Lagrasse: Verdier, 1982.

--- *Le Rythme et la vie*, Lagrasse: Verdier, 1989.

--- *La Rime et la vie*, Lagrasse: Verdier, 1990.

--- *Politique du rythme, politique du sujet*, Lagrasse: Verdier, 1995.

Milner, Jean-Claude, 'Accent de vers et accent dans l'alexandrin classique', *Cahiers de Poésie Comparativiste* 15 (1987): 31-77.

Milner, Jean-Claude and François Regnault, *Dire le vers: Court traité à l'intention des acteurs et des amateurs d'alexandrins*, Paris: Editions du Seuil, 1987.

Molino, Jean and Joëlle Tamine, 'Des rimes, et quelques raisons...', *Poétique* 52 (1982): 487-98.

Moreau, François, *Six études de métrique*, Paris: S.E.D.E.S., 1987.

Moreau, P, *La tradition français du poème en prose avant Baudelaire*, Paris: Archives des lettres modernes, Jan-Feb 1959, 3:19-20.

Murat, Michel, ed., *Le Vers français: Histoire, théorie, esthétique*, Paris: Champion, coll. 'Métrique Française et Comparée', 1999.

--- ed., *L'Invention des formes poétiques, de Rimbaud au surréalisme*, Paris: P.U.F., coll. 'Perspectives littéraires', 2000.

Olovsson, Halvar, *Etude sur les Rimes de trois poètes romantiques: Musset, Gautier, Baudelaire*, Lund: C. Bloms boktryckeri, 1924.

O'Meara, Maurice A., 'La suggestivité des structures spirales dans cinq poèmes-clé de Baudelaire, Verlaine, Mallarmé et Apollinaire: Harmonie avec le mouvement cosmique', *Language and Style* 19:4 (1986): 368-76.

Parent, Monique, *Etudes sur le poème en prose*, Paris: Klincksieck, 1960.

--- ed., *Le Vers français au XXe siècle. Actes du colloque organisé par le Centre de Philologie et de Littérature Romanes de l'Université de Strasbourg, du 3 mai au 6 mai 1966*, Paris: Klincksieck, 1967.

Pensom, Roger, *Accent and metre in French: A theory of the relation between linguistic accent and metrical practice in French, 1100-1900*, Berne: Peter Lang, 1998.

--- 'The Stylistic Function of Metre in Some Imparisyllabic Lyrics of Verlaine', *French Studies* 49:3 (1995): 292-307.

--- 'Verlaine et le vers-librisme', in *Verlaine: 1896-1996*, ed. by Martine Bercot, Paris: Klincksieck, 1998: 265-77.

Philip, J. A., *Pythagoras and Early Pythagoreanism*, Toronto: University of Toronto Press, 1966.

Pirsig, Robert M., *Zen and the Art of Motorcycle Maintenance*, London: Vintage, 1974; 1991.

Poe, Edgar Allan, *Complete Poems and Selected Essays*, ed. by Richard Gray, London: Everyman, 1993.

Poulet, Georges, *La Poésie éclatée: Baudelaire / Rimbaud*, Paris: P.U.F., 1980.

Quicherat, Louis-Marie, *Traité de versification française*, Paris: Hachette, 1850.

Quitard, Pierre-Marie, *Dictionnaire des rimes, précédé d'un traité complet de versification*, Paris: Garnier, 1869.

Richelet, Pierre, *Dictionnaire des rimes*, Paris: Nyon, 1762.

Roubaud, Jacques, 'Mètre et vers (Deux applications de la métrique générative de Halle-Keyser)', *Poétique* 7 (1971): 366-87.

--- *La Vieillesse d'alexandre: essai sur quelques états récents du vers français*, Paris: Maspéro, 1978; Paris: Ramsay, 1988.

--- 'Dynastie: études sur le vers français. Sur l'alexandrin classique (1ère partie)', *Cahiers de poétique comparée* 13 (1986): 47-109.

--- *La forme du sonnet français de Marot à Malherbe*, 2 vols., Paris: Publications Langues'O: Cahiers de poétique comparée 17-19, 1990.

Sandras, Michel, *Lire le poème en prose*, Paris: Dunod, 1995.
Sauvanet, Pierre, 'Ordre et chaos ou du rythme en philosophie', *Ritm* 1 (1991): 125-33.
Scott, Clive, *French verse-art: A study*, Cambridge: C.U.P., 1980.
--- *A Question of Syllables*, Cambridge: C.U.P., 1986.
--- *The Riches of Rhyme*, Cambridge: C.U.P., 1988.
--- *Vers Libre: The Emergence of Free Verse in France 1886-1914*, Oxford: Clarendon Press, 1990.
--- *Reading the Rhythm: The Poetics of French Free Verse 1910-1930*, Oxford: Clarendon Press, 1993.
--- *The Poetics of French Verse: Studies in Reading*, Oxford: Clarendon Press, 1998.
Scott, David H. T., *Sonnet Theory and Practice in Nineteenth-century France: Sonnets on the Sonnet*, 'Occasional Papers in Modern Languages' 12, University of Hull Publications, 1977.
--- 'La structure spatiale du poème en prose', *Poétique* 59 (1984): 295-308.
Sommer, Edouard, *Petit Dictionnaire des rimes françaises, précédé d'un Précis des règles de la versification*, 1850; Paris: Hachette, 1859.
Soucy, Anne-Marie, 'Difficulties in the Genre of Prose Poetry', *Iris: Graduate Journal of Critical French Studies* 3:1 (1987): 53-64.
Souza, Robert de, *Le Rythme poétique*, Paris: Perrin, 1892.
Starobinski, Jean, 'Le Voile de Poppée', in *L'Œil vivant*, Paris: Gallimard, 1961; 9-27.
Steinmetz, Jean-Luc, *La poésie et ses raisons*, Paris: José Corti, 1990.
--- *signets. essais critiques sur la poésie du XVIIIe au XXe siècle*, Paris: José Corti, 1995.
Straka, Georges, 'Les rimes classiques et la prononciation française de l'époque', *Travaux de linguistique et de littérature* 23:1 (1985): 61-138.
Suberville, Jean, *Histoire et théorie de la versification française*, Paris: Editions de "l'Ecole", 1965.
Surenne, Gabriel, *French Pronouncing Dictionary*, Edinburgh: Oliver & Boyd, 1880
Tamine, Joëlle, 'Sur quelques contraintes qui limitent l'autonomie de la métrique', *Langue Française* 49 (1981): 68-76.
Ténint, Wilhelm, *Prosodie de l'école moderne*, Paris, 1844; ed. by Patricia Joan Siegel, Paris: Champion, 1986.
Tobler, Adolf, *Le vers français ancien et moderne*, transl. by Karl Breul and Léopold Sudre, pref. by Gaston Paris, Paris: 1885; Geneva: Slatkine, 1972.
Todorov, Tzvetan, *Poétique de la Prose*, Paris: Editions du Seuil, coll. 'Poétique', 1971.
--- 'La Poésie sans le vers', in *Les Genres du discours*, Paris: Editions du Seuil, 1978.
Vadé, Yves, *Le Poème en prose*, Paris: Belin, 1996.
Valéry, Paul, *Œuvres*, ed. by Jean Hytier, 2 vols., Paris: Gallimard, coll. 'Bibliothèque de la Pléiade', 1957 and 1960.
Verlaine, Paul, *Œuvres en prose complètes*, ed. by Jacques Borel, Paris: Gallimard, coll. 'Bibliothèque de la Pléiade', 1972.
Verluyten, Paul, 'Contraintes syntaxiques à la césure', in *Linguistique en Belgique* 4, ed. by Marc Dominicy and C. Peeters, Brussels: Didier, 1980: 219-52.
--- 'Historical metrics: the caesura in French', in *Papers from the 5th International Conference on Historical Linguistics*, ed. by Anders Ahlqvist, Amsterdam: John Benjamins, 1982: 356-61.

--- *Recherches sur la prosodie et la métrique du français*, doctoral thesis, University of Antwerp, 1982.

--- 'Prosodic structure and the development of French schwa', in *Papers from the 6th International Conference on Historical Linguistics*, ed. by Jacek Fisiak, Amsterdam: John Benjamins, 1985: 549-59.

--- 'L'Analyse de l'alexandrin: Mètre ou rythme?' in *Le Souci des apparences*, ed. by Marc Dominicy, Brussels: Editions de l'Université, 1989: 31-74.

Verrier, Paul, *Le Vers français*, 3 vols., Paris: Didier, 1931-32.

Vincent-Munnia, Nathalie, 'Premiers poèmes en prose: le spleen de la poésie', *Littérature* 91 (1993), 'Prose de poètes': 3-11.

--- *Les Premiers poèmes en prose: généalogie d'un genre dans la première moitié du XIXe siècle français*, Paris: Champion, 1996.

Volkoff, Vladimir, *Vers une métrique française*, Columbia, South Carolina: French Literature Publications Company, 1978.

Watson, Lawrence and Rosemary Lloyd, eds., *Patterns of Evolution in Nineteenth-Century French Poetry*, Deddington: Tallents, 1991.

Wing, Nathaniel, *The Limits of Narrative: Essays on Baudelaire, Flaubert, Rimbaud and Mallarmé*, Cambridge: C.U.P., 1986.

Zink, Gaston, *Phonétique historique du français*, 1986; 3ᵉ édition, Paris: P.U.F., 1991.

BIBLIOGRAPHY II. BAUDELAIRE

Primary texts

Baudelaire, Charles, *Œuvres Complètes*, ed. by Claude Pichois, 2 vols., Paris: Gallimard, coll. 'Bibliothèque de la Pléiade', 1975-76.

--- *Correspondance*, ed. by Claude Pichois, 2 vols., Paris: Gallimard, coll. 'Bibliothèque de la Pléiade', 1973; vol. 1 reprinted in 1993 with supplement; vol. 2 reprinted in 1999.

--- *Les Fleurs du Mal*, ed. by Graham Chesters, London: Bristol Classical Press, 1995.

--- *Les Fleurs du Mal*, ed. by John E. Jackson, Paris: Librairie Générale Française, 'Le Livre de Poche. Classique', 1999.

--- *Nouvelles lettres*, ed. by Claude Pichois, Paris: Fayard, 2000.

Secondary texts

Abou Ghannan, Anis 'Sur le sonnet baudelairien', *Poétique* 79 (1989): 349-62.

Antoine, Gérald, 'Pour une nouvelle exploration "stylistique" du *gouffre* baudelairien', *Le Français Moderne* 30 (1962): 81-98.

Antoine, Gérald, *et al*, *Baudelaire. Actes du colloque de Nice (25-27 mai 1967)*, Annales de la Faculté des Lettres et Sciences Humaines de Nice, Paris: Minard, 1968.

--- 'Expansion sémantique et sonore dans Les Fleurs du Mal', *Etudes baudelairiennes* 8, Neuchâtel: A la Baconnière, 1976: 9-45.

Bandy, William T., *Index des rimes des Fleurs du Mal*, Nashville: Vanderbilt University, 'Publications du Centre d'Etudes baudelairiennes', 1972.

Bauer, Franck, 'Le poème en prose: un joujou de pauvre?', *Poétique* 109 (1997): 17-37.

Beebee, Tom, 'Orientalism, Absence and the Poème en Prose', *Rackham Journal of the Arts and Humanities* 2:1 (1981): 48-71.

Bercot, Martine, *Baudelaire, Les Fleurs du Mal: L'Intériorité de la forme, Actes du colloque du 7 janvier 1989*, Paris: S.E.D.E.S., 1989.

Bercot, Martine, and André Guyaux, eds., *Dix Etudes sur Baudelaire*, Paris: Champion, 1993.

Blanchot, Maurice, 'L'échec de Baudelaire', in *La Part du feu*, Paris: Gallimard, N.R.F., 1949: 133-51.

Broome, Peter, *Baudelaire's Poetic Patterns: the secret language of 'Les Fleurs du Mal'*, Amsterdam: Rodopi, 1999.

Burton, Richard D. E., *Baudelaire in 1859, A Study in the Poetic Sources of Creativity*, Cambridge: C.U.P., 1988.

--- , 'Destruction as Creation: 'Le Mauvais Vitrier' and the Poetics and Politics of Violence', *Romanic Review* 83:3 (1992): 297-322.

Cargo, Robert T., ed., *A Concordance to Baudelaire's Les Fleurs du Mal*, Chapel Hill: University of North Carolina Press, 1965.

--- ed., *Concordance to Baudelaire's Petits Poèmes en Prose*, University of Alabama Press, 1971.

Cassagne, Albert, *Versification et métrique de Charles Baudelaire*, Paris: Hachette, 1906; Geneva: Slatkine, 1982.

Cellier, Léon, *Baudelaire et Hugo*, Paris: José Corti, 1970.

Chesters, Graham, *Some Functions of Sound-repetition in 'Les Fleurs du Mal'*, University of Hull Publications, 'Occasional Papers in Modern Languages' 11, 1975.

--- 'Baudelaire and the Limits of Poetry', *French Studies* 32 (1978): 420-34.

--- 'The Transformation of a Prose-Poem: Baudelaire's 'Crépuscule de soir'' in *Baudelaire, Mallarmé, Valéry*, ed. by Malcolm Bowie, Alison Fairlie and Alison Finch, Cambridge: C.U.P., 1982: 24-37.

--- 'Baudelaire et un problème de versification: voyelle + e atone', *Bulletin des études parnassiennes* 7 (1985): 12-26.

--- *Baudelaire and the Poetics of Craft*, Cambridge: C.U.P., 1988.

Cohn, Robert Greer, 'Baudelaire's Beleaguered Prose Poems', in *Textual Analysis: Some Readers Reading*, ed. by Mary Ann Caws, New York: Modern Languages Association of America, 1986: pages unknown.

Compagnon, Antoine, 'Baudelaire et les deux infinis', *Le Genre humain* 24 (1992), 'Fini & infini': 115-34.

Cornulier, Benoit de, *Les Fleurs du Mal de Baudelaire*, relevé métrique, base de données MS Works 2.0 sur MacIntosh, Nantes: Centre d'Etudes Métriques, 1987.

--- 'Métrique des *Fleurs du Mal*', in *Les Fleurs du Mal: l'intériorité de la forme*, ed. by Martine Bercot, Paris: S.E.D.E.S., 1989; 55-76.

--- 'Pour une analyse du sonnet dans Les Fleurs du Mal', in *Lectures des Fleurs du Mal*, ed. by Steve Murphy, Presses Universitaires de Rennes, 2002; 197-236.

Cunen, Frédéric, 'Le Gouffre et l'Abîme de Baudelaire', *Travaux de linguistique et de littérature* 15:2 (1977), 109-41.

Dayan, Peter, 'De la traduction en musique chez Baudelaire', *Romance Studies* 18:2 (2000): 145-55.

Deguy, Michel, 'L'Infini et sa diction ou de la diérèse (Etude baudelairienne)', *Poétique* 40 (1979): 432-44.

Delabroy, Jean and Yves Charnet, eds., *Baudelaire: nouveaux chantiers*, Lille: Presses Universitaires du Septentrion, 1995.

Derrida, Jacques, *Donner le temps 1: La fausse monnaie*, Paris: Galilée, 1991.

Emmanuel, Pierre, *Baudelaire, la femme et Dieu*, Paris: Editions du Seuil, coll. 'Points', 1982.

Fairlie, Alison, 'Reflections on the successive versions of 'Une gravure fantastique'', *Etudes baudelairiennes* 3, Neuchâtel: A la Baconnière, 1973: 217-32.

--- '"Mène-t-on la foule dans les ateliers?": Some remarks on Baudelaire's variants', in *Order and Adventure in Post-Romantic French Poetry*: ed. by E. M. Beaumont, J. M. Cocking and J. Cruickshank, Oxford: Blackwell, 1973: 17-37.

Fondane, Benjamin, *Baudelaire et l'expérience du gouffre*, Paris: Seghers, 1947; Brussels: Editions Complexe, 1994.

Froidevaux, Gérald, *Baudelaire: représentation et modernité*, Paris: José Corti, 1989.

Galand, René, *Baudelaire: Poétiques et Poésie*, Paris: Nizet, 1969.

Gendre, André, 'Examen syntaxique et stylistique de quelques sonnets baudelairiens', *Etudes baudelairiennes* 8, Neuchâtel: A la Baconnière, 1976: 46-94.

Godfrey, Sima, 'Baudelaire's Windows', *L'Esprit Créateur* 22:4 (1982): 83-100.

Goulbourne, Russell, 'The Sound of Silence... Points de suspension in Baudelaire's *Les Fleurs du Mal*', *Australian Journal of French Studies* 36 (1999): 200-13.

Grojnowski, Daniel, 'De Baudelaire à Poe: l'effet de totalité', *Poétique* 105 (1996): 101-9.

Guiette, Robert, 'Vers et prose chez Baudelaire', in *Journées Baudelaire*, Brussels: Académie Royale de Langue et de Littérature Françaises, 1968: 36-46.

--- 'Des 'Paradis artificiels' aux 'Petits Poèmes en Prose'', *Etudes baudelairiennes* 3, Neuchâtel: A la Baconnière, 1973: 178-85.

Guiraud, Pierre, 'Le champ stylistique du *gouffre* de Baudelaire', *Orbis Litterarum*, supplement (1958): 75-84.

Hiddleston, J. A., *Essai sur Laforgue et les 'Derniers Vers', suivi de 'Laforgue et Baudelaire'*, Lexington: French Forum, 1980.

--- *Baudelaire and Le Spleen de Paris*, Oxford: Clarendon Press, 1987.

Hirt, André, *Baudelaire: l'Exposition de la Poésie*, Paris: Editions Kimé, 1998.

Hogarth, William, *Analyse de la Beauté, destinée à fixer les idées vagues qu'on a du goût*, 1753; trans. by Jansen, rev. by Serge Chauvin, pref. by Bernard Cottret, Paris: Ecole nationale supérieure des Beaux-Arts, 1991.

Inoue, Teruo, *Une Poétique de l'Ivresse chez Charles Baudelaire*, Tokyo: Editions France-Tosho, 1977.

Jackson, R. F., 'Baudelaire, "Le Gouffre" and the Critics', *Australian Journal of French Studies* 11:1 (1974): 41-53.

Jakobson, Roman, 'Une microscopie du dernier Spleen dans *Les Fleurs du Mal*', in *Questions de poétique*, Paris: Editions du Seuil, 1973: 420-35.

--- 'Les Chats', in *Questions de poétique*, Paris: Editions du Seuil, 1973: 401-19.

Jamison, Anne, 'Any Where Out of this Verse: Baudelaire's Prose Poetics and the Aesthetics of Transgression', *Nineteenth Century French Studies* 29 (2001) 256-86.

Johnson, Barbara, *Défigurations du langage poétique: La seconde révolution baudelairienne*, Paris: Flammarion, 1979.

Journées Baudelaire: Actes du Colloque Namur-Bruxelles 10-13 octobre 1967, Brussels: Académie Royale de Langue et de Littérature Française, 1968.

Lawler, James R., 'The Prose Poem as Art of Anticlimax: Baudelaire's "Kaleidoscope"', *Australian Journal of French Studies* 36:3 (1999) 327-38.

Leakey, F. W., *Baudelaire and Nature*, Manchester University Press, 1969.

--- *Baudelaire. Collected Essays 1953-1988*, Cambridge: C.U.P., 1990.

Leakey, F. W., and Claude Pichois, 'Les Sept Versions des "Sept Vieillards"', *Etudes baudelairiennes* 3, Neuchâtel: A la Baconnière, 1973: 262-89.

Lloyd, Rosemary, 'Horrifying the Homais: The Challenge of the Prose Poem', *Esprit Créateur* 39:1 (1999): 37-47.

Loncke, Joycelynne, *Baudelaire et la Musique*, Paris: Nizet, 1975.

Lüdi-Knecht, Karin Edith, 'La dialectique du nombre chez Baudelaire', doctoral thesis, dir. by Georges Poulet, Zurich: Juris Druck & Verlag, 1974.

Murphy, Steve, 'Le Mauvais Vitrier ou la crise du verre', *Romanic Review* 81 (1990): 339-49.

--- 'L'Hiéroglyphe et son interprétation: l'association d'idées dans 'Le Tir et le cimetière"', *Bulletin baudelairien* 30:2 (1993): 61-84.

--- 'Le Complexe de supériorité et la contagion du rire: Un plaisant de Baudelaire', *Travaux de littérature* 7 (1994): 257-85.

--- 'Haunting Memories: Inquest and Exorcism in Baudelaire's "La Corde"', *Dalhousie French Studies* 30 (1995): 65-91.

--- 'La scène parisienne: lecture d'"Une mort héroïque" de Baudelaire', in *Le Champ littéraire, 1860-1900: études offertes à Michael Pakenham*, ed. by Keith Cameron and James Kearns (Amsterdam: Rodopi, 1996): 49-61.

--- ed., *Lectures des Fleurs du Mal*, Presses Universitaires de Rennes, 2002.

--- *Logiques du dernier Baudelaire*, Paris: Champion, 2003.

Nøjgaard, Morten, *Elévation et expansion*, Odense University Press, 1973.

Nuiten, Henk, *Les Variantes des 'Fleurs du Mal' et des 'Epaves' de Charles Baudelaire*, Amsterdam-Academic Publishers Associated: Holland University Press, 1979.

Pellegrin, Jean, 'Rythmes baudelairiens', *Cahiers de Sémiotique Textuelle* 14 (1988): 51-63.

Pensom, Roger, 'Le poème en prose: de Baudelaire à Rimbaud', *French Studies* 56:1 (2002): 15-28

Poulet, Georges, *Etudes sur le temps humain*, vol. 1, ch. 16, Paris: Plon, 1952.

Robb, Graham, *La poésie de Baudelaire et la poésie française 1838-1852*, Paris: Aubier, 1993.

Ruff, Marcel A., 'Baudelaire et le poème en prose', *Zeitschrift für französische Sprache und Literatur* 77 (1967): 116-23.

Sainte-Beuve, Charles-Augustin, *Vie, Poésies et Pensées de Joseph Delorme*, 1829; ed. by Gérald Antoine, Paris: Nouvelles Editions Latines, 1956; Paris: Editions d'Aujourd'hui, coll. 'Les Introuvables', 1985.

Scott, Clive, 'A privileged syllable: the articulated a in *Les Fleurs du Mal*'; in *A Question of Syllables*, Cambridge: C.U.P., 1986: 86-117.

--- *Translating Baudelaire*, University of Exeter: North Western University Press, 2001; ch. 2, 'Translating Rhythm'.

Scott, David H. T., 'Le Poème en prose comme symptôme de crise littéraire: Hétérogénéité et déconstruction dans *Le Spleen de Paris* de Baudelaire', *Esprit Créateur* 39:1 (1999): 5-14.

Sieburth, Richard, 'Gaspard de la nuit: Prefacing Genre', *Studies in Romanticism* 24:2 (1985): 239-55.
Soucy, Anne-Marie, 'Baudelaire's Prose Poem and Contemporary Theory', *Forum for Modern Language Studies* 24:1 (1988): 27-36.
Stephens, Sonya, *Baudelaire's Prose Poems – The Practice and Politics of Irony*, Oxford: O.U.P., 1999.
Thélot, Jérôme, *Baudelaire, violence et poésie*, Paris: Gallimard, coll. 'Bibliothèque des Idées', 1993.
Trahard, Pierre, *Essai Critique sur Baudelaire Poète*, Paris: Nizet, 1973; ch. 7, 'Baudelaire versificateur'.
Tucci, Nina S., 'Baudelaire's "Les Sept vieillards": The Archetype Seven, Symbol of Destructive Time', *Orbis litterarum* 44:1 (1989): 69-79.
Wright, Barbara, and David H. T. Scott, *La Fanfarlo and Le Spleen de Paris*, London: Grant & Cutler, 1984.

BIBLIOGRAPHY III. RIMBAUD

Primary Texts

Rimbaud, Arthur, *Œuvres Complètes*, Paris: Gallimard, coll. 'Bibliothèque de la Pléiade', 1972.
--- *Illuminations*, ed. by Nick Osmond, London: Athlone Press, 1976.
--- *Œuvres complètes*, vol. I, ed. by Steve Murphy, Paris: Champion, 1999.
--- *Poésies, Une saison en enfer, Illuminations*, ed. by Louis Forrestier; 1965 edition, revised 1999, Paris: Gallimard, coll. 'Folio Classique', 1999.

Secondary Texts

Argote, Joel Thompson, 'Colliding Fragments: The *Illuminations* as Collage', *Romance Notes* 37:2 (1997): 199-206.
Aroui, Jean-Louis, 'Rimbaud: les rimes d'une *Larme*', *Parade sauvage* 13 (1995): 24-44.
--- review of Fongaro's 'Segments métriques', *Parade sauvage* 13 (1995): 156-59.
Arouimi, Michel, 'L'enjeu métaphysique de Rimbaud', *Sud* 'Arthur Rimbaud: bruits neufs' (1991): 61-79.
Backès, Jean-Louis, 'Rimbaud musicien', *Romantisme: Revue du Dix-Neuvième Siècle* 12:36 (1982): 51-63.
Bandelier, Danielle, 'La prosodie des *Romances sans paroles* et des *Derniers vers*', *Versants* 9 (1986): 49-60.
--- 'Les rimes de Verlaine et de Rimbaud: l'aventure poétique de la contestation du vers', in *Arthur Rimbaud: Poesia e avventura*, ed. by Mario Matucci, Pisa: Pacini, 1987: 181-88.
Bivort, Olivier, 'Ecriture de l'échec, écriture du désir', *Parade sauvage colloque 2* (1990): 207-15.
--- 'Le tiret dans les *Illuminations*', *Parade sauvage* 8 (1991): 2-8.
Bivort, Olivier and André Guyaux, *Bibliographie des 'Illuminations' (1878-1990)*, Paris: Champion, 1991.

Bivort, Olivier and Steve Murphy, *Rimbaud: publications autour d'un centenaire*, Torino: Rosenberg and Tellier, 1994.

Bobillot, Jean-Pierre, 'Rimbaud et le "vers libre"', *Poétique* 66 (1986): 199-216.

--- 'Rimbaud moderne? Absolument!', *Impressions du Sud* 29 (1991).

--- 'Entre mètre et non-mètre: le "décasyllabe" chez Rimbaud', *Parade Sauvage* 10 (1994): 29-44.

--- 'Le *clinamen*, d'Arthur Rimbaud. Travail du rythme et matérialisme dans les vers de 1872', in *Rimbaud 1891-1991. Actes du colloque d'Aix en Provence et de Marseille*, ed. by André Guyaux, Paris: Champion, 1994.

--- review of *Rimbaud. Tradition et Modernité*, ed. by Bertrand Marchal, *Parade sauvage* 13 (1995): 133-43.

--- 'Vaches, mouches, figures: *Les Reparties de Nina, Chanson de la plus haute tour, Chanson de la plus haute tour*', *Parade Sauvage* 14 (1997): 19-32.

Bonnefoy, Yves, *Rimbaud par lui-même*, Paris: Editions du Seuil, 1961.

Borer, Alain, ed., *Rimbaud Multiple. Colloque de Cerisy, dirigé par Alain Borer, Jean-Paul Corsetti et Steve Murphy*, Gourdon: D. Bedou et J. Touzot, 1986.

Carter, William C. and Robert F. Vines, *A Concordance to the 'Œuvres Complètes' of Arthur Rimbaud*, Athens: Ohio University Press, 1978.

Chadwick, Charles, *Etudes sur Rimbaud*, Paris: Nizet, 1960.

--- 'La poésie des *Illuminations*', *La Revue des Lettres Modernes* 370-73 (1973): 43-61.

--- *Rimbaud*, London: The Athlone Press, 1979.

Charolles, Michel, 'Le texte poétique et sa signification: Une lecture du poème intitulé "Mouvement" (Illuminations) et de quelques commentaires qui en ont été donnés', *Europe*: 529-30 (1973): 97-114.

Chataigné, Henriette, review of Fongaro's 'Segments métriques', *Parade Sauvage* 13 (1995): 155-56.

Coates, Carrol F., 'Structuration phonémique et poétique iconoclaste: Les vers métriques de Rimbaud', *Parade Sauvage colloque 3*, 'Rimbaud cent ans après' (1992): 87-103.

--- 'Phonemic Structuration and the Reading of the Poem: Rimbaud's "Le Châtiment de Tartufe" and "Cocher ivre"', in *Understanding French Poetry: Essays for a New Millenium*, ed. by Stamos Metzidakis, New York: Garland, 1994: 87-97.

--- '"A": sur l'"Ophélie" de Rimbaud', *Degrés* 25:104 (2000), h.

Cornulier, Benoit de, "Métrique du vers de 12-syllabes chez Rimbaud", *Le Français Moderne*, 48:2 (1980): 140-74.

--- *Poésies complètes d'Arthur Rimbaud*, relevé métrique, base de données MS Works 2.0 sur MacIntosh, Nantes: Centre d'Etudes Métriques, 1988.

--- 'Mètre "impair", métrique "insaisissable"? Sur les "derniers vers" de Rimbaud', in *Le Souci des apparences*, ed. by Marc Dominicy, Brussels: Editions de l'Université, 1989: 75-91.

--- 'Sur la métrique des "premiers vers" de Rimbaud', *Parade Sauvage colloque 2* (1990): 4-15.

--- 'L'alexandrin zutique métricométrifié', *Parade Sauvage colloque 3*, 'Rimbaud cent ans après' (1992): 83-86.

--- 'La chambre ouverte d'un *Jeune Ménage*; sur un poème de Rimbaud', in *De la musique à la linguistique, Hommages à Nicolas Ruwet*, ed. by Lilianne Tasmowski and Anne Zribi-Hertz, Ghent: Communication and Cognition, 1992: 57-70.

330 *Rhythm, Illusion and the Poetic Idea*

--- 'Lecture de "Qu'est-ce pour nous, mon cœur" de Rimbaud comme dialogue dramatique du poète avec son cœur', *Studi Francesi* 106 (1992): 37-59.

--- 'Illuminations Métriques: Lire ou faire des vers dans la prose à Rimbaud', in *Rimbaud 1891-1991. Actes du colloque d'Aix-en-provence et de Marseille*, ed. by André Guyaux, Paris: Champion, 1994: 103-23.

--- 'Le violon enragé d'Arthur pour ses *Petites Amoureuses*', *Parade Sauvage* 15 (1998): 19-32.

--- 'Rimbaud rimeur étourdi des *Premières Communions*', *Cahiers du Centre d'Etudes Métriques* 4 (1999): 159-83.

Corsetti, Jean-Paul, 'Victor Hugo et Arthur Rimbaud: mimétisme et parodie', *Parade sauvage* 3 (1986): 18-25.

--- *Essais sur Rimbaud*, Charleville-Mézières: Musée-Bibliothèque Arthur Rimbaud, coll. 'Bibliothèque sauvage', 1994.

Décaudin, Michel, 'Des 'vers nouveaux' aux 'illuminations'. Une aventure de l'écriture', in *Arthur Rimbaud: Poesia e avventura*, ed. by Mario Matucci, Pisa: Pacini, 1987: 7-12.

Dednam, Sabine, 'Poésies et musique dans les Lettres du voyant de Rimbaud', *Revue d'Histoire Littéraire de la France* 89:2 (1989): 220-229.

Didier, Béatrice, 'Le motif musical dans l'œuvre de Rimbaud', in *Arthur Rimbaud. Poesia e Aventurra*, ed. by Mario Matucci, Pisa: Pacini, 1987: 13-32.

Dobay Rifelj, Carol de, 'Rimbaud's "A la musique": Language and Silence', *Romance Notes* 21 (1980): 174-77.

Doerry, Hilda, 'Une comparaison de structures: 'Une Mort héroïque' de Baudelaire et 'Après le déluge' de Rimbaud', *Chimères: A Journal of French and Italian Literature* 18:2 (1986): 67-74.

Dominicy, Marc, '*Tête de faune* ou les règles d'une exception', *Parade Sauvage* 15 (1998): 109-88.

Dragacci-Paulsen, Françoise, 'Ironie et subversion dans *Mauvais Sang* ou le rêve rimbaldien d'expansion du Moi', *Parade sauvage* 10 (1994): 76-93.

Ducoffre, David, 'Lecture d'"A une Raison"', *Parade sauvage* 16 (2000): 85-100.

Eigeldinger, Frédéric, 'Rimbaud et la transgression de "la vieillerie poétique": Ponctuation et rejets dans ses alexandrins', *Revue d'Histoire Littéraire de la France* 83:1 (1983): 45-64.

--- '*Une Saison en enfer' d'Arthur Rimbaud: Table de concordances rythmique et syntaxique*, Neuchâtel: A la Baconnière, 1984.

--- '*Poésies' d'Arthur Rimbaud: Table de concordances*, Neuchâtel: A la Baconnière, 1986.

--- *Table de concordances rythmique et syntaxique des 'Illuminations' d'Arthur Rimbaud*, Neuchâtel: A la Baconnière, 1986.

Eigeldinger, Frédéric, Gérald Schaeffer and André Bandelier, eds., *Table de concordances rythmique et syntaxique des 'Poésies' d'Arthur Rimbaud*, 2 vols; vol.1 *Poésies 1869-1872*, vol.2 *Table de concordances*, Neuchâtel: A la Baconnière-Payot, 1981.

Eigeldinger, Marc, 'L'inscription du silence dans le texte rimbaldien', in *Lumières du mythe*, Paris: P.U.F., coll. 'Ecritures', 1983.

Fongaro, Antoine, 'Les Vers mesurés dans "Illuminations"', *Littératures* 8 (1983): 63-79.

--- *Sur Rimbaud. Lire 'Illuminations'*, Les Cahiers de *Littératures*, Publications de l'Université de Toulouse-Le Mirail, 1985.

--- *'fraguements' rimbaldiques*, Les Cahiers de *Littératures*, Presses Universitaires du Mirail-Toulouse, 1989.

--- 'Matériaux pour lire Rimbaud', Les Cahiers de *Littératures*, Presses Universitaires du Mirail-Toulouse, 1990.

--- *Segments métriques dans la prose d'Illuminations*, Presses Universitaires du Mirail-Toulouse, 1993.

--- *Rimbaud: texte, sens et interprétations*, Presses Universitaires du Mirail-Toulouse, 1994.

Fusco, Susan Wirth, *Syntactic Structure in Rimbaud's Illuminations: A Stylistic Approach to the Analysis of Form in Prose Poetry*, University of Mississippi, Romance Monographs, 1990.

Girard, Alain, 'Statues de silence: Note sur le statut de la poésie dans la communication à travers la question du sujet chez Rimbaud et Mallarmé', *Les Lettres Romanes* (1993): 75-99.

Gouvard, Jean-Michel, '*La Chanson de la plus haute tour* est-elle une chanson? Etude métrique et pragmatique', *Parade Sauvage* 10 (1994): 45-63.

Guyaux, André, 'Pour l'analyse des *Illuminations*' in *Le Mythe d'Etiemble: hommage, études et recherches*, Paris: Didier Erudition, 1979: 93-101.

--- ed., *Lectures de Rimbaud*, Editions de l'Université de Bruxelles, 1982.

--- *Poétique du fragment: Essai sur les 'Illuminations' de Rimbaud*, Neuchâtel: A la Baconnière, 1985.

--- 'Aspects de la réception des Illuminations (1886-1936)', *Revue d'Histoire Littéraire de la France* 87:2 (1987): 191-99.

--- *Duplicités de Rimbaud*, Paris: Champion, 1991.

--- 'Mystères et clartés du guillemet rimbaldien', *Parade Sauvage* 8 (1991): 26-34.

--- 'Entre prose et vers', in *Rimbaud, tradition et modernité*, ed. by Bertrand Marchal, Mont-de-Marsan: Editions InterUniversitaires, 1992: 17-33.

--- ed., *Rimbaud 1891-1991. Actes du colloque d'Aix en Provence et de Marseille*, Paris: Champion, 1994.

--- 'Les variantes dans les poésies de Rimbaud : leur relation avec la "mécanique du vers"', *Parade Sauvage* 11 (1994): 59-66.

--- 'Les variantes et la mécanique du vers', *Romanic Review* 86:3 (1995): 463-72.

Hackett, C. A., *Rimbaud. A Critical Introduction*, Cambridge: C.U.P., 1981.

Hambly, P. S., 'Lecture de *Ma Bohème*', *Parade Sauvage bulletin* (March 1988): 27-41.

Henry, Albert, 'Lecture de quelques *Illuminations*', Paris: Palais des Académies, 1989.

--- 'Le Thème de la création poétique dans les *Illuminations*', *Parade Sauvage colloque 2* (1990): 187-98.

--- 'Le loup criait sous les feuilles', *Parade Sauvage* 10 (1994): 67-75.

--- 'Lecture de *Conte*', *Parade Sauvage* 11 (1994): 103-6.

--- *Contributions à la lecture de Rimbaud*, Brussels: Académie Royale de Belgique, 1998.

--- 'Est-elle almée?...', *Parade Sauvage* 15 (1998): 40-8.

Hier, L., 'D'une irrégularité dans la disposition des rimes, chez Rimbaud', *Centre Culturel Arthur Rimbaud* 11 (1991): 2-3.

Hirai, Hiroyuki, 'Un mémoire sur la *Mémoire* de Rimbaud', *Parade Sauvage* 8 (1991): 91-99.

Hubert, Renee Riese, 'The Use of Reversals in Rimbaud's "Illuminations"', *L'Esprit Créateur* 9:1 (1969): 9-18.

Jutrin, Monique, 'Parole et silence dans 'Une Saison en enfer': L'Expérience du 'moi divisé'', *La Revue des Lettres Modernes* 445-49 (1976): 7-23.

Kim, Jong-Ho, 'Le vide et le corps des *Illuminations*', Charleville-Mézières: Musée-Bibliothèque Arthur Rimbaud, coll. 'Bibliothèque sauvage', 1993.

Kittang, Atle, *Discours et jeu: essai d'analyse des textes d'Arthur Rimbaud*, Presses Universitaires de Grenoble, 1975.

Laurent, Emmanuelle, 'Le 'pleur qui chante': sur les chansons des Derniers Vers', *Parade Sauvage* 7 (1991): 16-30.

Little, Roger, *Rimbaud: Illuminations*, London: Grant & Cutler, 1983.

--- ed., 'Rimbaud: Bruits neufs', *Sud: Revue Littéraire*, numéro hors-série, 1991.

--- 'L'innommable et l'indicible dans les *Illuminations*', *Parade sauvage* 11 (1994): 113-22.

Macklin, Gerald M., 'A Study of Beginnings and Finales in Arthur Rimbaud's *Illuminations*', *Neophilologus* 68:1 (1984): 22-36.

--- 'Aspects of the Rimbaldian Prose Poem: Pattern and Disorder in the *Illuminations*', *Orbis Litterarum* 45:3 (1990): 248-72.

--- 'Rimbaud mystificateur: Distancing the Reader in the *Illuminations*', *French Studies Bulletin* 56 (1995): 8-12.

Mandrant, Jacqueline, 'Rythmes de l'oubli, cadences de la mémoire: l'ombre du doute et sa représentation', *Parade Sauvage* 3 (1986): 78-96; *Parade Sauvage* 4 (1986): 39-54.

Marchal, Bertrand, ed., *Rimbaud, Tradition et Modernité*, Mont-de-Marsan: Editions InterUniversitaires, 1992.

Marshall, Lindsay, 'Poetic Doctrine in Three of Rimbaud's Verse Poems', *Orbis Litterarum* 38:2 (1983): 124-39.

Matucci, Mario, ed., *Arthur Rimbaud: Poesia e Avventura: actes du colloque de Grosseto, 11-14 sept 1985*, Pisa: Pacini, 1987.

Meyer, Bernard, 'Chanson de la plus haute tour', *Parade Sauvage* 9 (1994): 32-58.

--- *Sur les 'Derniers Vers'. Douze lectures de Rimbaud*, Paris : L'Harmattan, coll. 'Poétiques', 1996.

--- 'Honte', *Parade Sauvage* 16 (2000): 29-44.

Mortier, Roland, 'La Notion d'harmonie dans les *Illuminations*', in *Mélanges à la mémoire de Franco Simone, IV: Tradition et originalité dans la création littéraire*, Geneva: Slatkine, 1983: 442-49.

Murat, Michel, 'A propos de *Mouvement*', *Parade Sauvage* 4 (1986): 69-77.

--- 'Du vers à la prose : le dégagement de l'écriture', in *Arthur Rimbaud : Poesia e Avventura*, ed. by Mario Matucci, Pisa: Pacini, 1987: 59-68.

--- 'Rimbaud et la poétique du sonnet', *Parade Sauvage* 13 (1996): 5-23.

--- 'Rimbaud et le vers libre. Remarques sur l'invention d'une forme', *Revue d'Histoire Littéraire de la France* 100:2 (2000): 255-76.

Murphy, Steve, *Le Premier Rimbaud ou l'apprentissage de la subversion*, Paris: Editions du C.N.R.S. / Presses Universitaires de Lyon, 1990.

--- '"Une Saison en enfer" et les "Derniers vers" de Rimbaud: Rupture ou continuité?', *Revue d'Histoire Littéraire de la France* 95:6 (1995): 958-73.

Plessen, Jacques, *Promenade et Poésie: L'expérience de la marche et du mouvement dans l'oeuvre de Rimbaud*, Paris: Mouton, 1967.

--- 'Après le déluge: une lecture', *Parade sauvage* 4 (1986):11-22.

--- 'The Tribulations of the Alexandrine in the Work of Rimbaud: A Contest between Innovation and Convention', in *Convention and Innovation in Literature*, ed. by Theo D'haen, Rainer Grubel and Helmut Lethen, Amsterdam: Benjamins, 1991: 253-72.

Reboul, Yves, 'A propos de l'*Homme juste*', *Parade Sauvage* 2 (1985): 44-54.

--- 'Lecture de Michel et Christine', *Parade Sauvage colloque 2* (1990): 52-59.

Ribi, Max, *Essai d'une rythmique des 'Illuminations'*, Zurich: Uto, 1948.

Ricciulli, Paola, 'J'écrivais des silences...', *Parade sauvage* 15 (1998): 73-85.

Richard, Jean-Pierre, 'Rimbaud ou la poésie du devenir', in *Poésie et profondeur*, Paris: Editions du Seuil, 1955.

Richter, Mario, 'Echos baudelairiens dans le 'prologue d'*Une saison en enfer* de Rimbaud', *Parade sauvage* 15 (1998): 86-90.

--- '"La Beauté", clef de lecture d'*Une saison en enfer*', in *Les Valenciennes* 13 (1990), 'Malédiction ou révolution poétique: Lautréamont/Rimbaud, Colloque de Cerisy-la-Salle, 15-22 juillet 1989', ed. by Jean-Paul Corsetti and Steve Murphy: 167-73.

Robinson-Valery, Judith, *Rimbaud, Valéry et "l'incohérence harmonique"*, Paris: Lettres Modernes Minard, 1979.

Sacchi, Sergio, '"Aube": temps et rythmes de l'Illumination', in *Poesia e Avventura*, ed. by Mario Matucci, Pisa: Pacini, 1987: 93-108.

--- ed., *Rimbaud: Le Poème en prose et la traduction poétique*, Tubingen: Gunter Narr Verlag, 1988.

Steinmetz, Jean-Luc, 'Ici, maintenant, les Illuminations', *Littérature* 11 (1973): 22-45.

--- *Arthur Rimbaud. Une question de présence*, Paris: Tallandier, 1991.

Thisse, André, *Rimbaud devant Dieu*, Paris: José Corti, 1975.

Watson, Lawrence, 'Rimbaud et le Parnasse', *Parade Sauvage colloque 1* (1987): 18-29.

Wing, Nathaniel, *Present Appearances: aspects of poetic structure in Rimbaud's 'Illuminations'*, University of Mississippi, Romance Monographs, 1974.

York, R.A, 'Aspects of Intersentence Connection in Rimbaud's "Les Illuminations"', *Language and Style: An International Journal* 13:2 (1980): 146-55.

Yuasa, Hiroo, 'De la franchise première à la nouvelle harmonie', *Etudes de Langue et de Littérature Françaises* 36 (1980): pages unknown.

--- 'La Tentative du "je-autre" ou l'"approche de l'inconnu"', in *Rimbaud Multiple*, ed. by Alain Borer, Gourdon: D. Bedou et J. Touzot, 1986: 228-44.

Zissmann, Claude, *Des 'Fleurs du Mal' aux 'Illuminations'*, Paris: Le Bossu Bitor, 1991.

BIBLIOGRAPHY IV. MALLARMÉ

Primary texts

Mallarmé, Stéphane, *Œuvres Complètes*, ed. by Bertrand Marchal, vol.1, Paris: Gallimard, coll. 'Bibliothèque de la Pléiade', 1998.

--- *Igitur, Divagations, Un coup de dés*, Paris: Gallimard, coll. 'Poésie', 1976.

--- *Correspondance complète 1862-1871. Suivi de Lettres sur la poésie 1872-1898*, ed. by Bertrand Marchal, Paris: Gallimard, coll. 'Folio Classique', 1995.

--- *Correspondance*, ed. by Henri Mondor and Lloyd James Austin, Paris: Gallimard; I, *1862-1871*, 1959; II, *1871-1885*, 1965; III, *1886-1889*, 1969; IV, *1890-1891*, 1973; V, *1892*, 1981; VI, *Jan. 1893-July 1894*, 1981; VII, *July 1894-Dec. 1895*, 1982; VIII, *1896*, 1983; IX, *Jan.-Nov. 1897*, 1983; X, *Nov.1897-Sept.1898*, 1984; XI, *Nov.1897-Sept.1898*, 1985.

--- *Correspondance: compléments et suppléments*, ed. by Lloyd James Austin, Bertrand Marchal and Nicola Luckhurst, Oxford: Legenda, 'Research Monographs in French Studies' 2, 1998.

Secondary texts

Abastado, Claude, 'Expérience et théorie de la création poétique chez Mallarmé', *Archives des Lettres Modernes* 4:119 (1970).

--- 'Lecture inverse d'un sonnet nul', *Littérature* 6 (1972): 78-85.

Austin, Lloyd James, *Essais sur Mallarmé*, ed. by Malcolm Bowie, Manchester University Press, 1995.

Backès, Jean-Louis, *Poésies de Mallarmé*, Paris: Hachette, 1973.

--- 'Hérodiade et le faune', in *Stéphane Mallarmé: Actes du colloque de la Sorbonne du 21 nov. 1998*, ed. by André Guyaux, Paris: Presses de l'Université de Paris-Sorbonne, 1998: 133-44.

Bernard, Suzanne, *Mallarmé et la Musique*, Paris: Nizet, 1959.

Betz, Dorothy, ' "Un Coup de dès': Mallarmé as Poet of the Absurd', *South Atlantic Bulletin* 43:4 (1978): 37-46.

Blanchot, Maurice, 'Le mythe de Mallarmé' and 'Le mystère dans les lettres', in *La Part du feu*, Paris: Gallimard, 1949: 35-48 and 49-65.

Bobillot, Jean-Pierre, 'Histoires de césure: contre-remarque sur la versification de Mallarmé', *Revue de Littérature Française et Comparée* (1998): 151-62.

Bourgain-Wattiau, Anne, *Mallarmé ou la création au bord du gouffre*, Paris: L'Harmattan, 1996.

Bowie, Malcolm, *Mallarmé and the Art of Being Difficult*, Cambridge: C.U.P., 1978.

Bowie, Malcolm, Alison Fairlie and Alison Finch, eds., *Baudelaire, Mallarmé, Valéry: New Essays in Honour of Lloyd Austin*, Cambridge: C.U.P., 1982.

Breatnach, Mary, *Boulez and Mallarmé: A Study in Poetic Influence*, Aldershot: Scolar, 1996.

Brooker, Jewel Spears, 'Poetry and Truth in Mallarmé', *College Language Association Journal*, 26:1 (1982): 49-57.

Brown, Calvin S., 'The Musical Analogy in Mallarmé's *Un Coup de des*' (1967) in *Musico-Poetics in Perspective: Calvin S. Brown in Memoriam*, ed. by Jean-Louis Cupers and Ulrich Weinstein, Amsterdam: Rodopi, 2000: 167-89.

Brown, Peter, *Mallarmé et l'écriture en mode mineur*, Paris-Caen: lettres modernes minard, 1998.

Brunel, Pierre, 'Musicienne(s) du silence', *Corps Ecrit* 12 (1984): 159-65.

Campion, Pierre, *Mallarmé, poésie et philosophie*, Paris: P.U.F., 1994.

--- 'La raison poétique chez Mallarmé', in *Mallarmé ou l'obscurité lumineuse*, ed. by Bertrand Marchal and Jean-Luc Steinmetz, Paris: Hermann, 1999: 155-72.

Chisholm, A. R., *Mallarmé's Grand Œuvre*, Manchester University Press, 1962.

Coates, Carrol F., 'Sound Structuring in Mallarmé's "Le Vierge..."'; in *Translation Perspectives IV: Selected Papers, 1986-87*, ed. by M. G. Rose, Binghampton: Research & Instruction Program, State University of New York Press, 1988: 37-50.

--- 'Une évolution vers la norme sonore? (quelques sonnets de Mallarmé)', *Currents in Comparative Romance Languages and Literatures* 101, 'Poésie et poétique en France, 1830-1890', ed. by Peter J. Edwards, New York: Peter Lang, date unknown: 227-49.

Cohn, Robert Greer, *Mallarmé's Prose Poems*, Cambridge: C.U.P., 1987.

Cornulier, Benoît de, 'Métrique de Mallarmé: analyse interne de l'alexandrin', in *Analyse et validation dans l'étude des données textuelles*, ed. by Mario Borillo and Jacques Virbel, Paris: Editions du C.N.R.S., 1977: 197-222.

--- 'Métrique de l'alexandrin de Mallarmé', *Annales de la Faculté des lettres de Dakar* 9 (1977): 77-129.

--- 'Remarques sur le sonnet "*Le vierge, le vivace et le bel aujourd'hui...*" de Stéphane Mallarmé', *Studi Francesi* 64 (1978): 59-75.

--- 'Remarques sur la métrique de Mallarmé', *Cahiers du Centre d'Etudes Métriques* 4 (1999): 69-88.

Davies, Gardner, *Vers une explication rationnelle du 'Coup de dés'*, Paris: José Corti, 1953.

--- *Mallarmé et le drame solaire*, Paris: José Corti, 1959.

--- *Mallarmé et le rêve d'Hérodiade*, Paris: José Corti, 1978.

--- *Mallarmé et la 'Couche Suffisante d'Intelligibilité'*, Paris: José Corti, 1988.

Dayan, Peter, *Mallarmé's 'Divine Transposition'*, Oxford: Clarendon Press, 1986.

--- 'Do Mallarmé's *Divagations* tell us not to write about musical works?', *Word and Music Studies* (2001): 65-80.

Décaudin, Michel, '"La retrempe" ou le vers libre', *Romancia Wratislaviensia* 18 (1982): 5-11.

Dujardin, Edouard, *Mallarmé par un des siens*, Paris: Albert Messein, 1936.

Durand, Pascal, 'Du sens des formes au sens du jeu: itinéraire d'un apostat', in *Mallarmé ou l'obscurité lumineuse*, ed. by Betrand Marchal and Jean-Luc Steinmetz, Paris: Hermann, 1999: 87-114.

Elwert, W. Theodor, 'Mallarmé entre la tradition et le vers libre: Ce qu'en disent ses vers de circonstance' in *Le Vers français au 20e siècle*, ed. by Monique Parent, Paris: Klincksieck, 1967: 123-40.

Engstrom, Alfred G., 'Mallarmé and the Death of God: The 'Sonnet en -yx'', *Romance Notes* 22:3 (1982): 302-7.

Franklin, Ursula, *An Anatomy of Poesis: The Prose Poems of Stéphane Mallarmé*, Chapel Hill: University of North Carolina Press, 1976.

Gill, Austin, 'Mallarmé on Baudelaire'; in *Currents of Thought in French Literature: Essays in Memory of G. T. Clapton*, ed. by J.-C. Ireson, Oxford: Blackwell, 1965; 89-114.

--- *The Early Mallarmé*, 2 vols., Oxford: Clarendon Press, 1980 and 1986.

Goebel, Gerhard, '"Poésie" et "litérature" chez Baudelaire et Mallarmé: Analyse du changement d'un concept', *Romantisme* 12:39 (1983): 73-83.

Gouvard, Jean-Michel, 'Métriques de l'alexandrin chez Mallarmé et Dario', *Littérature et Nation* 15 (1995), Université de Tours: 139-56.

--- 'L'alexandrin de Mallarmé et la poésie française (1850-1865)', *Cahiers du Centre d'Etudes Métriques* 4 (1999): 89-137.

Guyaux, André, ed., *Stéphane Mallarmé: Actes du colloque de la Sorbonne du 21 nov. 1998*, Paris: Presses de l'Université de Paris-Sorbonne, 1998.

Hambly, Peter, 'Mallarmé et la musique: Réflexions sur "Sainte", "Feuillet d'album" et "Une dentelle s'abolit"', *Nottingham French Studies* 29:1 (1990): 21-34.

Huot, Sylvain, *Le 'mythe d'Hérodiade' chez Mallarmé*, 1956; Paris: Nizet, 1977.

Ishida, Hidetaka, 'Le Rythme-sujet des poèmes mallarméens et la poétique du sacré: Autour d'Hérodiade (La "Scène" et l'"Ouverture ancienne")', *Etudes de Langue et Littérature Françaises* 54 (1989): 35-52.

Jenny, Laurent, 'Mallarmé: musique, espace, pensée', *Po&sie* 85 (1998): 115-22.

Kearns, James, *Symbolist Landscapes*, London: Modern Humanities Research Association, 1989.

Kinloch, David, and Gordon Millan, eds., *Situating Mallarmé*, Oxford: Peter Lang, coll. 'French Studies of the Eighteenth and Nineteenth Centuries' 10, 2000.

Kravis, Judy, *The Prose of Mallarmé: The evolution of a literary language*, Cambridge: C.U.P., 1976.

La Charité, Virginia A., *The Dynamics of Space: Mallarmé's Un Coup de dés jamais n'abolira le hasard*, Lexington, Kentucky: French Forum, 1987.

Lees, Heath, '"... depuis Wagner, la poésie". Mallarmé and the All-Embracing Word Work', in *Situating Mallarmé*, ed. by David Kinloch and Gordon Millan, Oxford: Peter Lang, 2000: 13-32.

Lowe, Catherine, 'Le mirage de ptyx: implications à la rime', *Poétique* 59 (1984): 325-45.

Marchal, Bertrand, *Lecture de Mallarmé*, Paris: José Corti, 1985.

--- *La Religion de Mallarmé*, Paris: José Corti, 1988.

--- 'Le fantôme d'Hérodiade', in *Stéphane Mallarmé, actes du colloque de la Sorbonne du 21 nov. 1998*, ed. by André Guyaux, Paris: Presses de l'Université de Paris-Sorbonne, 1998: 123-32.

--- 'Les Noces du "Livre"', in *Situating Mallarmé*, ed. by David Kinloch and Gordon Millan, Oxford: Peter Lang, 2000: 143-56.

Marchal, Bertrand and Jean-Luc Steinmetz, eds., *Mallarmé ou l'obscurité lumineuse: Actes du colloque de Cerisy, 13-23 août 1997*, Paris: Hermann, 1999.

Marvick, Louis W., 'Mallarmé and Wagner on Rhythm', *Rivista di Letterature Moderne e Comparate* 50:1 (1997): 43-50.

Mazaleyrat, Jean, 'Note technique sur les sonnets de Mallarmé', *Littératures* 9-10, (1984): 185-90.

Meschonnic, Henri, 'Mallarmé au-delà du silence', in *Stéphane Mallarmé, Ecrits sur le livre: choix de textes*, Paris: Editions de l'Eclat, 1986: 13-62.

Miller, George A., 'The magical number seven, plus or minus two: some limits on our capacity for processing information', *Psychological Review* 63:2 (1956): 80-97.

Miner, Margaret, 'Music Obscured: Mallarmé's Hermetic Mandore', *Dalhousie French Studies* 33 (1995): 35-54.

Paxton, Norman, *The Development of Mallarmé's Prose Style*, Geneva: Librairie Droz, 1968.

Pearson, Roger, *Unfolding Mallarmé: The Development of a Poetic Art*, Oxford: Clarendon Press, 1996.

Pellegrin, Jean, 'Rythmes mallarméens', *Ritm* 1, 'Rythme et écriture 2', (1991): 137-58.

Porter, Laurence M., 'The Disappearing Muse: Erasure of Inspiration in Mallarmé', *Romanic Review* 76:4 (1985): 389-404.

Poulet, Georges, *Espace et Temps Mallarméens*, Neuchâtel: A la Baconnière, 1950.

--- 'La Distance intérieure', in *Etudes sur le temps humain*, vol.2, Paris: Plon, 1952.

Rancière, Jacques, *Mallarmé. La politique de la sirène*, Paris: Hachette Livre, coll. 'Coup double', 1996.

--- 'La rime et le conflit', in *Mallarmé ou l'obscurité lumineuse*, ed. by Bertrand Marchal and Jean-Luc Steinmetz, Paris: Hermann, 1999: 115-41.

Reisinger, Deborah Streifford, 'Le Retour au rien: La Circularité mallarméenne à travers 'Sonnet en –yx' et 'Salut'', *Romance Notes* 37:3 (1997): 273-80.

Robb, Graham, *Unlocking Mallarmé*, London: Yale University Press, 1996.

Ronat, Mitsou, 'Cette architecture spontanée et magique', in *Mallarmé, Un Coup de dés jamais n'abolira le hasard*, ed. by Mitsou Ronat, Paris, Editions Change errant / d'atelier, 1980: 1-7.

--- 'Le Coup de dès forme fixe?', *Cahiers de l'Association Internationale des Etudes Françaises* 32 (1980): 141-47.

Scepi, Henri, *Mallarmé et la prose*, Magnac / Touvre-Charente: la licorne, 1998.

Scherer, Jacques, *Grammaire de Mallarmé*, Paris: Nizet, 1977.

--- *Le Livre de Mallarmé*, Paris: Gallimard, 1978.

Scott, Clive, 'Mallarmé's Mercurial E', *Forum for Modern Language Studies* 34:1 (1998): 43-55.

Staub, Hans, 'Le mirage interne des mots', *Cahiers de l'Association Internationale des Etudes Françaises* 27 (1975): 275-88.

Steinmetz, Jean-Luc, 'Le paradoxe mallarméen: les poèmes en prose', *Europe* (1976): 134-60.

Szondi, Peter, 'Sept leçons sur *Hérodiade*', *Poésies et poétiques de la modernité*, Presses Universitaires de Lille, 1982: 73-141.

Temple, Michael, *The Name of the Poet: Onomastics and Anonymity in the Works of Stéphane Mallarmé*, University of Exeter Press, 1995.

Van Laere, François, 'L'ordonnance d'un livre de vers', in *Stéphane Mallarmé, actes du colloque de la Sorbonne du 21 nov. 1998*, ed. by André Guyaux, Paris: Presses de l'Université de Paris-Sorbonne, 1998: 221-28.

APPENDIX. DATES OF TEXTS

I. Baudelaire

Graham Robb gives a list of 'les poèmes que l'on peut dater avec certitude, ceux qui ont été datés par les contemporains de Baudelaire, et ceux que les commentateurs s'accordent à assigner à l'époque en question'.[1] I include poems from the section 'Poésies écrites en collaboration; Poésies attribuées à Baudelaire' of the 1975 *Pléiade* edition, the unfinished 'Epilogue' texts and the 'Bribes'. I do not include the poems of 'Bouffonneries' and 'Amœnitates Belgicae' (satirical verse from the 1860s), 'Le Pauvre diable', 'D'un esprit biscornu...', the poems written in collaboration with Banville and Auguste Vitu for the 'Salon caricatural de 1846' and the latin verse. This gives a total of 187 texts. Up to 1852, the periods are those suggested by Robb. Poems are written in alexandrines unless otherwise indicated in brackets.

1) 1838-1841. Early *poésies de jeunesse* not kept for publication. (10)

'N'est-ce pas qu'il est doux...'	'Il est de chastes mots...'
'Il aimait à la voir...'	'Vous avez, chère sœur...'
'Je n'ai pas pour maîtresse...'	'Hélas! qui n'a gémi...'
'Quant à moi, si j'avais...'	'Epitaphe'
'Tout là-haut...'	'Tout à l'heure...' (8s)

2) Poems from the 1840s poems which cannot be dated more precisely. (9)

'La Muse malade'	'Remords posthume'	'Les Chats'
'Le Soleil'	'La Muse vénale'	'Tristesses de la lune'
'La Béatrice'	'La Beauté'	'Sépulture' (8s)

3) Poems composed before 1843. (27)

'Le Mauvais moine'	'Sed non satiata'
'Don Juan aux enfers'	'Une nuit que j'étais près...'
'Je t'adore à l'égal...'	'A une dame créole'
'Je n'ai pas oublié...'	'La servante au grand cœur...'
'Allégorie'	'De profundis clamavi'
'Le Crépuscule du soir'	'Le Crépuscule du matin'
'L'Albatros'	'Bohémiens en voyage'
'L'Ame du vin'	'Le Vin des chiffonniers'
'Le Vin du solitaire'	'Paysage'
'Le Rebelle'	'La Géante'
'Les Deux bonnes sœurs'	'Les Yeux de Berthe'
'A une Malabaraise'	
'Le Vin de l'assassin' (8s)	'Le Raccommodeur de fontaines' (8s)
'Le Chat (XXXIV)' (10/8)	'Combien dureront nos amours?' (8/4)

---

[1] *La poésie de Baudelaire et la poésie française 1838-1852*, Paris: Aubier, 1993; 'Appendice II', pp.385-92.

4) Poems composed between 1843 and 1846. (31)

'Je vis, et ton bouquet…' 'A Madame du Barry'
'A une belle dévote' 'A une jeune saltimbanque'
'Avril' 'Sonnet cavalier'
'A Ivonne Pen-Moore' 'Sur l'album de Mme Emile Chevalet'
'Tous imberbes alors…' 'Sur l'album d'une dame inconnue'
'L'Idéal' 'Parfum exotique'
'Harmonie du soir' 'Correspondances'
'La Chevelure' 'Sur *Le Tasse en prison*'
'A Théodore de Banville' 'Un voyage à Cythère'
'La Destruction' 'Bénédiction'
'La Lune offensée' 'La Vie antérieure'
'J'aime le souvenir…' 'Tu mettrais l'univers…'
'Femmes damnées' 'Delphine et Hippolyte' (st.1-21)
'Lesbos' 'Une gravure fantastique'
'A une mendiante rousse' (7/4)
'Noble femme au bras fort…' (12/8)
'J'aime ses grands yeux bleus…' (12/6)

5) Poems written between 1847 and 1849. (2)

'Les Litanies de Satan' 'Abel et Caïn' (8s)

6) Poems written between 1850 and 1852. (17)

'L'Homme et la mer' 'La Cloche fêlée'
'Spleen' I-IV 'La Fontaine de sang'
'Le Reniement de saint Pierre' 'Le Tonneau de la haine'
'Le Mort joyeux' 'Châtiment de l'orgueil'
'Le Guignon' (8s) 'La Pipe' (8s)
'La Rançon' (8s) 'A Celle qui est trop gaie' (8s)
'La Mort des amants' (10s) 'La Musique' (12/5)

Since Robb's study stops in 1852, I propose the further periods:

7) Poems composed between 1853-1857. (23)

'Le Balcon' 'Au Lecteur' 'L'Aube spirituelle'
'Les Phares' 'Réversibilité' 'Que diras-tu ce soir…'
'L'Ennemi' 'Le Flacon' 'Le Flambeau vivant'
'Causerie' 'Semper eadem' 'Delphine et Hippolyte' (st.22-26)[1]

---

[1] 'Poulet-Malassis écrivait à Asselineau que les cinq dernières strophes […] "avaient été écrites d'inspiration, puis revues et corrigées en prévision de l'intervention du parquet, quelques jours avant la publication"[…] on peut imaginer que le poème jusqu'en 1857 se terminait au vers 84' (O.C.I: 1127).

'Hymne' (8s) 'L'Héautontimorouménos' (8s)
'L'Irrémédiable' (8s) 'Tout entière' (8s)
'Le Vampire' (8s) 'L'Irréparable' (12/8)
'Confession' (12/8) 'Le Beau navire' (12/8)
'Le Poison' (12/7) 'L'Invitation au voyage' (5/7/8)
'Le Jet d'eau' (8/6/4)

8) Poems composed between 1858 and 1859.[1] (12)

'Sisina' 'A une Madone'
'Le Masque' 'Le Cygne'
'Les Sept vieillards' 'Les Petites vieilles'
'Danse macabre' 'Le Voyage'
'Sonnet d'automne' 'L'Albatros' (stanza 3)
'Chant d'automne' 'Le Squelette laboureur' (8s)

9) Poems composed in the 1860s. (24)

'Le Rêve d'un curieux' 'Le Gouffre'
'Obsession' 'La Voix'
'L'Imprévu' 'Le Coucher du soleil romantique'
'Recueillement' 'Le Couvercle'
'Epilogue I' 'Epilogue II'[2]
'Alchimie de la douleur' (8s) 'La Prière d'un païen' (8s)
'Horreur sympathique' (8s) 'Bien loin d'ici' (8s)
'Les Plaintes d'un Icare' (8s) 'Rêve parisien' (8s)
'L'Avertisseur' (8s) 'L'Examen de minuit' (8s)
'Madrigal triste' (8s) '... M. Honoré Daumier' (8s)
'Fin de la journée' (8s) 'Un Fantôme' (10s)
'Chanson d'après-midi' (7s) 'Les Promesses d'un visage' (12/8)

10) Poems for which the date of composition is unknown or unsure. (32)

'Elévation'[3] 'Avec ses vêtements...'[4]
'La Mort des pauvres' (pre-1851) 'Métamorphoses du vampire' (pre-1851)
'La Mort des artistes' (pre-1851) 'Mœsta et errabunda' (pre-1855)
'Ciel brouillé'(pre-1857) 'Les Bijoux' (pre-1857)
'Brumes et pluies' 'Le Jeu' (1857-58?)
'Duellum' (1858?) 'Le Goût du néant' (1858?)

---

[1] See Richard D. Burton, *Baudelaire in 1859*, Cambridge: C.U.P., 1988.
[2] Since the manuscript presents a largely unfinished text, only those provisionally completed alexandrines are counted: 26.
[3] Given its similarities with the late 1830s poem 'Tout là-haut...', 'Elévation' may have been written in the early 1840s (O.C.I: 838).
[4] 'Sans doute inspiré par Jeanne [...] mais pas nécessairement un poème de jeunesse' (O.C.I: 887).

'Hymne à la Beauté'[1]   'Je te donne ces vers...' (pre-1857)
'Le Possédé' (1858?)   'L'Horloge' (post-1857)
'L'Amour du mensonge' (1860?)   'A une passante' (1860?)
'Les Aveugles' (1860s?)   'Bribes'[2]
'Le Chat (LI)' (8s) (1850s?)   'Le Vin des amants'(8s) (pre-1857)
'Le Revenant' (8s)   'Les Hiboux' (8s) (pre-1851)
'Le Monstre' (8s)   'Epigraphe pour un livre condamné' (8s)
'Le Léthé' (10s) (pre-1857)   'Le Serpent qui danse' (8/5)
'Une Charogne'[3] (12/8)   'Une Martyre' (12/8) (pre-1857)
'L'Amour et le crâne' (8/5)
'Elégie refusée aux jeux floraux' (12/8) (pre-1851)

II. Rimbaud

Based on the Champion edition (1999) meticulously compiled by Steve Murphy, poems are grouped as follows:

1) 'Les Etrennes des orphelins': published 2 January 1870, *La Revue Pour Tous*.

2) 'Les Cahiers de Douai' (23):

    (i) 1er Cahier, dated / undated:

'Sensation'	(March-May 1870)
'Soleil et Chair'	(May 1870)
'Credo in Unam'	(36 lines cut, between ll.80-81)
'Ophélie'	(May 1870)
'Vénus anadyomène'	(July 1870)
'Première soirée' (8s)	(August 1870)
'Les Reparties de Nina' (8/4)	(August 1870)
'*Morts de Quatre-vingt-douze...*'	(Sept. 1870?)
'Les Effarés' (8/8/4)	(Sept. 1870)
'Roman'	(Sept. 1870)
'A la musique'	
'Bal des pendus' (8s and 12s)	
'Le Châtiment de Tartufe'	
'Le Forgeron'	
'Le Mal'	
'Rages de Césars'	

---

[1] Either pre-1857, and omitted from the first edition for its similarity to 'La Beauté', or written between 1857 and 1861. Pichois suspects the former (O.C.I: 876-77). According to Graham Chesters, the poem was written in 1859 (*Baudelaire and the Poetics of Craft*, Cambridge: C.U.P., 1988, p.133).

[2] 'Ces fragments peuvent [...] être d'époques différentes.' (O.C.I: 1172)

[3] 1843 and 1853 are two possible dates (O.C.I: 889).

(ii) 2ème Cahier, dated / undated:

'Rêvé pour l'hiver'	(Oct. 1870)
'Le Buffet'	(Oct. 1870)
'L'Eclatante Victoire de Sarrebrück'	(Oct. 1870)
'La Maline'	(Oct. 1870)
'Au Cabaret-Vert'	(Oct. 1870)
'Le Dormeur du val'	(Oct. 1870)
'Ma bohème'	

3) 'Poésies 1871' (21):

Although Murphy suggests that the composition of these poems might date from late 1870 to early 1872, I use the title 'Poésies 1871', the year in which the majority were written. Undated texts (right-hand column) are inserted among dated texts (left-hand column) according to Murphy's suggestions as to possible dates of composition.

> 'Les Sœurs de charité' (March-April 1871?)
> 'Les Assis' (spring 1871?)
> 'Voyelles' (spring 1871?)
'Le Cœur supplicié / du pitre' (8s) (May-June 1871)
'Chant de guerre parisien' (8s) (May 1871)
'Mes petites amoureuses' (8/4) (May 1871)
'Accroupissements' (May 1871)
> 'Les Mains de Jeanne-Marie' (8s) (May 1871?)
> 'Les Poètes de sept ans' (May 1871?)
'L'Orgie parisienne' (May 1871)
'Les Pauvres à l'Eglise' (June 1871)
> 'Les Douaniers' (first half 1871?)
'L'Homme juste' (July 1871)
'Les Premières Communions' (July 1871)
'Ce qu'on dit au poète...' (8s) (July 1871)
> 'L'étoile a pleuré rose...' (summer 1871?)
> 'Oraison du soir' (1871?)
> 'Le Bateau ivre' (Sept. 1871?)
> 'Les Chercheuses de poux' (end 1871?)
> 'Tête de faune' (10s) (1871-72?)
> 'Les Corbeaux' (8s) (Jan.-Mar. 1872?)

4) 'Album zutique' (Winter 1871 – Spring 1872) and *textes para-zutiques*: (27)

23 poems featured in Murphy's edition and the 1999 Gallimard 'folio' edition, revised by Louis Forestier. These include 'L'Idole', 'Mais enfin...' and 'Bouts-rimés' (absent from this section in the 1972 'Pléiade' edition), but not 'L'Enfant qui ramassa les balles'.

Also included are the texts Murphy classes as *para-zutiques*: the two poems of 'Vers pour les lieux' ('De ce siège si mal tourné' and 'Quand le fameux Tropmann') and an additional two poems from the 'Stupra' ('Les anciens animaux...' and 'Nos fesses...').

5) 'Poésies 1872' (20)

This title replaces 'Derniers vers' or 'Vers nouveaux et chansons' in both Murphy's and Forestier's editions. In the absence of sufficient evidence to mix dated and undated texts, I follow Murphy's lead, grouping undated poems alphabetically after the dated ones.

May:	'Comédie de la soif'
	'Bonne Pensée du matin'
	'La Rivière de Cassis'
	'Larme'
	'Bannières de mai'
	'Chanson de la plus haute tour'
	'L'Eternité'
June:	'Age d'or'
	'Jeune ménage'
July:	'Est-elle almée?'
August:	'Fêtes de la faim'
September:	'L'Enfant qui ramassa les balles'
Undated:	'Entends comme brame...'
	'Honte'
	'Le loup criait...'
	'Mémoire'
	'Michel et Christine'
	'O saisons, ô châteaux!...'
	'Plates-bandes d'amarantes...'
	'Qu'est-ce pour nous, mon cœur...'

6) 'Vestiges'. (6)

I do not include the 'Récritures minimales', where Rimbaud alters only one word in each of two stanzas by Blanchecotte, nor the 'Reconstitutions par Labarrière'.[1] I do, however, include the text entitled 'La plainte du vieillard monarchiste' in the 1872 'Pléiade', and Murphy's 'Reconstitutions par Delahaye', part of the 'Bribes' section of the 'Pléiade':

'Au pied des sombres murs...'
'Oh! Si les cloches sont de bronze...'
'Derrière tressautait...'
'Brune, elle avait seize ans...'
'La plainte des épiciers'
'Lettre à Loulou'

---

[1] Murphy's Champion edition, pp.879 and 883-84.

I.iii Mallarmé

Poems are grouped, as far as possible, according to their date of composition. A complete chronological presentation of publications and manuscripts can be found in Carl Paul Barbier and Charles Gordon Millan's edition.[1] All page references are to Bertrand Marchal's 'Pléiade' edition (1998).

1) 'Poésies de jeunesse' (1854-1861), pp.169-238 (55)

2) 1862-1865. (26) Poems in alexandrines:

1862	'L'Enfant prodigue'	p.63	
	'Mysticis umbraculis'	p.64	
	'Contre un poète parisien'	pp.54-55	
	'Le Guignon'	pp.125-26	
	'Placet'	p.124	
	'Le Sonneur'	p.118	
	'Tristesse d'été'	p.124	
	'Haine du pauvre'	p.64	
	'A un mendiant'	p.122	→ ('Aumône', 1887)
	'Vere novo'	p.119	→ ('Renouveau', 1887)
1863	'Parce que de la viande...'	p.65	
	'Les Fenêtres'	p.117	
	'Apparition'	p.7	
1864	'Image grotesque'	p.129	→ ('Une négresse par...', 1887)
	'L'Azur'	p.120	
	'Les Fleurs'	p.121	
	'A une putain'	p.119	→ ('Angoisse', 1887)
	'Lassitude'	p.123	→ ('Las de l'amer repos', 1887)
	'Le Pitre châtié'	p.128	
	'Soupir'	pp.15-16	
1865	'Brise marine'	p.122	
	'Le Jour'	p.127	

Poems in other metres:
1862	'Le Carrefour des demoiselles'	(8s)	pp.51-54
	'Soleil d'hiver'	(8s)	p.55
1863	'Le Château de l'espérance'	(8s)	pp.65-66
1865	'Sainte Cécile...'	(8s)	p.127

3) 'Hérodiade. Scène' (1865-66) pp.142-46
4) 'Le Faune, Intermède héroïque' (1865) pp.153-59
5) Ouverture d'Hérodiade (1866) pp.135-37

---

[1] Stéphane Mallarmé, *Œuvres complètes I, Poésies*, Paris: Flammarion, 1983, xviii-xxxii.

6) 1866-1868 (16):
Alterations made to poems sent to the *Parnasse Contemporain* in 1866, pp.103-10:

                             'Les Fenêtres'
                             'Le Sonneur'
('A une putain', 1864) → 'A Celle qui est tranquille' → ('Angoisse', 1887)
                             'Vere novo'   → ('Renouveau', 1887)
                             'L'Azur'
                             'Les Fleurs'
                             'Soupir'
                             'Brise marine'
('A un mendiant', 1862) →'A un pauvre' → ('Aumône', 1887)
('Lassitude', 1864) →   'Épilogue'   → ('Las de l'amer repos...', 1887)
                             'Tristesse d'été'

'Le Pitre châtié' (unpublished; p.1150)
'Sonnet allégorique de lui-même' (1868) → ('Ses purs ongles très haut...', 1887)

(8s):   'De l'orient passé...' (late 1860s)   → ('Quelle soie...', 1887)
        'De l'oubli magique...' (late 1860s)   → ('Quelle soie...', 1887)

7) 1870s. (6) All poems written in alexandrines:
    1871   'Dans le jardin'
    1873   'Toast funèbre'
    1875   'Improvisation d'un faune'
    1876   'L'Après-midi d'un faune. Églogue'
                   'Le Tombeau d'Edgar Poe'
    1877   'Sur les bois oubliés...'

8) 1880s. (26) Poems in alexandrines:
    1860s-1887? 'Quand l'ombre menaça...'
    1885   'Hommage (à Wagner)'
    1885-87   'Le vierge, le vivace...'
    1885/86   'Toujours plus souriant...' (p.131) → 'Victorieusement fui'
    1886   'O si chère de loin...'
    1887   'Le Pitre châtié'
                   'Victorieusement fui...'
                   'Méry Sans trop d'aurore...' (p.133) → 'Dame sans trop...'
                   'Ses purs ongles très haut...'
                   'Mes bouquins refermés...'
                   'La chevelure vol...'

Poems in other metres:
    1884   'Autre Éventail'   (8s)
    1884[1]   'Prose (pour des Esseintes)'   (8s)

---

[1] See Graham Robb, *Unlocking Mallarmé*, appendix 2.

1885	'Quelle soie…'		(8s)
1866-87?	'Triptyque'	I 'Tout orgueil…'	(8s)
		II 'Surgi…'	(8s)
		III 'Une dentelle…'	(8s)
1886	'M'introduire…'		(8s)
1889	'Chansons bas' I, II		(7s)
	'Types de la rue' I-VI		(7s)

9) 1890s (17) Poems in alexandrines:

    1893 'Remémoration d'amis belges'
    1894 'Le Tombeau de Charles Baudelaire'
    1897 'Tombeau (de Verlaine)'

Poems in other metres:

1890	'Eventail de Méry Laurent'	(8s)
	'Feuillet d'album'	(8s)
	'Billet (à Whistler)'	(8s)
1891	'Éventail'	(7s)
1893	'Salut'	(8s)
	'Petit air' II	(7s)
1894	'Petit air' I	(7s)
	'A la nue accablante tu'	(8s)
1895	'Hommage (à Puvis)'	(7s)
	'Petit air (guerrier)'	(7s)
	'Toute l'âme résumée'	(7s)
1896	'Rien, au réveil…'	(8s)
	'Si tu veux nous…'	(8s)
1898	'Au seul souci…'	(8s)

10. 'Les Noces d'Hérodiade. Mystère' (1898), pp.147-52:

    Prélude [I]
    'Cantique de saint Jean'
    Prélude [III]
    'Scène intermédiaire'
    Finale [I]
    Finale [II]

11. 'Vers de circonstance', pp.239-362

The vast majority of these verses date from the 1880s and 1890s, but since many cannot be dated more precisely, data from this category is counted together. Since the edition used is Marchal's 1998 'Pléiade', individual texts are referenced as 'page no., poem no.'.

INDEX OF AUTHORS

INDEX OF WORKS BY BAUDELAIRE, RIMBAUD, MALLARMÉ

Figures in italics denote a reference in the footnotes.

I. Baudelaire

II. Rimbaud